ENDING THE GAUNTLET:

Removing Barriers to Women's Success in the Law

Lauren Stiller Rikleen

ISSN 0-314-96037-6

DEDICATION

To Elaine and Joe Stiller and Rebecca and Alexander Rikleen for the gift of devoted parenting. To Sander Rikleen for the gift of devotion, and to Ilyse Rose and Alex William Rikleen for making parenting such a joy.

ACKNOWLEDGMENTS

I have often been struck by the deep sense of appreciation authors express in their acknowledgements. I now understand why. Book-writing may be a peculiarly lonely endeavor, but its successful completion can require a vast network of support.

This particular effort could not have even begun without the leap of faith taken by those lawyers, male and female, who gave hours of their time to talk to me about their experiences and perspectives. These confidential interviews enriched the writing of this book in ways that research of publications alone could never have accomplished. For their trust, their time, their intelligence, and their honesty, I am truly grateful.

Nor could this effort have been completed without the complete support of my partners at Bowditch & Dewey. Although I do not write about myself or my firm in this book, a few words here seem appropriate.

I came to my firm in 1988 as a lateral hire from the world of government and the non-profit sector. I was asked to build an environmental law practice where there was none, and I did. Along the way, I was elected an income partner, and shortly after, an equity partner. However, in spite of the fact that I was succeeding at what I was asked to do, something was wrong. When I came to work each day in my firm of 70 lawyers, I felt painfully lonely. The fact was, there was no one else there like me.

Throughout my years as an equity partner, I have been the only mother, a status that has set me apart in countless ways. Most of the partners in the firm came as associates and stayed. They grew up together as professionals, sharing history and life experiences. I shared none of these. Even as I was asked to create something that did not exist, I had very little help and no mentors. I saw other women arrive at the firm, struggle, and leave. Yet even as my own feelings of isolation grew, I continued to succeed in my assignment. Our firm's environmental practice became among the most respected in the region, but I never felt like I belonged. I used my sole voice to speak openly, and many of my partners would say quite bluntly, about my frustrations with the hurdles women faced as they tried to run a gauntlet of subtle barriers that were daunting.

Then a few years ago, an interesting thing happened that demonstrates the fundamental message of this book: strong leadership from the top can change firm culture. Our firm's Managing Partner, Robert Longden, saw the need to address the issues relating to the retention and advancement of women at Bowditch & Dewey, and he did it in the only way it could be successful. He devoted his own time and efforts, as well as firm resources, in a comprehensive, multi-pronged process.

These efforts have moved forward in ways that have had a strong impact on the culture of the firm and the creation of a respectful workplace. In the course of that journey, my voice no longer felt isolated and alone. My law partners became colleagues and the efforts became collective ones. There is much work still to do, but when culture shifts, the possibilities for change are limitless. I will always be grateful to Bob Longden for his leadership on this issue and his kindness on all others. I am also proud of the Management Committee and my partners who are willing travelers on this journey of change.

I feel a special bond with, and appreciation for, the very talented women of Bowditch & Dewey, lawyers, administrative, and support staff alike, for their strength and enthusiasm. Their interest in and support of this book was inspiring. I am particularly grateful to my colleague, Kim Stone, for her thoughtful comments on an earlier draft.

I am also grateful to the wonderful Framingham office support staff for their never-wavering and cheerful help. Within the midst of all that help, I am especially appreciative of Alexis Allfrey, not only for her constant interest, enthusiasm, and hard work, but for being so much fun to be around. Thanks also to Richard Foote, with whom I have serendipitously made the journey from Boston College Law School, to the Environmental Protection Agency, and to Bowditch & Dewey, for helping chart the next phase of my efforts to see women thrive in this profession.

There are two others at Bowditch & Dewey for whom I could never buy enough chocolate or thank enough. Our firm librarian, Byron Hill, was an invaluable resource whose prompt response to endless emails and late night phone messages was incredible. His humor is worthy of Leno or Letterman (and he should know that I have kept copies of all his emails). Deb Hanley has served as an extraordinary assistant and demonstrated constant enthusiasm for this seemingly endless project. Without her, this book would still be a work in progress. Her dogged dedication, which included the Herculean task of mastering Bluebook, meant more than I can ever express.

There are others whose impact on this book was indirect, but invaluable. I am grateful to the academic institutions that helped bring intellectual rigor to youthful idealism and, in various ways, led to my interest in these issues. First to my alma mater, Brandeis University, where I was exposed to outstanding courses and programs in women's studies. Second, to Boston College Law School, a law school which provides unparalleled teaching in an atmosphere of equality, creates community for all its students, and which introduced me to my life-long friend, Ann Williams, who was the reason for my career in environmental law. And third, to Clark University, a crown jewel of private research universities and the special place where I met my husband, Sander. Clark truly produces students who challenge convention and work to change the world.

Every lawyer should feel a debt of gratitude to the organized bar which devotes itself to the ideals and aspirations of our profession. These institutions exist and thrive because thousands of lawyers care deeply about their profession and are willing to devote their time and energy to improving the way in which the law serves society. The Boston Bar Association remains true to its proud heritage by its willingness to serve as a leader on so many issues important to our profession. I am proud to have served as its President and I am particularly grateful to the members of the BBA Task Force on Professional Challenges and Family Needs, whose 1999 report, *Facing the Grail: Confronting the Costs of Work-Family Imbalance*, helped spark a nation-wide interest by other bar associations in the issues addressed in the report. I am humbled by the legacy of leadership from the past presidents of the BBA who have inspired and encouraged my efforts, and I am proud of my successors for continuing the tradition of innovation.

The Women's Bar Association of Massachusetts provides a critical voice on behalf of women lawyers and also has a proud legacy of leadership on issues relating to the retention and advancement of women. Many members of that bar association have encouraged and supported my efforts on this project. The American Bar Association has never been so important in ensuring that our country understands the precious link between liberty and the rule of law. ABA President Michael Greco has demonstrated an unwavering focus on values and I am grateful for the confidence he has shown in appointing me to the ABA Commission on Women in the Profession.

At its essence, this book is about ensuring the rightful prioritization of family in the day-to-day lives of busy professionals. For me, no words of gratitude will ever seem sufficient enough for my family, whose men and women have been equally dedicated to the nurturing of the family unit. The boisterous genius of the Rikleen family has long been a special part of my life. I am particularly appreciative of Sander's mom, Rebecca, whose incredible skills as a parent helped ensure terrific grandchildren. My own family, immediate and extended, has been my steady lifeline. The Stiller/Brodie clan and the wonderful spouses who have joined the pack are a constant reminder that family matters more than anything else. My loving mom, Elaine Stiller, my dearly-missed dad, Joe Stiller, my brother, Mel Stiller, and my "sister", Claire Newman, provided the best foundation of all, unconditional love and patience. All of my family has supported this project with tremendous enthusiasm, and I am grateful for the gift of time to write.

My husband, Sander, who still is the smartest person I know, has been everything to me for my entire adult life. Throughout the 35 years we have been together, he has been an unwavering source of strength and encouragement. His contribution to this book is as critical as it is in every other area of my life. His crunching of years of Massachusetts Lawyers Weekly data analyzing statistics on women in law firms, an effort undertaken before I wrote the first words for this book, demonstrated how real the problems addressed in this book are. His great title for the book is only another example of his creativity.

Finally, I am most honored and humbled by the best title of all: mommy. Our children, Ilyse and Alex, bring happiness to our lives each and every day. They are the reasons this book matters so much to me. May they continue the rich legacy they have inherited from both sets of grandparents: a curious mind, sharp intellect, empathy, humor, and a sense of purpose.

May this book inspire others to create a workplace which understands that nurturing our children and caring for clients are mutually reinforcing values.

PROLOGUE

Imagine that you are a senior partner in a large, nationally-recognized law firm, meeting with a client who is excitedly describing his latest proposed business venture.

"I've been offered an opportunity to run a large business."

Your lawyer-like caution is emerging, since your client already works hard. "But don't you already have a full-time job?"

"Sure, but that's the great thing about this new challenge - I can do it part-time."

His response worries you. "The business must have quite a management structure in place, if it can operate with a part-time CEO." You make this statement with the sinking feeling that your client is about to get in way over his head.

"Well...it's not the kind of business that relies much on managers. The people there are very independent. They just go out and make money."

"Is there middle management in place to support the Chief Executive?"

"Of course, there's some. Each group of professionals has a leader, although it's not that clear what the leaders' specific roles are. And there's a Management Committee that works closely with the Chief Executive."

"Are there job descriptions? How is their performance measured?"

"Everyone's performance in the organization is measured pretty much the same way: by how much money they bring into the company."

"So there are no defined management responsibilities?"

"The folks that work there would not take well to being told what to do."

"Then how much time do they spend as managers?"

"They manage part-time. Most of the time they're out making money, too."

"How are they selected for the position?"

"I've been told they are chosen based on who is the least objectionable to the other moneymakers."

"So these 'least objectionable' people manage the different groups on a part-time basis? Are they involved in recruiting and hiring?"

"That will vary. Most of these managers hate to interview, so they delegate as much as possible to some of the very bright and talented people who work for them."

"Do these people also want to help manage the company some day?"

"Hard to say. Most of them leave after a few years."

"Isn't it incredibly expensive to lose all these people?"

"Not that I've been told. It appears that they just go out and hire replacements."

"How do they make their money? Are they manufacturers?"

"No. It's a professional services business. They bill clients hourly for giving advice."

"But the profitability potential of this business is limited. After all, if you bill hourly, there's a lot of pressure to be extremely efficient and to keep the rates low."

"That doesn't seem to be the case, as far as I can tell. That's why this seems like such a great opportunity. Hourly rates have soared over the past several years, and clients keep paying them!"

"OK, so you are looking at a highly profitable professional services business, which has an enormously independent worker population, little structural management, high turnover, and profits based on how many hours in a day the workers can bill. Seems like you are totally dependent on your workforce talent to survive. How do you keep them happy and motivated?"

"They are paid a lot."

"That's it?"

"It seems to be."

"Tell me about the people that you've met already. You know that it's important to understand the problems you are inheriting in a new venture. Who have you talked to?"

"I spoke to a variety of people there. The young men are real go-getters! I heard some stories that demonstrate great business development acumen."

"What about the women professionals?"

"I didn't really get to talk to them. I was told they keep to themselves a lot—pretty much stay in their offices and grind out the work that's brought in to them."

"Are there women in senior positions?"

"A few. Apparently a lot of them have left, so they can be with their children."

"Have you reviewed any of the company policies?"

"Seems to be the standard fare. There's a part-time policy, but I was told not too many people use it. Probably better for the company, anyway, since it cuts into those billable hours."

"Have you looked at whether the business provides any of the initiatives and procedures that some highly successful companies are now offering their workforce, such as parental leaves, flexible work arrangements, or telecommuting?"

"Well, I know they provide their employees with cell phones, beepers, and personal computers, so they can be fully accessible at home. I also understand that they have a state-of-the-art day care center which employees can use on nights and weekends. I hear they even offer dog-walking services!"

You have now heard enough. Your initial astonishment has changed to an emerging flicker of recognition. You feel increasingly uncomfortable as you realize that this strangely organized business he is describing is your own.

INTRODUCTION

A Profession at the Tipping Point

This book is, in many ways, a personal story of the many women lawyers who so graciously shared stories about their deeply moving struggles to succeed in their chosen profession. It is also an analysis of law firms that, even in its focus on women lawyers, reveals a range of issues that are negatively impacting men as well.

For me, it is a critical look at a profession that I love. The legal profession remains, for all its flaws, filled with generous people full of ideals who are willing to contribute time and money to important societal needs.

Throughout my years in private practice, I have marveled at the generosity of lawyers who volunteer, without hope of even indirect compensation, in countless different ways to improve our world. Look at any successful nonprofit organization and you will likely find within it lawyers contributing tirelessly to its success.

These observations are consistent with studies which demonstrate that lawyers choose this profession because they hope to make a contribution, to have an impact on the world around them. This motivation is a recurring theme in the stories of the women interviewed for this book. Most began their careers excited and optimistic about what they could accomplish with their law degree. They expected to work hard. What they did not anticipate was the lack of professional fulfillment and the unsustainable personal sacrifice they encountered.

In the field of epidemiology, a "tipping point" occurs when a small change causes a critical mass to be reached, thereby "tipping" a disease into an epidemic.[1] This epidemiological concept also applies to the ways in which ideas, behaviors, and new products move through a population, similar to the contagious patterns of a disease.[2] Malcolm Gladwell described this one dramatic moment of sudden change as the "Tipping Point," which can also be observed in business and social policy.[3] Also, we have seen, in law.

For approximately two decades, law firms have undergone profound changes which have impacted all aspects of their organizational structure and behavior. These changes have moved through the profession with the speed of an epidemic. With each change, however, firms have tipped further out of balance.

Examples of the profession's vulnerability to "Tipping Points" are instructive. In the fall of 1999, the venerable law firm of Hale & Dorr[4] instituted a policy allowing its attorneys to dress casually every day.[5] The rationale? The firm believed that the younger, high-tech entrepreneurs were more likely to hire lawyers who dressed comfortably and looked less "buttoned-down." This was a shocking development in a city known for its business-like (if somewhat frumpy) couture, and where "Casual Fridays" were generally a summertime treat.

Almost immediately after Hale & Dorr's announcement, most major law firms in Boston were reluctantly preparing to institute their own full-time casual dress policy. One lawyer described the Hale & Dorr change as being similar to hearing that the Berlin Wall had fallen.[6] In effect, the firm's new policy served as the moment of critical mass, the Tipping Point for an emerging casual dress epidemic in the City's legal profession.

In another example with far more significant consequences, the former Boston law firm of Testa, Hurwitz & Thibeault[7], once renowned for its entrepreneurial high-tech client base, announced in early 2000 that it was raising the starting salaries of its new associates.[8] The firm justified this salary hike as the necessary response to the increased competition it was facing from internet firms and other high-tech companies offering huge salaries to attract top law school graduates.

Large law firms in Boston immediately perceived Testa's decision as a direct threat to their own ability to recruit high-quality legal talent. Accordingly, the bidding war began as other firms instituted similar hikes in starting salaries and bonuses.[9] This precipitous jump in the compensation of fledgling lawyers had a cascading effect throughout all levels of law firms, as more experienced attorneys sought corresponding salary increases commensurate with their level of experience. In a matter of weeks, the decision of one Boston law firm to adjust its compensation levels for new lawyers served as a "Tipping Point" which resulted in spiraling compensation demands and a concomitant impact on other components of law firm life which have reverberated throughout the profession.[10]

Most law firms have grown enormously in the past decade, while retaining an antiquated, unsustainable business model, much like a high-rise building without any foundation. This business model has a particularly deleterious impact on the increasing number of women attorneys who entered the profession during this time of unprecedented growth.

Throughout my numerous interviews with women lawyers, it was hard to escape the visual image of the "canary in the coal mine." Historically, canaries were used to detect the presence of toxic gases in underground mines; if they exhibited signs of distress or illness, it was a clear signal to miners that the conditions below were dangerous. Many of the women lawyers interviewed for this book similarly saw themselves as the harbinger of an unhealthy work environment. Impacted in greater numbers by the extraordinary demands of the modern law firm, their higher-than-average attrition rates serve as a warning.

However, the "canary in the coal mine" metaphor suggests a pessimistic result: the canary either dies or takes ill, yet conditions in the mine do not change. A more optimistic view of the future of the legal profession is warranted, however, as long as the warnings are heeded.

In the world of the Tipping Point, radical change is a certainty.[11] For the legal profession, radical change is both a certainty and a necessity. The profession is moving towards its own Tipping Point, and each woman who leaves the practice of law brings it closer to the edge. Their continued departures are ignored at the profession's peril.

There is no question that law firms are capable of dramatic positive changes. Just as salaries escalated and wardrobes changed in an instant, the ways in which law firms operate can also change quickly, and for the better. Law firms are enormously susceptible to outside influences and capable of decisive actions where a response is needed.

Part One of this book identifies the gauntlet that women experience—the challenges and roadblocks they face as they struggle to succeed in law firms. Part Two weaves together the voices and issues unique to women and the often divergent perspective of the Managing Partners. Part Three sets forth recommendations for change, describing concrete actions which law firms can implement.

Those firms which move aggressively to change will have the distinction of playing a key role in charting a new and successful course for the future, one in which women can take their rightful place as equals in the legal profession.

Endnotes for Introduction

1. Paul McFedries, *Tipping Point*, Word Spy *at* http://www.wordspy.com/words/tippingpoint.asp (posted on June 16, 2004).

2. Malcolm Gladwell, The Tipping Point: How Little Things Can Make A Big Difference (2002) (2000).

3. Gladwell, The Tipping Point: How Little Things Can Make a big Difference (2002) (2000). Gladwell highlights three characteristics which help define how any type of epidemic, be it a social epidemic or a disease, moves through the population: the first is the characteristic of "contagiousness;" second is the notion that "big changes can follow from small events," a concept which, Gladwell cautions, runs counter to our expectations of proportionality; and third is the moment of sudden change. At 9-14.

4. In 2004, as the result of a merger with Wilmer Cutler Pickering LLP, the law firm was renamed Wilmer Cutler Pickering Hale & Dorr.

5. Steven Wilmsen, Law Suitless: *Change in Clientele Spurs Casual Dress at Legal Firms*, Boston Globe, Nov. 19, 1999, at A1.

6. Steven Wilmsen, Law Suitless: *Change in Clientele Spurs Casual Dress at Legal Firms*, Boston Globe, Nov. 19, 1999, at A1.

7. On January 14, 2005, the partners of Testa, Hurwitz & Thibeault voted to disband. For an analysis of its demise, *see* Carlyn Kolker, *The Wages of Denial*, The American Lawyer, Mar. 2005, at 17.

8. Diane E. Lewis, *Law Firms Up Salary Ante to Fight Associates' Flight to Dot-Coms*, Boston Globe, Feb. 8, 2000, at D1.

9. Diane E. Lewis, *Hale & Dorr Hikes Lawyers' Pay*, Boston Globe, Feb. 9, 2000, at D7.

10. *See, e.g.* Diane E. Lewis, *High Anxiety over Attorneys' Soaring Pay*, Boston Globe, Feb. 11, 2000, at E1.

11. Gladwell, The Tipping Point: How Little Things Can Make a big Difference 13-14 (2002) (2000).

PART ONE

CHAPTER 1

THE ROAD FROM OVERT TO BENIGN EXCLUSION

For centuries, the practice of law was conducted with a comfortable consistency and closed to women. Margaret Brent, who came to the colonies in 1638, is known to be the first woman lawyer in America.[1] Incredibly, more than 200 years passed before history recorded the names of any other women lawyers.[2]

It was not until the 1860s that women began to seek entrance into the legal profession in earnest.[3] However, these intrepid women faced daunting challenges: sexual discrimination was deeply routed in the legal system, and the profession itself posed more barriers to the entry of women than any other in the nineteenth century.[4] To gain entry, women had to file lawsuits in state and federal courts, as well as seek the passage of statutes that would specifically permit women to practice law.[5] As a result of these aggressive efforts, by the turn of the 20th century, 35 states and territories and the District of Columbia had opened the profession to women.[6]

These efforts by women to enter the profession coincided with a significant transformation that was taking place in the education of aspiring lawyers. Until approximately the 1870s, few law schools existed; most lawyers earned their place at the bar through an apprenticeship system in which they trained under another lawyer.[7] In the second half of the 19th century, however, law schools began to emerge as the critical gateway into the legal profession.[8]

Just as apprenticeships were closed to women, however, similar barriers prevented them from entering law schools.[9] Columbia University Law School Dean Harlan Stone earned his place in ignominy by dismissing a female applicant's inquiry about why women were not admitted with this reason: "We don't because we don't."[10]

It took until the 1920s for many law schools to finally begin opening their doors, albeit begrudgingly and in a limited way; women comprised but a small minority in a male-dominated setting.[11] Interestingly, the elite law schools remained the most reluctant to alter their admittance restrictions, with the last holdout refusing to allow women into its school until 1950.[12]

Even as law schools slowly opened their doors, the opportunities for women in the law remained limited. A national pattern of discrimination in the early 1900s created pervasive barriers which greatly hindered opportunities for women.[13] Women lawyers lucky enough to be employed were relegated to solo practices or office work outside the courtroom; others found work as stenographers or law clerks.[14]

These barriers to meaningful work persisted throughout the mid-20th century. Women law school graduates were frequently told directly that, despite outstanding qualifications, the law firms' doors were closed to them.[15] One law professor advised a Harvard Law School admittee that she should attend secretarial school after obtaining her law degree to guarantee landing a personal secretarial position for a senior partner at a high-prestige firm.[16]

Perhaps the most famous example of the overt discrimination women faced in their early careers is the often-told story of the first woman to serve on the United States Supreme Court, Sandra Day O'Connor. Upon her graduation from Stanford Law School (as number three in her graduating class), she was unable to obtain an offer from any law firm, except for a position as a legal secretary.[17] Justice O'Connor's story vividly demonstrates that informal barriers persisted long after formal prohibitions on women's entry into the profession were lifted.

By the early 1960s, women comprised approximately 3% of the legal profession.[18] Amazingly, more than 300 years after Margaret Brent came to America, women seeking entry in the legal profession were still pioneers.

It was nearly another decade before gender-based restrictions were formally eliminated in all accredited law schools.[19] When the American Association of Law Schools prohibited its member schools from gender discrimination in their admissions, one of the last formal legal barriers was eliminated and the floodgates to the profession opened.[20] In 1970, 8.5% of incoming law students and approximately 5% of all law firm associates were women.[21] By 2001, women constituted approximately half of the entering law school students and about 30% of the profession.[22]

However, just as women had finally overcome centuries of obstacles and began to take their place in law schools and as new lawyers, the profession itself underwent a radical transformation. To truly understand the daunting hurdles women in the legal profession face at the dawn of the 21st century, it is necessary to understand the challenges facing the profession itself. In less than three decades, revolutionary changes in the practice of law have resulted in working conditions that have significantly impeded women's opportunities to succeed.

Through the years following World War II, law firms were generally considered stable entities with manageable growth.[23] Even the "big" law firms at that time were markedly smaller than today's behemoths; in the late 1950s, only 38 firms had more than 50 lawyers. In 1985, more than 500 firms had over 50 lawyers.[24] By 2005, the top 100 law firms ranged in size from 197 to just under 3,000 lawyers.[25]

Until the early 1970s, associate attorneys in law firms were primarily men who could expect that the firms they entered were secure institutions, that they had a reasonable opportunity to succeed and be elected partner, and that, even if a billable-hour requirement were articulated, it would likely be around 1,700 hours a year.[26] However, the law firms women entered in large numbers in the 1980s were changing rapidly: billable-hour demands grew dramatically, law firms were exploding in size and gross revenues, some law firms broke up, lateral hiring increased, and firms engaged in hiring and promotional practices which varied from the associate-to-partner model that had long been the hallmark of the law firms' organizational structure.[27]

It is this confluence of circumstances, women's entry into a drastically changing profession, that is analyzed in this book.

For years, those concerned by the grim statistics which chronicled the small percentage of women who became law firm partners were offered the same rationale: that the disparity was attributed to the low numbers of women in law schools. According to this "pipeline" theory, once women graduated in larger numbers and began working in private practice as associate attorneys, they would emerge triumphantly as partners in ever-increasing numbers.

This optimistic projection was strongly rooted in the success women were experiencing in law school. After all, the progression of women accepted to and graduating from law school has been on a steady upward trajectory for more than two decades. Until the early 1970s, women were consistently much less than 10% of the entering class; by 1980, more than a third of the first year students were women.[28]

The significant progress continued as women comprised more than 40% of the entering class by the mid-1980s. However, the statistical gains in entry during these decades tell only a small part of the story. These were years in which women faced overt discrimination in all aspects of their efforts to practice law. Many of these experiences have been fully chronicled in reports conducted by state bars or judicial task forces.[29] One Managing Partner of a mid-sized law firm interviewed for this book told of his star senior partner who, in the late 1970s, was given an offer to join the law firm where she clerked while in law school. The offer was contingent, however, on her working in the Business Practice Group because the firm did not think it "proper for a young lady to try cases."

By the turn of the 21st century, women were close to half of the first-year law school population. For more than two decades, therefore, there has been a sufficiently large pool of female law school graduates in the pipeline to warrant a proportional increase in women partners.[30] However, that has not happened.

In 1987, the American Bar Association created the Commission on Women in the Profession, recruiting as its first chair a Little Rock attorney named Hillary Rodham Clinton. The Commission's first major task was to identify the barriers that were preventing women attorneys from fully participating in the profession. The ABA President who appointed the first Commission members articulated the critical need to recognize and acknowledge gender differences as an important step towards achieving equality: "Clearly, the quest for gender equality must become a central objective of the legal profession if we are to be faithful to the professional ideal of opposing all forms of discrimination, and if we are to achieve full integration and equal participation of women."[31]

However, in the years since the Commission issued its first report, many of the obstacles remain in place, notwithstanding the continued attention focused on these issues. In 1983 and 2000, the ABA Journal polled lawyers to determine how women were progressing in the profession. Although the comparative results demonstrate progress in certain areas, particularly with respect to opportunities to obtain the first job after law school, it is startling that the data reveals that substantial ground has actually been lost.[32]

For example, in 1983, 38% of the women polled stated that they had to work harder than male lawyers to get the same result; by 2000, that number increased to 56.9%. The responses also demonstrated that, in 2000, significantly fewer women and men believed that high-level responsibilities, prospects for advancement, high salaries, and opportunities for direct client contact were equally available to men and women.[33] Also, of even greater concern, fewer men and women were confident that women could realistically combine their role as lawyer with that of wife and mother successfully.[34]

Numerous studies and reports confirm the slow progress. For example, in 2002, the NALP Foundation reported that women accounted for only 16.3% of the partners in the nation's major law firms.[35] A detailed study by Catalyst reported that, even assuming a conservative 10-year track to partnership: "the rate of increase in the percentage of women partners and equivalent senior positions has lagged behind the rate of increase in the percentage of women in the profession overall."[36] As of 2000, Catalyst reported that women represented 15.6% of law firm partners and only 13.9% of the equity partners.[37]

After more than two decades of observing the pipeline clog and develop leaks, however, it is clear that the simple mathematical progression anticipated was an expectation built on flawed assumptions. Instead of taking their place at the top of the profession, women are leaving in disproportionate numbers.

As the Catalyst study revealed, men and women begin their legal careers in law firms, but then proceed along divergent paths. "Of those graduating in the 1970s, only 30 percent of the women law graduates are still in law firms, as opposed to 51 percent of the men. Thus, of 1970s law graduates, twice as many women as men are currently in the education and corporate sectors rather than in law firms. Thirty-five percent of the women law graduates from the 1980s and 51 percent of the women law graduates from the 1990s are still in firms."[38]

So what has happened? Why do statistics demonstrate that too many women in law firms are stalled in their career path, even as their male colleagues vault over them? Why, even as the overt barriers of gender discrimination have been crumbling, do law firms remain an inhospitable environment for women?

The answer can be found in the short-sighted decisions and flawed management structures that currently permeate the profession. Modern law firms have exploded in size, wealth, and complexity. As they have grown, however, they have failed to develop an infrastructure which could channel the energies that have led to huge financial success into a coherent management framework. The result is a series of internal, unstructured organizational units which often have more in common with life in the frontiers of the Old West than they do with sophisticated businesses.

However, within this challenging framework, lawyers are delivering sophisticated legal services in a country which has been transformed into a service economy. In light of this shift from the "production of goods to production of services," it is critical to understand the impact to organizations when the firm's primary output is human capital, rather than an industrial product.[39] Unfortunately for the legal profession, there has been far too little focus on the proper management of the human capital that is critical to any law firm's success: lawyers.

Yet, law firms are prominent institutions in our society and, as such, the modern law firm is a critical source of power and influence. In describing lawyers as the "gatekeepers of our nation's justice system," the American Bar Association's Commission on Women in the Profession calls for attorneys to be the "trailblazers in promoting equality."[40] The importance of this challenge to our profession grows as the authority of lawyers extends even further into American society. Today, there are approximately one million practicing lawyers in the United States.[41] Lawyers have a seat at the table in important board rooms of major businesses and institutions, and corporations today rarely make decisions without attorneys at their side, serving as advisor and protector. The large corporate law firm has been described as the authoritative center of the legal profession—the primary function of the legal system.[42] Writing of the elite law firms, one author observed that such firms were bound together by "their representation of America's major banks, financial institutions and corporations, the country's greatest concentrations of economic power."[43]

Large law firms also set the standard for their smaller counterparts, thereby exerting a significant influence throughout the legal community as a whole.[44] Also, private practice itself remains the largest employment setting for lawyers.[45]

Moreover, law firms serve as significant training grounds for those who become major societal figures of influence. Lawyers who have achieved critical authoritative positions in our society, such as judges, high government officials, or members of Boards and Commissions, tend to move into such positions from a partnership in a major law firm.[46] In 1994, the majority of U.S. Senators and nearly half the members of the House of Representatives had law degrees, and law continues to be the dominant profession of the members of Congress.[47] Former President Clinton, the 25th lawyer to serve in the White House, appointed 13 attorneys to his 18 member cabinet. [48]

"Lawyer-dominated legislatures and bureaucracies now extend their reach into every corner of contemporary American life. ... The positions that lawyers occupy throughout the corporate, financial, and commercial worlds are no less strategic. Judges increasingly seem to have the last word on the most divisive and hotly contested questions of the times."[49] These words, written more than a decade ago by Harvard Law School Professor Mary Ann Glendon, have proven prophetic in light of the pivotal role of the Supreme Court in the 2000 presidential election, as well as the role of the state judiciaries in ruling on such societal issues as whether homosexual couples have the right to marry.

The importance of lawyers to our democratic society, therefore, means that we all have a stake in this profession whose influence extends far beyond its office towers. The distinguished New York Court of Appeals Judge Judith Kaye, noting the profound changes that have taken place in the profession, wisely summarized why lawyers must address their own issues of equality in their workplace: "Indeed, the legal profession, concerned with the rights of others, should be in the forefront of meaningful reform to effect genuine integration and equality within its own ranks."[50] Judge Kaye added that such reform, in addition to serving the interest of justice, "also serves the selfish interest of attracting and keeping the best available talent."[51]

However, the state of the profession at the turn of the new century is troubling. Women lawyers still face a grueling gauntlet of challenges. The factors that have derailed the career expectations of too many women now threaten the future of the profession: spiraling compensation demands that are seldom satiated; unpredictable (and frequently, unfathomable) decisions about who will be elected to partner status; loosely-formed, intermediate management positions where lawyers inexperienced in such roles often serve with ambivalence; and a workplace reluctant to invest in the well-being of its primary asset—the human capital by which it is able to continue feeding its hunger for growing revenues.

These issues are all interrelated and, together, form a barely penetrable barrier through which only a small number of women pass. For those that emerge on the other side, the price of transport has been high, and is frequently accompanied by a bewildering disappointment.[52]

After centuries of facing—and overcoming—intractable obstacles, the scenario facing many women today is still daunting. Even if a woman has persevered and finally achieved that long, sought-after goal of partnership, she is likely to experience disappointment in a system that makes no more sense as an insider than it did during the brutally hard years she worked to achieve that status.

Consider the profession that today's newly elected partner enters. In this new role, she realizes that she is still vulnerable to losing her job if she does not bill enough hours or bring in enough clients, notwithstanding her considerable legal skills. She has no greater control over her life, as technology has made her accessible around the clock. Her partnership status has not altered the fact that she feels the same pressures she was feeling as a senior associate.

In the midst of these concerns, she realizes that the firm itself is in danger. Clients are constantly complaining that their bills are too high, even as they pay the firm's exorbitant rates. Many are also questioning why so many different people work on their cases. These once loyal clients are now shopping around to her competitors to see if they can get better rates.

Equally disquieting, she is privy to information about her colleagues that alarms her. Several are threatening to leave unless they receive a significant increase in their compensation. Others are at war over who should receive financial credit for ongoing work from a large firm client. The Management Committee is quietly trying to deal with several partners whose issues range from drinking too much to communicating inappropriately with young associates and secretaries. If she then does a "reality check" with one of her law school classmates who has also recently been elected partner at another law firm, the conversation will likely have a haunting familiarity. Expecting support, and maybe even hoping for encouragement to join her friend's firm where those problems do not exist, she, instead, hears the same observations and fears. She finds little comfort in knowing that she is not alone.

Endnotes for Chapter 1

1. Karen Berger Morello, The Invisible Bar—The Woman Lawyer in America: 1638 to the Present 3 (1988) (1986).

2. Morello, The Invisible Bar—The Woman Lawyer in America: 1638 to the Present 8 (1988) (1986). Morello reminds us of the enormously restricted society women faced: "[W]ell into the nineteenth century married women could not vote, serve on a jury, get a professional education, hold elective office, enter into a contract, obtain custody of their own children, or control their own money, even when they had earned it. ... Society had become so formal...that restrictions on race, sex and class prevented the emergence of any successors to Margaret Brent." Morello, The Invisible Bar—The Woman Lawyer in America: 1638 to the Present 8, 9 (1988) (1986).

3. Virginia G. Drachman, Sisters in Law: Women Lawyers in Modern American History 1 (2001).

4. Drachman, Sisters in Law: Women Lawyers in Modern American History 2 (2001). Drachman wrote: "Law in the late nineteenth century was even more masculine than other male-dominated professions: it was characterized by an all-male bar, all-male judges, and the shared belief that law was the natural province of men, not women." At 11. Science writer Deborah Blum noted the extensive roots of such prejudice: "In the days before women were admitted to college, male scientists insisted that girls were born too fragile and emotional to even handle higher education." Deborah Blum, *Solving for XX*, Boston Sunday Globe, Jan. 23, 2005, at E5.

5. Not all efforts were successful. Most notably, in 1872, the United States Supreme Court denied a woman named Myrna Bradwell the right to practice law. *Bradwell v State of Illinois*, 83 U.S. 130 (1873).

6. Drachman, Sisters in Law: Women Lawyers in Modern American History 12 (2001), noting also that, in 1879, the United States Congress authorized women to practice before the United States Supreme Court.

7. Drachman, Sisters in Law: Women Lawyers in Modern American History 39 (2001).

8. Drachman, Sisters in Law: Women Lawyers in Modern American History 40 (2001). At that time, high school graduates could attend most law schools without the prerequisite of a college degree.

9. Drachman and Morello provided detailed chronicles of women's struggles to obtain entry into law school, particularly, those in the Northeast. Both books contain startling quotations from law school deans and professors refusing to admit women; for example, Drachman quoted the University of Pennsylvania Law School Dean E. Spencer Miller who, in reaction to the law school application of Carrie Burnham, stated: "I do not know what the Board of Trustees will do, but as for me, if they admit a woman I will resign for I will neither lecture to niggers nor women." Drachman, Sisters in Law: Women Lawyers in Modern American History 42 (2001), citing to M. C. Klingelsmith, *A Pioneer Woman Lawyer of Pennsylvania*, 9 Women Lawyers' Journal 18 (1920).

10. Drachman, Sisters in Law: Women Lawyers in Modern American History 143 (2001).

11. Drachman, Sisters in Law: Women Lawyers in Modern American History 148 (2001).

12. Drachman, Sisters in Law: Women Lawyers in Modern American History 138 (2001).

13. Drachman, Sisters in Law: Women Lawyers in Modern American History 219-20 (2001). Women "knew that the meritocracy in the legal profession was not working for them and that discrimination was a central aspect of their careers in law." At 221. Drachman further noted that these pervasive barriers impacted the ability of women to practice in the courtroom; by 1920, only 6% of women lawyers specialized in trial work and criminal law. At 223.

14. Drachman, Sisters in Law: Women Lawyers in Modern American History 241 (2001).

15. *See, e.g.*, Morello, The Invisible Bar - The Woman Lawyer in America: 1638 to the Present 136 (1988) (1986), describing a distinguished Columbia Law School graduate of 1935 who ranked second in her class being told by a Wall Street lawyer: "What a shame…with your record, we would hire you on the spot - if you were a man."

16. Morello, The Invisible Bar—The Woman Lawyer in America: 1638 to the Present 105 (1988) (1986).

17. Supreme Court Historical Society, *Sandra Day O'Connor,* (March 2, 2000), *available at* http://www.supremecourthistory.org/myweb/justice/o'connor.htm. Justice Ruth Bader Ginsberg, the second woman to serve on the Supreme Court, obtained a clerkship with a District Court judge through the heavy-handed assistance of a professor who overcame "the Judge's reluctance to hire a woman clerk, particularly one with a young child, by guaranteeing him a male backup as a replacement should he be unable to work with her, and threatening to cut off the Judge's future supply of Columbia clerks should he be unwise enough to refuse to give her a 'trial run.'" Herma Hill Kay, *Symposium Celebration of the Tenth Anniversary of Justice Ruth Bader Ginsburg's Appointment to the Supreme Court of the United States*, 104 Colum. L. Rev. 1, 9 (Jan. 2004).

18. ABA Comm'n Women in the Prof., The Unfinished Agenda: Women and the Legal Profession 13 (2001).

19. ABA Comm'n Women in the Prof., The Unfinished Agenda: Women and the Legal Profession 13 (2001).

20. Morello, The Invisible Bar—The Woman Lawyer in America: 1638 to the Present 86 (1988) (1986).

21. Eleanor M. Fox, *Being a Woman, Being a Lawyer and Being a Human Being - Woman and Change*, 57 Fordham L. Rev. 955, 957 (1989).

22. ABA Comm'n Women in the Prof., The Unfinished Agenda: Women and the Legal Profession 13 (2001). Of note, the 2001 Catalyst study reported that 63% of the Class of 2003 at the University of California at Berkeley (Boalt Hall) were women; and women comprised 53% and 51% respectively, at Yale Law School and Harvard Law School. *See also,* Catalyst, Women In Law: Making the Case 9 (2001).

23. Marc Galanter & Thomas Palay, Tournament of Lawyers: The Transformation of the Big Law Firm 20 (1991).

24. Galanter & Palay, Tournament of Lawyers: The Transformation of the Big Law Firm 46 (1991), noting that not only were there more big firms, but they were growing at a much faster rate.

25. *The Am Law 100*, The American Lawyer, July 2005, at 111-121.

26. *See, e.g.,* Mona Harrington, Women Lawyers: Rewriting the Rules 17-21 (1995) (1994).

27. *See, e.g.,* Sussman, *The Large Law Firm Structure: An Historic Opportunity,* 57 Fordham L. Rev. 969, 970 (1989).

28. ABA Network, *First Year Enrollment in ABA Approved Law Schools 1947-2002 (Percentage of Women)* at http://www.abanet.org/legaled/statistics/femstats.html (June 20, 2003).

29. See, for example, U.S. Ct. App., 1st Cir., Report of the First Circuit Gender, Race and Ethnic Bias Task Forces (1999) at v, which noted: "Among attorneys, many more women than men reported that either an attorney, court employee or judge 'made inaccurate assumptions regarding their professional status.'...Women were also more likely than men to report sexually suggestive comments or advances, comments about their physical appearance or clothing, demeaning or derogatory comments and that their opinions or views were not taken seriously." *See, e.g.,* Report and Recommendations of the Florida Bar Special Committee for Gender Equality in the Profession, July 1992 Fla. Bar Assoc., *available at* http://www.flabar.org.

30. *First Year Enrollment in ABA Approved Law Schools 1947-2002 (Percentage of Women) at* http://www.abanet.org/legaled/statistics/femstats.html (June 20, 2003). The U.S. Equal Employment Opportunity Commission requires law firms that employ 100 or more employees to file EEO-1 reports which compile data on the employment status of women and minorities. In 2003, the EEOC issued a comprehensive analysis of its data over a period of years and confirmed the well-stocked pipeline, noting: "In large, national law firms, the most pressing issues have probably shifted from hiring and initial access to problems concerning the terms and conditions of employment, especially promotion to partnership." U.S. Equal Employment Opportunity Comm'n, Diversity in Law Firms 15 (2003) at http://www.eeoc.gov/stats/reports/diversitylaw/index.html, (Dec. 8, 2005).

31. Robert MacCrate, *What Women Are Teaching a Male-Dominated Profession,* 57 Fordham L. Rev. 989, 990 (1989).

32. Hope Viner Samborn, *Higher Hurdles for Women,* 86 ABA J. 30, 30 (Sept. 2000).

33. Hope Viner Samborn, *Higher Hurdles for Women,* 86 ABA J. 30, 31 (Sept. 2000).

34. Hope Viner Samborn, *Higher Hurdles for Women,* 86 ABA J. 30, 32 (Sept. 2000).

35. NALP Found., *Presence of Women and Attorneys of Color in Large Law Firms Continues to Rise Slowly but Steadily,* (Oct. 3, 2002), at http://www.nalp.org/press/details.php?id=18 (Dec. 6, 2005).

36. Catalyst, Women In Law: Making the Case 8 (2001).

37. Catalyst, Women In Law: Making the Case 26 (2001).

38. Catalyst, Women In Law: Making the Case 13 (2001).

39. Ronald J. Gilson and Robert H. Mnookin, *Coming Of Age In A Corporate Law Firm: The Economics Of Associate Career Patterns,* 41 Stan. L.Rev. 567, 570 (1988). *See also,* Cynthia Fuchs Epstein, Carroll Seron, Bonnie Oglensky, and Robert Sauté, The Part-Time Paradox: Time Norms, Professional Lives, Family, and Gender (1999). In writing of the "elite" firms of more than 100 lawyers, the authors stated: "These lawyers provide legal and financial advice to the commanding heights of the world economy." At 12.

40. ABA Comm'n Women in the Prof., *Preface to* Unfinished Business: Overcoming the Sisyphus Factor 3 (1995). *See also*, U.S. Equal Employment Opportunity Comm'n, Diversity in Law Firms, (2003) *at* http://www.eeoc.gov/stats/reports/diversitylaw/index.html, (Dec. 8, 2005): "Lawyers are very often key players in designing and activating the institutional mechanisms through which property is transferred, economic exchange is planned and enforced, injuries are compensated, crime is punished, marriages are dissolved and disputes are resolved. The ideologies and incentives of the lawyers engaged in these functions directly influence the lived experience of Americans, including whether they feel fairly treated by legal institutions." At 2.

41. NALP Found. & Am. B. Found., After the JD: First Results of a National Study of Legal Careers 19 (2004) *available at* http://www.NALPFoundation.org.

42. Harrington, Women Lawyers: Rewriting the Rules 16 (1995) (1994).

43. Stewart, The Partners: Inside America's Most Powerful Law Firms, 14 (1983). Author Robert Nelson observed: "As legal counsel to major corporations, the large law firm participates in transactions and disputes that have enormous consequences for society." Robert L. Nelson, Partners with Power: The Social Transformation of the Large Law Firm 1 (1988).

44. See, e.g., Suzanne Nossel & Elizabeth Westfall, Presumed Equal: What America's Top Women Lawyers Really Think About Their Firms xiii (1998).

45. ABA Comm'n Women in the Prof., Basic Facts from Women in the Law: A Look at the Numbers (1995); *see also,* ABA Comm'n Women in Prof., A Current Glance at Women in the Law (2005) at http://www.abanet.org/women/womenstatistics.html.

46. Harrington, Women Lawyers: Rewriting the Rules 16-17 (1995) (1994). See also David B. Wilkins, From *"Separate is Inherently Unequal" to "Diversity is Good for Business": The Rise of Market-Based Diversity Arguments and the Fate of the Black Corporate Bar*, 117 Harv. L. Rev. 1548, 1600 (2004), noting that: "Corporate law jobs sit atop both the income and status hierarchies of the bar and serve as a gateway to prominent positions in government, business, and civil society."

47. Mary Ann Glendon, A Nation Under Lawyers: How the Crisis in the Legal Profession is Transforming American Society 12 (1994). See also, Mildred L. Amer, Membership of the 109th Congress: A Profile, Congressional Research Service Report for Congress, (updated October 25, 2005).

48. Press Release, ABA Div. for Media Relations and Communications Services, Stories of America's Lawyer-Presidents to Be Told in New Museum Exhibit, Chicago: Sept. 2004, available at: http://www.abavideonews.org/ABA296/release1.htm; and Glendon, A Nation Under Lawyers: How the Crisis in the Legal Profession is Transforming American Society 12 (1994).

49. Glendon, A Nation Under Lawyers: How the Crisis in the Legal Profession is Transforming American Society 12-13 (1994).

50. Judith S. Kaye, *A Prologue in the Guise of an Epilogue*, 57 Fordham L. Rev. 995, 996 (1989). An ABA Journal article observed: "Women have had a significant impact on law and the profession through pressure, influence and gut-level work on laws and practices concerning the workplace, family leave, reproductive rights, domestic violence and other

issues...." Yet, the impact of women on the law has been more successful than the profession's impact on their careers: "The reverse impact - what the legal profession has done to women - has been more brutally Hobbesian. Women's idealism, goals and solidarity often have been blunted not just by sexist hurdles and glass ceilings, but also by a profession that fortuitously changed in harsh and fundamental ways just as they came to it in considerable numbers." Carter, *Paths Need Paving*, 86 ABA J. 34, 35 (Sept. 2000).

51. Judith S. Kaye, *A Prologue in the Guise of an Epilogue*, 57 Fordham L. Rev. 995, 996 (1989).

52. In describing the confusing progress women have experienced in the past few decades, one author stated: "The lip service paid to equality makes the reality of discrimination even more confusing." Mary Pipher, Ph.D., Reviving Ophelia: Saving the Selves of Adolescent Girls 27 (1994).

CHAPTER 2

"WHAT'S MY LINE?"

In the 1950's hit quiz show, What's My Line, the panelists had to guess a contestant's occupation by asking a series of questions which could only be answered "yes" or "no." For each "no" answer, the contestant won $5. The game was over when either 10 "no" answers were given by the contestant, or the contestant's occupation was correctly identified.[1]

If that game were played today, it would be interesting to imagine how panelists would fare against a contestant whose occupation was a law firm manager. Most large law firms have similar management structures: one or two "Managing Partners" who are at the top of the firm's hierarchy; a Management or Executive Committee which meets regularly with the Managing Partner(s); and Department Managers and Practice Group Leaders who preside over each of the firm's substantive law specialties (for example, a Corporate Practice Group, a Litigation Practice Group, a Trusts and Estates Practice Group, a Real Estate Practice Group and, frequently, sub-specialties within each of these broad practices).

Although this seems like a well-organized structure, in actual practice it is generally not. Most lawyers resist being managed and dislike managing. Moreover, most management positions are filled by firm lawyers who are simultaneously engaged in the full-time practice of law. In fact, most firms pride themselves on the fact that their busiest and most successful lawyers are often the ones serving as managers. However, the busiest practitioners have little time to engage in management and even less inclination to be trained for the position. The result is generally an unwieldy system with no coherent management framework.

So imagine being a member of a "What's My Line" panel where the contestant's job title is: Chair, Corporate Law Practice, Large Law Firm. As a panelist, you only know that the contestant has some kind of management function. You begin the questioning:

> Question 1:   "Are your responsibilities limited to management?"

Answer 1:   "No."

Question 2:   "Do you spend more than half your time on management issues?"

Answer 2:   "No."

Question 3:   "Do you engage in annual goal setting with your group to develop specific team targets for accomplishment over the next year, and then revisit those team objectives on a regular basis throughout the year?"

Answer 3:   "No."

Question 4:   "Are you regularly engaged in communicating information to your team?"

Answer 4:   "No."

Question 5:   "Is there a comprehensive training program defined for each member of your team which helps them achieve increasing levels of expertise and maximize their promotion potential?"

Answer 5:   "No."

Question 6:   "Is every senior member of your group involved in the mentoring of the more junior employees, to help them learn both the formal and informal ways to achieve success in your business?"

Answer 6:   "No."

Question 7:   "Do you have a clear and well-understood process for distribut-

ing assignments among team
members to ensure fairness?"

Answer 7:   "No."

Question 8:   "Are you compensated in a way
                 that takes into full account your
                 own management responsibili-
                 ties?"

Answer 8:   "No."

Question 9:   "Do you have specifically articu-
                 lated goals to achieve diversity
                 and a well-organized plan to try
                 to accomplish those goals?"

Answer 9:   "No."

Question 10:   "Has a woman ever served in
                 your position?"

Answer 10:   "No."

Under the "What's My Line?" Game Show rules, the contestant would
have won $50 as a result of his 10 successful "No" answers. In the real life of
a law firm, however, these responses reveal the inherent structural flaws that
are bad for all lawyers and, in particular, negatively affect women's careers.

Ironically, libraries and bookstores are filled with volumes on management theories offering in-depth analyses of major corporations, studies of
their successes and failures, and chronicles of their chief executives. Comparatively little, however, has been written about the "business" of law and how it
functions. Law firms have resisted the significant management changes that
are necessary to address the sophisticated business institutions they have
become. This is a dramatic distinction from other types of businesses where
the management of the entire institution is understood to be critical to its
financial success.

Concerns about law firm management have been recognized since women
began to enter the profession in larger numbers. One commentator reported
that a study of the structure of large law firms in 1981: "marveled that attorneys engaged in the most sophisticated legal practice were working in organi
zational structures that were so remarkably unsophisticated, when compared

to the upper tiers of corporations or even the leading organizations of other professionals, such as universities or accounting firms." [2]

Many firms have attempted to address these issues by hiring non-lawyer managers to focus on firm finances, marketing, technology, and other such functions. In noting this rise of the non-lawyer managerial class, *The American Lawyer* magazine highlighted challenges for the modern law firm that were not imaginable 25 years ago: "A billion-dollar business with hundreds of partners spread out among a dozen or more offices requires professional, full-time attention. This has led to bands of non-lawyer administrators who run important parts of the firms, and often get paid as though they were partners. These are the chiefs: operating officer, financial officer, marketing officer. Once firms were run by part-time managing partners who liked reading spreadsheets. There are still a few that try. Most can't bear to give up practice. Some don't require much sleep; others have deputies who carry the weight. None would advise their clients to follow their example."[3]

Few firms, however, have put into place the critical structures needed to manage and develop the careers of the firm's life blood—the lawyers. Moreover, as noted by *American Lawyer* writer, Andrew Longstreth, to manage significant growth: "large firms have adopted structures that place power in fewer hands."[4]

A scholar who has written extensively on women in the law observed the failure of firms to incorporate business management strategies for lawyers in the structuring of their workplace: "As experts often note, the state of human resources initiatives in most law offices is nothing short of 'Dickensian.'...Seldom do managing attorneys receive formal training in personnel issues, and seldom have they made adequate use of research on employment satisfaction."[5] Even those firms that acknowledge the importance of certain managerial practices generally fail to implement appropriate management incentives and rewards for performance. Professional services consultant, David Maister, highlighted the dilemma: "In most firms, 'business-getting' *is* indeed 'where it's at,' and individual partners do not perceive coaching, training, engagement leadership, skill-building, and contributing to retention as high on their priority list; these activities frequently receive more lip service than day-to-day attention."[6]

The limited focus on the day-to-day management of law firms has been further exacerbated by changes in partner mobility, as lawyers move laterally from one firm to another in the pursuit of better opportunities and higher compensation. This degree of lateral mobility was rare up until the late 1990s, when higher turnover became a fixture on the landscape of the modern law firm. However, much of this lateral movement has been poorly managed and very costly. Most law firms do not even track the economic impact caused by the departures of partner-level attorneys on whom they have spent significant resources trying to attract in the first place.

An article in *The American Lawyer* noted the management failures contributing to the high rate of partner-level departures.[7] These include, for example, too much attention to the anticipated fees from clients that the lawyer hopes to bring with him to his new firm, and too little attention paid to whether there is a good cultural fit between the potential new partner and the existing partnership. Poor management can also lead to the hiring of partners with an incompatible client base, which may include clients who are unwilling to pay the high hourly rates of the new law firm, or whose work may pose a conflict of interest with other work in the firm. Frequently, too, the management team fails to examine properly whether the new lawyers are bringing complementary skills that offer synergistic opportunities for the firm. However, failure to integrate lateral hires is only one, albeit expensive, example of ways in which the lack of attention to day-to-day management issues in law firms is economically unsound.

The women interviewed for this book uniformly described management roles in their law firms that are loosely organized and lack accountability, resulting in significant inconsistencies in the way in which lawyers are treated. One litigation partner described the varieties of management styles she has observed in her large firm:

> *Some practice groups are, depending on the leader, very good, very organized....And they try to be very fair so there are no inter-team rivalries. Other teams are just really loose-knit groups: there's no management, no strategy and, at best, if they talk about who is on their team, it is whoever their protégé is-whoever they want to plug. ...In [some groups, the team leader] is just trying to grab every case for himself. Not trying to spread things around, not thinking about succession issues...which I think is a serious issue.*

Yet there was also an appreciation for the complexity of the issues which managers must face, even as doubts were expressed about whether the firms were properly organized to address them. One young partner, appointed to an internal committee, was amazed at the extraordinary responsibilities facing the full-time lawyers involved in managing the firm:

> *Two years into my partnership I remember think-ing: There's a lot of partners, a lot of sophisticated materials, a lot of sophisticated presentations, and a lot of thought into running and managing a partner-ship. How the Managing Partners were able to prac-tice law at the same time, I don't know.*

Many women expressed concern that their firm lacked formalized com-munication structures, leaving people to obtain their information through individual relationships, to the detriment of those less-connected to important sources of knowledge within the firm. In a structure where women are often marginalized, this informal network is less accessible and, therefore, they fre-quently may not receive valuable communications. A retired female partner summarized her experiences:

> *It just became clear that I didn't hear the same things that other people heard. I didn't get the same respect that other people got. The real decisions here get made in the men's room.*

A young female partner at a large law firm echoed these frustrations with a description of her firm's multiple layers of management that did nothing to facilitate internal communications:

> *Women have to rely more on formal information flow, because they have less of an informal network. There are so few of us, we can barely create our own network, and we're excluded from the boys' network. So unless you have the formal network going on, you really have women who don't get enough information.*

She further observed that most law firms have a flawed management structure because they do not understand the difference between a manage-ment job and true leadership:

> *I think that the cultivation of leaders is a major*
> *problem in law firms. Look at the number of and lev-*
> *els of leaders we have, and how little leadership*
> *development we do, how little attention we give to*
> *how people treat each other, and the messages they*
> *send by how they listen, how they speak, how they*
> *interact in a meeting. You know, all of that stuff is not*
> *paid any attention to in law firms. You've got Depart-*
> *ment Chairs, you've got Department Managers,*
> *you've got Executive Committees, you've got the*
> *Management Committee, you have leaders in multi-*
> *ple levels, none of whom have been cultivated as*
> *leaders.*

Overall, the concept of management in law firms is an anathema, since the prevailing cultural assumption is that lawyers, by their very nature and training, will resist being managed. As a result, there is an institutional bias against investing significantly in management functions, since it is assumed no one will pay attention anyway.[8]

A weak management structure invariably means that there is also little attention paid to team building. One senior attorney, who worked in two firms before accepting a public sector opportunity, expressed her frustration with the tension between the need for sensible business practices and the organizational constraints of law firms:

> *There seems to be more team building in corpo-*
> *rate America. There seems to be more of an agree-*
> *ment that teamwork is appropriate. In law firms, it is*
> *a totally different structure, and the more team build-*
> *ing you have, the higher the cost to the client because*
> *you have too many people on one case.*

A young associate at a midsize firm also expressed frustration with the differences between law firm management and other business models:

> *[T]he structure of law firms...just seems...a bad*
> *business model. The way they function and the way*
> *they work, it is a very different way than most busi-*

nesses do: ...The people who become managers aren't people who necessarily have great managing skills.

She then recounted an anecdote about a senior partner who was attempting to reassure a young associate that her feelings of frustration were normal:

And he said to her, 'Well, you know, the first few years you're here you're going to get a lot of papers back with a lot of red marks on them. And you're going to be supervised pretty heavily, have partners really looking over your shoulder. And then after a while, they'll give you some space to grow. And that's just the way it is here. The way it's always been.' And I thought: 'Here's someone who's actually trying to help, but he's got that party line in him: 'That's the way it's always been." Which is ridiculous. I mean, why? Why? Why is it? ...

There is so much: '...And you're just going to be thrown into the fire and you've got to sink or swim.' I think that's what he meant. 'You will be frustrated, so deal with it.'

She noted that her firm was undergoing a transition in leadership, and the heir-apparent Managing Partner historically had no prior involvement in management issues. She described his current role in the firm:

He'll come in, do his job. He just wants to get his work done and leave. He never really addresses the global picture. It's like he can't be bothered. His practice is so busy, and he comes in, and he works and he wants to leave.

Yet the expectation in the firm was that he would likely become the next Managing Partner because, notwithstanding his lack of involvement in firm management issues, there was no other likely successor to that role.

These observations succinctly highlight a major flaw in the management structure of most firms: the selection of law firm managers has little to do with any inherent management qualities of the individual selected. In general, there is no formal process for selecting Practice Group Leaders, and no established criteria for the skills required to become a member of the firm's Executive Committee or the Managing Partner. Often, the selection is based on qualities having nothing to do with management abilities and everything to do with successful lawyering such as rainmaking skills and high billable hours.[9] Remarking upon the need for effective leadership at the Managing Partner level, one commentator noted: "Unlike senior executives at large corporations, who are typically nurtured through formal leadership development programs, the heads of law firms often reach their positions because of their experience as practice heads and executive committee members. Leadership skills and qualities have little to do with it."[10]

In fact, there was remarkable unanimity among the interviewees when they described how managers in their firms were selected. The prevailing description was best summarized by this female partner:

> *Number one, it's the least common denominator.*
> *The person who is most acceptable or least objection-*
> *able is the best way of putting it. Until they become*
> *objectionable, then they are replaced. And then you*
> *go through the cycle again.*

This informal process for selecting firm leaders presents few opportunities to identify and train women for a seat at the decision-making table. A survey of women in leadership roles conducted by the professional services consulting firm, Hildebrandt International, revealed that the largest firms have few women in leadership positions. For example, women comprise only 12% of the total leadership positions in firms of 1,000 or more attorneys, and only 19% in firms with 500-1,000 attorneys.[11] A young partner described the process in her large firm:

> *In our firm, department chairs get chosen by the*
> *department from the ranks of the equity partners. So*
> *they first look at who is willing, and then there is the*
> *discrete: 'Well, who would have credibility outside*
> *the firm? Who has time? Who is respected as being a*
> *good lawyer?' Any number of criteria. The Executive*

> *Committee has to approve it but, in the end, the*
> *department decides who they want to be chair, and*
> *there are no performance criteria.*

With an informal system of part-time managers selected because they may be less objectionable than their other colleagues, it follows that enormous differences exist among practice groups. The Litigation Department, for example, may have a completely different way of operating than the Corporate Department or the Intellectual Property Group. The young partner expressed her candid assessment of these variations.

> *In a large firm, what is not transparent to people*
> *on the outside is that every department has its own*
> *personality, has its own way of operating, has its own*
> *culture, has its own power structure, and information*
> *sharing structure, and networking structure. Every-*
> *thing is different.*

These cultural variations among the different departments have particularly negative consequences for women. Leaders generally are not held accountable for specific management objectives relating to retention, promotion, work-load distribution, or teamwork. With few role models in senior partner positions, and with no systematic way of obtaining important information throughout the firm, women frequently are excluded from learning about opportunities that could be critical to their future success. It is not surprising, therefore, that women do not advance quickly. Again, the young partner commented on the impacts of an informal system that lacks accountability:

> *There are no performance criteria [for the*
> *advancement of women]. Whether women advance,*
> *or they don't advance, no one is holding you account-*
> *able for it, and that's true in all the ranks of this firm.*
> *No one is looking and saying, 'Where are the women*
> *managers?' Or, in Accounting: 'Where are the women*
> *managers? Why are they accounts receivable clerks,*
> *instead of the manager?'*

Many interviewees noted that by failing to engage women in management roles, firms are missing a valuable opportunity. As one prominent woman partner stated:

> *When it comes to running organizations...women should be cultivated to take on these roles as managers, because they do understand: the multi-tasking role; the training element; running the organization in a way that brings collegiality; decision-making in a collaborative way, as opposed to by fiat. Those are the kinds of things that women should be brought along and rewarded for doing.*

However, women remain largely excluded from management through an ad hoc structure that negatively impacts women at all levels in the firm.[12] A comprehensive study of women in large law firms observed that the dearth of women on Executive or Management Committees may be rooted in old stereotypes: that women lack aptitude for business matters.[13] One report quoted the CEO of a national management consulting business who observed that, in the decade of strategic mergers and acquisitions that he had seen, no women lawyers played a significant role representing the law firm at the table.[14] The ABA Commission on the Status of Women described the lack of women in such important leadership committees as Compensation and Firm Governance as the "second glass ceiling."[15]

An attorney from the Midwest, who has been a national voice on issues of concern to women, decried the lack of women in leadership positions:

> *Nationally, I think it is still remarkable that women are not at senior-level partnership, chairs of departments of large law firms, chairs of substantive areas, or Managing Partners in significantly greater numbers than they are....[C]orporations...are a whole lot better at it than law firms. And they do it in two or three different ways. They earmark talent from the beginning, and probably...have a skewed development path for those that are tagged as significant leadership potential....The next is that they make an awful lot of effort—a great deal of effort—in develop-*

> *ing talent. And law firms do [continuing legal educa-*
> *tion], but they don't do talent development as well*
> *they should.*

Professional services consultants Patrick McKenna and David Maister list behaviors which group leaders should be "absolutely, one hundred percent intolerant of" including, for example: (1) abuse of power or position, (2) any disrespect shown by anyone to anyone else, (3) bullying, (4) hiding from accountability, (5) lack of teamwork, (6) intimidation, and (7) delegating by throwing work on the desk and walking away.[16] Unfortunately, these are some of the same behaviors continually described in the interviews.

Many interviewees reported feeling adrift because they did not see anyone ever looking out for them. Key decisions about their role in the firm were often made without their knowledge or opportunity to respond. One mid-level associate told of her frustration with the firm's failure to provide the training it had promised her when she first interviewed. Before she was hired, she was told that she would participate in an associate rotation program where she would work in each of the firm's departments, and then she could select the area in which she would concentrate her practice long-term. For staffing reasons, however, she was not provided the opportunity to develop expertise in one particular area, as promised. Her frustration was palpable:

> *I think it is extraordinarily frustrating to be what*
> *I am now. I'm going into my seventh year... not feel-*
> *ing particularly adept in any one area. I can kind of*
> *do a lot of things....I can get up to bat, I can hit a sin-*
> *gle or a double, but never a home run in any one*
> *area. And I think that is really a function and part of*
> *this really poor management....No one takes respon-*
> *sibility for anything. There aren't good avenues to fol-*
> *low when you want to get a problem resolved.*

A partner in a large firm said she felt foolish for trying to seek advice from her firm's senior management about her decreased work load during an economic downturn:

> *I selected about three of four people: the chair of*
> *the firm, the Managing Partner of [the local] office,*

*and then one other fellow who was a relatively prom-
inent partner. And I talked to each one of them and I
said, 'Here is my situation.' I had done a lot of work
previously with [a major business generator who had
left the firm]. I no longer had that source of work to
do, combined with the economy going down....So I
had all this time, and work was slow, and I went to
see them: 'Perhaps if I developed an industry specialty? Or, what sort of suggestions might you have?'*

*One told me, 'You have a real problem.' I was
really astounded. Because I thought, if you were a
CEO of a corporation, and you had a very competent
employee who, for various reasons the job she had
been doing didn't need to be done right now, and you
needed to reallocate or redeploy them, you would do
that....*

*I should have kept my mouth shut, burrowed
ahead, and when the economy picked up, things
would have probably gotten better. So lesson learned:
You respond like a woman in a man's world, and
sometimes it doesn't go so well.*

This lack of a clear process to help lawyers resolve such problems can be
particularly disastrous for those suffering the vagaries of an abusive or inappropriate manager. One former associate described her two and a half years
working for an emotionally abusive partner whose intimidating behavior
included: frequently screaming at her in her office; demeaning her; altering
documents in her computer without her consent; engaging in what she viewed
as inappropriate billing practices; and demanding that she never reveal that
she had done work on client documents for which he took credit. When she
finally sought help from another senior partner involved in the supervision of
her work, he offered to protect her as "best he could," but only on the condi-
tion that she tell no one else of her frightening circumstances:

*So through all this, eventually my back went out
so badly I spent two months in bed....I couldn't even*

> *go downstairs....And, meanwhile, I had all this work to do and I wanted to keep it up, so I'm taking pain killers...and the FedEx's were coming, and I'd take conference calls from my bed....*

> *I was completely emotionally abused to the point of being physically incapacitated....[My] superior was part of this whole male thing where these two guys are partners, they play golf together, get together with their wives socially—they were friends!... He was protecting the partner [who was mentally abusing me].*

At first she felt that her only alternative was to accept the senior partner's minimal assistance, believing that there was no one else in the firm who would help her. If a supervising partner could provide only limited help, and only on the promise of secrecy, she feared that any breach of that promise of confidentiality would result in even worse repercussions. Yet, in her interview, she revealed that what she needed most at that time was something her firm lacked—a management structure that would be receptive to an associate who sought help. She stressed how important it is for a Managing Partner to state clearly to all lawyers in the firm:

> *You can come to me anytime as Managing Partner with a problem you are having in this firm, and I will do my best to help you.*

She then added:

> *Unfortunately, that's not a message I have ever heard delivered.*

A former partner referred to law firm management as "a cycle of abuse," adding:

> *[A]ssociates...are treated so poorly.... And how can you expect them to be good managers when they [are treated badly]?*

*Experts at Hildebrandt International empha-
sized the importance of investing in effective management: "Growing a firm requires a significant
investment in both time and actual dollars (for
recruiting, for ramp-up time, for marketing activities,
etc.)....In the broadest perspective, practice management means managing the legal work, managing clients and managing the professionals (lawyers and
other fee earners)."[17] However, most interviewees
described practice group managers whose focus was
seldom on actual management. For example, a partner in a small law firm described her practice group
leader at the East Coast firm where she had once
worked as an associate:*

*He would never get to the firm until 10:30 or
11:00 in the morning. He went to the gym every
morning.... He was well respected because he was
the rainmaker, but his personal skills were just awful.
He would immediately start yelling about where certain files were, and why wasn't something on his desk.*

She described similar circumstances with respect to a verbally abusive
senior partner at the first firm where she worked. There, too, the firm did nothing to reign in his behavior:

*On his bad days, he always wanted to fire the
administrative staff and he would yell and scream and
throw things and have tantrums. And people complained about him a lot, but the partnership never, as
far as we saw, never did anything about it, because he
had so many clients. He was a huge rainmaker for the
firm. Everybody was like: 'Oh, that's just how [he] is.
Just ignore him. It's fine. We know it's not you.' But he
went through associates. Everybody quit.*

Through all these experiences, she was frustrated by a management that failed to set limits on senior partners who acted inappropriately, and who could not contain their intolerance of the limitations of new lawyers:

> *I think there is a big disconnect between what partners expect out of young attorneys, and what those young attorneys are capable of delivering without any training.... They do not remember how little these kids know. And they don't have time to teach them, but they get very frustrated with the work product....*
>
> *As far as management goes, I think they need to take a look at that, and, instead of getting mad, they need to do something about it. I think a lot of times they just don't have the time.*

She attributed much of the failing to a management model that selects rainmakers as managers, rather than appointing individuals with specific skills to do the job. When asked how her former law firm addressed such management issues as equity in the assignment process or problems with difficult partners, her answer revealed a bottom-line driven focus:

> *At one of the firms, they would have workload meetings where they would actually go around and see who's busy and who is not. But then their solutions were something like: 'Well, we're going to rank all the associates in terms of how many hours they bill each month.' And if you are above the line, then you are fine. But if you are below the line, then you are in trouble, and you get a letter from the Management Committee. That is not good motivation.*

Scholar Mona Harrington questioned how lawyers who bill extraordinarily high hours can adequately serve in a key managerial role in a law firm. She noted that: "[A] person consumed by work knows too little of life, thinks too little about the functions of law and its connections to the society, and has too dim a grasp of the individual views, needs and interests of others in the firm to make balanced judgments about the common enterprise."[18]

For so many of the lawyers interviewed, good management was something they longed for, but did not experience. They were frustrated by their firms' failure to understand that inadequate or inept managers can pervade the culture of an entire firm, and have a tremendous impact on an attorney's career success. They all concurred that good management is most needed, and frequently hardest to find, in the control of work flow and assignments to the lawyers.

Endnotes for Chapter 2

1. *1950-1967 Version: How the Game was Played, A Tribute to "What's my Line?"* at http://www.geocities.com/televisioncity/4439/wml50.html (Feb. 2, 2003).

2. Fern S. Sussman, *The Large Law Firm Structure: An Historic Opportunity*, 57 Fordham L. Rev. 969, 970 (1989).

3. Aric Press and Susan Beck, *Almost a Revolution*, The American Lawyer, May 2004, at 77, 80.

4. Andrew Longstreth, *Partner in Name Only?*, The American Lawyer, (Mar. 2005), at 65.

5. Deborah L. Rhode, In the Interests of Justice: Reforming the Legal Profession 45 (2000).

6. David H. Maister, Managing the Professional Service Firm 203 (1993). Maister has also described the failure of many professional services firms to pay attention to effective practice group management: "The people in the practice-group leadership roles are not chosen for their interest in being coaches, leaders, or managers, but instead on some other basis, such as business-getting ability or professional eminence. Too, the compensation system contains no recognition of either leadership or managerial activities. All practice-group leaders are expected to carry as full a client workload as any other professional - and then to manage on top of that! Of course, this is an impossible task." David H. Maister, True Professionalism: the Courage to Care About Your People, Your Clients, and Your Career 72 (1997).

7. Nathan Koppel, *Hello, I Must Be Going*, The American Lawyer, Mar. 2005, at 106. Koppel summarizes the dangers law firms face through the poor hiring and management of lateral attorneys: "Firms spend a fortune interviewing and vetting partner candidates, and another fortune on recruiters' fees, which average 30 percent of a new partner's first-year compensation. Much of this investment is lost when a recent hire walks out the door. Firms' reputations can also take a beating if they consistently disgorge their lateral hires." At 108.

8. The lack of attention to the management of people in law firms can have a particularly detrimental effect on the past-Baby Boom generations, as a former Wall Street lawyer observed in his book on managing Generation X: "I was struck by the fact that, with few exceptions, the more senior lawyers in the firm didn't have a clue about how to manage people my age. ... The closest they came to treating Xers as a special management concern was to dump us in the hands of Baby Boomers, who insisted on misinterpreting our behavior in terms of their own disgruntled youth." Bruce Tulgan, Managing Generation X: How to Bring Out the Best in Young Talent (2000) (1996) 17-18.

9. In a study of large law firms, author Robert Nelson noted: "Most entrepreneurs of the large firm sit on the relatively small governing committee of the firm. With few exceptions these are partners who bear the greatest responsibility for clients. Their governing authority is not as formal as that of their corporate analogues." Robert Nelson, Partners with Power: The Social Transformation of the Large Law Firm 70 (1988).

10. Peter Haapaniemi, *Key Word: Leadership*, Law Biz, Summer/Fall 2005, at 16.

11. Susan Raridon Lambreth, Written materials provided at the Developing Women Leaders in the Legal Profession Conference, (June 10, 2005) sponsored by the Hildebrandt Institute and Thomson/Glasser LegalWorks (unpublished; on file with the author).

12. *See, e.g.,* N.Y. St. Bar Comm. on Women in L., Gender Equity in the Legal Profession: A Survey, Observations and Recommendations 21 (2001) *available at* http://www.nysba.org/ Content/ContentGroups/News1/Reports3/womeninlawreport-recs.pdf (Dec. 1, 2005), which reported that women in private practice: "were more likely to be on committees addressing diversity and associates, but much less likely to be on executive management committees, partnership selection, or business development/marketing committees." One study observed that high-hour demands: "reduce access to powerful positions for those unwilling to tolerate excessive work hours early in their careers. This selection process may have the effect, although not the intent, of keeping a disproportionate number of qualified women out of leadership positions in business and professional organizations. It may also be that the male and female professionals who emerge victorious from a rat race are those who are personally the least well equipped to address the consequences that shifting demographics have for professional and managerial employment relationships." Renée M. Landers, James B. Rebitzer, and Lowell J. Taylor, *Rat Race Redux: Adverse Selection in the Determination of Work Hours in Law Firms,* 86 American Economic Review 329-348 (1996).

13. Cynthia Fuchs Epstein, Robert Sauté, Bonnie Oglensky, & Martha Gever, *Glass Ceilings and Open Doors: Women's Advancement in the Legal Profession,* 64 Fordham L. Rev. 291, 338 (1995 Rpt. to The Assoc. B. City N.Y., Comm. Women Prof.). For an example of this issue as covered in the media, *see* Scott Olson, *Few Women Scale Managing Partner Peak,* 25 Indianapolis. Bus. J., 19A, 16 (2004).

14. *The Crucial Next Phase: Facilitating the Success of Women in Private Practice,* 2003, Strategic Communications, & NorthStar Conf. (unpublished material on file with Levick Strategic Communications, LLC).

15. ABA Comm'n Women in the Prof., Empowerment and Leadership: Tried and True Methods for Women Lawyers 5 (2003). A preliminary study by the Boston Bar Association revealed that significantly fewer women than men perceived that they had input into management decisions in their law firms. *See* BBA Comm. on Gender and the Practice of Law, Preliminary Report of the Boston Bar Association Study of the Role of Gender in the Practice of Law 16 (1988).

16. Patrick J. McKenna & David H. Maister, F1rst Among Equals 149-150 (2002).

17. Susan Raridon Lambreth & Amanda J.Yanuklis, *Achieving the Benefits of Practice Management,* Hildebrant Int'l, (Aug. 30, 2001), *at* http://www.hildebrandt.com/Documents.aspx?Doc_ID=547 (Dec. 8, 2005). The authors further noted that: "Running a practice group in a medium to large firm is equivalent to running a business unit of a major company and requires the same level of management attention and calculated focus on skillset development." *See also,* Susan Raridon Lambreth & Amanda J.Yanuklis, *Practice Groups - Selecting the Most Effective Partners as Leaders,* Hildebrant Int'l, *at* http://www.hildebrandt.com/Documents.aspx?Doc_ID=1062 (Dec. 8, 2005). The authors stated that the typical way practice group leaders had historically been selected is because they fit one of the following four profiles: a major business generator; an egotistical partner needing a "title"; an under-productive partner who may have the time and interest to manage but may not have the skills or credibility; or a partner with an interest in marketing and business development. All four offer poor choices because their background does not suggest the skill sets needed to be an effective leader and manager.

18. Harrington, Women Lawyers: Rewriting the Rules 39 (1995) (1994).

CHAPTER 3

"PLEASE SIR, I WANT SOME MORE ASSIGNMENTS"

For associates, work assignments are the lifeblood. The "right" work assignments can set you on a path of career success. The "wrong" work can crash your career with greater force than race cars colliding on a speedway. The American Bar Association Commission on the Status of Women described the assignment process as playing: "a crucial role in mentoring, training, compensation, and promotion, in short, all attorney development..."[1]

Law firm management consultant David Maister described the work assignment process as: "the single most important managerial activity in a professional service firm....Over time, the pattern of assignments given to professionals will profoundly influence their *professional development*, their worth to the firm and to clients, their *satisfaction* with the firm, and, as a result, their *motivation* and *productivity*."[2]

However, like most critical aspects of law firm life, the assignment process is steeped in mystery and riddled with discretion. New attorneys are exposed early to the internal grapevine. They learn quickly which partners are the "important" ones from whom they should seek assignments and which are the ones to avoid. The information is widespread and not always accurate, but persists as part of the subculture of associate life.

From an associate's perspective, the categorization of partners as either important, or not important, can be simplistic in its criteria. Associates pay significant attention to whether the assignment is coming from a "powerful" partner, and there are only a limited number of ways to be perceived as powerful in a law firm: be someone who brings in a lot of business, or...be someone who brings in a lot of business.

Even a deadly boring assignment is acceptable if it comes from the firm rainmakers. Want to spend six months in a warehouse full of dusty boxes reading technical reports? Yes and happily, if it comes from someone perceived to be critical to the wealth of the firm.

Concomitantly, even the most interesting assignments evoke disappointment if they are from a partner who seems low on the status scale. One retired woman partner at a mid-sized firm, expressing frustration at her own lack of economic clout, described her experience with a new associate:

> *They brought in an associate from another firm who is the most ambitious, walk-on-your-grave type of person I have ever seen. He decided within a week that he didn't have to pay any attention to me.*

The fact that this woman managed important client work for her partner colleagues did not seem to matter to a young male lawyer intent on cementing relationships with those he perceived as powerful. Her experiences were consistent with the findings of a comprehensive study of Colorado attorneys which observed: "Women report that <u>gender is a factor in the distribution of firm resources</u> which hampers their ability to get their work done. This can occur when associates give preference to the work assigned by senior male colleagues because they know who has the power in the firm."[3]

One former large firm partner described all of the nonverbal cues by which one could determine who were the "stars" and who were not:

> *It's a whole subculture in and of itself....It's almost like: who's cool and who's not?...[A]nd part of it is where your office is, you know? I mean, real estate, like where your office is, plays. I never realized it's so important where you are in the office scheme. Because if you're way out, and you don't get a chance to mingle with people during the day, you are out of the loop....[W]hen we moved [to a different building], it was amazing to see the work fall off: the position of where you were in the firm and who you were close to made a huge difference.*

She then added that, based on her observations, there was one other way that women got the good assignments: if they were "attractive" and if they had a "sparkly personality."

The assignment process can make a tremendous difference in how, or whether, an associate succeeds. The sophistication and type of work assigned, the amount of client contact (if any), and the internal exposure to a variety of partners all contribute to developing the skills and relationships needed for professional success. The study conducted for The Association of the Bar of the City of New York noted that if younger attorneys are not provided, through the assignment process, opportunities to develop relationships with potential clients, then their chances for partnership may be diminished as they are being deprived of an important way to demonstrate business generation skills.[4] Yet few law firms focus sufficiently on this clear link between the assignment process and professional growth. David Maister wrote that "[M]any firms take an unstructured, even haphazard, approach to staffing projects. There may be an assignment committee, but in the day-to-day press of events, it is often circumscribed. Junior staff are assigned to whichever project appears most pressing, or to the senior partner who screams the loudest."[5]

In a system in which work is likely to be distributed in an arbitrary or disorganized manner, the ability to understand and affect the results of that system can matter a great deal. However, women tend to have a difficult time working this system to their advantage. Women frequently described their initial feelings of arriving at their firms excited by the opportunity to focus on the substantive challenges: to do interesting work and to do it well. As many interviewees observed, the male associates more frequently arrive hardwired to develop a quick understanding of the internal politics of the firm. A respected woman partner, lamenting the difference in political savvy that male associates exhibit, noted:

> *The men come in saying, 'Who are the important partners?' 'Who should I get to work for?' 'What are the best areas?' I don't know how they know this, but they come in right out of law school and they'll ask around. They pay a lot more attention to structuring their climb.... Women are more interested in: 'I want to do good work.' 'I like the work I do.' 'I get a lot of satisfaction out of it.' Men are much more likely to do things they just hate doing, because their goal is to make partner. Whereas, generally, I think that is not the goal that the women had in mind. We want to be good lawyers.*

The notion that women may be more attuned to the quality of, and their interest in, the work while adjusting to a variety of different role models, and that men tend to be more focused on assignments as a tool of career advancement can create an early, subtle dynamic that begins the process of differentiating between many of the male and female associates. In their study of Colorado lawyers, Reichman and Sterling observed the impact of gender in the assignment process, noting: "The distribution of assignments is socially constructed in a world where gender stereotypes still operate. Thus, when an assignment is not given to a woman because someone thinks she won't want to travel, or because someone thinks the client is too tough or too sexist for her to handle, or simply because she is pregnant, that woman is not given equal opportunity to be productive."[6] When the professional services firm of Deloitte & Touche held a series of workshops to explore why women perceived they had fewer career opportunities than men, it became clear that fewer women were assigned to high-profile, high-revenue assignments: "because male partners made assumptions about what they wanted...."[7]

Even where women voluntarily undertake tasks which demonstrate their good organizational citizenship, the efforts tend not to be recognized. In a study demonstrating the significant relationship between "organizational citizenship behavior" and performance evaluations, women who were judged to perform higher levels of such behavior than their male colleagues did not receive higher performance evaluations.[8] The implications of this and related research is that women facing the institutional impediment of an inequitable or arbitrary assignment process do not necessarily benefit by proving their value through involvement in those firm committees where the work is neither recognized nor rewarded.

Throughout the interviews for this book, women expressed frustration with an amorphous assignment process that frequently resulted in their receiving lower status, less engaging work than their male colleagues. The research supports these personal observations. For example, the study conducted for The Association of the Bar of the City of New York reported that women attorneys perceived that they were more frequently assigned pro bono matters, resulting in reduced opportunities to network with potential client contacts.[9]

In addition to describing male associates who understood better how to manipulate the system to ensure they got the plum assignments, many women interviewed often felt ignored by male senior partners who favored associates who were more like them. A female senior associate in a mid-size law firm described her shock at learning that, while she was working on a small matter for a firm client, a male attorney of equal experience was handling a more interesting and complex problem for the same client. Both had received their assignments from the same senior partner. This experience correlates with the study for the Association of the Bar of the City of New York. Which observed that women are devalued in the way work is assigned by: "a process of discriminatory selection by senior male partners favoring male associates for interesting and complex work, leaving the more routine tasks to the women associates...."[10]

A nationwide survey of women lawyers reported responses from litigators who felt relegated to research and writing tasks while men were assigned to depositions and court appearances. Concomitantly, women corporate lawyers reported being assigned due diligence tasks while their male colleagues were involved in the frontline negotiation of the deals.[11] The survey authors noted that the Respondents further highlighted the critical nature of the assignment process, noting that: "failure to secure increasingly complex and challenging assignments will doom an attorney's prospects for advancement."[12]

As much as associates may try to jockey for position, it is, of course, the partners who decide to whom they will distribute their work. One publication reported advice given by a department chair to a new associate: "A law firm is not any different than the Army...that there are two things you have to know to succeed. First, who gives out the assignments. Second, when and where do you get your meals."[13] In some firms, each partner can assign work independently; in others it may be a more coordinated process.

However, like everything else in law firm life, those who generate the business usually can select whomever they choose to work on their matters. Since these individuals are usually successful senior male partners, a subtle dynamic is added to the early differentiation between how male and female associates are treated. As described by one young female partner in a highly regarded large firm:

> *We don't have partners saying, 'I'm not giving you work because you have ovaries.' They just fail to give you work, and they give it to people who look just like them, typically white men. And I think that's a lot of what goes on in large firms like mine.*

The intent may not be purposeful discrimination, but the result can be just as detrimental. As Susan Estrich noted: "Unconscious discrimination is harder to recognize and more difficult to prove, which makes it a more insidious problem for women."[14]

This theme of disparate work assignments was repeated often in the interviews. One former partner described the process at her firm:

> *It was very haphazard...you kind of grabbed people in the hall. And then somebody...started to analyze people's hours and figure out who wasn't being utilized so that you would call that person first. That would never happen. You call the person you want to work with. That's really what happened.*

Echoed another young partner from a large firm:

> *More intervention is needed in the assignment process. Right now it's all free market and the free market doesn't work.*

A senior partner in a Western office of a national law firm addressed the lack of coordination in her firm's case assignment process:

> *If a big case comes in to [her branch office],...then they are assigned out to the people that person feels comfortable with....If I am going to send a case to [another branch office], I don't call the head, I will call an attorney there who I like the way he does a case. Be it man or woman. And that is what they do. They will call and say, 'I have a client who got sued out there, would you do this case?' And they do not go through the head [of the departments]. Because if they go through the head, they take it all.*

A senior associate, who gave up her high salary for a job in the non-profit sector, succinctly summarized the uphill battle women face in obtaining important assignments:

> *For a young associate, the distribution of work assignments is one of the more critical elements of a successful career path toward partnership. Every law firm has its share of "dog" cases which no one*

ever wants to work on: work that is either from a difficult client, is not challenging, requires mind-numbing hours of document review, or offers little opportunity for demonstrating one's creative talents. The assignment distribution process is a critical impediment to women's success in large law firms. Invariably, and particularly in the highly prized litigation and corporate departments, women do not get high-quality work.

Often, these disparate results happen without anyone in firm management even recognizing the issue. A litigator described her conversation with the firm's Managing Partner who was questioning why he was perceived as being "not female friendly":

And I said, 'Well, could it be because you don't have a single female [working on your cases]?' And remember, this guy worked 2,800 hours [a year], had all the biggest pieces of litigation in the firm, and not one of them had a female in the second position on any of his cases. He could not put a female in that second position.

One nationally recognized attorney dryly commented:

Assignments are being made by men based on the same crummy masculine model.

The way in which cases are assigned is the first step in a longer-term winnowing out process that results in both intended and unintended consequences. It is also, however, the first glimpse into a workplace that is loosely, if at all, managed. The assignment process is, therefore, frequently perceived as arbitrary and oddly-conceived because it is reflective of a management structure which, as it has developed, often defies coherent management principles.

In general, what the women I interviewed most wanted from their firm's management was a demonstrated commitment to their growth and development as professionals. However, instead of a management structure focused on working with associates to develop their talents and capabilities, there was generally only one message that was widespread and consistent across departments: keep your billable hours as high as possible if you want to succeed.

Endnotes for Chapter 3

1. ABA Comm'n Women in the Prof., Fair Measure: Toward Effective Attorney Evaluations 26 (1997).

2. Maister, Managing the Professional Service Firm 175 (1993).

3. Nancy Reichman & Joyce S. Sterling, Gender Penalties Revisited 43 (2004).

4. Epstein, et al., *Glass Ceilings and Open Doors: Women's Advancement in the Legal Profession*, 64 Fordham L. Rev. 291, 336 (1995 Rpt. to The Assoc. B. City N.Y., Comm. Women Prof.). Studies consistently demonstrate that women tend to be less satisfied with specific aspects of their work relating to: job opportunities; recognition for work done; opportunities for advancement; and control over the amount and manner of their work. *See, e.g.*, Reichman & Sterling, Gender Penalties Revisited (2004); *see also* Heinz, et al., *Lawyers and Their Discontents: Findings from a Survey of the Chicago Bar*, 74 Ind. L. J. 735 (1995).

5. Maister, Managing the Professional Service Firm 156 (1993).

6. Reichman & Sterling, Gender Penalties Revisited 42 (2004). Sometimes, gender disparities in the assignment process can play out on national television for all the world to observe. Donald Trump's first "apprentice" winner, a male, was allowed to choose one of two positions: overseeing the construction of the Trump International Hotel and Tower in Chicago or managing the Trump National Golf Club in Los Angeles. The second apprentice chosen, another male, had a choice between the Trump International Hotel and Tower in Las Vegas or the $4 billion dollar Trump Place project in Manhattan. In the third season, the selected apprentice was a woman. Her choice of projects? She could either organize the Miss Universe Pageant or oversee the renovations of Donald Trump's Palm Beach mansion.

7. Douglas M. McCracken, *Winning the Talent War for Women: Sometimes it Takes a Revolution*, Harv. Bus. Rev., (Reprint R00611) (Nov./Dec. 2000), at 6.

8. Sharon E. Lovell, Arnold S. Kahn; Jennifer Anton, Amanda Davidson, Elizabeth Dowling, Dawn Post & Chandra Mason, *Does Gender Affect the Link Between Organizational Citizenship Behavior and Performance Evaluation?*, Sex Roles: J. Research (Sept. 1, 1999) at 4, *available at* 1999 WL 18705871. The article cited to research demonstrating disparate impacts in evaluating gender-based behaviors: "A mother who changes her baby's diaper is not considered to have accomplished a praiseworthy act, but a father who engages in the same behavior will often receive praise for it. Likewise, a mother who does not change her baby's diaper will receive far more disapproval than will a father who neglects his baby.

9. Epstein, et al., *Glass Ceilings and Open Doors: Women's Advancement in the Legal Profession*, 64 Fordham L. Rev. 291, 337 (1995 Rpt. to The Assoc. B. City N.Y., Comm. Women Prof.).

10. Epstein, et al., *Glass Ceilings and Open Doors: Women's Advancement in the Legal Profession*, 64 Fordham L. Rev. 291, 337 (1995 Rpt. to The Assoc. B. City N.Y., Comm. Women Prof.).

11. Nossel & Westfall, Presumed Equal: What America's Top Women Lawyers Really Think About Their Firms xviii (1998).

12. Nossel & Westfall, Presumed Equal: What America's Top Women Lawyers Really Think About Their Firms xviii (1998).

13. *The Crucial Next Phase: Facilitating the Success of Women in Private Practice*, 2003, Levick Strategic Communications, & NorthStar Conf. (unpublished material on file with Levick Strategic Communications, LLC).

14. Susan Estrich, Sex & Power 10 (2000). Estrich further observed that an additional problem with unconscious discrimination is that it allows a guilt-free attitude to prevail: "If the men on top don't think they're discriminating-and most of them don't…what's the reason to change?" At 147.

CHAPTER 4

THE COIN OF THE REALM

The most valuable currency in any culture is called "The Coin of the Realm." In law firms, the Coin of the Realm is the billable hour. Hours are measured and evaluated on an annual basis: the more billable hours a lawyer produces in a year, the more valuable that person is to the firm.

For more than two decades, there has been a growing body of literature on the subject of career dissatisfaction among lawyers. Each time, the same culprit is identified: the time famine created by high billable-hour demands. In 1990, the American Bar Association conducted an in-depth survey of lawyers to compare the extent of dissatisfaction in the legal profession with data that the ABA had previously collected in a 1984 survey.[1] The results revealed a significant increase in the number of lawyers who reported not having enough time for themselves and their families. The data offers a clear explanation why: in 1984, 35% of the Respondents reported working in excess of 200 hours per month; by 1990, that number grew to 50%.[2] Similarly, *The American Lawyer* compared data from its 2005 survey of mid-level associates with results from its 1986 survey and found that today's associates report billing 16% more than their 1986 counterparts.[3]

Moreover, the ABA study disputed the contention that lawyers have always worked hard by noting the changed nature of the hours lawyers are working: "The pressures and demands of law firms and clients, the element of speed created by the advent of fax machines and computers, and the increasing lack of courtesy between lawyers...have together changed the quality of the hours worked so that 200 hours in today's practice is far more stressful than 200 hours in the 1960s."[4] Importantly, the ABA noted that this is not a gender-based problem; in addition to a majority of both the men and women reportedly not having enough time, 71% of the men and 84% of the women reported feeling increasingly worn out at the end of the workday.[5]

In fact, the intense pressure fostered by technology's expanded opportunities for instant communications and even faster results may be the most significant factor affecting the profession today. The impact of technology on the pressure and quality of each billable hour requires immediate attention. As

The American Lawyer recently reported: "A straight comparison of hours also ignores the impact of technology on productivity...Older partners had the luxury of occasionally leaving work at the office, while lawyers today are on call 24/7. Associates are no longer shackled to their desks, but they now sleep with their cell phones close at hand."[6]

As the billable-hour demands have grown with each passing year, today's lawyers are under unprecedented pressure to bill extraordinarily high hours. One commentator noted: "Indeed, the time demands of most law firms now approach the impossible for anyone, female or male, who needs or wants to have life consist of anything more than a job."[7]

These time demands are at the heart of a fundamental discontent with legal practice today which is driving so many lawyers out of the profession. The particular impact on women can be traced to the unprecedented expansion which law firms underwent in the decades when women were entering the profession in large numbers.

For example, in the early 1980s, as more women were finding their way into law schools, the "large" law firm was undergoing significant growth. Firms of approximately 50 lawyers in the 1970s may have increased five fold and more, adding offices in the United States and abroad by the late 1980s.[8] Before 1980, no firm in this country had gross revenues exceeding $60 million dollars; by the late 1980s, however, it was not unusual for the gross revenues of major New York law firms to exceed $200 million dollars.[9] By 2004, four law firms had gross revenues in excess of a billion dollars and more than 60 firms reported gross revenues exceeding $300 million dollars. Of these firms, most had more than 500 lawyers; ten had more than 1,000.[10]

The enormous impact of this explosive growth is felt in the brutal billable-hour system.[11] Up until the mid-20th century, most lawyers did not keep track of their time at all. In the past several decades, however, the billable hour has become the dominant mechanism by which law firms are paid for their legal services. In many cases, billable time is measured in six-minute segments.[12]

As recently as the early 1980s, it was not unusual for a large firm's annual billable-hours expectation to be approximately 1,600 to 1,700 hours a year. By the end of that decade, however, as firm size and revenues were exploding, annual expectations were climbing towards 2,000 hours and higher.[13] One commentator reported that some New York law firms were actually budgeting associates at 2,500 billable hours a year.[14] Even then, the early seeds were planted for some firms which, today, have increasing numbers of attorneys billing 3,000 hours or more a year. For the most part, the law firm of the 21st century is making more money simply by working longer hours at higher rates.[15]

Even relatively young lawyers note the dramatic difference in billable-hour requirements compared to when they first entered the profession. Observed one senior associate:

> *I've been practicing at this firm for 10 years, and it's been astonishing to me how law firms in general have changed and how, institutionally, the practice of law has changed. When I first started, I think the bill-able-hour requirement was 1,725....I probably was still billing 2,200 hours, but it is nice to know that is what the requirement was. Now the [stated] require-ment is 1,950. The fact is, if I now wanted to be part-time, it would just bring me back down to the require-ment that was full-time when I started here.*

The demand for associate leverage and increased hours has also caused firms to compete fiercely for the top law school graduates. Firms that once hired a small number of new lawyers each year began to hire large entering classes of associates.[16] Law firms further competed by enticing these new recruits with ever-increasing starting salaries.[17]

The giant salaries, however, came with a formidable price tag: firms expected their highly paid lawyers to bill more hours in order to justify their compensation, even as they imposed more pressure for non-billable activi-ties.[18] Pressure is not just driven by law firms trying to wrestle out every last moment of productivity from its lawyers, but from clients who, paying ever-increasing hourly rates, demand immediate access. An article in *The American Lawyer* painted a grim picture of the pace of life in the modern law firm: "Once clients summoned busboys and secretaries with discrete buzzers; now they summon their million-dollar lawyers with BlackBerries. That thin bulge can ruin the drape of a fine suit or the rare family conversation; it's hard to be a Master of the Universe if you're always on call. It's not just that there is nowhere to hide, it's that the whole velocity of the practice has changed, and with it the spike in tension and mistake. 'As soon as possible' once allowed a decent interval for thought, research, and delivery. Over the last 25 years, that evolved from Special Delivery, to courier, to overnight delivery, to send-me-the-attachment-now!"[19]

The relentless drive for increased billable hours has clearly had a negative effect on the profession as a whole. Recognizing that the billable-hour model has had detrimental impacts and unintended consequences to the profession, the American Bar Association created a Commission on Billable Hours. Its purpose was to analyze how the billable-hour system affects the delivery of legal services.[20] The Commission's list of the "corrosive impacts" of the billable-hour system is instructive to this book's analysis:[21]

1. a decline in the collegiality of firm culture and concomitant increases in associate departures;[22]

2. discourages pro bono work;[23]

3. fails to encourage project or case planning;[24]

4. provides no basis for the client to predict cost;[25]

5. may not reflect a value to the client;[26]

6. penalizes the efficient and productive lawyer;[27]

7. discourages communication between lawyer and client;[28]

8. encourages skipping steps;[29]

9. fails to discourage excessive layering and duplication of effort;[30]

10. fails to promote a risk/benefit analysis;[31]

11. does not reward the lawyer for productive use of technology;[32]

12. puts client's interest in conflict with the lawyer's interest;[33]

13. client runs the risk of paying for the lawyer's incompetence or inefficiency;[34]

14. client runs the risk of paying for associate training;[35]

15. client runs the risk of paying for associate turnover;[36]

16. client runs the risk of paying for aggressive time reporting;[37]

17. itemized bills tend to report mechanical functions instead of valuing progress; and[38]

18. lawyers compete based on hourly rates.[39]

The Commission attributed the prominence of the billable hour as resting on "interlocking and reinforcing pressures: simplicity, familiarity, profitability, efficiency, and amiability."[40] This powerful combination of characteristics, however, has resulted in a system that has wreaked havoc on the profession.[41]

For women, these unrelenting billable-hour demands have been described as one of the greatest impediments to their movement up the career ladder at large law firms. This impact was highlighted in a study of Wisconsin lawyers which noted that women tend to bill fewer hours: "Women with family responsibilities statistically are caught up short (1) it is difficult to put in the 70- or 80-hour weeks; and (2) the billable-hour system does not reward any efforts for efficiency in work habits."[42] The study conducted for the Association of the Bar of the City of New York summarized the pervasive impact on law firm life: "Billable hours not only reflect actual time spent on a case; they have also become a benchmark for ascertaining commitment to the firm. As one of the few measurable elements in a system of evaluation marked by subjective criteria, billable hours are also symbolic in expressing dedication and willingness to sacrifice for the good of the firm." [43]

A senior partner noted the increased pressures she has experienced since she began practicing law:

> *When I was an associate, I had 1,800 hours pretty much every year, maybe 1,850. And I might have had 50 hours of something else, but that's what I did. I hit my billable target....and if somebody had told me that I had to put in 2,200 hours, I would have left, too.*

As billable hours have become the benchmark by which law firms define one's commitment to the profession, there is no time left for other relationships. A former associate at a large law firm recalled the painful memories of her first year as a young lawyer:

> *As a first-year associate [I was working on a large case]....For two months I didn't have one meal with my husband, except on a Saturday night at 8 p.m. when he met me downtown... Not a breakfast. Not a lunch. Nothing. So that was around the clock....And I just assumed that this is what was expected of me.*

> *Similarly, a third-year associate at a successful East Coast law firm stated that, to maintain her bill-*

able hours in excess of 2,000 hours per year, she does not make plans with friends unless they understand that the plans are likely to be broken at the last minute. She was skeptical of her firm's description of itself as a meritocracy where gender does not have any impact on success. She observed that, in law firm parlance, the real meaning of meritocracy is equated with physical presence at the firm:

> *Being exceptionally bright is not enough to succeed. You have to be available.*

The relentless hourly pressure and the constant need to disrupt evening and weekend plans contributed to her decision to leave the firm. She noted that the difference between annually working 1,900 hours and 2,100 hours has a tremendous impact on one's personal life, emphasizing that those extra 200 to 300 hours equals an extra four weeks of work each year. Another attorney who fled the associate life at her former law firm recalled her horrified reaction to the business card of a Washington lawyer which included her cell phone number, home phone number, pager number and every other means by which she could be reached any hour of the day.[44]

In fact, the advent of email and the BlackBerry has become another opportunity for capturing more time to bill, rather than devices which save time or provide flexibility. As one senior partner observed:

> *Now with the arrival of not just cell phones, but BlackBerries..., it presents a set of challenges as well. It certainly allows you to be out more. But what does it do to the quality of that time? I don't know. I was talking to a therapist the other day, and she said, 'What is it with you lawyers? You all have BlackBerries.' She said she doesn't see any other patient base that looks like we do....*

> *There's a law firm that has a rule that you cannot be beyond ear-shot of your BlackBerry. So if you're in the gym, or wherever you are, you have to be able to*

hear it. So I'm a little worried. Yes, we may give you your flex time, but it may not be worth it.

A former associate in a large New York law firm lamented that, by her second year of practice, she was billing nearly 2,400 hours a year and expressed excitement if she was home by 10 p.m. during the week:

> *Weekends were generally in the office; 2,300 hours cannot be reasonably managed. It requires constant work....But to do more interesting work assignments, you have to have the experience which you only develop by working hard.*

One former partner candidly described the different types of client billable hours, noting that some assignments can justify constant work by a larger team, where other matters are hoarded by senior lawyers so their own hours remain high:

> *There are easy hours to bill and then there are difficult hours to bill. If you are litigating, it is easy to be working on the train home, working on a brief; you know, constant work....[B]ut if you are not generating that kind of work for your associates, especially in the transactional world, one deal, you know, a few months go by before there is anything significant. I mean, your senior partners have to be really jamming it down and all the senior partners are doing that work, because they are hanging onto those hours. And so, I think that creates a whole host of problems.*

Lawyers frequently observe a significant inconsistency between how firms represent themselves during the interviewing process when they are trying to recruit new associates, and the reality of life in the firm once they are on the inside. For example, this effort to present one's law firm in the best light possible for recruitment purposes was observed in a survey conducted for law students which asked women in private practice about their law firms.

The authors noted that, based on the nature of the comments accompanying the survey: "it could be argued that some respondents, particularly partners, chose to focus exclusively on the positive aspects of firm life in an effort to buoy their firm's position in the eyes of potential recruits." [45]

A former partner of a large law firm, who left to become general counsel of a major business, summarized this experience succinctly:

> *Firms market as the Peace Corps, but they're really the Marines.*

This observation corresponds with the disparity between what firms articulate as their billable-hour requirement, and what is actually required to succeed. A senior partner in the New York City branch office of a national law firm commented on her firm's ever-evolving approach to what associates should be told:

> *We change our philosophy every year in terms of what is stated and what is not stated. I think that anything below 1,800 would certainly be unacceptable. If you want to get large bonuses, you would need to be over 2,200. Somewhere in between, anywhere over 2,000, you probably could still get a bonus.*

One lawyer noted that associates are told that the billable-hour "target" in her firm is 1,850, but, in reality, those who become partners are billing in excess of 2,300 hours a year. A young partner reported that her firm's articulated requirement of 1,900 billable hours was recently augmented by an edict requiring all lawyers to report on their time sheets an annualized 2,500 hours which includes direct client-billable and other non-billable activities (such as, for example, business development and training). Another partner reported that her firm tells its associates that they should be targeting between 2,000 and 2,200 billable hours per year. She then observed, however, that if an associate achieves 2,000 billable hours, that person would not be considered a "superstar."

As a result, women frequently criticize their own naiveté in accepting the articulated standard, which invariably turns out to be a lower number than the one which actually matters when compensation and partner elevation decisions are made. A former senior associate described her average week trying to meet the stated "recommendation" of 2,000 hours. Even though she was working nights and weekends, she was informed that her elevation to partner was in jeopardy because she was not billing as much as others in her department which, she came to understand, frequently exceeded 2,500 hours. To avoid what she felt was the disgrace of not being elected partner in an "up or out" system, she threw herself into her work:

> *I was crazy sick, physically, nervous, everything.*
> *It was the thought of not making partner that was*
> *more humiliating to me than anything else, even*
> *though I knew I was getting positively used.*

As she recounted her sorrow during what turned out to be her final months in the firm, she recalled what it first felt like when she started six years earlier:

> *You are overwhelmed at how wonderful it is. You*
> *have this beautiful office and you have a secretary*
> *and you're working on all these great assignments*
> *and it's really a wonderful experience. And then*
> *everything fell apart.*

A female partner from that same law firm seemed not to realize her own inconsistency in responding to questions identifying whether there was a disparity between her firm's articulated billable-hour requirement and what was really needed to succeed:

Question:	What is the billable-hour expectation?
Answer:	For associates, it is 2,000 hours.
Question:	And is that a real 2,000?
Answer:	It's pretty real.
Question:	Can you make partner at 2,000?
Answer:	Yeah.
Question:	So it's not "2,000, but you'll only really be considered if you're at 2,400?"

Answer: Nope....I mean, most of the peo-
                 ple who do go on to become part-
                 ner actually do work more. We
                 are pretty neurotic people here.

One veteran of two large firms who ultimately accepted a prestigious position in the public sector, summarized the pressures:

If you are going to make it as a partner in a big firm, you are giving up your weekends, you are giving up your nights, and you are doing a lot of travel. And you have to decide whether that fits into your life. That "drop everything and do it for the client" is a given. The revolution failed because we didn't change the workplace.

Many of the women interviewed expressed frustration with the workaholic role model by which they constantly felt they were being measured. The pace they described felt like an out-of-control freight train, with the lead car barreling forward, dragging all the other cars along to an uncertain destination. It is unclear whether the train is driven by the client's demands or the firm's competitive fears, but both seem to drive each other to even faster speeds. The study conducted for The Association of the Bar of the City of New York noted the vicious cycle: "It is not simply that clients expect and demand immediate attention to their needs and thus determine the prevailing ethos of these firms. The competition for clients drives each of these firms to set standards that will ensure its future existence."[46] Consider one senior woman lawyer's description of her former Managing Partner:

He was a workaholic. When I was there, he would often be there past 11 p.m. or midnight, and in at 7:30 a.m. He loves to practice law and he spends all of his time there. But he also holds other people to that standard.

In addition to senior partners who modeled a workaholic approach to their job, women lawyers frequently felt frustrated by male contemporaries who exhibited similar behavior to gain greater competitive advantage. One émigré from a large national firm described an associate colleague:

There was a male associate, very cut-throat, ambitious, and was at the office every single night until late. And then about 8 p.m., he would make the rounds, and see who was there so everybody could see him. [Whenever I worked in the evenings] he would come in and say to me, 'Why aren't you home with your children?' And I said 'Why aren't you home with yours?' And he'd answer 'because my wife is with them.' And then, the same guy, after his third child was born, took off Sunday. He did it once on a Sunday to be with his newly born baby.... He became a partner very quickly.

This anecdote captures the difficulties experienced by women attorneys which are mirrored by women throughout the workforce. As the Report of the Sloan Work-Family Policy Network observed: "The culture and organization of paid work, domestic care work, and community organizations remain predicated on the breadwinner-homemaker model. Thus, jobs, schools, medical services, and many other aspects of contemporary life operate on the assumption that someone (a wife) is available during the typical workday to care for children after school, during the summer, or on snow days, to take family members to the doctor or the dog to the vet, or to have the refrigerator fixed."[47]

This male model of equating extraordinarily long hours with success results in many women feeling as though they must engage in super-human efforts to demonstrate the same level of commitment to their work.[48] One woman interviewed described a former senior associate who worked incredibly long hours, including during the last weeks of her pregnancy. Even as she went into premature labor, she was anxiously trying to convince her husband to allow her to deliver documents to her partner on the way to the hospital. She continued to work full-time after the birth of a second child. One evening, after a recent surgical procedure, she came back to work late at night. As she checked her emails, there was a message from one of her partners complaining about her absence from the office earlier that day. That was when she finally quit.

A prominent attorney who left private practice in dismay over the changes she has seen in the profession, stated:

*The billable hour is a sick thing without respect
to gender. It promotes bad lawyering and inefficiency.*

In its analysis of minimum billable-hour requirements, the ABA Commission on Billable Hours stated: "Some argue that minimum requirements...shift the focus of the new lawyer's work from doing the job and deriving satisfaction from that endeavor to a preoccupation, even an obsession, with logging the number of hours required for retention, promotion, and bonuses....Further, the combination of required hourly minimums and the shift of responsibility can lead to questionable billing practices, ranging from logging hours for doing unnecessary research to outright padding of hours. These are not imaginary fears; researchers report numerous instances of over-billing, many involving exaggerated hourly entries."[49]

In its survey of midlevel associates, *The American Lawyer* reported that nearly 4% of its respondents stated that: "[I]nflating their hours on time sheets is an accepted practice at their firms.... Many agree that the tendency to inflate hours is an unavoidable, albeit unfortunate, by-product of the bill-or-burn culture of big-firm life."[50]

Similarly, an ABA Journal Article noting the obstacles to advancement that women in the profession have faced, stated: "Law firms have moved more and more to eat-what-you-kill compensation and billing expectations that challenge the veracity of a 24-hour clock."[51] A number of interviewees corroborated that the pressure for billable hours can result in clients being billed for unnecessary time. One attorney stated that, by the time she left her large firm, she felt significant pressure to round her time upwards. Another described her frustration with a senior partner who refused to address client concerns in his billing practices:

> *I would waste my time on something, like we all
> do inadvertently, so there would be two hours of
> research and I would realize that I shouldn't have
> done it this way to begin with.... I can't bill the client
> for this, because it is not fair to bill the cost. Or the
> summer associates would be working on something,
> and I would spend forever training them, and would
> take way too long, and the client was not getting the
> value. This would include my time talking with the*

senior partner about [the specialized area of law that
he knew nothing about].

Then I, as the communication point with the cli-
ent, was called and told, 'You can't bill me for this.'
And I would have to say, 'You're making a really good
point. Let me get back to you.'

Then I would have to go back to [the senior part-
ner] and he would say, 'No!'...He was insisting that
every penny be billed.... And I was furious...because I
felt that the client was getting cheated.

An associate at a large firm reported that she would be asked to work on client matters that the senior partner did not want to bill. Because the partner did not want his own billing attorney statistics to be impaired by write-downs, he would pressure her to leave the time off her daily time sheet, thereby negatively impacting her own billing statistics, resulting in her having to work even longer hours to make up the "missing" time.

Another outgrowth of the relentless focus on client billable hours is the marginalization of all other important firm work. Participation on firm committees, involvement in the hiring process, and other roles demonstrating good firm citizenship are not generally recognized by the firm in its compensation process. As a result, attorneys are asked to perform functions which contribute significantly to the firm, but for which no billable-hour credit is given. One associate expressed her frustration with these substantial but unrecognized efforts.

In our practice area, we are constantly updating
and revising our forms. So this morning, I was
researching and rewriting the forms that we do for all
of our clients, and at the meeting today I have to
explain to the partners and the members of that com-
mittee why we need to make these changes. So it is
real legal work, I've been instructed to do it, but it
doesn't count.

In reality, what firms do not measure tends not to matter. As a result, lawyers respond to the statistics that are tracked and used in the attorney evaluation process and which contribute to one's overall prestige within the firm. Too frequently, these internal measures fail to include activities which are critical to the over-all success of a law firm, focusing instead on short-term profitability rather than the long-term health of the organization. As David Maister stated: "Unfortunately, in many law firms, the reporting systems do not provide equitably for...varying paths to profitability."[52] In particular, firms that place excessive emphasis on one's personal billable hours actually end up promoting behaviors that result in hoarding work, instead of promoting operational efficiencies - including more business generation activity.[53]

The Career Development Office at Yale Law School developed a model to demonstrate how many actual hours in the office may be necessary to achieve certain billable-hour milestones. Setting forth some reasonable assumptions about the length of an average workday as well as assumptions about the number of vacation and paid holidays, the model demonstrates that, to achieve a target goal of 1,800 billable hours, it is likely that a lawyer will spend in excess of 2,400 hours actually at the office. Similarly, to achieve a targeted goal of 2,200 billable hours requires a likely time commitment of in excess of 3,000 hours. Although the model recognizes time spent for meals and rest room breaks, it does not account for time spent on personal issues, participation in bar or other committee work, writing an article, or other involvement in community activities.[54]

Other articles have also addressed the practical impacts of high billable-hour demands by recognizing that not every working hour can reasonably be billed. Although the projections vary, the impact is equally grim. For example, one author noted that, to bill 2,000 hours a year, a lawyer must work six 10-hour days each week; to bill 2,400 hours would require 12-hour days, six days a week.[55] Another article reported that: "Studies show that lawyers need to spend about three hours in the office for every two hours of billable time. Ergo, under that measure (assuming an hour for lunch), billing six hours means working a 10-hour day, which in turn generates between 1,500 and 1,600 hours of billable time a year."[56]

An article addressing the continued impediments women face in the legal profession reported: "It takes approximately 1.5 hours of actual working time to produce a billable hour...."[57] One former large firm practitioner stated in her interview that, according to her calculations, a fully profitable associate needs to bill four times one's own salary. Her analysis, she feared, had dramatic negative ramifications for the future: in an environment where partners insist on large increases in compensation each year, requiring corresponding increases in associate pay to attract top law school talent, the implications of having to bill four times one's salary would mean ever-increasing billable-hour demands on associates.

Even as women lawyers struggle valiantly to meet their firm's billable-hour expectations, they are still losing ground to their male colleagues who have recognized that bringing large amounts of business into the firm is fundamental to becoming a partner and achieving even higher compensation.

Endnotes for Chapter 4

1. *See, The State of the Legal Profession: 1990*, 1991 ABA Young Law. Div.

2. *The State of the Legal Profession: 1990*, 1991 ABA Young Law. Div. 22.

3. Amy Kolz, *Don't Call Them Slackers*, The American Lawyer, Oct. 2005, at 115. One article minced no words in describing the profession's sentiment towards the billable hour: "Both reviled and ubiquitous, the billable hour is the cockroach of the legal world." Douglas McCollam, *The Future of Time,* Litigation 2005, (Suppl. The American Lawyer & Corp. Couns.), 2005, at 64.

4. *The State of the Legal Profession: 1990*, 1991 ABA Young. Law. Div. 23-24. Note that the study was conducted before electronic mail changed the pace of the profession even more dramatically.

5. *The State of the Legal Profession: 1990*, 1991 ABA Young Law. Div. 24.

6. Amy Kolz, *Don't Call Them Slackers*, The American Lawyer, Oct. 2005, at 117.

7. S. Elizabeth Foster, *The Glass Ceiling in the Legal Profession: Why Do Law Firms Still Have So Few Female Partners?*, 42 U.C.L.A. L. Rev. 1631, 1651 (1995). *See also* Steven Keeva, *Take Care of Yourself*, 90 ABA J. 80, 80 (Dec. 2004), noting: "Billing by the hour is extraordinary in the way in which it so nakedly equates money with time. It thereby offers no incentive at all to stop working. The taskmaster par excellence, it can reduce grown professionals to slavish piece workers."

8. Harrington, Women Lawyers: Rewriting the Rules 25 (1995) (1994). *See also*, Andrew Longstreth, *Partner in Name Only?*, The American Lawyer, (Mar. 2005), at 65: "In 1986 there were four firms in The Am Law 100 [*The American Lawyer* 100] that had 500 lawyers or more. By 2003, that number had grown to 62."

9. Harrington, Women Lawyers: Rewriting the Rules 25 (1995) (1994).

10. *See The Am Law 100*, The American Lawyer, July 2004, at 103.

11. Law firms budget for billable hours on an annualized basis.

12. Epstein, et al., *Glass Ceilings and Open Doors: Women's Advancement in the Legal Profession*, 64 Fordham L. Rev. 291, 379 (1995 Rpt. to The Assoc. B. City N.Y., Comm. Women Prof.). A national career counselor interviewed for this book attributed part of the "tyranny of the billable hour" to the rise of the consultants in the late 1960s and early 1970s who encouraged firms to increase revenue by "breaking the hour into one-sixth of an hour pieces." For a glimpse into how life used to be, an article noted that, in 1958, an ABA publication observed that there were approximately 1,300 "fee-earning" hours in a year. *See* Cary Griffith, *Creative Billing: Is the Reign of the Almighty Billable Hour Over?*, Lawcrossing, *available at* http://www.lawcrossing.com/article/index.php?printerflag=P&id=627 (July 22, 2005).

13. Harrington, Women Lawyers: Rewriting the Rules 26 (1995) (1994). *See also*, Linda Bray Chanow, *Results of* Lawyers, Work & Family: A Study of Alternative Schedule Programs at Law Firms in the District of Columbia (2000), Women's Bar Assoc. D.C., Women's Bar Assoc. Found. D.C., and Am. U. Wash. Coll. of Law, Gender, Work and Family Proj. (2000).

14. Sussman, *The Large Law Firm Structure: An Historic Opportunity*, 57 Fordham L. Rev. 969, 971 (1989). Discussing the impact of the increased billing pressures on the lives of lawyers, Professor Eleanor M. Fox wrote: "There is no more luxury to learn the law at the feet of the great people of the profession." Fox, *Being a Woman, Being a Lawyer and Being a Human Being - Woman and Change*, 57 Fordham L. Rev. 955, 958 (1989).

15. *The American Lawyer*'s analysis of the top 100 law firms showed that in 2004: "Revenue per lawyer grew more quickly than head count...suggesting that firms increased rates and lawyers worked longer hours." *The Am Law 100*, The American Lawyer, July 2005, at 107. *See also* Alison Frankel, *The Case of the Missing Associate*, The American Lawyer, July 2005, at 96.

16. *See, e.g.,* Harrington, Women Lawyers: Rewriting the Rules 25 (1995) (1994).

17. *See, e.g.,* Harrington, Women Lawyers: Rewriting the Rules 25 (1995) (1994). *See also,* Diane E. Lewis, *Law-Firms Up Salary Ante to Fight Associates' Flight to Dot-Coms*, Boston Globe, Feb. 8, 2000, at D1; Diane E. Lewis, *High Anxiety over Attorneys' Soaring Pay*, Boston Globe, Feb. 11, 2000, at E1.

18. Harrington, Women Lawyers: Rewriting the Rules 26 (1995) (1994). *See* Terry Carter, *Paths Need Paving*, 86 ABA J. 34, 37 (Sept. 2000), observing: "Lawyers in big firms are much like MRI machines in medical practices, they must be utilized days, nights and weekends to recoup the capital investment." *See also,* ABA Comm'n Women in the Prof., The Unfinished Agenda: Women and the Legal Profession 17 (2001), "Twelve hour days and weekend work are typical of many practice settings."

19. Aric Press and Susan Beck, *Almost a Revolution*, The American Lawyer, May 2004, at 77, 79.

20. ABA Comm'n on Billable Hours, ABA Commission on Billable Hours Report: 2001-2002 *available at* http://www.abanet.org/careercounsel/billable/toolkit/bhcomplete.pdf (Dec. 13, 2005).

21. The ABA Commission was blunt in its recognition of the problem: "It has become increasingly clear that many of the legal profession's contemporary woes intersect at the billable hour.... The billable hour is fundamentally about quantity over quality, repetition over creativity. With no gauge for intangibles such as productivity, creativity, knowledge or technological advancements, the billable-hour model is a counter-intuitive measure of value." ABA Comm'n on Billable Hours, ABA Commission on Billable Hours Report: 2001-2002 ix (2002) *available at* http://www.abanet.org/careercounsel/billable/toolkit/bhcomplete.pdf (Dec. 13, 2005). *See also,* Hannah C. Dugan, *Does Gender Still Matter in the Legal Profession?*, 75 Wis. Law. (Oct. 2002), *available at* WL 75-OCT Wis. Law. 10, noting: "Even though the attorney's work product meets the client's needs, the billing system works against the lawyer's professional development, her partnership track, and her income."

22. The ABA Commission noted: "Unfortunately, the increased need for billable hours has caused the pace of law practice to become frenetic and has had a negative effect on mentoring, associate training and collegiality. Lawyers no longer are being recognized primarily for the quality of their work and their talent. As a result, the quality of law firm cultures are in decline and the pressure for hours makes it impossible for many lawyers to achieve balance in their lives." ABA Comm'n on Billable Hours, ABA Commission

on Billable Hours Report: 2001-2002 5 (2002), *available at* http://www.abanet.org/careercounsel/billable/toolkit/bhcomplete.pdf (Dec. 13, 2005).

23. The ABA Commission stated: "The well-meaning associate who desires to participate in pro bono work is often challenged by the attitude of law firms that value only billable work." ABA Comm'n on Billable Hours, ABA Commission on Billable Hours Report: 2001-2002 5 (2002), *available at* http://www.abanet.org/careercounsel/billable/toolkit/bhcomplete.pdf. (Dec. 13, 2005).

24. The Commission observed that: "[A]bsent a request from the client, hourly billing arrangements do not require, or even encourage, the lawyer to prepare a project plan or case plan at the beginning of a client engagement. Rather, hourly billing allows lawyers simply to start working and reporting the hours." ABA Comm'n on Billable Hours, ABA Commission on Billable Hours Report: 2001-2002 5-6 (2002), *available at* http://www.abanet.org/careercounsel/billable/toolkit/bhcomplete.pdf (Dec. 13, 2005).

25. The Commission highlighted the frustration of clients: "Hourly billing does not offer any predictability for the client. It is not until the matter concludes that the client knows the ultimate cost." ABA Comm'n on Billable Hours, ABA Commission on Billable Hours Report: 2001-2002 6 (2002), *available at* http://www.abanet.org/careercounsel/billable/toolkit/bhcomplete.pdf (Dec. 13, 2005).

26. As the Commission highlighted: "Every legal project has an intrinsic value to the client. The value may be greater than a fee based on the total of the hours billed. Or the value may be less. More importantly, with hourly billing the client does not have the information necessary at the outset to evaluate whether to or how to pursue a matter." ABA Comm'n on Billable Hours, ABA Commission on Billable Hours Report: 2001-2002 6 (2002), *available at* http://www.abanet.org/careercounsel/billable/toolkit/bhcomplete.pdf (Dec. 13, 2005).

27. The Commission identified a common frustration: "The inefficient and less productive lawyer ends up billing more hours." ABA Comm'n on Billable Hours, ABA Commission on Billable Hours Report: 2001-2002 6 (2002), *available at* http://www.abanet.org/careercounsel/billable/toolkit/bhcomplete.pdf (Dec. 13, 2005).

28. The Commission noted how billable hours exacerbate a communication gap: "Clients may be discouraged from communication with their lawyers because they are concerned such action will start the billing clock." ABA Comm'n on Billable Hours, ABA Commission on Billable Hours Report: 2001-2002 6 (2002), *available at* http://www.abanet.org/careercounsel/billable/toolkit/bhcomplete.pdf (Dec. 13, 2005).

29. The Commission identified the poor results that can flow from the competing interests: "In situations where the pressure is on the lawyer to save money or cut costs, hourly billing may result in the lawyer cutting out necessary steps in litigation or transaction planning." ABA Comm'n on Billable Hours, ABA Commission on Billable Hours Report: 2001-2002 6 (2002), *available at* http://www.abanet.org/careercounsel/billable/toolkit/bhcomplete.pdf (Dec. 13, 2005).

30. Without clear client direction, the incentives are misaligned: "Hourly billing does not encourage the responsible partner to limit the number of lawyers and paralegals assigned to a file. In fact, it promotes duplication of effort by not providing any incentive to limit the number of lawyers participating at a given event or to take advantage of research on the shelf." ABA Comm'n on Billable Hours, ABA Commission on Billable Hours Report: 2001-2002 6

(2002), *available at* http://www.abanet.org/careercounsel/billable/toolkit/bhcomplete.pdf (Dec. 13, 2005).

31. The Commission observed the problem that arises from the absence of predictable costs: "Hourly billing does not encourage lawyers to conduct a risk/benefit analysis with regard to determining how to proceed on matters.... Hourly billing results in work being conducted that may not be necessary, or work being performed prematurely or at a cost that is not justified." ABA Comm'n on Billable Hours, ABA Commission on Billable Hours Report: 2001-2002 6 (2002) *available at* http://www.abanet.org/careercounsel/billable/toolkit/bhcomplete.pdf (Dec. 13, 2005).

32. The Commission reported that the increased technology has failed to result in monetary rewards for improved efficiency and investment in technology; rather, technology: "ironically creates additional pressure to bill more hours." ABA Comm'n on Billable Hours, ABA Commission on Billable Hours Report: 2001-2002 6-7 (2002), *available at* http://www.abanet.org/careercounsel/billable/toolkit/bhcomplete.pdf (Dec. 13, 2005).

33. The Commission juxtaposed the client's interest in resolving a matter efficiently and quickly with the fact that a lawyer billing hourly: "will earn a lower fee than an inefficient and slow lawyer. Because of this, hourly billing fails to align the interest of the lawyer and client, and under many circumstances puts their interests in conflict." ABA Comm'n on Billable Hours, ABA Commission on Billable Hours Report: 2001-2002 7 (2002), *available at* http://www.abanet.org/careercounsel/billable/toolkit/bhcomplete.pdf (Dec. 13, 2005).

34. The Commission bluntly observed: "Excessive hours due to incompetence and inefficiency are likely to be billed to the client and paid?." ABA Comm'n on Billable Hours, ABA Commission on Billable Hours Report: 2001-2002 7 (2002), *available at* http://www.abanet.org/careercounsel/billable/toolkit/bhcomplete.pdf (Dec. 13, 2005).

35. The Commission noted that: "As hour requirements increase, the amount of time available for partners to interact and teach associates, as well as the time available for associates to train, decreases." As a result, the Commission stated: "clients end up, in effect, paying for associate 'on the job' training." ABA Comm'n on Billable Hours, ABA Commission on Billable Hours Report: 2001-2002 7 (2002) *available at* http://www.abanet.org/careercounsel/billable/toolkit/bhcomplete.pdf (Dec. 13, 2005).

36. The Commission also identified the high cost to clients resulting from associate turnover: "When an associate leaves the firm and a new associate is assigned to a file, the client may end up paying for the hours involved in getting the new associate up to speed." ABA Comm'n on Billable Hours, ABA Commission on Billable Hours Report: 2001-2002 7 (2002) *available at* http://www.abanet.org/careercounsel/billable/toolkit/bhcomplete.pdf (Dec. 13, 2005).

37. The Commission stated that: "[H]igh hourly requirements can put subtle pressure on lawyers to be aggressive rather than conservative in recording their time. Under those circumstances, a lawyer may be less likely to carefully evaluate the quality of the time spent. Hourly billing tends to lead to simple quantitative recordings of time without qualitative judgments being applied." ABA Comm'n on Billable Hours, ABA Commission on Billable Hours Report: 2001-2002 7 (2002), *available at* http://www.abanet.org/careercounsel/billable/toolkit/bhcomplete.pdf (Dec. 13, 2005).

38. The Commission observed further ways in which billable hours results in a mechanized legal bill: "The recording of hours for hourly billing tends to focus the lawyer on mechanical functions rather than on accomplishments or substantive progress." ABA Comm'n on Billable Hours, ABA Commission on Billable Hours Report: 2001-2002 7 (2002), *available at* http://www.abanet.org/careercounsel/billable/toolkit/bhcomplete.pdf (Dec. 13, 2005).

39. As the Commission noted: "[H]ourly billing makes the billing rate the primary factor for clients when they shop for legal services." But, the Commission added, selecting the best rate: "may not convert to the best overall cost." ABA Comm'n on Billable Hours, ABA Commission on Billable Hours Report: 2001-2002 7 (2002), *available at* http://www.abanet.org/careercounsel/billable/toolkit/bhcomplete.pdf (Dec. 13, 2005).

40. ABA Comm'n on Billable Hours, ABA Commission on Billable Hours Report: 2001-2002 11 (2002), *available at* http://www.abanet.org/careercounsel/billable/toolkit/bhcomplete.pdf (Dec. 13, 2005).

41. In its report on the state of the legal profession, the ABA noted: "The competitive business climate is felt to be undermining one's sense of ethics. Pressure and demands placed on attorneys have rendered practices that used to be unethical or inappropriate simply 'What you do' today." C&R Research, *Pulse 2002: The State of the Legal Profession* 2002 ABA 13.

42. Hannah C. Dugan, *Does Gender Still Matter in the Legal Profession?,* 75 Wis. Law. (Oct. 2002), *available at* WL 75-OCT Wis. Law. 10.

43. Epstein, et al., *Glass Ceilings and Open Doors: Women's Advancement in the Legal Profession,* 64 Fordham L. Rev. 291, 339 (1995 Rpt. to The Assoc. B. City N.Y., Comm. Women Prof.). *See also* Maryann Hedaa, *Attracting - and Keeping - the Best & Brightest,* Hildebrandt Int'l, at http://www.hildebrandt.com/Documents.aspx?Doc_ID=827 (Spring 2001), noting: "For years, consulting firms and investment banks have been measuring performance, while law firms have been measuring productivity and putting undue emphasis on the *quantity* of hours billed rather than the *quality* of the work product or the potential gains from a long-term client relationship."

44. The study for The Association of the Bar of the City of New York observed that even though partners may carry as demanding a schedule as associates, the hierarchical organizational structure of law firms results in significant frustration for associates because of their total lack of control over the timing of assignments or other aspects of their schedule. Epstein, et al., *Glass Ceilings and Open Doors: Women's Advancement in the Legal Profession,* 64 Fordham L. Rev. 291, 387-388 (1995 Rpt. to The Assoc. B. City N.Y., Comm. Women Prof.).

45. Nossel & Westfall, Presumed Equal: What America's Top Women Lawyers Really Think About Their Firms xv (1998).

46. Epstein, et al., *Glass Ceilings and Open Doors: Women's Advancement in the Legal Profession,* 64 Fordham L. Rev. 291, 383 (1995 Rpt. to The Assoc. B. City N.Y., Comm. Women Prof.). See also, Stephanie Francis Ward, 2,000+ Club Stays Open 24/7, 91 ABA J. 32, 32 (Feb. 2005). This article focused on ways in which several lawyers maintain their consistently high billable hours. Of interest, one male lawyer who had been billing between 2,700 and 2,800 hours a year acknowledged that his work schedule may have been "partially to blame" for his divorce. Another, who claims to commonly bill in the 3,000 range, "appreciated" that his spouse did not object to the enjoyment he finds in his work.

47. Lotte Bailyn, Robert Drago, & Thomas A. Kochan, Work-Family Policy Network, MIT Sch. Mgmt., Integrating Work and Family Life: A Holistic Approach 1 (2001). Bailyn et al. identify the dichotomy between the work places as they have historically been structured, and the difficulty of meeting the challenges of modern life today: "In the last half century, we have moved from a division of labor depending generally on men as breadwinners and women as family caregivers to a way of life in which both men and women are breadwinners." At 6.

48. Generally, however there is not a corresponding decrease in their other obligations. See Bailyn et al., Work-Family Policy Network, MIT Sch. Mgmt., Integrating Work and Family Life: A Holistic Approach 7 (2001): "The default solution to the work and family challenge is increasingly long hours of work and an unchanged reliance on the care work of women."

49. ABA Comm'n on Billable Hours, ABA Commission on Billable Hours Report: 2001-2002 43 (2002) available at http://www.abanet.org/careercounsel/billable/toolkit/bhcomplete.pdf (Dec. 13, 2005). See also, the study conducted for The Association of the Bar of the City of New York, which stated: "If there is more play in the system than is immediately observable or reported, there is a conspiracy of silence about it. Complaints about the time demands may mask certain rhythms that permit at least senior men to play golf and spend time at their country homes, as well as attending sports events that are referred to as important to bringing in business. Perhaps men's leisure and work pursuits are more firmly intertwined than women's (although some women do have similar schedules), and therefore the reported hours worked include social time spent with clients." Epstein, et al., *Glass Ceilings and Open Doors: Women's Advancement in the Legal Profession*, 64 Fordham L. Rev. 291, 379 (1995 Rpt. to The Assoc. B. City N.Y., Comm. Women Prof.). The study also reported on frustrations expressed by women who suggested that: "[M]en may report hours more generously than women, who may under-report time actually spent on a case." At 379.

50. Helen Coster, *The Inflation Temptation*, The American Lawyer, Oct. 2004, at 129. Coster noted that the associates attribute their billing irregularities to "hefty billing requirements, a downturn in business, inadequate training, and the difficulty of accurately recording six-minute intervals of work." At 129.

51. Carter, *Paths Need Paving*, 86 ABA J. 34, 35 (Sept. 2000).

52. Maister, Managing the Professional Service Firm 32 (1993). Maister noted that most firms are revenue-driven, without enough detailed analysis to determine whether the coveted "top-line" volume of fees actually produces profitable work, even as firms reward those with the highest volume. This tends to result in misplaced recognition due to: "the lack of a good profitability reporting system that allows them to know which work is truly profitable and which is not." At 37.

53. See, e.g., Maister, Managing the Professional Service Firm 43-44 (1993).

54. Yale Law School Career Development Office, The Truth About the Billable Hour, at http://www.law.yale.edu/outside/pdf/Career_Development/cdo-billable_hour.pdf (May 2005). See also Ward, Billing Basics: Associates Need to Learn Nuances of Billing Before Start ing Big Projects, 90 ABA J. 42, 42 (Oct. 2004), noting that: "Associates who want to look like they know what they're doing may even underestimate their billable hours on a project, to give the appearance of being efficient."

55. Carl T. Bogus, *The Death of an Honorable Profession*, 71 Ind. L. J. 911, 926 (Fall, 1996).

56. Douglas McCollam, *The Future of Time*, Litigation 2005, (Suppl. Am. Law. & Corp. Couns.), 2005, at 68.

57. Alison G. Orchant, The Status of Women in the Legal Profession, Monster Legal, at http://legal.monster.com/articles/womenstatus (Nov. 12, 2003).

CHAPTER 5

THE SUN ALWAYS SHINES ON THOSE WHO MAKE RAIN

If the currency of law firms is the billable hour, it can only be derived from a steady flow of legal work from new and existing clients. The lawyers responsible for bringing significant new business into the firm are called "rainmakers." They provide the fuel which feeds the compensation demands from partners and associates alike. As the study conducted for The Association of the Bar of the City of New York observed: "In most firms there is clear stratification between the rainmaking partners and the partners who service these clients."[1]

Like so many of the other issues analyzed in this book, the overwhelming pressure to bring in new business, and its importance as a criterion for future success, exploded in importance as women were entering the profession in large numbers. For many women, the impact of this cultural shift in the profession has been devastating, affecting both their opportunities for advancement to partnership and their economic standing within the firm.[2]

The term "rainmaker" has been described as a word which connotes magic, suggesting that business generation is the result of a natural gift which does not require hard work.[3] This image of rainmaking as a natural gift further devalues the efforts of women who are working hard to bring in new clients. The fact is, few women have achieved the exalted title of "rainmaker." One retired partner succinctly summarized how her failure to achieve that status impacted her life at her firm:

I'm not a rainmaker, I never was. If I had been a
rainmaker, I would have been given more deference.

She then noted that none of the other women in her firm had been rainmakers either, an observation routinely made during the interviews.

A frequently expressed theme in the interviews was that women are not comfortable in the business generation role. This perception, that women are confident doing the work but not pursuing it, is at the heart of any analysis of women and business generation. However, the reasons for discomfort with the business generation role are deeply rooted in law firm culture and the traditional ways in which client generation activities have been conducted, ways which often exclude women overtly, and offer few opportunities to learn the "business" of business generation. Said one women in-house counsel who had previously worked at two law firms:

> *My belief is that there are less females who have the inherent skills for rainmaking.*

Even women who became partners in their firms echoed this observation. Said one:

> *We are not good at asking for the business. We are good at doing it, but we are not good at asking for it. I think it just doesn't come. I know I don't feel comfortable.... I just can't ask for the business and that is true with women who are in business. I just don't feel comfortable doing this. I would much rather do a good job and hope that they'll give me the business. I think there is just something different about women's make-up.*

A former partner in a national law firm emphasized the differences between how men and women approach business development. She recalled the words of a male partner in a New York law firm who told her:

> *I can be friends with someone who will give me business, and I can be friends with people who don't...but why would I...*

Other women interviewed compared their own inhibitions to the more natural talent they observed in their male colleagues, particularly with respect to using sports as a tool for marketing:

> *Golf is a big part [of business generation]. I know a lot about sports, but it's just not the same as a woman. You don't have the same ability to pat somebody on the back over a beer and say, 'Hey, this is a*

great game, but you've got to give me some business, buddy.' I don't know how they do it, but they're just better at it.

A senior partner at a Northwest law firm echoed this sentiment:

I continue to think that business development for women lawyers is harder than it is for men, because you don't have that same gender camaraderie when you are trying to bring in business from men who are strangers....

I am not interested in sports. And they are not interested in Clinique gifts.

However, the real problem is that the role models for success against which women are comparing their own skills are frequently men who generate business through their social networks and activities. Women perceive a world in which men are better able to draw on college friendships and sports activities to develop business.[4] Interviewees expressed frustration with senior partners who would invite male associates to a variety of social events, golf outings, after-work drinks, even bachelor parties, which had the effect of solidifying relationships and opening doors for informal training and mentoring of these male colleagues.

Silvia Coulter, a noted consultant to law firms in the area of business development and strategy, observed: "[W]omen are so good at establishing rapport that they can become quite close to the target. The irony is that sometimes they feel that they cannot ask for business from someone so close."[5] One interviewee admired the ability of her male colleagues to understand the importance of life-long relationships in building a practice:

I think women are not as good at that. Men do business with people they have been friends with all their lives, and in law school, and they keep those contacts.... I don't even see anyone I went to school with. I don't have any of those contacts. Mine all come from my work. It is a different way, but I think it is an easier way to do it the way the men did it.

Many women expressed their discomfort with such traditional forms of marketing as inviting clients and prospective clients to social events. They worried that socializing for business development reasons with members of the opposite sex would be misinterpreted. The study conducted for The Association of the Bar of the City of New York noted that inviting clients to dinner as a form of marketing can be a source of discomfort for female attorneys, particularly among women lawyers who are not married and have no children.[6] A former large-firm partner interviewed for this book recalled how she lacked exposure to clients because the partner with whom she worked had a "mistrustful wife" who would not let him travel with her. Similarly, a partner in a Western law firm spoke of women excluded from opportunities because male attorneys were concerned with "how it looks" if they traveled with a female colleague.

A senior partner in a major law firm echoed similar concerns:

I think it's harder for women to market in some ways. I struggle with "the-box-at-the [athletic event]" form of marketing. I'm sorry, but I'm just not comfortable taking a guy out to a sports event. I don't know anything about sports, I don't like sports, period. I'm sure his wife wouldn't be happy about the evening, either. I mean it's just not comfortable. So in that sense, that kind of traditional marketing is hard. I just am not good at it and I don't do it. I just don't do it.

Often, women linked their discomfort undertaking business development activities with the observation that they had never been taught "how" to market their services. A marketing consultant noted that law firms lag far behind the corporate sector in directing the needed resources to help women develop these skills:

Corporations will train people to do the job. Law firms just expect the good ones to know such things intuitively.

One prominent woman partner summarized the dilemma:

Women in other businesses may have studied marketing and know how to do it, but marketing and sales is not something that law firms build in. Those first couple of years, when you are learning, all the various [substantive law] training opportunities, who teaches you how to market and sell anything? And yet, at some point in your career, you are moving along toward being considered for partnership, and at some point they start saying, 'Well, so are you bringing business in yet? How are you cultivating business? And are you cultivating business?'

Another young partner echoed these sentiments:

You are just told that you should be doing what you need to do to develop business. It's very mushy.... I'm not a rainmaker type at all. I'm basically the kind of person who sits in my office and works my tail off.

Numerous interviewees noted their frustration with the lack of training in business-generation skills, as summarized by one attorney who left her large firm for a more family-friendly practice:

People had occasionally said at firm-wide things, 'Of course it is important to bring in business' speaking in generalities. We never had any training or even good conversations with people about how to really bring in business. You can hear these things that you know to be true like, 'Everything is potentially a marketing opportunity.'... But nobody had ever really seemed honestly to teach it in a serious enough way

so you felt like you had to do it. So I had never really
gotten out there and tried to bring in work.

The diminished respect women face for what they perceive as their own plodding efforts was best described by a former large firm associate. As a senior associate, she tried to develop a niche practice, spending considerable time learning her selected specialty by writing articles and seeking other ways to develop her new practice. Having worked extraordinarily hard to develop her expertise, she was shocked when the firm's national Managing Partner stated bluntly at her performance evaluation:

I've got to tell you, in the history of the firm, I
haven't seen anyone who is less profitable than you
are.

A woman who had left her mid-sized firm after a number of unhappy years was frustrated by her firm's inconsistent messages. Her own "Tipping Point" was reached when, after being encouraged by the firm to accept a prominent, non-profit volunteer opportunity, she then bore the brunt of their snide comments criticizing her absences which were necessary for her to carry out her responsibilities. In addition, the firm complained about the amount of time she spent preparing and presenting at a major seminar, even though her efforts were for business development purposes.

I have a feeling that I can't win. My level of frus-
tration has reached a critical mass.

Many interviewees contrasted the apparent smoothness of the business-generation process among men, which seems like a well-understood ritual between the attorney and the potential client, compared with the frequent awkwardness of the process among women. One in-house attorney noted her discomfort at being the object of a female partner's business-development efforts:

I never got the sense from her that she felt like a
senior partner. She was very, very focused on market-
ing. She was very open about this. She would say,
'I'm talking to you because it's a marketing opportu-
nity. I'm inviting you to dinner because it's a market-

ing opportunity.'.... I don't think that went over very
well. But I think she must have felt a lot of pressure to
market.

A similarly clumsy approach was highlighted by a former senior associate of a large firm who ultimately became the General Counsel of an institution which had once been her firm's client. She described her former firm's efforts to maintain the client relationship. Even though most of the lawyers familiar with this client were men, the firm sent a delegation of women attorneys, presumably because the client's small in-house legal staff was comprised of women. Then, rather than taking the time to learn about the client's changing legal needs, the delegation focused only on what they wanted to do as outside counsel:

> *They had this impression that we had this enor-*
> *mous budget. Their pitch was that: 'We're supposed to*
> *be seeing the whole picture, understanding when we*
> *need to go out for specialized help....' That's not the*
> *job of the outside law firm.... They had pitched it...as*
> *if...they could understand all of it, and they'd provide*
> *such great service because they would understand the*
> *whole institution. But that's what we're here for.... I*
> *knew these women...and it just appalled me that they,*
> *first of all, took that approach. If they had thought*
> *about it for 10 minutes, they would have realized that*
> *was going to [be unsuccessful]. So it bombed.*

In recounting that experience, the General Counsel also recognized that it was indicative of an ineptly implemented cultural shift taking place at the law firm. Previously, there had been no pressure to market for new business because there was no need. She observed:

> *They were all partners, but they had been operat-*
> *ing on the model of: 'We get so much work already*
> *that we don't need any. We are doing just fine with the*
> *people we have.' Then they were told, 'You've got to*
> *sell yourselves, so let's go.' It may have been just that*
> *they hadn't sat down and said, 'Let's think about this*

> *whole thing from [the General Counsel's] perspective for a minute, and pitch it to her in a way that is adequate.' Because what they did is to make her feel inadequate.*

Still, for most women, the frustration is that they lack a network of women professionals necessary for business development opportunities. Said one young partner:

> *I'd like to be bringing in more of my own clients instead of just servicing the other partners' clients. I think it would be easier to do that if I had more women who are at my level to recruit work to me or women who are in-house counsel to send me work. And when I think about the women in my law school class who I am still in touch with, most of them have dropped out of the law for one reason or another....*

> *I tried to stay in touch with women lawyers that I know, because I think that might be, at some point, a powerful network for me to be a part of. But you know, it is hard, because there just aren't any contemporaries of mine that are in law.*

This diminished pool of women left in private practice correlates with the limited amount of time available to those women who have stayed. The simple fact is that women already have too many obligations in their lives to be able to devote significant time to the outside activities required to generate business. According to the study conducted for The Association of the Bar of the City of New York, time pressures are frequently cited as an impediment to business development by women. In fact, both men and women respondents stated their belief: "that women are disadvantaged in their ability to bring in business because they possess fewer contacts than men, have less time to devote to client development, and are not part of the networks in which business is generated." The study further reported that women tend to develop business by promoting their expertise through lecturing, writing, working hard to ensure client satisfaction, and seeking opportunities to develop contacts with other women.[7]

The study also noted that the pressure to develop business can be particularly stressful for female junior partners who are also facing intensified family responsibilities.[8] A former partner recalled the challenge of trying to reconcile her clients' obligations and her attendant business development responsibilities, noting that:

> *Women do not have the same amount of time to spend on marketing as men do because of their family obligations.*

A former partner at a national law firm described how her business generation activities diminished as her family obligations grew:

> *I had actually seen my originating billings drop after I had my second child. I just couldn't...I just didn't have the time for client development.*

One former partner ruefully expressed an understanding of why she may not have been given work from her in-house counsel friend, stating that whenever they would get together:

> *All we did was complain about how we were working too hard. Then I was thinking, 'Well, if you were going to hire somebody, why would somebody hire me when I am telling them that...I don't want to be there at nine at night.'*

The study conducted for The Association of the Bar of the City of New York also reported a similar observation expressed by a woman in-house attorney, who remarked that: "when women in a firm and in-house get together, they are apt to talk about personal issues, making it difficult to translate these meetings into business relationships in the future."[9]

Some women expressed frustration with the contradiction between what firms say and what they actually rely upon as their measure of success. These contradictions can be at their most stark when it comes to business development expectations. One senior in-house attorney who left a large law firm noted that associates were regularly told not to worry about generating business:

> *They emphasize that it is an associate's job to*
> *learn the law, serve the firm's clients well, and be*
> *responsive to the partners who are assigning them*
> *work. The reality, however, is different. When it comes*
> *time to make judgments about who should be ele*
> *vated to partnership, the same associates are judged*
> *by their likely ability to generate business.*

Ironically, as firms grow dramatically in size, some align their expectations of significant attrition with the desire to get as much billable time out of each associate while they are there, rather than encouraging rainmaking activities. A former senior associate in a large East Coast law firm recalled how her own interest in networking activities had been discouraged:

> *I thought I would try…and get involved and try to*
> *meet people through associations. And [the firm] was*
> *less inclined to appreciate a lawyer away from the*
> *office or leaving early to go to an event because I do*
> *not think they cared. I think they thought it was such a*
> *long shot that anyone would make partner there any-*
> *way, that it wasn't a realistic thing for me to be*
> *spending my time on.*

> *I would say, 'I am going to leave and go to this*
> *bar association dinner.' And the partner would say,*
> *'No, you are not, because you have this and this and*
> *this to do. And that is what you need to be working*
> *on.' He would say something like that. So I was*
> *always afraid to do anything.*

Women who were not pressured to generate business expressed frustration with a system in which they were, nonetheless, marginalized for not having it. A young partner in a large firm commented on the half-hearted marketing initiatives at her firm:

> *We had this brochure with all the women part-*
> *ners, and it sits in a box because no one really uses it*
> *for marketing purposes.*

Law firms which aggressively send their lawyers on business development pitches tend to be very ad hoc in these efforts. There is little training on how to do it, nor are there tight controls on the nature of the work that is sought, particularly if the prospective client has the potential to generate a significant number of billable hours for the firm's attorneys. Accordingly, some lawyers may offer to do work outside their areas of expertise. The same partner observed:

> *Men are far more willing to pitch business they have no business pitching than women are. They figure out how to staff it later. But there is a risk [in accepting that business]. The question for me is: Are women supported in their risk taking? Men have a network, they have a support system, and so they figure: 'I am not going to fall on my butt all by myself; I am going to take some people with me.'*

Another partner in a large national firm commented that she frequently heard women complain that they were not included in firm networking opportunities. She felt that this exclusion placed women at a greater disadvantage because of their inherit reluctance to market as aggressively as men:

> *Men make marketing a holistic part of who they are, carrying cards and distributing them at social events.*

This woman then offered a shocking example of why she believes women do not "get" the business development game the way men do. She explained that she had spent considerable time working up the courage to ask for business from a close, long-time friend who worked in-house at a giant national corporation. The response, after she finally summoned her courage to make the request? She never heard from her friend again.

This example comports with the analysis of women's relationships in the workplace in which authors Pat Heim and Susan Murphy observed that: "[W]omen can react negatively to the feeling that someone has taken the female inclination toward developing friendships and turned it into an opportunity for self-promotion and business development....Business can be like playing poker to men: they know it's a game, and they'd be stupid to tip their hand. But women often don't see work as a game; rather they can view it as a network of connections."[10]

Even those firms with a less ad hoc approach and which encourage the creation of business development plans frequently fail to follow through with support and guidance. Observed one female partner in a national law firm:

> So if you really make no effort in business development, and you keep busy, then you can get away with [or ignore] it, essentially.

The interviewees described another impediment to business development which affects men and women alike: their high hourly rates. One senior associate stated that the firm increased her hourly rate without any notice to her. She observed that it negatively impacted her ability to recruit new clients, because most of the relationships that she would have at this stage in her life would be people who could not yet afford her high rates.

Similarly, a former partner was frustrated by her firm's messages about the importance of bringing in business, even as the billing rates were set too high for many attorneys to seek work from their own peers in the business world:

> There is that pressure that you can't cut your rate, so you are not going to be taking small clients.... [I]t is really tight.... [I] mean, kids coming out of [business school], they can't afford $500 an hour.... [T]hey can barely afford $200 an hour.

She tried to find ways around the firm's billing system by, for example, stretching the time worked on a matter over several months, which gave her the opportunity to write off a certain amount each month and stay within the firm's billing guidelines. It also allowed the client to have several months to pay. Her experiences led her to believe that firms should not require lawyers who are unsuited for rainmaking to be measured by their business development achievements. Rather, firms should simply empower those who are good at it to focus most of their time on these efforts:

> It got to be a real challenge, because, again, the only work that you can do [is for a] big institutional client where you are a small cog. You are not driving the relationship.... [S]ee we're talking about going to

these multinational companies, and how do you do it?
And strategically, how do you get there and who should
do it? You should have a small dedicated team that
feeds the masses all the work that needs to be done....

She then identified another barrier: the failure of firms to promote team-work in business development efforts, causing lawyers to work against each other, rather than in the common purpose of bringing more work into the firm. In recounting her experience with a colleague who was jealous of her relation-ship with his client, she observed that the younger male lawyers could be more difficult to work with than the older partners:

These older guys were a product of the 1960s.
They marched, they were for civil rights, they had
kind of a social conscience. The young guys, many of
them had wives that didn't work, and were so...jeal-
ous of their client relationships.... I remember one fel-
low in particular that was so leery that I was involved
with his client. Talk about teamwork. I was enhancing
the relationship. He was so afraid that the relation-
ship was going to somehow come to me. It wasn't my
client. I was just doing the best that I could....

His insecurity about her relationship with the client led him to make derogatory remarks about her to others. When she learned of this she con-fronted him directly:

[H]e was really caught off guard. I sort of walked
away from that thinking: 'You petty, small-minded
person. If you are going to be in charge of this
department it is not going to go anywhere.' You know,
it is not going to go anywhere....

[S]ome of the guys that are in positions where
they are taking over the firm...are not big-minded
thinkers. You know, sort of small, territorial, and you
would like to think that the people coming into power
are magnanimous and have a sense of business.

> *Her experience with colleagues who are reluc-*
> *tant to encourage direct client contact is consistent*
> *with the ABA Journal poll which reported that women*
> *today believe they have fewer opportunities for direct*
> *client contact than they did 20 years ago.*[11]

Paradoxically, as law firms take increasingly longer to evaluate and pro-mote associate attorneys into the partnership, the delay has a detrimental impact on their ability to attract business. Potential clients generally want partners to be in charge of their work, not associates. Said one senior associate in a mid-size law firm:

> *I was a senior associate for so long, and it's hard*
> *to get business. It's hard to feel good about yourself.*

As a result of their lengthy associate status, women frequently feel squeezed on both ends. Their extended time as associates limits their business generation opportunities, as clients generally prefer to give their business to a partner. Moreover, at the age at which they might become young partners, their family responsibilities generally take precedence over early morning or late evening networking opportunities.

Ironically, just as many women are finally hitting their stride with fewer family obligations, law firms are lowering their mandatory retirement age. One female senior partner observed that early mandatory retirement hurts women more than men:

> *Women generally hit their stride later, because*
> *family constraints inhibit their ability to market*
> *aggressively in their earlier years.*

In an environment in which high hourly rates, long periods in the lower status position of associate, and less time for external activities as a partner exacerbate the difficulty of bringing new clients to the firm, the inheritance of business from an existing client can make or break a younger attorney's career. A former partner in a large firm, describing the bond between a senior partner in her practice group and a male colleague of equal experience to her, expressed frustration that her colleague would clearly be the one to inherit the client work of the partner. This reflects a prevailing perception of existing clients as chattel which can be passed down from one lawyer to another. In most instances when that happens, the work is infrequently passed to a female attorney.

Just as women generally do not get to inherit work, they also can be excluded from the client development process. The study conducted for the Association of the Bar of the City of New York, for example, described a "glass ceiling that occurs when senior men with whom they work are unwilling to share contacts or credit for client development."[12] A senior woman partner in a large firm reported that men in her firm rarely made a special effort to include women in their business development pitches to prospective clients:

> *It's not that they exclude [women], it's just that they don't recognize that their team is all guys....I don't think they really intend it, but they literally do not notice it. And then you have to be careful when you point it out because they think they are being accused of being sexist.*

She then summarized the advice she regularly gives to other women to help them address this challenge:

> *You're better off spending a couple of years not having billable hours on the table, but going out and trying to develop your own client base in one form or another, whether it's outside the firm, or whether it's getting a good contact from someone in the corporate area who will refer your work.*

This is particularly sound advice for succeeding in an environment in which business generation is not only the engine which drives the billable-hour machine, but also serves as the basis upon which attorneys can be extraordinarily compensated. The atmosphere of today's law firm is permeated by senior partners who measure their own self-worth and evaluate all others around them by the simple test of how much business they bring into the firm. The payoff is a coveted listing in major publications which rate the top revenue-generating firms in the country, and those who have the highest profits per partner.

Endnotes for Chapter 5

1. Epstein, et al., *Glass Ceilings and Open Doors: Women's Advancement in the Legal Profession*, 64 Fordham L. Rev. 291, 332 (1995 Rpt. to The Assoc. B. City N.Y., Comm. Women Prof.). One writer vividly described the distinction between the rainmaker and others in the firm who do not bring in business: "In today's law firm, there are the rainmakers, and there are the sponges, who absorb the work as best they can, producing thousands upon thousands of billable hours through a painful metabolic process involving 18-hour work days, 24-hour word processing departments, and piles of late-night delivery menus." *See* T. Z. Parsa, *The Drudge Report,* New York Mag., June 21, 1999, at 29.

2. *See, e.g.*, Nossel & Westfall, Presumed Equal: What America's Top Women Lawyers Really Think About Their Firms (1998). In this nationwide survey of women attorneys, senior women lawyers in particular noted the importance of business generation as: "a critical factor for promotion to partner and for advancement within partnership ranks." At xviii.

3. See, e.g., Reichman & Sterling, *Recasting the Brass Ring: Deconstructing and Reconstructing Workplace Opportunities for Women Lawyers*, 29 Cap. U. L. Rev. 923, 943 (2002).

4. Epstein, et al., *Glass Ceilings and Open Doors: Women's Advancement in the Legal Profession*, 64 Fordham L. Rev. 291, 332 (1995 Rpt. to The Assoc. B. City N.Y., Comm. Women Prof.). This survey further observed that some women did not believe that the senior men in the firms were helping them develop such contacts.

5. Silvia L. Coulter, The Woman Lawyer's Rainmaking Game: How to Build a Successful Law Practice 10-4 (2004).

6. Epstein, et al., *Glass Ceilings and Open Doors: Women's Advancement in the Legal Profession*, 64 Fordham L. Rev. 291, 335 (1995 Rpt. to The Assoc. B. City N.Y., Comm. Women Prof.).

7. Epstein, et al., *Glass Ceilings and Open Doors: Women's Advancement in the Legal Profession*, 64 Fordham L. Rev. 291, 302-303 (1995 Rpt. to The Assoc. B. City N.Y., Comm. Women Prof.).

8. Epstein, et al., *Glass Ceilings and Open Doors: Women's Advancement in the Legal Profession*, 64 Fordham L. Rev. 291, 334-335 (1995 Rpt. to The Assoc. B. City N.Y., Comm. Women Prof.).

9. Epstein, et al., *Glass Ceilings and Open Doors: Women's Advancement in the Legal Profession*, 64 Fordham L. Rev. 291, 339 (1995 Rpt. to The Assoc. B. City N.Y., Comm. Women Prof.).

10. Pat Heim, Ph.D., Susan A. Murphy, Ph. D., MBA & Susan K. Golant, In the Company of Women 177-178 (2003).

11. Hope Viner Samborn, *Higher Hurdles for Women*, 86 ABA J. 30, 31 (Sept. 2000).

12. Epstein, et al., *Glass Ceilings and Open Doors: Women's Advancement in the Legal Profession*, 64 Fordham L. Rev. 291, 334 (1995 Rpt. to The Assoc. B. City N.Y., Comm. Women Prof.). The study further reported that several women interviewed stated that "a few senior men make claims to clients even when women have had a hand in creating a business opportunity."

CHAPTER 6

PAVLOV'S LAWYERS

The critical role of billable hours and client marketing converge in the law firm compensation process, the time of year when the firm's Compensation Committee passes judgment on the amount each lawyer should earn. It is a decision that goes to the heart of a lawyer's sense of self-worth and perception of value within the hierarchical structure of the institution: lawyers measure themselves against their colleagues, their contemporaries in other law firms, and against published statistical measures that provide a further benchmark as to whether they should feel satisfied or angry.

In this process, it is rarely about the absolute dollars one earns. Rather, it is the comparative analysis that results in an ever-spiraling and unquenchable need for a larger slice of the economic pie.

The internal life of lawyers within a law firm can be summarized in three simple words: compensation drives behavior. If you want to understand the firm's culture, then look first at the way in which partner profits are distributed. Knowledge of a particular firm's compensation system provides the key to understanding the behaviors and interpersonal relationships that are likely to exist among that firm's attorneys.

By rewarding certain behaviors over others, firm management has an opportunity to influence the types of behaviors it hopes to encourage in its attorneys.[1] A recent NALP Foundation study analyzing the conflicts attorneys face in their efforts to meet both their work and family responsibilities noted: "For many attorneys working in law firms, the pressure to devote time to fee-generating activities largely stems from compensation systems based on objective criteria such as hours billed or collected and business origination."[2] The problem, however, is that most firms fail to use this powerful tool to change firm culture and to promote active management.

For those unfamiliar with the way in which lawyers (particularly partners) are paid, compensation is usually decided by a small committee which analyzes certain key measures that each firm weighs differently in establishing its own compensation model. These measures generally include:

1. Individual Time-Keeper Statistics - Two sets of statistics matter here: the amount of billable time that an individual lawyer worked and the fees brought into the firm as a result of those billable hours.

2. Client Origination Receipts - This statistic tracks fees generated from each client and credits the lawyer "responsible" for bringing the client into the firm. It is a measure frequently fraught with controversy, as it can be very difficult to agree on which attorney(s) are actually responsible for either bringing a new client into the firm or generating new matters from existing clients. The fundamental dilemma is as follows: which attorney has the right to claim that a client's business is at the law firm solely because of that individual lawyer's efforts? How do you allocate credit for a client's engagement of a law firm among: those lawyers who may have originally been involved in persuading the client to consider the firm, those lawyers who are responsible for keeping the client happy on a day-to-day basis by the quality of the work that they perform, and those lawyers who may have brought in additional work from that same client to a different practice area of the firm? Very rarely is the same lawyer responsible for all aspects of a client's business.

3. Subjective Factors - Firms which consider subjective factors in their compensation model may look at some or all of the following:

   • is the lawyer a "good firm citizen" who participates in various committees which are critical to the effective functioning of the organization?

   • is the lawyer active in outside organizations? What is the lawyer's reputation in the community?

   • how well does the lawyer get along with colleagues? Does the attorney treat support staff respectfully?

   • does the lawyer contribute to the profession through, for example, participation in bar association activities?

Each firm weighs these factors differently, resulting in nearly as many compensation systems as there are law firms, each with their own nuances designed for the firm's particular culture. Some interviewees observed that their firms continue to use outdated compensation models that may have worked when the firm was smaller, but no longer fits in a firm of several hundred lawyers. As one senior associate in a large firm noted:

The compensation system is a very strange thing.... It's kind of like any institution, historical practices that may have worked in a firm with 30 lawyers..., but now it's 450 lawyers. So they are trying to adjust to that, but it is really hard to change.

Invariably, each adjustment to the system can provide fodder for internal disagreement and dismay over what the firm "values." Regardless of the individual nuances, however, the amount of compensation available for distribution is largely dependent on the production value of billable hours. In fact, the relentless drive for increased billable hours and the ever-burgeoning compensation demands of lawyers have become inextricably linked.

The combination of these forces resulted in the large salary hikes in associate pay that so many law firms instituted in the year 2000. The origin of this dramatic pay hike was a Silicon Valley law firm which significantly raised starting salaries to stem the loss of associates who were responding to the lure of high tech firms needing their own in-house lawyers. News of the firm's dramatic increase in associate compensation spread quickly, and it was only a matter of months before other firms across the country were following suit.[3]

This widespread salary increase, in effect, has further tightened the golden tether which binds associates to the clock.[4] A comprehensive survey of associate attrition undertaken by the NALP Foundation quoted associates referring to their six-figure salaries "as a curse, rather than a cure."[5] The NALP Foundation further stated that this associate "disaffection evolves from higher billable expectations and an undercurrent of resentment from partners who struggle to accept the wages paid to 'novice' lawyers."[6] Clients, too, are unhappy with the increased costs and are less willing to tolerate any added personnel on their matters that are not clearly necessary.[7]

A senior associate in a large regional firm described the relentless pressures she felt as a result of her firm's reliance on a compensation system built on high billable hours and high hourly rates:

Now it's not enough to bill hours, but you have to have a high enough billable rate so your receipts are higher.

A former partner in a national law firm is blunt in her assessment of the impossible demands of most firms' compensation systems:

I think the compensation system, the way it was designed, is really bullshit. Because you are forcing lawyers to be good at five different things and nobody is good at five different things....I should have been devoted exclusively to client development. That's where all my time should have gone. Because I have that natural salesman personality and other people in the firm are horrible at it and they hate to do it.

Among all the women interviewed, there was both resignation and resentment towards the increasingly high compensation of top partners whose unrelenting billable-hour demands were driving lawyers to the brink. They described firms blindly focused on luring lawyers who bring in significant business. Much like the competition that exists in professional sports, they viewed their firm's management as being in constant fear that their multi-million dollar producers will leave for another law firm if they are not making the top salaries.

Because these top producers are usually men, most compensation systems feel inherently biased to the women interviewed, and for good reason: surveys demonstrate a clear and long-standing wage gap between male and female lawyers which widens over time.[8] For example, surveys of Colorado lawyers in 1993 and 2000 revealed continued and pervasive income disparities between male and female attorneys.[9] An in-depth survey of Washington law firms also revealed startling gender disparities at all levels.[10] Similarly, preliminary findings from the longitudinal study of lawyers graduating in the year 2000 has shown that women are earning significantly less than their male counterparts, and that the gender-based wage gap persists even in large law firms.[11]

Even more recently, a 2005 Economics of Law Practice Survey conducted on behalf of The Massachusetts Bar Association revealed a wide gap between the earnings of men and women. This gap was greatest at the higher income levels. For example, 32% of the men earned $151,000 or more, compared to just 12% of the women. Concomitantly, 73% of the women earned less than $101,000 compared to 47% of the men.[12]

In her book analyzing the continuing pay inequities between men and women at all levels, former Massachusetts Lieutenant Governor Evelyn Murphy wrote of "everyday discrimination" which erodes women's pay.[13] She described the "below-the-threshold experiences" in which the biased expecta tions and behaviors of others hold women back and damage their compensation. She also stressed the need to recognize and understand that the more subtle forms of discrimination, the failure to be given credit for work accomplishments, the exclusion from client-development opportunities, being only one female member of an all-male management team, all have a bottom-line impact on the pay gap.

Analyzing the significant disparity between the economic success of men and women, researchers Babcock and Laschever traced the roots of these differences to the way in which women negotiate their own starting salaries. Even modest wage gaps early in one's career will lead to significant economic differences over time because of this initial differential. Their study reports that men frequently outperform women in negotiating their own compensation packages because they are willing to seek bigger goals at the outset: "People who go into negotiations with more ambitious targets tend to get more of what they want than people who go in with more moderate goals."[14]

In the world of law firms, the significant lateral movement among attorneys and the variable bonus pools should provide significant opportunities to assert one's own voice in the compensation process. One former partner expressed frustration that, the year she left, none of the women received a compensation increase, even though there was additional money available to distribute due to the retirement of another partner:

> *And we were furious. Because you would at least make a gesture in that direction...and I said something about it. I said, 'You ought to think about how that looks.' And somebody said to me with the greatest seriousness: 'You aren't saying we discriminate?' And I waited a long time and I said, 'Not deliberately.'*

However, the bottom line is, lawyers modify their behavior based on qualities rewarded by their compensation system, resulting in repercussions felt throughout the firm. This is particularly troubling in firms whose compensation models do not make appropriate adjustments as lawyers transition into new roles. For example, one common compensation model requires partners to share credits with other partners involved with a client, but they do not have to share credits with associates. As a result, associates can receive large amounts of work from a valued client, which keeps their billable hours high, while the assigning partner retains financial credit for all of the work being done.

Once the associate is elected to partner, however, the work flow may suddenly cease. Partners become reluctant to share financial credit with those former associates who have achieved partnership, even though they previously provided excellent client service. Instead, the work is transitioned to other associates, until they become partners. This is not only devastating for newly-elected partners but highly inefficient for clients.

An in-house counsel described the impact of this system at her former firm where senior associates, who had spent years servicing equity partners in their practice group, were without work once elected as income partner, because the equity partners were unwilling to subject themselves to the sharing of billing credits. She described lawyers who felt cast adrift by partners to whom they gave years of dedication and service, and who had never encouraged them to make any effort to generate their own business.

Both men and women are impacted by a compensation model which results in this behavior. The effect is that only those who can transition to developing their own clients can successfully progress in their firms.

Like other structural issues which have a negative impact on lawyers of both sexes, this flawed model has a disproportionate effect on women. However, a system does not need to discriminate deliberately to have biased effects. In a system easily manipulated, the power of personal relationships matter. A senior litigation partner described circumstances she continually observed throughout her career:

> *If a man or a male partner or a younger partner does not get credit in terms of seeing the numbers show up in the column, then the rainmaker partner usually takes care of the male partner, so it is reflected in the compensation. And what happened, and I think the women saw this repeatedly, is that you don't get credit at any point along the way. Not only were the numbers not showing up in your column, but these people were not speaking up for you at the end of the day, when the firm committee was deciding compensation. And if you have a system like that, it is going to inherently work to the disadvantage of anyone who does not have the same degree of leverage. And once you get yourself into that situation, it is very hard to get out of it.*

She also noted that many newly-elected women partners have left her firm because, once they were no longer associates, they lost their source of billable hours. She was indignant at the inefficiency of a system which allows senior partners to remove high-quality lawyers from their client matters once they become junior partners, reassigning important client work to less experienced hands:

> *People would not use them.... [But it is ineffective to] have associates running these kinds of cases. And the rainmakers don't have the time to do it and a lot of times they don't have the ability to do it. That's not what they are good at.*

This practice had a particularly disproportionate impact on women:

> *It is very disheartening to realize that you are being excluded from basically the internal partnership network - all the referrals of work. It was a slap in the face to realize that as soon as you made partner, that the partners you had worked extremely closely with for the last seven years dropped you like a hot potato.*

> *And what is interesting is that people say, 'Well, you're a partner now, you are supposed to go get your cases, your own clients, that's what part of being a partner is.' No one ever mentored us or clued us in to that.... And, in fact, as is probably true at most firms, there are a handful of rainmakers, and the rest of the people are very good lawyers who work on the cases. And that's fine because everybody has different talents. And also you do different things at different stages of your career.*

> *What other women did notice is that the male associates who became partners at the same time as we did didn't get dropped. And they continued to get work from male partners. The other inequity that*

exists just in terms of the compensation system, how you give credit internally as either origination or billing credit, the male partners will share credit with male partners and, historically, have not shared credit with the women partners. And that is a really serious issue because it obviously affects your compensation. It affects how you are perceived within the firm, especially as you get larger.

She described how this sharing of credits among the male partners impacted her own compensation. She reviewed her firm's compensation data, and realized that, over a period of many years, one of her contemporaries earned in excess of $9 million dollars more than she did:

He got the business handed to him. He had a mentor who gave him his work, and I had kids.

The damage caused by a partner's reluctance to share billing or origination credits was described by a former junior partner at a large law firm:

One of the things that has become abundantly clear is that this firm abandons people when they become income partners...they don't have to share anything. They share credit if they feel like sharing credit. It's not as if the system doesn't note that you've worked on this deal, but in terms of the credit that the firm hears about, it's got to be formalized by the partner-in-charge. You've always got these situations where women are in the supplicant position because there are so few [women] equity partners.

The idea of "sharing" credit for a client's work is particularly problematic when the client entity's relationship with the firm dates back to a time before many of the lawyers were born. The senior litigation partner recounted her frustrations with a compensation system that encouraged lawyers to scramble to succeed to the billing credit for long-time institutional clients, even where the originating attorney had retired or died:

> *Nobody owns these clients, though lots of people*
> *claim that they do. But these clients have had a rela-*
> *tionship [with the firm] that goes back a hundred*
> *years or 50 years.*

The phenomenon of treating clients like one's own property was described in a law journal article as resulting from the profession's transition to a client production system which devalues teamwork and rewards individualism. The authors noted that: "In the heyday of law firm growth, clients were viewed as firm clients and not clients of the individual lawyers....By the 1990s, the transition to a client production system transformed clients into the property of individual lawyers who collect profits from 'their clients' work. In this new environment, a client has come to be defined as a 'scarce' commodity."[15] The former junior partner summarized her frustration by stating that, if she had the opportunity to make any change of her choosing, she would alter the entire compensation system because of its impact in the firm and its detrimental effect on women:

> *Because money drives this firm, it drives the part-*
> *ners, it drives the way we do business, so I would*
> *change the compensation system.... Women don't get*
> *credit for the things they should get credit for. There is*
> *no question men will allow kudos to arrive and then*
> *will not be gracious about [crediting a female attor-*
> *ney with] with all the work. No question about it.*

In some instances, women described examples where the reach for client origination credit led to more than unfair treatment, it led to irrational behavior. For example, a former associate described a senior partner who would demand that she hide her role in producing the work product presented to a client:

> *He would come in late at night when there were*
> *few people around and shut my door.... He would*
> *say, 'When you work for this client you are not to tell*
> *anybody that this came from you. This is me. This is*
> *mine. I'm going to take the credit for it.'*

This former associate identified another source of dissension within most compensation structures deriving from the ways in which firms calculate bonuses. Like the allocation of client origination credits for a new matter, interviewees frequently observed the bonus pool being used as an arbitrary means of additional payment to their male colleagues:

> *The guys got the bonuses because they'd hang out with the male partners who would dispense the bonuses. It was so clear, it was so clear. It was grossly unfair.... Only partners could get bonuses for work they bring in. Why is that? So any piece of business that I brought in had to be assigned a partner who would get the bonus.*

She further noted that the system is also adverse to the best interests of the client:

> *We've all seen this where one big client comes in for one piece of work to one person. Another lawyer in a different department develops business through another piece of work for this client. And, yes, the introduction is from that [first] lawyer, but when that other lawyer develops a big piece of the business, [credit] usually goes to that [first] lawyer....*

> *If my contacts had never heard of [the originating partner], but they see him on the bills, they think, 'Who is this? Why is there time on this and why is he billing me for work [when he's from a different practice group]?' ... There always has to be a supervising partner, and he wanted to remain the supervising partner on my work, so he could get the bonus, which was the worst possible structure. So the whole thing was ridiculous. The guys got better bonuses because there was nothing they did to deserve them except hang out with the partners and drink beer after work and play golf with them.*

Law firm compensation is often described as an "eat-what-you-kill" system. For many women, that means feeling hungry unless someone is willing to take the time to teach them the rules of the hunt.

Endnotes for Chapter 6

1. Two Stanford University Law School professors noted that the way firms divide profits may be: "the most revealing aspect of law firm organization because it displays the balance the firm has selected between risk-sharing and incentives...." Ronald J. Gilson and Robert H. Mnookin, *Coming Of Age In A Corporate Law Firm: The Economics Of Associate Career Patterns,* 41 Stan. L.Rev. 567, 567 (1988).

2. NALP Found., In Pursuit of Attorney Work-Life Balance: Best Practices in Management, 19 (2005).

3. See, *e.g.,* Carter, *A New Breed,* 87 ABA J. 37, 37 (Mar. 2001).

4. Interestingly, although the increase in associate salaries that took place in the year 2000 was dramatic and had a tremendous reverberation across the profession, it is not the only time that firms have used increases in starting salaries as a lure for top law school gradu- ates. For example, by the late 1980s, bidding wars had begun to have a significant impact on the profession. *See, e.g.,* Eleanor M. Fox, *Being a Woman, Being a Lawyer and Being a Human Being - Women and Change,* 57 Fordham L. Rev. 955, 958 (1989) noting: "Having bid up the 'price' for entering lawyers... the firms are demanding yet more billable hours from each associate."

5. NALP Found., Keeping the Keepers II: Mobility & Management of Associates 15 (2003) *available at* http://www.NALPFoundation.org. Nonetheless, the compensation climb con- tinues. *See, e.g.,* Kimberly Blanton, *Associates' Bonuses Up at Top Hub Law Firms,* Bos- ton Globe, Dec. 22, 2004, at C1. Professor Deborah Rhode noted that: "The median income for attorneys is now over five times that of other full-time employees, and the legal profession has become the second highest paying occupation. Yet while wealth has been rising, satisfaction has not, and there is little relationship between income and fulfillment across different fields of practice." Deborah L. Rhode, In the Interests of Justice: Reform- ing the Legal Profession 31 (2000).

6. NALP Found., Keeping the Keepers II: Mobility & Management of Associates 15-16 (2003) *available at* http://www.NALPFoundation.org.

7. *See, e.g.,* Bryan Rund & Bill Kisliuk, *D. C. Salary Watch: Hiring Strategies to Match a Hot Market,* Legal Times, (Feb. 1, 2001) *available at* http://store.law.com/newswire_results.asp?lqry=Salary+Watch&x=8&y=8. The article reported that law firms were having to alter the way they train associates as clients refuse to pay for the training that used to be done at their expense, such as attendance at depositions.

8. Rebecca Korzec, *Gender Bias: Continuing Challenges and Opportunities,* 29 ABA Litiga- tion 14, 14-15 (Spring 2003). Interestingly, the writer reported that marriage is associated with a decrease in income for women attorneys, and an increase for men.

9. Reichman & Sterling, Gender Penalties Revisited 6, 8 (2004). Their data showed that the overall gap between the earned income of women lawyers to men in the seven-year period between the two surveys narrowed a mere one percent from 59 cents for every dollar earned by a male lawyer to 60 cents.

10. Wash. St. Sup. Ct., Comm'n on Gender & Just. and The Glass Ceiling Task Force, Self- Audit for Gender and Racial Equity: A Survey of Washington Law Firms 24 (Final

Report-Administered by the NorthWest Research Group) (2001). The study reported that: "Seventy-seven percent (77%) of all lawyers receiving the top 25% monetary compensation are male lawyers. Comparatively, sixty-two percent (62%) of all lawyers receiving the bottom 25% monetary compensation are female lawyers."

11. NALP Found. & Am. Bar Found., After the JD: First Results of a National Study of Legal Careers 58 (2004) *available at* http://www.NALPFoundation.org. *See, e.g.*, N.Y. St. Bar Assoc. Comm. on Women in L., Gender Equity in the Legal Profession: A Survey, Observations and Recommendations 16, 42 (2001) *available at* http://www.nysba.org/Content/ContentGroups/News1/Reports3/womeninlawreport-recs.pdf (Dec. 1, 2005).

12. Bill Archambeault, *MBA Survey Reflects Income, Gender Trends*, Mass. Bar Assoc'n Lawyers J. Oct. 2005, 21.

13. See, in particular, chapter 8 of Evelyn Murphy with E. J. Graff, Getting Even: Why Women Don't Get Paid Like Men and What to Do About It (2005). Murphy noted that: "[A]lmost every woman has a story of the time she lost out, on recognition, or praise, or promotion, or pay, simply because she was Working While Female." At 175. For further discussion about the gap between the earnings of men and women lawyers, *see, e.g.*, Hannah C. Dugan, *Does Gender Still Matter in the Legal Profession?*, 75 Wis. Law. 10, 10 (Oct. 2002), *available at* http://www.wisbar.org.

14. Linda Babcock and Sara Laschever, Women Don't Ask: Negotiation and the Gender Divide, 132, (2003). Importantly, Babcock and Laschever analyzed significant research demonstrating that, although women may be uneasy negotiating on behalf of themselves, that same unease does not translate into their ability to negotiate successfully on behalf of others. At 154-157.

15. Reichman & Sterling, *Recasting the Brass Ring: Deconstructing and Reconstructing Workplace Opportunities for Women Lawyers*, 29 Cap U. L. Rev. 923, 945 (2001).

CHAPTER 7

SOMEONE TO WATCH OVER ME

The simple truth is that, behind nearly every successful lawyer is a mentor who truly cared about his or her career.[1] If success in a law firm depends on a combination of challenging assignments and exposure to clients, it generally takes a mentor to make it happen. It is impossible to over-emphasize the importance of a strong mentoring relationship to a young lawyer's career. Its importance was highlighted by nearly everyone interviewed for this book as a fundamental key to women's advancement.

Historically, the legal profession has had a long tradition of mentoring that served as the critical underpinnings of a new lawyer's career path.[2] In these relationships, a senior partner would take an active role in promoting the career of his young protégé. The fundamental basis of this model is that it is reliant on the personal relationship that develops between two people who work closely together and the bonds that form between them. For women associates, this has generally meant exclusion from the informal mentor network.

The findings in the nationwide survey of women attorneys conducted for law students resoundingly corroborated the importance of strong mentoring relationships: "Almost without exception, mentoring was cited as essential to advancement and, at many firms, women were reported to be less likely to be mentored than men."[3] The report of the survey results further identified the reason why women frequently are excluded from the benefits of a strong mentoring relationship: "As numerous respondents observed, men far outnumber women in firm partnerships, and because people are more likely to take under their wing young colleagues with whom they personally identify, informal relationships tend to favor male associates."[4] Professor Lani Guinier, noting how informal models can result in exclusion, linked the importance of mentoring to legal success: "Who succeeds at learning the job once given a chance is partially a function of mentoring and communications skills. And we tend to mentor those we know or those who remind us of who we once were."[5]

One in-house attorney who had previously been an associate in several large law firms stated that she never observed true mentoring. Instead, she saw what she described as "protection":

This resulted in certain associates being better taken care of than others by the partners in the firm who protected them.

The idea of a mentor as protector can have both negative and positive connotations, depending on whether the umbrella of protection extends to a broad and diverse group, or is limited to a chosen few. Moreover, protection is just one form of the assistance a great mentor can provide in addition to serving as teacher, advisor, and career strategist. The study conducted for The Association of the Bar of the City of New York detailed the importance of each of these aspects of a mentoring role. As teachers: "mentors may be involved in training their younger colleagues by providing challenging and varied assignments, teaching the craft of lawyering, offering strategies on how to deal with clients, and sharing insights about how to negotiate the organizational systems and politics of firm life." As to the advisor role: "This would be someone with whom the junior colleague can share personal difficulties, for example, about the stresses of balancing work and family responsibilities, and someone whom the junior colleague can identify with and emulate." In the career advocate role, "senior lawyers offer sponsorship by recommending protégés for special assignments; they provide opportunities for protégés and their work to be exposed or showcased to influential partners in the firms...and they offer protection in controversial situations."[6]

The in-house counsel who had left her large law firm after being told she would not become a partner distinguished her own experiences with respect to these roles:

There were two men there who became my mentors...I did a lot of work for them.... I learned a lot from them.... It was all professional guidance as far as: 'The [area of specialty] works this way.' There was never any guidance as: 'You should really get to have a better relationship with [name of influential partner], he is the guy who matters here.' Nobody ever told me things like that.

This type of navigational guidance within the firm is extraordinarily valuable, but usually results from informal relationships. It is also the reason why many suggest that a formalized mentoring system, while necessary, is not as effective, because it lacks these crucial subtleties. For example, a former associate from a New York law firm acknowledged the importance of her firm's efforts to create multi-layered formal mentoring programs, but expressed doubts as to whether these formal efforts could ever impact a career as much as the informal relationships do.

The ABA Commission on Women in the Profession observed that this lack of access to informal mentoring networks poses a significant hurdle to the careers of women: "The result is that many female lawyers remain out of the loop of career development. They aren't adequately educated in their organization's unstated practices and politics. They aren't given enough challenging, high visibility assignments. They aren't included in social events that yield professional opportunities. And they aren't helped to acquire the legal and marketing skills that are central to advancement."[7]

Women interviewed for this book frequently expressed a sense of exclusion from the informal mentoring networks which were available to their male colleagues. This dynamic was described by a former senior associate at a large firm, who recalled the visibly uncomfortable demeanor of her departmental co-chair when he told her that she was not going to be promoted to partnership:

> *There is a difference between the way the partners relate to women associates and men associates. So, for example...everyone knew that [the co-chair of the department] did not know how to talk to women.... I don't know how he got to be so successful because he doesn't have a lot of social skills. And when he came to apologize to me for not making junior partner, he was in the chair like so scrunched up....*

> *But yet he plays golf with some of the guys there, and I know there is one particular guy, he attended this guy's wedding and he is now a partner. So there was somebody that he sort of brought up [into the partnership].*

A female partner in a national law firm described her years of watching women being excluded from these relationships:

>	*Usually, if it's within the department and the senior litigation partner...is a rainmaker, they make sure the cases are staffed with people who they want to keep him happy. And, by and large, the partners that use this model have used guys. The partners historically have not included women in this umbrella of mentorship.... Within the firm, referrals from [one practice area to another], guys tend to refer to guys.*

In most law firms, there is a direct link between a good mentoring relationship and the referral of challenging work from important firm clients. A good mentor will provide opportunities to showcase an associate's talent and, ultimately, open the door to key client contacts which will be invaluable when partnership elections are near. Several interviewees expressed frustration with an informal mentoring process that frequently brought such benefits to their male colleagues only. As one senior partner stated:

>	*I think it's clear that mentoring, for whatever reason, as far as men handing down business to women, doesn't usually happen. It happens now and then, but generally speaking, it doesn't end up that way.*

Over and over again, the women interviewed would describe how they felt left out of the informal mentoring systems by which men ultimately inherit business generation credit for important clients and are exposed to other career-building activities. A senior partner described how the lack of a mentor could derail an associate's career:

>	*I definitely saw people getting lost in the shuffle because no partner had focused on them as: 'Oh, this is somebody I want to work with.' So you just didn't get a lot of work, and then your hours weren't there, and it was all cyclical like that.*

The ABA Commission on Women in the Profession noted that male attorneys may be reluctant to mentor female colleagues because of concern that the relationship will be perceived as inappropriate.[8] The study conducted for The Association of the Bar of the City of New York also described the discomfort that men can feel about their roles as mentors to women. Some expressed concern that the close ties forged by mentoring would lead either to suggestions of an inappropriate relationship or to possible charges of sexual harassment.[9]

In some instances, these concerns may arise from the experience of observing mentoring which did develop inappropriate aspects to the relationship. Here, too, the subtle tensions can have as negative an impact as more obvious forms of harassment. One woman described the overwhelming nature of her relationship with her mentor, a senior lawyer who jealously guarded access to her and who retreated from his relationship with her when she began doing work for other attorneys:

> *He was very into loyalty...I remember feeling that I now had to reassure him that I was there for him....He came into my office one day and he saw me working on [another partner's work] and there was nothing at the time that needed to happen on one of his matters. But he was so mad that I was working on it, that he actually stopped talking to me.*

> *I finally went to talk to him about a week later...I was scared to talk to him but I also felt really sure that I hadn't done anything wrong, so I said, 'I feel like you are bothered by the fact that I've got this other case.' And he said, 'Well, I think you are being irresponsible.' And I said, 'You know, people have called me some different things, but irresponsible is so far off of what I have ever been called before.' It actually gave me the strength to talk to him about it because I knew I hadn't been irresponsible....What he said was, 'I think you should think carefully about what your opportunities are, and I think you should think about the opportunities I've given you, because I've given you a great opportunity....'*

Many women regretted the lack of female mentors in private practice, and consequently, the lack of strong female role models. The dearth of female mentors is easy to understand: few women have reached the level of senior partner, and those who did succeed likely had no female mentor from whom they could have learned how to assist younger colleagues.

Respondents in the nationwide survey of female lawyers described the harmful effect on a woman's career that the lack of female mentoring can have: "There are too few female mentors to go around, and women partners are often not senior enough to exert the force necessary to help propel a young attorney's career."[10] As one woman partner succinctly stated, women don't mentor other women because they don't know how:

> *Nobody did it for them. They probably never worked anywhere but [here], so they may not even know what it means to mentor or how to mentor. I think a lot of the culture of law firms has to do with the fact that people have no other experience in life.*

This is particularly true for women who have succeeded in the profession by forging through obstacles with little help from others. Even where their success was aided by the helping hand of a senior mentor, it may not have resulted in feeling empowered to or capable of helping anyone else.

The study conducted for The Association of the Bar of the City of New York reported that a primary reason why women do not mentor is due to time constraints. The study also described as "striking" the "pervasive sense of guilt" some female partners felt for "not making themselves available to mentor junior women...." In addition, the study observed the feeling of ambivalence which, for some, was rooted in their lack of interest; for others, it was due to a belief that, just as they received no special treatment in their own careers, the younger generation of women should not be provided with special nurturing.[11]

The former senior associate, who described the formal relationship she had with her male mentors, expressed frustration with the more senior women in the firm who did not fill the gap by providing crucial informal assistance:

> *And I tried to cultivate women from the minute I got there. There were three women partners [in the practice group] and they were just as unreceptive as possible.*

One mid-level associate, reflecting on her own uncertain future at the firm, observed:

> *I think, for me, it is really a lack of female mentoring by the partners.*

Frustrated by the lack of a strong mentor relationship, many women begin to feel adrift, not yet aware of the even rockier shoals that lie ahead once they enter their child-bearing years.

Endnotes for Chapter 7

1. Epstein, et al., *Glass Ceilings and Open Doors: Women's Advancement in the Legal Profession*, 64 Fordham L. Rev. 291, 343 (1995 Rpt. to The Assoc. B. City N.Y., Comm. Women Prof.). "As in all fields, those in the legal profession who climb the ladder to success and those who are well integrated in the workplace proceed along tracks that are made available for them on courses that depend on assistance from experienced elders and gatekeepers." The report further highlights the importance of "collegial support," that is, "support from colleagues, supervising partners, and clients" as a crucial advancement factor. At 420.

2. Epstein, et al., *Glass Ceilings and Open Doors: Women's Advancement in the Legal Profession*, 64 Fordham L. Rev. 291, 343 (1995 Rpt. to The Assoc. B. City N.Y., Comm. Women Prof.). "In law, there has been a long tradition of mentoring, where older, more experienced partners in the large firms have taken junior colleagues under their wings, grooming and promoting them for partnership. This system created an informal network, a brotherhood."

3. Nossel & Westfall, Presumed Equal: What America's Top Women Lawyers Really Think About Their Firms xviii (1998).

4. Nossel & Westfall, Presumed Equal: What America's Top Women Lawyers Really Think About Their Firms xviii (1998). *See also* The New York State Bar Association study, which reported significant disparities in the way women viewed their professional development opportunities: only 41% of the female respondents (compared to 59% of the males) felt that assistance with professional development is actively provided; only 50% of the female respondents (compared with 64% of the males) believed they were in the career/professional development "loop"; and only 51% of the female respondents (compared to 66% of the males) reported that mentoring was valued. *See, e.g.*, N.Y. St. Bar Assoc. Comm. on Women in L., Gender Equity in the Legal Profession: A Survey, Observations and Recommendations 38 (2001) *available at* http://www.nysba.org/Content/ContentGroups/News1/Reports3/womeninlawreport-recs.pdf (Dec. 1, 2005).

5. Lani Guinier, Michelle Fine, and Jane Balin, Becoming Gentlemen: Women, Law School and Institutional Change 23 (2002) (1997).

6. Epstein, et al., *Glass Ceilings and Open Doors: Women's Advancement in the Legal Profession*, 64 Fordham L. Rev. 291, 334-345 (1995 Rpt. to The Assoc. B. City N.Y., Comm. Women Prof.).

7. ABA Comm'n Women in the Prof., The Unfinished Agenda: Women and the Legal Profession 16 (2001), further observing that these barriers become "self fulfilling," inhibiting a woman's ability to attract clients and obtain recognition: "This lack of external influence prevents women from demanding the internal opportunities that would help secure it."

8. ABA Comm'n Women in the Prof., The Unfinished Agenda: Women and the Legal Profession 16 (2001).

9. Epstein, et al., *Glass Ceilings and Open Doors: Women's Advancement in the Legal Profession*, 64 Fordham L. Rev. 291, 335 (1995 Rpt. to The Assoc. B. City N.Y., Comm. Women Prof.). The authors of this study observed that sensitivity to sexual harassment

concerns becomes a "two-edged sword" when it impacts mentoring: "Although it has served to alert the male partnership to the seriousness of engaging in sexist behavior, it has also made them cautious about their contacts with women lawyers." At 376.

10. Nossel & Westfall, Presumed Equal: What America's Top Women Lawyers Really Think About Their Firms xviii (1998).

11. Epstein, et al., *Glass Ceilings and Open Doors: Women's Advancement in the Legal Profession*, 64 Fordham L. Rev. 291, 334-355 (1995 Rpt. to The Assoc. B. City N.Y., Comm. Women Prof.).

CHAPTER 8

WHERE THE RUBBER MEETS THE ROAD

For a woman lawyer who learns she is pregnant, the joy of impending parenthood is sharply dampened by the fear of telling the partners with whom she works. The announcement of this seismic change in her life is usually received with tepid words of congratulations, soon followed by subtle, and sometimes not so subtle, changes in her relationship with the firm. As one former partner in a mid-size law firm wryly observed:

The line of demarcation is kids.

One interviewee from a mid-sized law firm noted that, at the moment her pregnancy was confirmed by her doctor, her immediate worry was how she should tell her Practice Group Leader, whom she knew would be unhappy with the news. When she shared the news with another senior partner, he commented that several partners had recently been discussing the likelihood she would soon become pregnant, and then opined that it would likely have a negative impact on her partnership potential.

Both men and women in law firms rank the conflict between work needs and family responsibilities as the number one barrier to success.[1] Professor Eleanor Fox observed that both her male and female students sought a textured life which included the ability to nurture relationships with families without sacrificing their professional opportunities: "Many worry about how to combine life and the practice of law. Most female students, however, seem unaware of the additional hurdles they will face just because they are women."[2]

The owner of a search firm which specializes in attorney placement summarized the experiences of many of the women who sought her services to find a new job:

> *I very seldom see people who can skillfully juggle*
> *the extraordinary time demands that law firms impose*
> *with a life that involves children and relationships.*

Interviews with women who were trying to raise children while pursuing their careers revealed a universal theme: their dual roles as lawyer and mother created enormous hurdles to their success in an environment that was unwilling to support their Herculean efforts to do both well. This was sadly consistent with the study conducted by the Association of the Bar of the City of New York which described the irony of women who approached their careers with greater focus after becoming mothers, yet were viewed by their colleagues and senior partners as less committed.[3] As Susan Estrich noted: "The assumption is that a man with children will work harder to support his family, while a woman with children will work less to be with her family."[4]

A Stanford Law professor and former Chair of the American Bar Association's Commission on Women in the Profession wrote about the impact of motherhood on a woman's career: "Assumptions about the inadequate commitment of working mothers adversely influence performance evaluations, promotion decisions, and opportunities for challenging assignments that are prerequisites for leadership roles."[5] Similarly, Harvard Law School Professor Mary Ann Glendon observed this differential impact, noting: "The women who are disadvantaged in the workplace are not women in the abstract, but women who are raising children."[6]

A senior partner succinctly described the dramatic change in her status at the firm where, for years, she had reliably served as a go-to litigator for her business colleagues' clients:

> *I was actually doing extremely well and was get-*
> *ting lots of internal referrals from the corporate*
> *side...until I had kids.... It was like hitting a brick*
> *wall.*

Similarly, a former partner in a large firm attributes her early fast rise to the freedom she had before starting a family:

> *I was advanced to partnership. Other people*
> *might have had to wait, if they had kids. I didn't have*
> *kids before I went on my partnership track. The*

women who had kids had a much more difficult time
on their partnership track because they couldn't put
in the hours.

A former litigator described the attitude of her male partners at the large law firm from which she subsequently resigned:

> *There was a general feeling...that you had to play*
> *in the man's world. It wasn't okay to be different and*
> *be a female. If you could do all the things a guy could*
> *do, you could bill long hours, either go out and drink*
> *with clients, all those kinds of things, then you might,*
> *you might, come up for partnership. But if you did ste-*
> *reotypical female things, like had children...that was*
> *pretty much going to derail you.*

A senior associate with two children recalled what she described as "family planning" advice she received from a senior partner after a more junior, and childless, female associate was elected a partner. The senior partner observed that perhaps the outcome would have been more positive for her as well, had she waited to have her children until after she became a partner.

A study in the Journal of Social Issues reported measurable impacts on women in the workplace once they became mothers: "[W]omen lost perceived competence and gained perceived warmth when they became mothers, looking significantly less competent than warm. Perhaps most noteworthy, participants expressed less interest in hiring, promoting, and educating the working mother compared to the childless woman."[7] In other words, childless working women were viewed as more competent and were, therefore, more likely to be promoted and trained. As a result of their study, the authors noted that: "in the workplace, working moms lose in both comparisons. Not only are they viewed as less competent and less worthy of training than their childless female counterparts, they are also viewed as less competent than they were before they had children. Merely adding a child caused people to view the woman as lower on traits such as capable and skillful, and decreased people's interest in training, hiring, and promoting her."[8]

The study conducted for The Bar of the Association of the City of New York reported that many women reduced their informal interactions at work to increase efficiency, for example, by eating lunch at their desks. This increased efficiency, however, comes at the expense of diminished social interactions and greater feelings of isolation.[9]

For many of the women interviewed, the few female partners in their law firm could not be relied upon as role models. A former large firm litigator reflected on her experiences:

> *As a woman at that firm, it would have been very, very difficult for me to even think about having a child. The role models, the female partners, were all approaching their 40s and none were thinking about having kids. So we had zero room almost for women who could have kids and either come back to work, or work part-time or something like that. It was very discouraging.*

These generational differences were observed in Reichman and Sterling's study of Colorado lawyers which noted that the earlier generation of women who succeeded felt that, to do so, required that their gender be invisible. As a result, even if senior women did have children, they: "tended to hide them from their coworkers."[10]

Sometimes, merely being of childbearing age can give rise to inappropriate comments. Some women described their feelings of discomfort at remarks from colleagues who refer to a possible future pregnancy several years away as if it were an inevitable event requiring immediate preparation. For example, one associate recalled being repeatedly asked by one of her senior partners when she planned to start a family, even though she had never raised the issue.[11]

Once there is an actual pregnancy to announce, the reaction can be outright hostility. One practitioner, recounting her early years of practice, recalled being told she had made a terrible mistake when she became pregnant as a second-year associate:

> *One of the senior partners said, 'This isn't the way you're supposed to do it. You're supposed to be at partnership level before you have a baby.' And I said, 'I'm 30 years old. I'm ready for a baby.' ...When I was pregnant with my second child, one of the part-*

ners said, 'You're pregnant again! You've just had a
baby. How many more babies do you plan to have?'

Several women described situations where partners responded to an announced pregnancy by increasing the workload pressure. For example, an associate described the behavior at her former firm as bordering on abusive, as partners loaded the schedules of women who were pregnant beyond what they had previously experienced. She noted that, on two separate instances, pregnant women were asked to serve as second chairs of trials with less than a month to go until their due date. Both women delivered premature babies.

Some women noted an increase in work pressures upon returning from maternity leave as a way of requiring new mothers to prove their professional credentials all over again. One senior associate described being the recipient of such treatment, noting that the behavior felt retaliatory and impeded her own adjustment to returning to work:

> *I felt like a first-year associate all over again. [It*
> *was like they were saying]: 'Okay you are back now.*
> *Prove that you mean it.'*

One successful, and childless, partner described the dynamic that she has observed over the years as the intensified pressures of legal practice often defeat a law firm's best intentions:

> *[O]ne of the reasons I came here was the percep-*
> *tion that [this firm] was an equal opportunity*
> *employer. That we had not just a kinder, gentler repu-*
> *tation, but...we were considered the "lifestyle" firm.*
> *We're considered the firm that is one of the most ori-*
> *ented toward the family [and engaged in the commu-*
> *nity]....This was the place to come if you wanted to*
> *practice high-quality law and be compensated*
> *accordingly, but at the same time have another life.*
>
> *Now what I have discovered is that...the reality*
> *hasn't meshed with that rhetoric. Part of it is the*
> *changing of the guard and the changing of the rules*
> *at all law firms. Everybody's bottom-line directed*
> *these days....So now I think the desire to be both*

politically correct and to try to have women brought along in ways that are comfortable for women have been trumped...by just the business proposition of running a law firm.

So, more and more, the issues that previously...got a lot of attention, like: 'Let's make sure that women associates can go start their families, but have part-time capabilities at firms.' All those things that grew up as an effort to make sure that everybody had that equal shot at the brass ring and could be contributors at whatever level they could best do that...While it still exists on the books, it's tougher and tougher to pull off....

I know women have complicated lives. What I hear more and more is: 'They're just not cutting it' in terms of their work product and I think that is masking a much bigger issue. These are women who came here because they came from the best law schools, had the best credentials, had the best writing samples...and they were going to shine....

More and more I see young women going off to do other things because they are told 'Your work product just wasn't good enough.' ... Everybody is driven by the number of hours and how much you're going to bill and how much business you're bringing in, so it takes more effort to bring a young woman along who has "complications" in her life like juggling small kids at home and juggling other types of responsibility.

Nor can the problem be blamed on an elder generation's narrower view of women in the workplace. Many interviewees expressed alarm that, as other male lawyers move into leadership positions, there has not been an improvement in firm culture and behavior. A partner recalled her former large firm with dismay:

[T]he younger partners...were the worst. They felt like they had given up their life and that if a woman made another decision, that was the conflict she chose. So actually, the younger men were the worst people, far worse than the more senior people. It was stunning to watch them with their colleagues.

Others expressed concern with their male colleagues' reluctance to embrace openly their parenting role at work. For example, although most law firms have paternity leave policies which permit men to take a leave around the birth or adoption of a new baby, very few take advantage of this policy other than, perhaps, a brief time at home.[12] One young partner in a national law firm expressed frustration with the lawyers in her firm who recently became new fathers:

Some are still around-the-clock. I don't understand. It's a real mess. No men have been willing to take a stand on paternity leave. I think the firm generally has some policy that allows for paternity leave, but I never heard somebody do it. No one is willing to be the standard for doing it. Men have made no progress with it here as far as I can tell.

A former associate expressed her concern that attitudes are not improving:

I think the issues of [feeling welcome], mentoring, receptivity to differences, a different way of practicing law, a different way of dealing with your schedule or your clients, are why there are so few [women]. It seems like if I'm a male partner in a traditional big firm, a white male partner, and you're different than me in how you practice law, and how you live your life, and how you handle your outside responsibilities, then you must be inferior. And I think that is an attitude that still very much pervades....

However, the reality is that, for many male attorneys, there is not a significant incentive to change. As a report of the ABA Commission on Women in the Profession stated: "Most male attorneys have spouses who assume the bulk of family responsibilities; most female attorneys do not."[13] Professor Joan Williams wrote that the gendered workplace: "is framed around the traditional life patterns of men and so discriminates against women. Women who now attribute their difficulties to work/family conflict inside their heads need to begin identifying the problem as discrimination that exists in the outside world."[14] Sometimes that may result in litigation, such as a recent decision upholding a lawyer's claim that she was discharged in retaliation for complaining that the managing partner of a firm's branch office became, among other things, verbally abusive after he learned she had a small child.[15]

An older woman partner confirmed the real life experiences that the data described:

> *I look around at associates who are making it. They have wives who either have no job or a very little job. For a woman to do it, she has to find a husband who's going to be that kind of a part-time worker and house-husband.*

A recently retired male partner from a national law firm echoed that perspective:

> *If you profile the management of...big firms, my guess would be that a disproportionate number of them meet the profile [of having a wife at home]. Management partners at [his former firm] always had a stay-at-home wife and sacrificed birthday parties and other things....*

> *So long as these are the success models, I believe that they literally lack the imagination to understand the impact...on people who want to do it a different way....*

The former large firm partner who rose quickly before she had children reflected on the changes she witnessed in her firm, as it grew from its roots as a collegial law firm to a larger institutional player:

[T]he growing pains in that shift make it very difficult to have two wage earners in a marriage. If you don't have a stay-at-home spouse, I honestly think it is a real uphill battle for men and for women....

Most of the men, even my compatriots, all had wives that were at home, that were not working. And you could go home late, dinner's on the table, the screaming kids are put to bed. I mean, life is never fair, but from an advancement standpoint, it was a huge advantage. Would I trade what I did for the world? No....[W]ould I be comfortable with a stay-at-home spouse? No. But I think that really is the institutional flavor of the job.

For women trying to fit within their firm's narrow definition of success while juggling family responsibilities, the isolation is painful. One partner described her struggle:

I do know that the women who have succeeded in the very upper levels either have no kids, are divorced and have no kids... [These] are the only people that have really gone to the upper levels of equity ranks and made it to management....It strikes me that there are not that many associates or partners with young kids who stick it out for long periods of time. I just think it's very difficult. The people that tend to succeed, at least here, to the very higher levels have a spouse at home taking care of everything. So, therefore, they can really dedicate themselves full-time. And it always has been men....Can they understand, at all, what my life is like on a daily basis? And I don't expect them to. Because they don't have to worry about 90% of the things that I am worried about on a daily basis....

Also, for a single parent, the isolation can feel even worse:

> *It was tough. It was 2,200 hours of work in one*
> *year. I have little support. It was just always a strug-*
> *gle. When I look back on those years I wonder how I*
> *survived. And frankly, in some ways, we didn't survive*
> *well. It was a constant 'I'm in the wrong place: I*
> *should be home; I should be here.' And it meant that*
> *you weren't good at any place. During those years,*
> *there was no flexibility, but I was in a position with no*
> *money, no anything. I didn't have the options, I was*
> *divorced, I had $80,000 worth of debt from law*
> *school. I had to have a good paying job or at least*
> *that's how I envisioned it.*

With disturbing frequency, interviewees reported that, in their experiences, the majority of the attorneys who were achieving success were men who were their family's primary, or sole, breadwinner. This created a particularly difficult, and subtly conveyed, dynamic that exacerbated the problem for women juggling their family and work responsibilities. How could male colleagues be supportive of their decision to work while raising a family, without, in effect, rejecting the choices their own families had made? After all, if a young partner's wife gave up her career to raise their children, then how could it be an acceptable alternative for the women lawyers in his firm to continue to do both? Perhaps to justify his own family choices, it is easier to believe that if female colleagues insisted on working while raising a family, then they cannot possibly be doing either well.

A study of the career movement of lawyers in the state of Colorado observed that women were treated differently after having children and were viewed as less committed to their work.[16] Similarly, the ABA Commission on Women in the Profession confirmed that working mothers are held to a higher standard of judgment than working fathers, even as they are criticized for their insufficient commitment to either their family or their profession.[17] The Commission's report succinctly summarized the double standard: "Those who seem willing to sacrifice family needs to workplace demands appear lacking as mothers. Those who want extended leaves or reduced schedules appear lacking as lawyers. Those mixed messages leave many women with high levels of stress, and the uncomfortable sense that, whatever they are doing, they should be doing something else. 'Good mothers' should be home; 'good lawyers' should not."[18]

However, studies report that many men today are also dissatisfied with the tradeoffs between their work and family commitments, and that close relationships with their children are as important to fathers as to mothers.[19] The American Bar Association president who established the Commission on Women in the Profession wrote of the new generation of lawyers who seek changes in the workplace to allow them to address the parental responsibilities of the two-career family.[20] Yet whether a more family-focused generation of younger male lawyers will help change their firm or simply join the growing ranks of attrition remains unknown.

The reality remains that, even as the incredible demands of today's law firms affect men as well as women, societal expectations still result in women generally assuming greater family responsibilities. As the authors of the nationwide survey of women in law firms stated: "Our decision to refer to women's issues arises from the recognition that women continue to perform the vast majority of caretaking, child-rearing, and homemaking functions in our society."[21] Nearly two decades after this survey, little has changed.

A lawyer who left private practice to become in-house counsel to a successful international corporation observed that it is societal pressures which ultimately prevent women professionals from succeeding once they become mothers:

> *All society revolves around the mother's role in addressing children. If a child is sick at day care, they automatically call the mom, instead of the dad. The expectation is that the mother is called by the teachers if there is a problem. It is the mother who attends school events and field trips. The whole educational system in society as a whole has unreasonable expectations for mom. As a result of all these pressures, women self-select to scale back or drop out.... Because of these societal pressures, your choice to remain in the workforce after having children is never reaffirmed.*

She also noted that, contrary to the view of most firms that work/family issues are a short-term problem for parents of babies, the management of her work and family responsibilities has been much more difficult since her children became teenagers. As Judge Judith Kaye wrote: "An atmosphere where individual value is measured solely by billable hours and tenths of hours would necessarily inhibit the rise of women with family responsibilities. During certain periods of their lives, hours are exactly what they have less of."[22]

As women struggled with the changed perception of their role in their law firm once they had children, they were struck by the irony of how men could undertake certain defined roles as fathers without any negative consequence. The study conducted for The Association of the Bar of the City of New York reported that, because motherhood is viewed as such an absorbing role, it conflicts with the other absorbing role of being a professional. The study states that: "[T]o be a true professional is to be defined by one's occupational role with the expectation that this will be given first priority."[23] On the other hand, as the study further noted, men are expected to combine fatherhood with their professional roles into what is viewed as a "normal life."[24] For many of the women interviewed, this translates into a double standard in which men are great dads because they coach their child's sports team, but women lack commitment to their work if they are home with a sick child.[25] One woman partner noted wryly:

> The "New Age" man's definition of success with families involves leaving early to go to his kid's soccer game. Men can get away with leaving early for this reason in law firms, but it's frowned upon for a woman to leave to take a child to a medical appointment, or any other reason that is not sports-related.

Women lawyers expressed their strong belief that their workplaces will not become more receptive to working mothers until working fathers are willing to clamor for the same changes. Said one associate:

> I used to say to young men who were off becoming fathers, 'Until you guys change, the system isn't going to change. Until you say, 'Wait a minute, it is important that I am home with my kids. It's important I take some time off when my kids are born....' For the most part, most men would say: 'Oh, no. Can't do that.'

A General Counsel recalled the words of her former Managing Partner when she told him she was expecting a second child:

He said to me, 'You're a transactional lawyer,
and your clients expect you to work full-time.'

The curious aspect of that quote, however, was that she had never asked to work part-time, nor did she intend to seek it as an option. However, the message was clear: if you are seeking to work a reduced-hours schedule, do not expect us to support you in your efforts.

Endnotes for Chapter 8

1.   Sheila Wellington, *Making the Case: Women in Law, in* The Difference "Difference" Makes: Women and Leadership 92 (Deborah L. Rhode ed., 2003). But even as both list work/family conflicts as a key barrier, women significantly outnumber men in ranking this concern: 74% to 59% respectively. *See also,* Epstein, et al., *Glass Ceilings and Open Doors: Women's Advancement in the Legal Profession,* 64 Fordham L. Rev. 291, 419 (1995 Rpt. to The Assoc. B. City N.Y., Comm. Women Prof.).

2.   Eleanor M. Fox, *Being A Woman, Being a Lawyer and Being a Human Being - Woman and Change,* 757 Fordham L. Rev. 955, 962 (1989). Professor Fox noted that she began to practice law in 1962 at a Wall Street law firm and that the only other woman associate left shortly after Professor Fox arrived. When she became a partner in 1970, only two women had ever succeeded to partner in a Wall Street firm. At 956-957.

3.   Epstein, et al., *Glass Ceilings and Open Doors: Women's Advancement in the Legal Profession,* 64 Fordham L. Rev. 291, 423 (1995 Rpt. to The Assoc. B. City N.Y., Comm. Women Prof.). *See also* Diane E. Lewis, *A Look Back, and Forward,* Boston Sunday Globe, May 30, 1999, at F4: "[A] working mother must still fight to retain her standing in a corporate world that assumes she will be less engaged in her job once her baby is born."

4.   Estrich, Sex & Power 33 (2000).

5.   Deborah L. Rhode, *The Difference "Difference" Makes, in* The Difference "Difference" Makes: Women and Leadership 10 (Deborah L. Rhode ed., 2003). *See also,* Reichman & Sterling, Gender Penalties Revisited 51 (2004), observing that: "[U]nintentional gender bias can be self-fulfilling. When people assess others on the basis of gendered assumptions, the behavior that results often re-affirms the stereotype."

6.   Mary Ann Glendon, *Feminism & the Family: An Indissoluble Marriage,* Commonweal, (Feb. 14, 1997) at 11, 13.

7.   Amy J. C. Cuddy, Susan T. Fiske & Peter Glick, *When Professionals Become Mothers, Warmth Doesn't Cut the Ice,* 60 J. Soc. Issues 701, 711 (2004). *See also,* Chapter 9 of Murphy & Graff, Getting Even: Why Women Don't Get Paid Like Men - and What to Do About It 194-213 (2005), which analyzes the economic penalty arising from stereotypical assumptions about a working mother's commitment and performance on the job.

8.   Cuddy et al., *When Professionals Become Mothers, Warmth Doesn't Cut the Ice,* 60 J. Soc. Issues 701, 711 (2004). *See also* Cecilia L. Ridgeway and Shelley J. Correll, *Motherhood as a Status Characteristic,* 60 J. Soc. Issues 683, 683 (2004), noting: "There is growing evidence that women suffer additional disadvantages in the workplace when they give evidence of being a mother." The authors added: "Furthermore, the discriminatory impact of a woman's status as a mother will be greatest in jobs with intensive, inflexible time demands such as hard-driving, '24/7' business and professional jobs...." At 697.

9.   Epstein, et al., *Glass Ceilings and Open Doors: Women's Advancement in the Legal Profession,* 64 Fordham L. Rev. 291, 421-422 (1995 Rpt. to The Assoc. B. City N.Y., Comm. Women Prof.).

10.   Reichman & Sterling, Gender Penalties Revisited 31 (2004).

11. Recent data suggests that women may still be making personal family decisions based on career concerns. The longitudinal study of law school graduates from the year 2000 reveals evidence of "differential sacrifice." Newer male lawyers are more likely to be married than newer female lawyers. And, in fact, more male attorneys are married when compared to the general population of a similar age group, and fewer women attorneys are married than their age cohort in the general population. *See* NALP Found. & Am. Bar Found., *After the JD: First Results of a National Study of Legal Careers* 59-60 (2004) *available at* http://www.NALPFoundation.org. *See also*, Ronald J. Burke, *Workaholism in Organizations: Gender Differences*, Sex Roles: J. Research., (Sept. 1999) *available at* http://www.findarticles.com/p/articles/mi_m2294/is_1999_Sept/ai_58469474 (Dec. 7, 2005). In this study of gender differences among those whose work patterns could be defined as "workaholic"; among the more statistically significant gender differences observed, the males were older, more likely to be married, in longer marriages, and, even had more children. Also of note, the women earned less and reported "greater job stress and greater perfectionism than males." Similar results were reported in a study by Sylvia Ann Hewlett: "[G]enerally speaking, the more successful the man, the more likely he will find a spouse and become a father. The opposite holds true for women...." Sylvia Ann Hewlett, Executive Women and the Myth of Having It All, Harv. Bus. Rev. OnPoint, April 2002, at 5.

12. ABA Comm'n Women in the Prof., Balanced Lives: Changing the Culture of Legal Practice, 18 (2001).

13. ABA Comm'n Women in the Prof., Balanced Lives: Changing the Culture of Legal Practice, 17 (2001). *See also* Harrington, Women Lawyers: Rewriting the Rules 26 (1995) (1994). It is interesting to note that in the study conducted for The Association of the Bar of the City of New York, the women lawyers surveyed had, on average, slightly fewer children than the male lawyers, but the women lawyers had substantially more paid child care. This fact was attributed to the large number of male attorneys whose wives did not work outside the home. Epstein, et al., *Glass Ceilings and Open Doors: Women's Advancement in the Legal Profession*, 64 Fordham L. Rev. 291, 427 (1995 Rpt. to The Assoc. B. City N.Y., Comm. Women Prof.).

14. Joan Williams, Unbending Gender: Why Family and Work Conflict and What to Do About It 271 (2000). Mona Harrington observed that: "[T]he problem for women lawyers is that the work rules currently in place tie into the social rules that so definitively assign the care of children to women...." Harrington, Women Lawyers Rewriting the Rules 35 (1995) (1994).

15. Gallina v. Mintz, Levin, Cohn, Ferris, Glovsky and Popeo, P.C., U.S. Ct. App. 4th Cir. No. 03-1883 (Feb. 2, 2005) Unpublished Opinion. Here, the Appeals Court both affirmed the jury's awarding of damages for a retaliatory discharge and found the district court erred by dismissing the plaintiff's claim for punitive damages.

16. Reichman & Sterling, *Recasting the Brass Ring: Deconstructing and Reconstructing Workplace Opportunities for Women Lawyers*, 29 Cap. U. L. Rev. 923, 951 (2002): "Deviations from linear, continuous models of career development can be perceived as a 'lack of commitment' to the firm."

17. ABA Comm'n Women in the Prof., Balanced Lives: Changing the Culture of Legal Practice, 17 (2001).

18. ABA Comm'n Women in the Prof., Balanced Lives: Changing the Culture of Legal Practice, 17 (2001). *See also* the study conducted for The Association of the Bar of the City of New York which stated: "'Mother' is a status charged with meaning. Everyone holds a view of the 'good mother,' and women are evaluated, and evaluate themselves, with regard to how close they come to the ideal. However, in actuality there is no consensus that defines the ideal, and norms that govern motherhood change." Epstein, et al., *Glass Ceilings and Open Doors: Women's Advancement in the Legal Profession*, 64 Fordham L. Rev. 291, 417 (1995 Rpt. to The Assoc. B. City N.Y., Comm. Women Prof.).

19. See, e.g., ABA Comm'n Women in the Prof., Balanced Lives: Changing the Culture of Legal Practice, 17 (2001). *See also* Patricia Wen, *GenX Dad*, Boston Globe, Jan. 16, 2005, (Magazine), at 22, reporting statistics from, among others, the Families and Work Institute in New York, showing a 50% increase in male participation in family life.

20. Robert MacCrate, *What Women Are Teaching a Male-Dominated Profession*, 57 Fordham L. Rev. 989, 994 (1989). Importantly, Attorney MacCrate has observed that the profession should be well-equipped to make these adjustments: "Historically, law practice accommodated male responsibilities for military service, political activity, and government service." Changes made to help men address these responsibilities provide sufficient precedent to guide firms in addressing today's unique challenges. As Attorney MacCrate noted: "Today a new generation of lawyers is asking their seniors to accommodate the parenting responsibilities of what is now commonplace, the two-career family." At 994.

21. Nossel & Westfall, Presumed Equal: What America's Top Women Lawyers Really Think About Their Firms xiv (1998).

22. Judith S. Kaye, *Women Lawyers in Big Firms: A Study in Progress Toward Gender Equality*, 57 Fordham L. Rev. 111, 122 (1988).

23. Epstein, et al., *Glass Ceilings and Open Doors: Women's Advancement in the Legal Profession*, 64 Fordham L. Rev. 291, 417 (1995 Rpt. to The Assoc. B. City N.Y., Comm. Women Prof.). In a column noting a study of the status of women at Duke University in which female undergraduates suppressed their academic intelligence and focused on their physical appearance, Anna Quindlen observed: "Now young women find themselves facing not one, but two societal, and self-imposed, straight jackets. Once they obsessed about being the perfect homemaker and meeting the standards of their male counterparts. Now they also obsess about being the perfect professional and meeting the standards of their male counterparts. ... [W]omen have won the right to do as much as men do. They just haven't won the right to do as little as men do." Anna Quindlen, *Still Needing the F Word*, Newsweek, Oct. 20, 2003, at 74.

24. Epstein, et al., *Glass Ceilings and Open Doors: Women's Advancement in the Legal Profession*, 64 Fordham L. Rev. 291, 417 (1995 Rpt. to The Assoc. B. City N.Y., Comm. Women Prof.). This perspective also leads to myopia about the gender disparities that arise as family responsibilities increase. As one commentator observed: "Some lawyers do not acknowledge work/family issues as gender bias issues at all. They argue that lawyers who cannot meet the demands of their law firms or the profession should leave." Rebecca Korzec, *Gender Bias: Continuing Challenges and Opportunities*, 29 ABA Litigation 14, 16 (Spring 2003).

25. In an op ed article decrying the double standard that high-performing women face in the judgments others make of their behavior, a former CEO wrote: "If a man leaves work early to watch his son play in Little League, he is lauded for being a balanced guy who has his priorities right. If a woman leaves work early to care for a sick child she is perceived as 'not in control of her life.'" David D'Alessandro, *The Boys of the Boardroom*, Boston Globe, Jan. 28, 2005, at A19. See also Sylvia Ann Hewlett and Cornel West, *Not Our Kind of People, 2005*, Boston Sunday Globe, Oct. 30, 2005, at E11.

CHAPTER 9

PART-TIME PAY, FULL-TIME WORK

If there is an emotional time bomb tucked into the underbelly of every law firm, it is the issue of "part-time" work. The mere mention of it can result in despair, anger, frustration, and disbelief at the inability of intelligent people to make a reduced-hours policy, when it even exists, function well in actual practice. Law firm efforts to fully integrate opportunities for parents both to reduce their full-time commitment to the practice of law and remain valued contributors to the law firm are generally dismal failures. These failures have had a particularly detrimental impact on women, resulting in painful decisions to leave their firms, unsupported in their attempts to reduce hours in a way that would allow them to serve both their clients and their families.

Ironically, most law firms today extol the existence of their written reduced-hours policies.[1] For many, it is a recruitment tool which demonstrates the firm's commitment to being "family-friendly." However behind the promises of the written documents are statistics that reveal their inherent failure. The ABA Commission on Women in the Profession reported that, even in organizations with formal part-time policies, studies show that most lawyers are too wary of adverse career repercussions to actually take advantage of them.[2] One commentator compared the 1997 data from the NALP Foundation, which reported that less than 3% of attorneys in law firms worked part-time, with 1997 Bureau of Labor Statistics data which reported that approximately 13% of those employed in a professional occupation worked part-time.[3] The Project for Attorney Retention observed that: "Balanced hour arrangements often are still treated as individual accommodations for a superstar."[4]

Law firms have difficulty implementing reduced hours policies because the policies are at fundamental odds with the flawed principle that commitment and success are defined by the number of hours billed. If a "good" lawyer bills 2,000 hours a year and a "great" one bills in excess of 2,500 hours, how many hours should a lawyer working a reduced schedule bill in order to be considered a valued member of the firm?

The reality is that one of the single biggest impediments to developing an effective reduced-hours program in law firms is the failure to develop a common language and consistency around the fundamental definitional issues. The intermingling of such separate descriptions as "part-time," "reduced hours," "flexible schedule," and other "arrangements" contributes to the confusion. Add to that the enormous disparity between the base hours required and the wide variance in compensation models, and it is no wonder that these limited efforts frequently end in anger and frustration.

The various "reduced-hours" arrangements endeavored by many of the women interviewed demonstrate the frustration of trying to define what it means to be "part-time" in the practice of law.[5] All too often, a law firm's culture supercedes any written policy which purports to bless a reduced-hours schedule. A former senior partner at a large firm summarized this bind:

> *...[I]f you weren't in, [my partners] assumed you were home with your kids. Even if you were out taking a deposition, the perception was you were home. Whereas other people could be away, and the perception was that they were off taking a deposition or something. [The firm had] a real macho, cowboy: 'We-are-the-toughest, We-work-the-hardest, We-work-the-longest' mentality, especially among the litigation partners.... When they would evaluate associates, they would make assumptions, particularly if you watched them evaluate women: 'Well, I never know where she is; I can't reach her.' You would say, 'Well, did you look for her?' But, no. 'I want to be able to walk down to her office and know where she is.'*

Another young partner recalled her difficult efforts to develop a consistent reduced-hours schedule:

> *I told them [when I was pregnant] that I would want to come back part-time. There was definitely opposition to that because they had tried it twice and it had not worked out. But they decided to give it another go and so when I came back... I was working five short days. So I was working eight to four, and that was considered 75% time, and I took a 25% pay cut.... The firm has an expectation of 1,800 billable*

hours from a full-time associate...and 100 to 200
non-billable hours for a total of 2,000 hours.... What
they expected was that I would work 1,500 total hours
and maybe 1,350 of that would be billable.... That
was a disaster for me personally... [F]inancially, I
was getting the short end of the stick. I was at that
time still fairly junior and so people liked having me
in the office every day.... But I never left at four, so
this was not a good situation for me.

Again and again, women pointed out the disparities between the existence and application of reduced-hours policies. Even in firms with written policies, many women noted that they still had to negotiate their own terms on an individual basis, with no ability to predict the result. As one woman partner observed:

You basically go in and strike your own deal. You
have to say, 'This is what I need and this is what I'm
going to need to make it work.'... You just sort of carve
out your own deal, and I think there is some policy
that if you go to a certain percentage, it is how it will
potentially delay you in terms of partnership, this is
the number of years it will take you to get there.

The stress of working in an organization where the same policy is applied so inconsistently takes its toll. Interviewees told stories of reduced-hours arrangements that varied wildly in their target requirements for billable hours and their lack of consistency in implementation. All expressed a common perspective that the process was inherently unfair. One reduced-hours associate reported the irony of being told by a senior partner that her 1,200 billable-hour requirement for her 60% schedule was equivalent to his full-time requirement when he began practicing law.

Throughout the interviews, women spoke of numerous efforts to tinker with their schedule to make it work. However, in each of these cases, those interviewed described their efforts as a fundamentally lonely endeavor. This was corroborated by the study of the Women's Bar Association of Massachusetts, which found that nearly two-thirds of its respondents who worked a reduced-hours schedule had no one at the firm to help them develop their arrangement.[6]

A senior associate, who left her firm several months after our interview, grew tired of the roller-coaster existence she experienced in her futile effort to balance her hours:

> *I've done everything, 70%, 80%, 90%, now I'm on 100% again, because I'm on trial. But when I was 70%, I was here every day. I was able to, at 70%, maybe leave on Friday at two in the afternoon to take my son out, at 70% of target! Which is a little bit insane! During the last six months, you didn't even know I was at all part-time. It's very difficult to do when you have a lot of other pressures, when you have expectations and targets you are supposed to meet in terms of marketing and client development...on top of everything else. That makes it more difficult.*

Even as women frantically adjusted their schedules to meet the needs of their law firms, they were left feeling as though they were never doing enough, a response that others at work were too often eager to confirm. The study of the Women's Bar Association of Massachusetts noted that nearly one third of its respondents reported a deteriorating relationship with partners in the firm after they began a reduced-hours schedule, and more than 25% of the respondents felt other attorneys began to devalue their skills.[7] A former associate summarized the frustration of trying to develop a mutually-acceptable schedule:

> *No matter what I did, they wanted me there more.*

According to the Project for Attorney Retention, "schedule creep" is one of the major reasons why lawyers trying to work a reduced-hours schedule ultimately abandon the effort. In fact, the Project noted the belief of some who: "have suggested that schedule creep is part of a semi-conscious policy to undermine reduced-hours schedules, to ensure that few people opt to work less than the standard schedule."[8]

One young partner described how her 80% schedule was completely over-whelmed one year by a series of litigation matters. The litigation demands were so difficult that she actually completed the year with among the highest billable hours in her department. Yet when she asked firm managers to adjust her 80% salary to match more appropriately her full-time hours, the firm refused.

Schedule creep can also take the form of an atmosphere in the firm that sends a disapproving message, no matter what the elements of a written policy might be. For example, an in-house counsel for a large corporation described the atmosphere that eroded her efforts to work a reduced-hours schedule, causing her to eventually leave her law firm:

> *Even if you're part-time, you want to look available all the time.... Working part-time made it bearable, but I didn't like working there... I was constantly feeling scrutinized.*

Another partner described the painful personal sacrifice she made while struggling to be flexible in her part-time schedule, hoping others would see how committed she remained to her practice:

> *I tried to come back at 80%, working four days a week at the office and one day out. My four days in the office were longer days, and what I found was that I wasn't seeing the kids for four days because I left when they were just getting out of bed in the morning and I came home when they were about to go to sleep. And I felt like I wasn't bonding with them, and I needed to spend more time with them. In the meantime, this case I was working on went to trial and I had to come back full-time to work on the case. So I came back full-time for at least six months... I didn't see the kids for about three months.*

Similarly, a former senior associate in a national law firm described her frustrating, and, ultimately, futile, efforts to vary her part-time hours to conform to her firm's standard of success.

> *At 60%, I was working 40 hours a week, and I was probably the only associate at the firm who exceeded my target billable hours. [The 60% was based on a target billable-hours' requirement of 2,200.]...I do remember being irate that the part-time people seemed to meet their target billable hours regularly, and none of the full-time people did. So [when I was at] 80%, I was probably billing the same as the 100% people.... And I had a 20% reduction in salary, and the difference was that I was in the office four days a week. But as we all know, part-time women spend their time in the office diligently working, versus hanging out down the hall and going out for lunch and doing all this 'stuff.' So [they are] physically around and get points for that, but [we] end up with the same net hours [which means that I was] generating more revenue to the firm, at a lower salary.*

A former partner on a reduced-hours schedule tried unsuccessfully to fit into the firm's culture:

> *I worked part-time from when our first kid came...until I left. I always worked 80%, although I did in different ways: sometimes five days a week, leaving early; sometimes four days a week, taking Fridays off. I always worked a lot more than 80%...but it always seemed like a losing proposition. I never felt comfortable saying I was full-time, but I also felt like I worked harder. It wasn't the money, but that was the problem, it was more for the respect.*

A successful New York partner wryly observed:

> *I think the only way part-time works is when the person who is trying to be part-time doesn't abide by it.*

Many women felt embarrassed by their failed efforts to keep to a reduced-hours schedule, because of the message that it sends to other lawyers. One partner described her discomfort with being a poor role model because of her long hours:

> *I think people look at us and I honestly think that they don't want our lives. I started keeping my door closed more, because I don't want [the female associate next door] to see how much I am here. It's scary. She'll run! It's really frightening, and we don't want to frighten them away.*

In general, those interviewed believed that firms tend to be more negative towards the concept of part-time litigators. One litigation partner endured frequent snide remarks from colleagues who disapproved of her reduced hours efforts, for example:

> *[The partner I used to work for] said things to me like, 'Don't you have back-up child care? Part-time means you're on-call the rest of the time, so you should always have the back-up care.'*

This myopic response to a female lawyer's efforts to balance her multiple responsibilities is particularly illogical in light of the fact that all lawyers with multiple clients are juggling commitments that require less than full-time attention to each client.9 The irony is not lost on one senior partner who recalled her long-ago efforts to address these issues relating to women's advancement at her large firm:

> *When we asked people on our management team whether they thought you could be a part-time litigator, they said, 'No, you can't.' And yet one of them had a practice which compelled him to be in London about half the time. He was only here about half the time. So who took care of his clients the other half of the time?*

Clients understand that attorney continuity is far more important than how outside counsel use their time when they are not working on their matters. In its study of quality of life issues in corporate law departments, the Project for Attorney Retention tested the prevailing theory among Managing Partners that clients do not want to work with attorneys on reduced-hours schedules. The Project found that many clients did not even know whether their outside counsel worked a reduced-hours schedule, and did not distinguish between an outside-counsel's unavailability due to other client work or responsibilities at home.[10]

Many women questioned whether the effort to work a reduced-hours schedule was worth the tension they felt when they were home. One partner described the constant demands she experienced on her "day off:"

> *[On the day] I stay home, it is incredibly stressful because work continues, and I often have things I have to do. So I'm home with my son feeling like I want to be paying attention to him and playing with him, but feeling like I have to be on a computer. Invariably, I have something that comes up, I have to talk to a client or something, so sometimes I have to put him in front of the TV or ignore him and walk away to have a conversation, and it ends up being incredibly stressful.... This is actually an advertisement for a lot of women in the office on why you shouldn't work part-time.*

Author Naomi Wolf described the "King Solomon's sword" which hangs over many women as they struggle to succeed in their jobs and have time for their children: "Women's willingness to sacrifice themselves for the good of their children is something that our society...relies upon. It is useful leverage in pressuring women of all classes into giving in, in different ways, to unequal deals, negotiated hesitantly from the place of vulnerability that is one's concern for one's child."[11] At its essence, the failure of reduced-hours arrangements is rooted in a law firm culture which insists on equating a person's commitment to the practice of law with long hours at work to the near-total exclusion of everything else.[12] It is a culture based on an inherently flawed premise, one which is particularly damaging to the careers of family caregivers. According to the Women's Bar Association of Massachusetts, 70% of the Partner Respondents reported that they were viewed as lacking commitment by their full-time colleagues.[13]

Women frequently described being treated differently as soon as they announce their part-time status, regardless of the number of hours they actually work. A partner, herself on a reduced-hours schedule, noted her own feeling of powerlessness as she observed the struggles of one of her colleagues:

> There is a woman who went part-time about a year ago. She's always been thought of as a star associate. She went part-time, but did everything she possibly could to be available at all hours of the day. She checked her e-mail, everything. But when she went part-time, the people that she generally got work from stopped giving her work. These were men who were type-A personalities, and if an associate is not committed...they don't see them there at seven every night...she basically was stigmatized. She recently went back full-time to get work because she wasn't getting good quality work. Of course, as soon as she came back full-time, she's getting dumped on, and she has all this work now; and I find it incredibly upsetting. To me it is a sign that certain people are not committed to who is working part-time.

As a woman partner watching the associate return to the full-time practice of law, she summarized the impossible circumstances in which the associate found herself:

> There are plenty of attorneys who feel that women are not committed if they are not working full-time, that they're not going to be available and don't have a strong work ethic. I mean this woman was nursing, she was pumping milk for the baby when she came back...during [a litigation proceeding] she would run into the bathroom in the middle, pump the milk, and respond to emails. I got emails from her on her BlackBerry.
>
> She had just gotten her associate review and a comment was made that, because she was still nurs-

ing and pumping, she wasn't as flexible as she other-
wise might have been. I was mortified. When she told
me this, my jaw just hit the floor. The partner who
made this comment is a completely...progressive
guy...but now that she is working full-time he has no
doubt that she has a strong work ethic.

She was saddened by the inability of law firms to address the changing demographics of its workforce:

I think that progress has been made, but it is
incredibly slow, and it concerns me that policies are
not applied consistently.... There are probably some
women out there that successfully work part-time, I
just haven't seen that.... In some cases, even type-A
personalities, people are going to flex their own mus-
cles, and there are a lot of huge egos out there. So
many women are getting negative reports on how it
can't be done and that women are stigmatized for
doing it. They are not respected for working part-
time, their hours aren't respected. They are expected
to stay in meetings when they need to leave to get
their kids. Or they are working full-time and getting
paid part-time, and I think it is unfortunate that so
many women have had that negative experience.

The study of Denver lawyers corroborated the opportunities for hypocrisy which arises when commitment is equated with physical presence within a law firm culture. The study reported that several men adopted a strategy of always leaving their door open, their lights on and a coat jacket hanging in the office to convey the impression that they were just temporarily out and their return was imminent, even though they had left for the day.[14] Their ruse demonstrates that "face time" is an illusory and meaningless measure of commitment to the practice of law.

A retired partner recounted her fury when one of her former partners questioned the commitment of a part-time lawyer:

It was just before I made partner, and I sat there and I thought: 'What can I do about this?' And I blew up. I said, 'For my entire legal career, I have been hearing about lack of commitment and it's just plain wrong. These women are not uncommitted. They are over committed! They are trying to raise your family, and they are trying to practice law and it's not a question of commitment.'

One woman who has studied these issues nationally observed:

The women all talk about the fact that the law firms want 150% of your time. [Their firms] are pretty inflexible. Even those folks that have gotten some kind of alternative work schedules typically are finding that the work assignments they are getting are not as challenging. Obviously, no matter what the firm says, they fall off the main track for prestigious assignments, the partnership, or almost anything else. So that seems to be pretty universal.

The impact of a reduced-hours schedule on an attorney's opportunities for partnership varies extensively from one law firm to another, and sometimes even within the same firm. Steeped in anecdotes of failure, the lack of clarity and uniformity regarding this issue has enormous adverse career consequences. The Women's Bar Association of Massachusetts reported that nearly three-quarters of its respondents believed their status had or would affect their advancement to partnership.[15]

Even if a woman becomes a partner while maintaining a flexible schedule, the disparate treatment and unfair compensation may push her back onto the full-time treadmill. One senior partner, who had previously worked a reduced-hours schedule, changed her status because she perceived that her identity as a part-time attorney had stigmatized her career. She realized that, even as she worked as hard as many of her male counterparts during her part-time years, she was not getting the same assignments and she was no longer placed on large corporate deals. She observed that she had been previously viewed as a "tough workaholic" before having children and, therefore, did not feel it would be honest to continue being called a full-time lawyer when she knew that she would not be available around-the-clock. However the change in attitude towards her was so palpable that she ultimately returned to full-time status to eliminate the stigma.

Similarly, another senior partner described the circumstances which ultimately drove her to make the transition from part-time to full-time:

> *I was part-time, so called, for a number of years.*
> *The first year I came back, in nine months I billed*
> *1,800 [hours] and they said, "Well, you said you were*
> *60%, so we're paying you 60%."...[They responded*
> *to my complaint that they were being unfair by cut-*
> *ting my compensation for the following year.] It was*
> *kind of a vicious cycle because it was intended to be a*
> *message that I should be grateful that they were let-*
> *ting me work part-time, which I was. And I did expect*
> *to take a hit, I mean I didn't expect total equality, but*
> *on the other hand...the first year that I billed the*
> *same as [a male associate of equal experience] and*
> *he was full-time, I was part-time, he got paid tens of*
> *thousands more than I did. I got paid 60%.*

As some women relinquished their reduced-hours status, others simply relinquished their jobs. A former junior partner described her response to her Managing Partner's suggestion that she consider an "of counsel" position to control her stress:

> *That would be great in the short-term, but you*
> *and I know what will happen. Other "of coun-*
> *sel"...still had the same pressures. They were paid*
> *less. They didn't get invited to the partnership meet-*
> *ings... You're still required to market, still required to*
> *bill hours, and then treated like second class citizens.*
> *Why would I want that on my resume? And he said,*
> *'You have a point there.'*

For many, being treated as a "second class citizen" means receiving less interesting work assignments. The study by the Women's Bar Association of

Massachusetts noted that 43% of its respondents reported a significant change in their work assignments after they commenced a reduced-hours schedule.[16]

One senior partner spoke regretfully of a friend who left her large firm because she stopped receiving interesting work assignments:

> *After her first child, she started getting much less complex deals. She was part-time, and she was getting leasing and she didn't want to do leasing. She wanted to work on some big deals and she wasn't getting them, so she ultimately left after having her second child. I think one of the reasons she left was that she wasn't as satisfied with her job as she used to be.*

She then identified one of the major challenges for women who have chosen a part-time schedule: a reduction in compensation that is not commensurate with the reduction in hours worked. She described the illusory choice that so many women on a reduced-hours schedule have made by being willing to work more than the agreed-upon schedule, and declining to seek additional compensation commensurate with the added time:

> *I've never wanted to make a big deal about my compensation because it is much less stressful to work more than I'm expected to. I would never want my allocation to go up substantially, because I don't want to work that hard next year. I prefer to work what everyone thinks I'm going to work.... So I think it would be better for me personally if my allocations stayed roughly the same, so I wouldn't feel the need to work extra hours.*

Although frustrated that their compensation generally did not keep pace with their actual time commitment to the firm, most women chose to be silent about this because of their fear that the pressures to work longer hours would increase even more. Few women were willing to challenge the inherent unfairness of a system in which they were paid for a reduced-hour schedule even as they were pressured to devote additional time to the firm.

The partner who so insightfully observed the struggles of the associate returning to a full-time schedule ignored similar issues in her own reduced-hours schedule, even as she unquestioningly accepted her lowered compensation:

> *I'm sure there were [full-time] associates who were working 80% but getting paid 100%, and maybe that's not fair. But I don't care because I'm giving up 20% of my salary so I can walk out of the office every day at 4:30 pm, so I can come in late, so I can work at home if I need to and there are no questions asked.... They know I'm working part-time, I take my salary cut and that is what I buy for myself.... I honestly have never resented the lower pay even when I'm working all the time.... To me, giving up that money is worth it for the flexibility even when I'm working at 11 o'clock at night. Plenty of people had said to me over the years, 'Why don't you just take full-time pay and do what you're doing?'...I out-bill many partners here, even at 80% status.*

The perception that women who choose a reduced-hours schedule are endangering their future potential for advancement was summarized by one former associate at a large firm:

> *If you go part-time, it's a death knell.*

The harsh reality is that many women are never able to regain their career track. A senior partner described how this dynamic played out in her former firm:

> *Once you got delayed as an associate, you fell into an abyss, a never-never land, and you couldn't get the people back on the train, even if you tried. It was always interesting to watch because you would have some women who would have kids early in their careers, and they would go off part-time, maybe having been there for three years, but having done excellent work and regarded by everyone as really stellar.*

And then they would be on a part-time schedule, particularly if they had more than one child, and this part-time continued, maybe another maternity leave continued.

And the doubts would begin to creep in. I remember saying, 'Wait a minute, this isn't based on any project, this isn't based on her not being available, this is based on your feeling of insecurity that you can't reach her when you need to or that maybe she is not as committed, whatever committed means.' You just couldn't pull the person back onto the track. I don't ever remember somebody getting back on who had gone off for any extended period of time. But if you went off and then came back and acted like a man, that was different.

She then recounted her firm's effort to revise its maternity-leave policy in a way that which would have exacerbated the already challenging hurdles for those considering parental leaves:

At one point...the Managing Partner wanted to change the maternity/paternity policy, and he had a committee of all men who re-wrote it. [He thought he] had to change it because some women have left and said that the policy wasn't really a policy. It was only afforded to the women whom [the firm] liked, and it was very discriminatory. It wasn't really as if you could take advantage of the policy. You could only take advantage of it if you were a superstar.

So [the Managing Partner] created this committee of all men who then re-wrote it. Shortly before it was distributed to the partner...he gave me a draft...and I looked at it and I said, 'What are you trying to do...' And he said, 'Well, we have this problem and I don't want people to think that it is not pos-

sible, because that's what people are saying, it's not feasible to take advantage of the policy.'...

He basically took what had been a pretty good part-time policy, although maybe people were right that it was only permitted for those women who are in good standing, and eliminated it. I mean, he basically broke it down to just the minimum provided by the federal law, and reserved all discretion to the firm. And so I said, 'Maybe this is what you're trying to do, but this is horrible. This is a horrible policy. If you want to look at it just from a recruiting standard...people are going to look at this and be astounded, the way I am, that really, you have no policy at all now.'

A former senior associate from a venerable law firm shared a moving story which starkly demonstrated all of the barriers faced by so many of the interviewees. As she began to work a reduced-hours schedule, she was perplexed over how to define "part-time" in her firm's full-time world:

[The firm] prides itself on not having a minimum number of hours, theoretically.... What I've heard is that there is such a big group of overachievers, that they are better off not putting a number down because they will all be working much harder than they ever expected, which is probably true. But the problem is, how do you define 80%?...What they recommend is 80%, either by going four days a week or by working five days a week, except leaving at five; nine to five [is their idea of an 80% schedule].

She then identified a theme echoed by many women interviewed: clients were far more respectful of her part-time schedule than were the partners in her law firm:

I had a much easier time carving out my day off with my clients than I did with the partners. I think

*that's because the clients have known me for a long
time and when I said to them, 'I'm not going to be in
on Friday, but if it's an emergency, I'll get back to
you,' they knew that I would get back to them on Fridays if it was an emergency. They knew that I would
get things done on Thursday if they needed it by the
end of the week.*

However, her openness about her schedule led to the disapproval of those
who believe that the label "part-time" is a scarlet stigma permanently affixed
to attorneys on a reduced-hours schedule:

*I then had a partner sit down and give me 'a little
chat' about 'a little piece of advice' she wanted to
share with me which was that, she had been part-
time, but found the best way to handle being part-
time at [this firm] is to never talk about it and that I
shouldn't mention it to anyone. I shouldn't tell anyone
that I'm reduced-time and that it really is 100% my
responsibility to try and make reduced-time work.
And I said to her that I really didn't believe that, that
I thought if the firm offered reduced time, I wasn't
embarrassed to take it. I didn't feel like it was a
reflection on my commitment to my career, and so I
didn't see any reason to hide the fact. In fact, it
seemed to me that if I did hide the fact that I was
reduced-time, there would be basically no chance
that I would have my day off. She said the way she
handled that was, and these are her words: 'I pur-
chased more child care than I ever needed. You
should have an evening nanny,' she said. 'And that
way you don't have to worry if you have to stay at
work or can't get home, because that way it is taken
care of.' I said that, for me, that just wasn't the point.
It wasn't the stress of needing to be home, it was the
fact that I wanted to be home.*

Her interview was full of anecdotes demonstrating the futility of her efforts to carve-out a reduced-hours schedule. She used her firm's emergency day care center for 35 out of the 52 Fridays that she had previously negotiated to be at home. On those rare Fridays when she did not come into the office, she worked from home. She was incredulous at how completely disconnected the partners were from her reality in their failure to recognize her commitment:

> *So I would try to do conference calls when my baby was napping and that sort of thing. Return documents in the morning before she woke, or whatever it was. And a great anecdote I have about that is the former head of my department called me into his office for a project, and said, 'Oh, by the way, my wife is wondering why she hasn't seen you in the music class for toddlers on Fridays,' because they live near me. And I said, 'I can't go to a music class for toddlers.' And he said, 'Why not? You've got Fridays off.' I said, 'Because the class is in the morning, and I can't leave the apartment while I'm on the phone or trying to finish documents.'... And then in the same meeting, he gave me a project that kept me working until 4 a.m. on a Thursday night.... So I often work until 1, 2, or 3 in the morning on Thursday to try and avoid going in. I'd still be home doing calls, but at least I didn't have to actually be in the office.*

She frequently felt sabotaged by the partners assigning her work, notwithstanding her diligent efforts to ensure that everything was done in a timely manner. One week, she had been deluged with assignments from a number of lawyers and, unable to resolve the conflicts, she sought the assistance of the chair of her department, as she had been told to do:

> *So I talked to the head of my department, who actually agreed that this is a problem, and tells me that I shouldn't keep the project. Now that's the way it is supposed to work. I'm supposed to go to the head of my department, they are supposed to assess my work load, decide if there are other capable people*

who are available, and redistribute. Well, the partner whose project I then turned down came into my office and said, 'Let me give you a piece of advice. I know you are reduced-time and I know that means you sometimes have to turn down work, but you shouldn't turn down mine.' ... He said to me, 'It turns out that this project is going to lead to other exciting work, and I'm not going to put you on it.'... I felt he was trying to say to me: 'There are repercussions of this both in terms of how I view you, but this could come up in your review, that you turned down my work. And I'm not going to give you what I see as good new work.' Even though I happened to feel that it wasn't good new work, but he did, and that was the point.

She also experienced the effects of another barrier to women juggling a career and their family obligations: the strategic move of law firms towards a national, and even international, practice which makes traveling a much bigger part of the job. In her case, the firm was oblivious to the ramifications of travel on her life:

When I was seven months pregnant, I spent...three or four days a week for five weeks in New York.... But that kind of thing is also very difficult for anyone with a family but [for]women in particular. For example, you can't be nursing your child and in New York four days a week.

She then ruefully reported an anecdote that she believed summarized the attitude of many of her partners towards efforts to integrate family considerations into the practice of law. In describing a firm-sponsored program on work-family balance, she stated:

One of my friends, who is an associate, had a senior partner walk into her office with the little flyer for the work-family balance program, put it on her desk, and go, 'Ha, ha, ha, ha' and then walk out.

151

The humor is lost on those fighting to meet their personal and professional obligations, trying to honor their family responsibilities while demonstrating their excellence as lawyers, and holding to their deeply-held belief that their schedule should not be a bar to the firm's acceptance of them as one of their own, a partner.

Endnotes for Chapter 9

1. For example, in a study conducted by the Women's Bar Association of Massachusetts, 90% of the responding firms reported that they have "some type of policy regarding reduced-hours arrangements." Employment Issues Comm., Women's Bar Assoc. Mass., More than Part-Time: The Effect of Reduced—Hours Arrangements on the Retention, Recruitment and Success of Women Attorneys in Law Firms 9 (2000).

2. ABA Comm'n Women In The Prof., Balanced Lives: Changing the Culture of Legal Practice, 16 (2001).

3. Deborah Epstein Henry, *The Case for Flex-Time and Part-Time Lawyering*, 23 Penn. Law. 42, 44 (2001). A survey of women lawyers in Utah reported that 94% of the respondents believed that taking a leave of absence to care for a child or working part-time would be somewhat likely or very likely to adversely impact their chances for advancement. *Report on 20th Anniversary Survey of Utah Women Lawyers,* 2001 Women Law. Utah 10.

4. Joan Williams & Cynthia Thomas Calvert, Balanced Hours: Effective Part-Time Policies for Washington Law Firms, Am. U. Wash. Coll. L., Project Att'y Retention 27 (Final 2nd ed. 2001). Other studies point to low utilization rates of reduced-hours policies, for example, see Employment Issues Comm., Women's Bar Assoc. Mass., More than Part-Time: The Effect of Reduced- Hours Arrangements on the Retention, Recruitment and Success of Women Attorneys in Law Firms 12 (2000).

5. Epstein, et al., *Glass Ceilings and Open Doors: Women's Advancement in the Legal Profession,* 64 Fordham L. Rev. 291, 393 (1995 Rpt. to The Assoc. B. City N.Y., Comm. Women Prof.). "There is little consensus among the firms studied on a single definition of part-time work."

6. Employment Issues Comm., Women's Bar Assoc. Mass., More than Part-Time: The Effect of Reduced-Hours Arrangements on the Retention, Recruitment and Success of Women Attorneys in Law Firms 17-18 (2000). The report noted: "Without such input, an attorney seeking an alternative work arrangement is left to guess what arrangement will be acceptable to the firm." At 18. Examples of other bar associations which have analyzed the need for effective reduced-hours policies include: Linda Bray Chanow, *Results of* Lawyers, Work & Family: A Study of Alternative Schedule Programs at Law Firms in the District of Columbia (2000), Women's Bar Assoc. D.C., Women's Bar Assoc. Found. D.C., and Am. U. Wash. Coll. of Law, Gender, Work and Family Proj. (2000); Ga. Assoc. Women L., Atlanta B. Assoc. Women in Prof. Comm., Ga. Comm. Women, It's About Time: Part-Time Policies and Practices in Atlanta Law Firms, (2004), *available at* http://www.gawl.org/gawl/docs/Its%20About%20TimeFinal.pdf; N.Y. St. B. Assoc. Comm. Women L., Report and Sample Policy on Alternative Work Arrangements (1995) *available at* http://womenlaw.stanford.edu/AltWork.htm (June 17, 2003).

7. Women's Bar Assoc. Mass. Employment Issues Comm., More than Part-Time: The Effect of Reduced-Hours Arrangements on the Retention, Recruitment and Success of Women Attorneys in Law Firms 20- 25 (2000).

8. Williams & Calvert, Balanced Hours: Effective Part-Time Policies for Washington Law Firms, Am. U. Wash. Coll. L., Project Att'y Retention 27 (Final, 2nd ed. 2001).

9. See , e.g., Keith Cunningham, *Father Time: Flexible Work Arrangements and the Law Firm's Failure of the Family*, 53 Stan. L. Rev. 967, 985 (Apr. 2001): "The reality is that while senior partners who are in the middle of a deposition are just as unavailable as a flextime parent spending time with his child, it is the latter scenario that is somehow viewed as suspect."

10. Am. U. Wash. Corp. Council Proj. Atty Retention, Better on Balance? The Corporate Counsel Work/Life Report, (Final 2003) at 51, available at http://www.pardc.org.

11. Naomi Wolf, Misconceptions: Truth, Lies, and The Unexpected on the Journey to Motherhood 228 (2003) (2001).

12. See, e.g., Justin Davidson, *The Changing Man*, Newsday, July 1, 2002, at B6: "In the fiefdom of law, dedication, drive, income, grit, responsibility, and sacrifice, all the ancient marks of manliness, are measured in hours clocked behind a desk. To work anything less than all the time is already a compromise with excellence."

13. Women's Bar Assoc. Mass. Employment Issues Comm., More than Part-Time: The Effect of Reduced-Hours Arrangements on the Retention, Recruitment and Success of Women Attorneys in Law Firms 21 (2000).

14. Reichman & Sterling, *Recasting the Brass Ring: Deconstructing and Reconstructing Workplace Opportunities for Women Lawyers*, 29 Cap. U. L. Rev. 923, 953 (2002).

15. Women's Bar Assoc. Mass. Employment Issues Comm., More than Part-Time: The Effect of Reduced-Hours Arrangements on the Retention, Recruitment and Success of Women Attorneys in Law Firms 29-30 (2000).

16. Women's Bar Assoc. Mass. Employment Issues Comm., More than Part-Time: The Effect of Reduced- Hours Arrangements on the Retention, Recruitment and Success of Women Attorneys in Law Firms 33 (2000).

CHAPTER 10

MAKING PARTNER, BREAKING HEARTS

In the hierarchal structure of the law firm, there are two primary categories of lawyers: partners, and everyone else. Those who entered the world of private practice tended to do so with the ultimate goal of becoming partner. The "promotion to partnership pattern" emerged as law firms evolved into more formalized and growing entities in the early 20th Century.[1] Yet even as firms developed greater structure, only a small minority of those hired as associates became partners, and for the most part, only white men needed to apply.[2] Although there may have been occasional consideration of an associate attorney's business generation capabilities, lawyers were generally elected to the partnership based on their "proficiency, hard work, and ability to relate to clients."[3]

This is the world that greeted women graduates of law schools when they first entered the profession in greater numbers by the early 1970's. The racial, ethnic, and gender barriers that previously restricted so many from the practice of law were just beginning to break down, at least at the entry level of hiring. For these women graduates, however, the path to partnership would be even more daunting than the statistical challenge facing their white male predecessors.[4] Those women entering the profession joined law firms with few, if any, female partners and where even simple maternity leave policies did not exist.[5] Their path to the top was generally a lonely one, and their success was based strictly on a male model of achievement. As one recently retired male partner observed of the early women pioneers in his firm:

> *We had powerful corporate women partners. But, unfortunately, every successful woman partner that you could point to was the role model that said, 'I gave it all up for the firm.'...You didn't end up with the women with...compassion in positions of power.*

A few simple statistics demonstrate just how high these barriers continue to be. In 1984, women comprised 25.4% of associates in the United States, and 4.9% of law firm partners. Eight years later, plenty of time to have made significant inroads relative to their increasing numbers, women were 37.6% of the associates and only 10.7% of the partners.[6] By the year 2000, only 55% as many women were partners as would have been expected in light of their representation in the profession.[7] In 2002, women were 42.4% of the associate and staff attorney talent, but only 16.3% of the partners.[8] A report issued by the American Bar Association Commission on Women in the Profession stated that the chance of a male becoming a partner in a law firm is two to three times higher than that of a woman.[9] Illustratively, a study of Colorado lawyers revealed that, of associates who were surveyed when they had approximately five years of experience and who were surveyed again seven years later, 67% of the men had been promoted to partnership compared to only 46% of the women.[10]

Today's law firms still have a dearth of women at the top. The failure of law firms to bring about the changes needed to alter the disparity have not gone unnoticed by the federal agency responsible for eliminating illegal discrimination from the workplace. In its 2003 report, the U.S. Equal Employment Opportunity Commission ominously stated that its: "[E]xamination of the...data on legal professionals in private law firms has several broad implications for civil rights enforcement. In large, national law firms, the most pressing issues have probably shifted from hiring and initial access to problems concerning the terms and conditions of employment, especially promotion to partnership."[11]

As the study conducted for The Association of the Bar of the City of New York reported: "There is near consensus that obtaining...the 'brass ring' of partnership hinges upon the demonstration of commitment to the firms' traditional standards of constant availability and unflagging dedication to professional life."[12] A highly regarded consultant to law firms lamented the lack of women partners:

It feels like we're going backwards. The 1990s and on have not been good for women in law.

For many, the partnership elevation process seems unfathomable and arbitrary, and contributes to an environment where women are judged more harshly than men. One junior-level partner expressed her frustration with the double standard at her large firm:

I have no doubt that, technically speaking, the women in this firm are superior to the men because we're judged to a higher standard.

In the path to partnership, the law firm evaluation process is vital to an attorney's future success. Yet the process is often blind to the subtle ways in which gender bias emerges in judging the characteristics of lawyers. In their study of Colorado lawyers, Reichman and Sterling described the way in which gender stereotypes impact the evaluation process: "women are evaluated on their performance; men on their potential with radically different career outcomes."[13]

In its in-depth study of ways law firms can more effectively increase their diversity, the Minority Corporate Counsel Association identified patterns that make it more difficult for women to be judged fairly, including: "in-group favoritism, status-linked competence assessments, attributional bias, and the problem of polarized evaluations."[14] The study summarized the experience expressed by many of the women interviewees: "Coldly objective judgment often is reserved for out-groups. In-group favoritism is the first reason why women lawyers have a harder time than men proving their competence....The higher a group's status, the more convincing the demonstration of incompetence will have to be."[15]

The MCCA cited to research demonstrating the double-edged sword women face as they move closer to partnership consideration: "[I]f women act in traditionally feminine ways, they are likely to be considered unqualified for partnership because they are not 'go-getters.' Yet if women act in traditionally masculine ways, they may trigger dislike that disqualifies them for partnership in a decision-making process in which assessments of compatibility play a central role."[16] Similarly, a study conducted by the Defense Research Institute's Task Force on Women Who Try Cases found that: "[W]omen likewise suffer from the contrasting perception that they are not too familial and 'soft' but too aggressive and 'hard.' Their male counterparts are uncomfortable with them and therefore unwilling to support their advancement."[17]

To alter these unfair and irreconcilable impressions, the MCCA stated that it is not women or other minorities who should be monitored to avoid bias, rather, further attention must be paid to the way in which members of the majority treat one another. It is only through such awareness that firms will be able to identify the common pattern of: "'leniency bias,' where objective rules are applied flexibly to in-group members, while out-groups find themselves treated 'strictly by the book.' Thus, a white man who lacks a certain qualifica tion will be interviewed nonetheless because he shows 'promise,' whereas a woman will be told she simply does not qualify because she does not meet the objective requirements of the job."[18]

The issue of leniency bias also emerges in studies of the relationship between gender, parental status, and the perception of job competence. For example, studies show that, not only are employed mothers judged more harshly than employed fathers, but the fathers are viewed both as better parents and professionals as compared to the employed mothers.[19] Critically, however, in a study of how certain job applicants were evaluated, although the authors predicted that mothers would be judged more strictly than women who had no children, the results revealed a different bias: "[I]t was *fathers* who were held to more *lenient* standards than men without children."[20] Particularly interesting is the fact that gender had less of an impact than did parenthood: "That is, non-parent male and female targets received comparable evaluations, were held to similar standards for hiring, and were hired and promoted at equal rates."[21] For parents in the workforce, this research is significant in its demonstration that fathers are actually held to a more lenient standard than both mothers and men without children.

Barbara Reskin, an expert on gender and race inequality in the workplace noted: "The unconscious beliefs most people harbor about women cast doubt on women's suitability for high-level jobs."[22] Reskin described how unconscious stereotyping creates hurdles for women seeking access to the top: "Within seconds of meeting a person, our brains automatically categorize them as someone like ourselves (a member of our ingroup: 'us') or unlike ourselves (a member of our outgroup: 'them')."[23] Because this categorizing is immediate, gender has a role in whether someone is placed in the "us" or "them" category. This places a particular hurdle in the path of women's advancement, because people favor ingroup members: "We trust them more than other persons, attribute positive traits to them while ignoring their negative characteristics...evaluate them more positively than others, cut them more slack when their performance falls short, and favor them when distributing rewards."[24]

In the end, this creates a dynamic in which women settle for less, even when they are entitled to more. As researchers Babcock and Laschever observed: "The woman may suspect that she has been unfairly evaluated, but because the criteria for evaluation are ambiguous, she can't prove it. She may conclude that something about her behavior has put her in the wrong and that what put her in the wrong was asking to be promoted in the first place. This may make her reluctant to actively pursue advancement in the future."[25]

Interviewees spoke of the frequency with which one bad evaluation can spread the seeds of doubt about an individual attorney's performance, causing a long-term negative impact to one's career. The ABA Commission on Women in the Profession noted: "Lawyers who have achieved decision-making positions generally would like to believe that the system in which they have succeeded is fair, objective, and meritocratic. If women, particularly women of color, are under-represented in positions of greatest prominence, the most psychologically convenient explanation is that they lack the necessary qualifications or commitment."[26]

The road to partnership is also frequently blocked by a lack of exposure to important matters and large clients. In many law firms, the ability to inherit both work and clients depends on the relationships developed with senior partners in a position to promote emerging careers. Observed one young partner:

> *I do see rainmaking partners giving their clients to others. I think that's got to help...with [their] elevation...*

However, senior partners generally do not even recognize their inherent favoring of male attorneys. A former partner recalled that her Managing Partner once asked her why he was perceived as someone who was not supportive of women in the law firm:

> *And remember, this guy worked 2,800 hours, had all the biggest pieces of litigation in the firm, and not one of them had a female in the second position on any of his cases.... "You have how many pieces of large litigation and not one female? Isn't there somebody who could do the job?" He didn't say anything. His face got all red and he left like I had insulted him personally.*

> *He sees himself as being equitable. Equitable is what you do. If you have the largest pieces of litigation, you put women on them. It's not an aberration that women are not rising in the firm when he*

> *doesn't have them leading any of the major pieces of litigation...*

Underlying the importance of passing important client work to a rising protégé is the idea that, to become a partner, an associate needs a strong proponent. One partner emphasized the critical role of the proponent in the partnership election process:

> *[Even] if you had gotten all good performance reviews, you had to have a proponent, period. There is no question that you had to have a proponent. Somebody had to be willing, based on your work, to get up and say, 'This person needs to cross the line because of these reasons.' And if you had nobody to say that, you are not going to cross the line...it was also important that the person who was your proponent was well-respected.*

This same attorney also observed the stereotypes that lawyers carry into the evaluation process, recalling the statement of a male colleague who openly expressed surprise that a pretty associate was also smart:

> *I remember saying to somebody afterwards, 'You can't say that...it's inappropriate.'... The only thing you should be looking at is work performance not whether she is gorgeous. But I remember sitting in an evaluation meeting and people would sit there and not even blush at the comment.... You just want to shake them and say, 'What is going through your mind when you make a comment like that?'*

One young partner described the frustration of witnessing other women fail because they lacked an important patron:

> *There is a woman here who has been here for years...not married, she doesn't have kids, she works really hard, very competent, but she doesn't have a lot of support to become a partner. She is not consid-*

ered a superstar, but she is very competent. She just tried a case on her own with a jury; everyone thought it was a dog of a case and that it shouldn't be tried, so all these other people passed up the case and she said, 'Sure, I'll see what I can do.' She has a lot of talent. She went to [Ivy League law school], but she doesn't have enough support.... I think it is a personal relationship thing.

This partner then described the firm's evaluation process for associates, a complicated scoring system which, at its essence, leaves significant room for subjectivity. An unusually high score could help brand a young associate for a bright future:

There is somebody this year who is a third- or fourth-year associate who got [the highest ranking]. We have a big pack of associates here and they are all really good.... This guy who got the [highest ranking], it was like he suddenly had this crown on his head.

Many women expressed frustration with vague criteria and little, if any, meaningful feedback. The study conducted for The Association of the Bar of the City of New York noted the critical role of feedback in encouraging a lawyer's pursuit of partnership: "Feedback is both psychologically empowering for the individual, reinforcing motivation, and a necessary channel of communication from the firm. Individuals who receive no feedback believe they are being negatively evaluated."[27] This lack of feedback was a common problem for many interviewees, as were the vagaries of the process itself, particularly with respect to the differing criteria among departments within the same law firm. Said one young partner:

One of the things we've learned is how...the criteria for equity partnership advancement [is different] in each of the departments.... Some departments are looking prospectively, some are looking retrospectively, and some are looking at both.

She noted that even if an individual got through the hurdles of the departmental evaluations, the associate would still be subject to the remaining process in which careers could be sabotaged for the flimsiest of reasons:

> *You get through this department, you go to the Executive Committee and then they vote. And then they decide who is actually going to go before the partnership, and then it is a free-for-all. Because anybody can get up at a partnership meeting and say, 'I once did a deal with [her] when she was a second-year associate, and she's so screwed up.' Anybody gets to say anything in the partnership meeting.*

However, a subjective evaluation process is not the only challenge for associates hoping to become new partners. As the study conducted for The Association of the Bar of the City of New York detailed, another key variable affecting advancement is the financial health of the law firm itself.[28] If the firm is facing an economic downturn, partners are less willing to expand their limited economic pie by electing new partners with whom they must share profits. Similarly, if a particular practice area is facing a slowdown, as evidenced by hours billed or revenues generated, then it is likely that the firm will not allow the practice group to nominate any of their associates for partnership until the bottom line improves.

A senior associate moved to a counsel position in her firm after several failed efforts to become a partner. Following each of these attempts, she was given specific goals that, if achieved, would, she was told, help ensure a successful result. Notwithstanding the fact that she achieved all of the ever-changing goals, she still was not elected because of the economic performance of her practice group. She observed the adverse impact of her experience on other women in the firm:

> *Almost all the associates in my practice group are women. Not voting me into the partnership was viewed as the firm's failure to recognize women who have achieved.*

A litigation partner in a national law firm described how the economic pressures of a practice group affected the partnership decision-making process:

[T]heir area economically was not doing well just because of the times and they were told, 'Sorry, you know, this isn't your year. We can't justify adding another partner to the group and that's not to say you're never going to make it. We just don't know. We'll have to wait and see if the economy picks up.' And, yeah, clearly there are issues about how many partners you can make and you have to watch what area you are doing it in. On the other hand, people really didn't have an inkling until right before it happened. Within a month or so these people were going to be told, 'No, this is not your year.' And that's another thing that was not handled well. It is what I'll call managing expectations not only on the part of the associate who's affected, but also on behalf of all associates, because what they saw was: 'This was so-and-so's year to be up and, oh, what happened?' They didn't make it.

The economic reality of law firm life is that, if the economy is bad, then the client development pressures are particularly intense. Yet even as firms have moved into a period of relative prosperity, the demands to generate new business can be relentless. The result is that business generation abilities now seem to be a pervasive criteria for partnership under any economic circumstances.[29]

The importance of business development as a key element of partnership consideration is a source of great frustration for women. Many recounted receiving the same advice early in their careers: work hard and bill a lot of hours. However, then they learned that, embedded in the firm's ultimately subjective evaluation process, it was important that the firm perceive them as potential rainmakers. One former associate described her frustration:

They never encouraged associates to bring in business, yet it was clear that was how they would be judged.

She further observed that even if she wanted to think about business development opportunities, the billing pressures left her with no time to do so.

For most interviewees, the inconsistency between the articulated message to bill more hours and the fact that, as prospective partners, they would be evaluated for their business generation potential served to underscore their frustration with the subjective nature of the process. Its inherent unfairness to women was identified a decade ago in the study conducted for The Association of the Bar of the City of New York which stated: "Additionally, because so few associates actually bring in any new business to their firms, partners make promotion decisions based on their expectations that an associate will bring in business. These expectations are largely based on subjective criteria that are very susceptible to being influenced by stereotypes about the roles and desires of women."[30]

One interviewee described the circular logic that arises in trying to judge such subjective criteria as one's business generation potential:

> *I've had this particular conversation, being told that it is the 'perceived ability to bring in business in the future' that is important as a factor for election. Yet, when questioned as to how they judge a 'perceived ability' for the future, I have been told that they base it on past, proven performance!*

Even as associates enter law firms with the inherent knowledge that "making partner" is supposed to be the end-game, the concept of what it actually means to be a partner is undergoing radical change. Understanding these changes are critical, because they ultimately have a direct impact on the advancement of women.

One significant change is that more firms are tiering their partnership levels or otherwise providing an increased diversity of partnership models. For example, of the 100 largest law firms in 2003 as measured by gross revenues, only 23 had one partnership tier, compared to 55 firms in 1994.[31] Firms similarly "held the line on equity partnership in 2004, opting to increase the non-equity ranks instead."[32]

In some respects, a multi-tiered model can be beneficial for women by increasing opportunities to engage in a challenging career, without the added burdens of equity partnership. The difficulty, however, is whether these alternatives are viewed as stages in one's career progress or an end-point and, if the latter, whether the firm can be structured in a way that provides a myriad of respected alternatives. The fact is, the lack of certainty in progressing to the next tier often adds to the stigma felt by those who remain at the junior partner level. A study of Colorado attorneys observed that tiered partnerships do not necessarily work to the advantage of women: "Rather, they have produced increased stratification within firms, creating a new form of 'employee' lawyer without change in the traditional professional model that informs most firm cultures and compensation structures."[33]

In today's law firm, achieving one level of partnership does not ensure graduation into the next level. As firms have increased in size, some lower-tiered partnerships have been described as not a stage, but a destination.[34] A *Boston Business Journal* article reported that, although the number of equity partners at top law firms increased by approximately 4.3% between 1997 and 2001, by 2003 that growth had slowed to 3.5%, and preliminary data for 2004 indicated even slower growth.[35]

Statistics from the nation's top law firms tell an even more compelling story. In an analysis of equity partner changes among the top 100 law firms, *The American Lawyer* reported that the average number of non-equity partners increased nearly 11% between 2002 and 2003, while the average number of equity partners grew by only 4%.[36] So although law firms have exploded in size in the past several years, the growth in the number of equity partners in many firms has flattened, or decreased.

The primary importance of the distinction in partnership tiers is that, under most compensation systems, it is the "equity" partners who share in the division of firm profits. As a result, even though the top law firms have far greater profits to share, an increasingly larger number of lawyers are earning significantly less than others in their firm, without any guarantee that they will ever enter the equity partner ranks.[37] One young partner observed that women are disproportionately impacted by the increased tiering of partnerships:

> *Many of the women equity partners here made it before there were two levels of partnership or at a time when the succession from income to equity was more automatic.*

As the tiering of partnerships has increased, so has the law firms' leverage, that is, the ratio of associates to partners, which is usually a key indicator of economic success. For example, as firms grew significantly between 1960 and 1985, the ratio of associates to partners increased an average of 28%.[38] So as profits have swelled, the passage into equity partnership has narrowed, and the need for leverage continues, although not necessarily unaffected by the economy.[39] The dramatic salary increases near the turn of this century have exacerbated the pressure on existing law firm attorneys to ensure that maximum value can be obtained from each lawyer: "More senior lawyers in these firms report finding themselves working more hours and spending even more time on client development at a point in their careers when many would expect they would be able to ease up on or at least control the pace of their practice."[40]

The widening gap between the number of equity partners and the number of non-equity partners and associates has become important for another reason: the numerous ranking systems that measure and publish annual report cards on law firm profitability. For example, for more than two decades, *The American Lawyer* magazine has ranked the top 200 law firms based on a statistical analysis that relied heavily on the firm's profits per equity partner. Law firms eagerly await the release of this compilation each summer as their relative ranking has become a critical data point in the recruitment and client development efforts. This is the place where size and profits truly matter.

With that focus on the rankings is an increased pressure on law firms to report the highest possible profits. One way to achieve that goal is to divide the firm's profits among a fewer number of equity partners.[41] The rationale is simple: by decreasing the number of equity partners, firms increase that all-important statistic of the profits per equity partner. An analysis of *The American Lawyer's* statistics for the top 200 law firms demonstrates the striking correlation between the closing of the equity partner gates and their growing financial success. Seventy of the top 200 law firms, nearly 35%, had fewer equity partners in 2004 than in 2003. Of those 70, only 10 also showed a decline in profits; 40 actually increased their profits by more than 10%.[42]

There is a price to be paid, however, in how others in the firm react to those changes.

One Managing Partner wryly observed that the huge profits per partner attributed to a competitor firm was solely attributable to how the other firm "counted" its partners:

> *The profit per partner they reported is just a question of manipulating the number of partners.... They only count one out of four partners. Their situation now is they have income and equity partners, but they all have one vote. They all participate in*

partner meetings. They all get compensated by the
same system.

Some law firms have become quite direct in communicating to the partnership the firm's goal of moving up in the rankings race. One partner told of a recent pronouncement by the management of her firm that they were planning to change the status of a number of lower-paid equity partners to the non-equity category, in order to secure a higher profits per equity partner ranking:

> *What I am seeing is that there is a lot of focus*
> *on...the list of the top 100 national firms based on*
> *average partners' salary. Our current management*
> *feels that the way to success is to move up on that list.*
> *We were on that list, but we're not particularly high,*
> *and so the strategy as far as I can figure out in man-*
> *agement right now revolves around how to move us*
> *up on the list.*

> *So, how to increase equity partner compensa-*
> *tion... You bring in better clients. You cut your*
> *expenses. But the other thing you do is, you knock off*
> *the lower paid partners. And so it has been announced*
> *that lower paid partners will be de-equitized, and*
> *there has even been an announcement as to where the*
> *cut-offs will be.*

She added that of the few women equity partners, most were in the lower end of the compensation scale:

> *It would really impact the women partners. We*
> *have a handful of women partners who have been*
> *very economically successful. But for the most part,*
> *they are in the lower salary tiers and they would defi-*
> *nitely be impacted.*

Even as law firms adjust their ratios to improve their rankings in *The American Lawyer*, however, the magazine has adjusted its formula to stay ahead of the continually changing partnership landscape. In 2004, the magazine observed that: "The range of nonequity partner models creates confusion in interpreting Am Law 100 data."[43] It also recognized how firms use these models to position themselves in the best possible light: "With so many components factoring into partner compensation, guaranteed draws, percentage shares, profit distributions, bonuses, firms can manipulate the number of equity partners to make themselves appear more profitable than they really are."[44] Accordingly, in 2005, *The American Lawyer* added a calculation to measure "Value Per Lawyer," as an alternative to its reliance on profits per equity partner.[45]

Ironically, as firms make partnership decisions with an eye towards the impact on relative rankings, *The American Lawyer* itself recognizes the daunting challenge of making significant changes in one's overall placement. In its own analysis of six years of data, the results demonstrated that: "[M]ost firms tended to finish in the same quintile as they started, despite unprecedented efforts at merging, opening new offices, and acquiring laterals. It may not be easy to keep a successful law firm afloat, but what is really difficult, according to the VPL measures, is moving a firm up in class."[46]

For all of the efforts to manipulate data to improve one's rankings, however, the set of statistics which should serve as an alarm bell to the entire profession are those analyzing the growing number of lawyers leaving law firm practice.

Endnotes for Chapter 10

1. Galanter & Palay, Tournament of Lawyers: The Transformation of the Big Law Firm 15 (1991).

2. Galanter & Palay, Tournament of Lawyers: The Transformation of the Big Law Firm 26 (1991).

3. Galanter & Palay, Tournament of Lawyers: The Transformation of the Big Law Firm 30 (1991).

4. Galanter & Palay, Tournament of Lawyers: The Transformation of the Big Law Firm 26-29 (1991), reporting on research conducted in the 1950s noting that the chance of becoming a partner varied from one in seven to one in 15; and the wait time for lawyers to become partners, around 1960, averaged just under 10 years.

5. *See, Minding the Gap*, The American Lawyer, May 2004, at 107.

6. *Minding the Gap*, The American Lawyer, May 2004, at 113. *See also* Marianne Sullivan, *Women Very Much in Minority Among Equity Partners*, Boston Bus. Journal, July 30, 2004, *available at* http://www.bizjournals.com/boston/stories/2004/08/02/focus2.html (Aug. 11, 2004).

7. Am. Bar Found., *Growth and Gender Diversity: A Statistical Profile of the Legal Profession in 2000*, 16 Researching Law: An ABF Update,10 (2005).

8. NALP Found., *Presence of Women and Attorneys of Color in Large Law Firms Continues to Rise Slowly but Steadily*, (Oct. 3, 2002), at http://www.nalp.org/press/details.php?id=18 (Dec. 6, 2005). *See also*, Marianne Sullivan, *Women Very Much in Minority Among Equity Partners*, Boston Bus. Journal, July 30, 2004, *available at* http://www.bizjournals.com/boston/stories/2004/08/02/focus2.html (Aug. 11, 2004).

9. ABA Comm'n Women in the Prof., The Unfinished Agenda: Women and the Legal Profession 8 (2001).

10. Reichman & Sterling, Gender Penalties Revisited 14 (2004).

11. U.S. Equal Employment Opportunity Comm'n, Diversity in Law Firms 16 (2003) at http://www.eeoc.gov/stats/reports/diversitylaw/index.html, (Dec. 8, 2005).

12. Epstein, et al., *Glass Ceilings and Open Doors: Women's Advancement in the Legal Profession*, 64 Fordham L. Rev. 291, 380 (1995 Rpt. to The Assoc. B. City N.Y., Comm. Women Prof.). Interestingly, the study noted that women fared poorly under the traditional "up or out" system of promoting partners, and some had better success when hired as laterals (*e.g.*, came into the law firm from another firm or from the public sector). Epstein, et al., *Glass Ceilings and Open Doors: Women's Advancement in the Legal Profession*, 64 Fordham L. Rev. 291, 358-359 (1995 Rpt. to The Assoc. B. City N.Y., Comm. Women Prof.).

13. Reichman & Sterling, Gender Penalties Revisited 55 (2004).

14. Minority Corp. Counsel Assoc., *The Myth of the Meritocracy: A Report on the Bridges and Barriers to Success in Large Law Firms*, 2003 MCCA Pathways 34, *available at* http://www.mcca.com/site/data/researchprograms/PurplePathways/index.html.

15. Minority Corp. Counsel Assoc., *The Myth of the Meritocracy: A Report on the Bridges and Barriers to Success in Large Law Firms*, 2003 MCCA Pathways 35, *available at* http://www.mcca.com/site/data/researchprograms/PurplePathways/index.html.

16. Minority Corp. Counsel Assoc., *The Myth of the Meritocracy: A Report on the Bridges and Barriers to Success in Large Law Firms*, 2003 MCCA Pathways 37, *available at* http://www.mcca.com/site/data/researchprograms/PurplePathways/index.html.

17. Shelley Hammond Provosty, *DRI Task Force Examines the Status of Women Litigators at Law Firms*, Of Counsel, July 2005, at 6.

18. Minority Corp. Counsel Assoc., *The Myth of the Meritocracy: A Report on the Bridges and Barriers to Success in Large Law Firms*, 2003 MCCA Pathways 34, *available at* http://www.mcca.com/site/data/researchprograms/PurplePathways/index.html.

19. Kathleen Fuegen, Monica Biernat, Elizabeth Haines, & Kay Deaux, *Mothers and Fathers in the Workplace: How Gender and Parental Status Influence Judgments of Job-Related Competence*, 60 J. Soc. Issues, 737, 740 (2004).

20. Fuegen et al., *Mothers and Fathers in the Workplace: How Gender and Parental Status Influence Judgments of Job-Related Competence*, 60 J. Soc. Issues, 737, 749 (2004).

21. Fuegen et al., *Mothers and Fathers in the Workplace: How Gender and Parental Status Influence Judgments of Job-Related Competence*, 60 J. Soc. Issues, 737, 750 (2004).

22. Reskin, *Unconsciousness Raising*, 14 Regional Rev.: Fed. Res. Bank Boston 33, 34 (Q1 2005).

23. Reskin, *Unconsciousness Raising*, 14 Regional Rev.: Fed. Res. Bank Boston 33, 34 (Q1 2005).

24. Reskin, *Unconsciousness Raising*, 14 Regional Rev.: Fed. Res. Bank Boston 33, 34 (Q1 2005).

25. Babcock and Laschever, Women Don't Ask: Negotiation and the Gender Divide, 91, (2003).

26. ABA Comm'n Women in the Prof., The Unfinished Agenda: Women and the Legal Profession 16 (2001).

27. Epstein, et al., *Glass Ceilings and Open Doors: Women's Advancement in the Legal Profession*, 64 Fordham L. Rev. 291, 362 (1995 Rpt. to The Assoc. B. City N.Y., Comm. Women Prof.).

28. Epstein, et al., *Glass Ceilings and Open Doors: Women's Advancement in the Legal Profession*, 64 Fordham L. Rev. 291, 363 (1995 Rpt. to The Assoc. B. City N.Y., Comm. Women Prof.).

29. Epstein, et al., *Glass Ceilings and Open Doors: Women's Advancement in the Legal Profession*, 64 Fordham L. Rev. 291, 364 (1995 Rpt. to The Assoc. B. City N.Y., Comm. Women Prof.). "Many associates and a number of partners are more likely to portray their firms as market driven entities, where decisions about partnership revolve around profitability."

30. Epstein et al., *Glass Ceilings and Open Doors: Women's Advancement in the Legal Profession*, 64 Fordham L. Rev. 291, 365 (1995).

31. Alison Frankel, *Veil of Tiers*, The American Lawyer, July 2004, at 92. The article, in noting the growing variation in partnership models in the nation's top 100 law firms, distinguishes

equity partners as those who are full voting members with an ownership interest, from non-equity partners (those who derive less than half their compensation from the firm's profits).

32. *Figuratively Speaking*, The American Lawyer, July 2005, at 106. The tiering of partnership opportunities also coincides with longer periods of time before a decision is made: "Over the past 15 years or so, law firm associates have seen the partnership track lengthen, stretching out to eight, nine, even as many as 12 years. And that goal is now often split into two tiers: the traditional and cherished equity partnership, and second-class, nonequity status." Terry Carter, *Homegrown vs. Lateral*, 91 ABA J. 30, 30 (Aug. 2005).

33. Reichman & Sterling, Gender Penalties Revisited 19 (2004).

34. Galanter & Palay, Tournament of Lawyers: The Transformation of the Big Law Firm 58 (1991).

35. Sheri Qualters, *Hurdles on the Partner Track*, Boston Bus. Journal., Apr. 1, 2005, at http://www.bizjournals.com/boston/stories/2005/04/04/story1.html, (with information cited from the *2005 Client Advisory*, Hildebrant Int'l, at http://www.hildebrandt.com/Documents.a spx?Doc_ID=2208, last visited Dec. 7, 2005).

36. Alison Frankel, *Veil of Tiers*, The American Lawyer, July 2004, at 92. Frankel described equity partnership, in which a lawyer is a full voting member of a firm with an ownership interest and a hefty share of profits as an increasingly elusive prize. At 92.

37. Alison Frankel, *Veil of Tiers*, The American Lawyer, July 2004, at 92. Frankel states, "Those wonderful profits per partner, in other words, are coming, in the aggregate, at the expense of partners who aren't truly owners of their firms.... The disparity is even wider when you compare profits per partner not to the average compensation of all partners, which includes the shares of equity partners, but just to the average non-equity partner compensation." Alison Frankel, *Veil of Tiers*, The American Lawyer, July 2004, at 92.

38. Galanter & Palay, Tournament of Lawyers: The Transformation of the Big Law Firm 59 (1991).

39. For example, *The American Lawyer* reported a decline in the total number of associates in its 2005 top 100 list, likely attributable to associates leaving in greater than expected numbers to take advantage of growing opportunities outside of private practice arising from an improved economy. Alison Frankel, *The Case of the Missing Associate*, The American Lawyer, July 2005, at 96.

40. Reichman & Sterling, Gender Penalties Revisited 20 (2004).

41. *See, e.g.,* Brenda Sandburg, *The New Math,* at http://www.law.com (April 27, 2004).

42. Analysis of data provided in *The Am Law 100*, The American Lawyer, July 2005, at 111-121; and *The Am Law 200*, The American Lawyer, Aug. 2005, at 77-122.

43. Alison Frankel, *Veil of Tiers*, The American Lawyer, July 2004, at 92.

44. Alison Frankel, *Veil of Tiers*, The American Lawyer, July 2004, at 92, 95.

45. "Value Per Lawyer" is calculated by dividing the total compensation to all partners (equity and nonequity) by the total number of lawyers in the firm. "VPL is a different cut on efficiency, putting in high relief which firms produce the same value at a faster rate. And are, therefore, stronger." Aric Press, *Adding Value*, The American Lawyer, July, 2005, at 88.

46. Aric Press, *Adding Value*, The American Lawyer, July, 2005, at 88.

CHAPTER 11

HEY, HEY, GOODBYE NOW

Attrition has become a significant economic challenge, and too few law firms are adequately addressing its pervasive impact. Dissatisfaction among lawyers is higher than in other professional groups.[1] Lawyers in private practice have greater dissatisfaction than lawyers in other law-related settings such as in-house counsel or government.[2]

The NALP Foundation has been collecting and publishing data which offers important insights into the study of associate attrition patterns. Its 1997 analysis of more than 10,000 associates, graduating in the period between 1988 and 1996, reported that nearly 10% left their firm within one year, 43% left within three years, and two-thirds left within five years.[3]

Between 1998 and 2003, the NALP Foundation conducted an additional comprehensive benchmark study of associate hiring and departures. With respect to entry-level associates, more than half of those hired in 1998 had left their law firms in less than five years.[4]

Consistent with other detailed analyses of patterns of attrition in the legal profession, a NALP Foundation study reported that: "Consistently working long hours may adversely affect attorney morale, satisfaction, and interest in continuing with the same employer."[5] The NALP Foundation study found, for example, that more than one-third of the law firm respondents expressed interest in changing employers during the next two years, a rate more than double that of in-house attorneys who answered the same question.[6] Significantly, when the respondents were asked what type of job they would most prefer if they were to change employers, only 13.3% of the respondents working in law firms stated that they would prefer private practice with a larger firm, a response rate equal to those who reported that they would prefer a non-legal job. Also of note, nearly 29% reported that they would prefer to be in a corporate legal department and more than 16% stated they would prefer service as a government attorney.[7]

The economic imperative to address the attrition crisis is compelling. Women in the profession are younger than men, and many have small children.[8] Their continued exodus from law firms results in layers of direct and indirect costs which too few firms even measure. In fact, although women may be leaving law firms in larger numbers, the costs - and many of the causes - of attrition are gender neutral. An *ABA Journal* article cited to "grueling schedules combined with lack of training and mentoring" as the primary reason why lawyers are leaving their law firms.[9]

A former president of the American Bar Association noted that, within less than four decades, the profession grew from 200,000 to approximately 700,000 lawyers, with women accounting for a large part of that increase.[10] In fact, the percentage of growth in women entering the legal profession is significant.[11] However the statistics demonstrating the rate at which women are heading for the exit make it clear that something is deeply wrong with the profession.[12]

Sadly, the one place in law firm life where women have caught up with, and even exceeded, their male counterparts is in the area of attrition.[13] After years of struggling to enter the doors of the legal profession on an equal footing with men, the steady exodus of women leaving the practice of law is a discouraging referendum on the profession's failure to adapt to its changing demographics. As the NALP Foundation reported: "Female and minority associates departed their law firm employers with greater frequency than males and non-minorities at almost every benchmark."[14] An article in *The American Lawyer* which reviewed major developments in the profession over the past 25 years noted: "Women escaped from the typing pool, filled law schools, entered the associate ranks, and discovered that a service business was not always healthy for parents, children, and other living things. While gender bias proved difficult to tame, and the biological clock an even more implacable foe, the law firm system itself treated most everyone equally when it came to lavishly recruiting, then spitting out, male and female associates with ease." [15]

One of the reasons so little seems to be done to stem attrition may be due to the general failure of law firms to monitor closely their attrition statistics and the concomitant impact on the firm's bottom line.[16] If they did, they might be surprised by what they found. The Midwest attorney who has long been involved in these issues noted:

> *The interesting part of it nationally is that women didn't want to hear about the fact that women are leaving the profession, or that women are leaving the large law firm practice to go elsewhere. Or that*

women are choosing a different quality of life and those who have children are sometimes opting out permanently. That is a discussion that nobody wanted to have before because they didn't want to really think that it was happening and they didn't want to discourage other women from choosing the profession.... But the facts are, for whatever reason, self-selection for quality of life, or self-selection because women don't see the certainty of advancement and, therefore, the price that they pay for that advancement is far too high, the men are willing to pay a price, because they have a certainty of advancement to the place of their choice....

Although there is limited publicly available data from existing law firms, the research that does exist is instructive as to this one key fact: attrition is expensive. Moreover, if law firms were to monitor all of the costs associated with constant turnover, they would also be unable to claim that such high-volume attrition is merely a weeding out of the unwanted. If, in fact, an honest appraisal of the attrition data proved otherwise, then firms would clearly benefit from a renewed analysis of their recruitment procedures to determine why they are hiring such poor fits.

Key studies and reports issued by the American Bar Association as well as the prominent consulting firm Catalyst, and other organizations and bar associations around the country corroborate the fact that, to date, firms have not paid enough attention to the significant costs of attrition. One nationally prominent attorney expressed her concern that firms do not appreciate the impact of their high attrition rates:

If it doesn't get measured, it doesn't get fixed. So firms [need to understand] the costs of attrition.

In its seminal study of associate attrition, the NALP Foundation stated that: "the hiring and attrition cycle has substantial direct costs and, sometimes, significant opportunity costs, both of which can impact the firm's profitability, client service, and attorney morale. When a law firm is unable to retain the 'keepers,' it may lose more than profits from the bottom line."[17]

In a detailed study, The Boston Bar Association Task Force on Professional Challenges and Family Needs undertook an economic analysis of the costs of attrition. The Report highlighted the primary ways in which associate attrition was costly to law firms.[18] Specifically, the BBA Task Force found that: first- and second-year associates at large and many medium-sized firms are generally an economic loss to their firms in these early years. Although the exact point at which an associate becomes profitable varies: "the primary return on a firm's investment in an entering associate occurs in years five to 10."[19]

More recently, Catalyst surveyed lawyers in 100 Canadian law firms to explore the relationship between how they perceive and manage work/family issues in their firm and the impact of that perspective on associate attrition.[20] The results of this study demonstrated a direct link between concerns about meeting one's family obligations while working in a law firm and attrition. Two-thirds of the women associates and nearly one-half of the men reported they intended to stay with their firm for only five years or less. Critically, the top factors cited as reasons to choose to work at another law firm were: choosing an environment more supportive of family and personal commitments; more control over work schedule; and an opportunity to work fewer hours. Also of importance, 63% of the women responding said that they would leave their firms for an environment more supportive of women.[21]

In this study, Catalyst quantified the average cost of an associate's departure at $315,000, approximately twice the average associate's salary.[22] In the model it developed, Catalyst analyzed investment costs such as salary and benefits, recruitment, training, and other capital expenses. Importantly, Catalyst also analyzed other costs incurred when an associate is separating from the firm, such as productivity losses in an associate's final weeks and months of tenure at the firm, file reassignment, career counseling services, exit interviews, and costs relating to severance (e.g., out-placement assistance).

Harder to quantify, but nonetheless real, are the intangible costs of attrition. For example, The Boston Bar Association Task Force on Professional Challenges and Family Needs described "relationship costs," arising out of the "recurring sense of loss" that is felt when coworkers depart.[23] Similarly, the Catalyst study observed that the intangible costs of associate turnover, although difficult to quantify, could: "have a longer, more enduring impact on a firm's profitability, morale, and client service."[24] None of these studies quantify the uniquely individual costs attributed to loss of clients who are unhappy with their firm's turnover rate or who leave to follow a departing lawyer to another law firm.[25]

Even as studies demonstrate that women are leaving law firms in larger numbers, their decision to leave is usually reached after significant failed efforts to improve their situation at work. This is contrary to popular cultural myths that professional women have been voluntarily "opting out" of work, a subject of intense media speculation.[26]

The fact is, few women have had the luxury of choosing a work environment that allows the effective integration of work and family responsibilities without a negative career impact. Accordingly, the choice implied by the term "opting out" is indeed a false one.

Recently, the New York Times reported that an email survey of women at two elite colleges revealed that more than half intended to cut back or cease working after having children.[27] However, even as the article, and ensuing media attention, raised concerns that high-achieving female college students were already accepting a traditional gender-based role, the key point seemed lost yet again.

The real question raised by the article should have been: What is the basis for these high-achieving women to imagine a workplace that would allow them the opportunity to manage both their careers and families according to the same high standards they have placed upon themselves their entire lives? As they observe their parents or other important role models who have struggled in unhealthy professional work environments, is it any surprise that these intelligent women contemplate an easier path for their own families in the future? Perhaps a more interesting survey would explore the circumstances under which these women would choose to remain in the workforce. If so, an instructive vision of a more flexible work environment would likely emerge, one that could ultimately retain these highly capable future professionals.

The fact is, the statistics refute the image that the popular media likes to portray of women opting out of the workforce entirely. As one important study reported, even when women do take a hiatus from their career, most (93%) want to return to work. A further finding which should sound an alarm to employers everywhere is this: "Only 5% of highly qualified women looking for on-ramps are interested in rejoining the companies they left. In business sectors, that percentage is zero."[28] In fact, research supports that female attorneys are less satisfied with their careers and, therefore, more likely to leave law firms at earlier stages.

Women are not, however, leaving the law.[29] Rather, they seek opportunities for positions that provide greater flexibility. They also seek opportunities to have an impact on their own workplace. A researcher analyzing the lower job satisfaction among female lawyers reported that the most important con tributing factor is lack of influence and opportunity: "What these outcomes show clearly is that female lawyers' lower job satisfaction is due mostly to their sense of not having enough influence, promotional opportunity, and financial compensation, rather than wanting a less demanding career."[30]

Research conducted on mid-career women demonstrates that the majority of the women who leave their workplace are not leaving: "to spend time at home, they are leaving because they are dissatisfied with their job growth and advancement, lack of flexibility, sex bias and discrimination, and they often go to competitors or start their own businesses."[31] These other options may lower compensation, but they offer a variety of alternative opportunities for job-related satisfaction.[32]

A senior partner in a New York law firm concurred with such research:

> *Here, you get rewarded on merit. But to be rewarded on merit, you have to put in a lot of hours. And because of that, I think women self-select out.... I don't believe women are leaving to go home....*

> *I see more people going in house, or choosing to do things differently, people getting out of the law and working, but not working the same kind of hours. But I don't see women staying home with children. I see them doing other things.*

Interviewees described law firms that invoked images of the legendary stories about law school Deans who, addressing new students on their first day of class, observed that many in the audience would not be part of the graduating class. Only, in these stories, the Deans could be replaced by law firm managers predicting the rate at which new associates will leave. Many interviewees reported that female colleagues who were part of the law firm's "entering class" of associates had moved on to other employers or had left the profession entirely. For example, one partner in a New York law firm stated that of her group of five close friends who graduated together from law school, only one remained in a large firm. Commenting on the cultural shock they all experienced in transitioning from law school to private practice, she stated:

> *Real punishment is when you start practicing law. They own you.*

A prominent partner summarized her numerous conversations with young associates who regularly confided in her:

> *Women, I do think, without drawing too many ste-*
> *reotypes, fewer women than men are locked into the:*
> *'I'm just here for one purpose.' We do as a group look*
> *for broader lives than that. Whether it's for our fami-*
> *lies or other types of involvement.... Stay-at-home*
> *moms, working moms, volunteers, we're trying to do*
> *all those things, but the model doesn't work very well*
> *within the economics [of a law firm]. There is just a lot*
> *of disappointment about feeling that this isn't neces-*
> *sarily what they want. That's what saddens me. This is*
> *not what they want to grow up to be, and they look at*
> *the partners and they don't see happy partners either.*

A former senior associate, who had worked at two large firms before she left the profession altogether, stated that, like many of her friends and colleagues, she had recognized early in her career that she could not remain. Her blunt assessment of her life as an associate was:

> *I felt like I was pushing a log up a hill.*

She further wryly observed that the law is the only profession with its own cottage industry of career counselors who are fully devoted to helping lawyers figure out what they want to do next so they can leave their law firms.

A third-year associate spoke of her decision to leave, noting her frustration with a workplace in which everyone was afraid to communicate realistically about workloads and deadlines. She described an example where a client, after letting a matter sit too long, called a partner who volunteered an immediate response to the client and then assigned her the work on a crisis basis over the weekend:

> *Why didn't he go back to the client and say, 'I*
> *value you and your work. To do a good job on this*
> *will take a little longer....'*

She then stated that the experience made her realize:

This is not how I want to live my long-term life.

One long-time career counselor was blunt in her assessment of the damaging effects to both men and women she has witnessed over the years:

> *There is a test that people often take for career guidance...and if you score high on three indices, it is very likely you are going to be counseled: 'You'd make a terrific lawyer.' And the three indices are: analytic, verbal, and autonomy.... The analytical capacity serves them well in a law firm. The verbal capacity serves them well in a law firm.*

> *But does the autonomy need serve them well in a law firm? Because there is no environment that is more rigid, formulaic, and intuitive than a law firm. Because they don't tell you what is expected of you, and if you don't do it, you get "dinged."... The people who have the highest autonomy needs of all usually leave first because they realize how rigid the environment is....*

> *So you got the guy who stays and he stays and he stays and ultimately, because a lot of his colleagues have left, he gets made partner because he is there....*

> *It is the kind of thing where there are a lot of people who remain in law firms simply because they don't have the vision or the guts to get out. And they are miserable, they are absolutely miserable. And then they go to inflict the same level of misery on the people who are beneath them.*

This perception of the profession's high misery index was reinforced by a social services professional who works with lawyers suffering from depression and other stress-related disorders. She noted that lawyers feel a constant and intense pressure to produce, which negatively impacts their personal life and sometimes leads to a downward spiral of impaired relationships and even destroyed practices. She added that these pressures can pose particular difficulties for women who feel prohibited from demonstrating characteristics which may be their greatest strength:

> *Women get co-opted by the dominant culture. So the characteristics that are strongest for women get thrown out the window, collaboration and teamwork.... The system doesn't allow for collegiality...*

A senior partner noted that, after two decades in private practice, she was contemplating alternative career options. She expressed sadness at the increased rate of attrition she observed among women associates, as well as women partners. As she spoke of her feelings about possibly leaving the firm, she felt struck by her lack of connectedness to her other partners:

> *I feel very little sense of: 'How could I leave my partners?' I don't have that feeling of belonging here...and I have thought about why that may be....*

> *You can come here, you can work, you can make partner, but you never really feel that you are part of a club in any way, part of the inside.... It is kind of like: 'You can be here, but you are not really one of us.' It is that sort of a feeling.*

> *I think that [as for] women in law firms, like other minorities...the presumption is that you can be here and be welcome, as long as you are performing superbly and everything is going well.*

She kept encouraging her firm's managers to recognize the increasing number of women associates resigning from the firm. She also highlighted that these departures coincided with the firm's sequential increases in both its billable and non-billable-hour expectations. However her efforts did not produce results:

They were pretty sympathetic, but nothing concrete was derived about what could be done. And I thought, when I was [entering the profession] there were few women partners that it was still a real accomplishment to become a partner. And you did it in large part just to prove it could be done. It was kind of like climbing a big mountain: you wanted to get to the top. And now, oddly, I think because there are [more] women partners, and people have done that, now, it is...no longer such an accomplishment that women are willing to make the sacrifices necessary to get there.

A struggling junior partner at a large firm believed that the women who try to stay tend to be poor role models for younger lawyers.

I wouldn't be surprised if one of the reasons for attrition begins to be: 'I don't really want that life.' We came here thinking that: 'We want this brass ring that's being held out to us.' I think the new associates coming in, women and men alike, are saying, 'I don't need this. I'm going to pay off my school loans, and have a balanced life.' And I would not be surprised if that happens more and more.

Echoed a senior associate in the same law firm:

I'll often go home at 5:30 or 5:00, and then come back after my kids are asleep at 9:00. And the people I work with, and I work with a large team of people and a lot of them are younger, usually women, and I think they look at me like I'm insane. But it's not like I'm complaining. That's what they see.

For some women, the strain of knowing they are role models to others, even if they feel like failures internally, becomes overwhelming. Consider the comments of this partner with young children who, even on a reduced-hours schedule, finds the competing demands of her work and her home impossible to balance:

> *I feel like I've been incredibly fortunate in my circumstances, but I almost regret that I'm in the position I'm in.... The burden of running a home and taking care of kids is on me, and the work is incredibly stressful. And once a month, I'm the one who is paying the bills and I could be earning more, but I'm not willing to do that. So I'm at the point where I'm considering walking away.*

> *But so many women associates in this office look to me as their role model, and I can't tell you how many people come into my office, women associates come into my office, and say, 'It's so great you're doing what you're doing. It's great. It's so exciting that you made partner and you have kids and you are doing it all.' And I feel this responsibility to these women, and I always joke with them and say, 'Please don't look at me as a role model. I'm a complete nut.' ... I feel this moral responsibility to the other women who see me as a role model. I want to stick it out. I don't want people to say, 'Oh, it can't be done. It was a mistake.'...*

> *I feel like there is no scenario where I could work it out here. The workload is so demanding. I just want to get away from the stress. There are so many women who are now working in alternative environments. Some women work for non-profit organizations or outside of law firms, and they do this because there is less stress than other work environments and they find a balance of family and work. It's preferable to be in a work environment that is not as stressful as you find in a private firm and that's what I'm hoping to find.*

I don't want to give up working. I don't want to
give up my career because I like what I do. But I
really, really want to reduce the stress. I feel like it
has taken years off my life with the pace that I'm try-
ing to keep up.

Throughout the interviews, women described their struggle to meet the obligations of their work and their family and, unable to feel like they could do either well, leave their firm, just as the partner quoted above subsequently did.[33] A former associate at a large firm stated her view of the "Tipping Point" which drives women out:

I don't think women leave after the first child; I
think they leave after the second one.

Her notion that the workplace becomes even less hospitable to women who have more than one child has emerging support. A study in the Journal of Social Issues noted: "There is some concern that two children...may truly signal a woman's lack of commitment to her job."[34] In other words, the perception that a woman is dedicated to her job is diminished as her family expands.

A female partner views these decisions to leave as logical ones:

Women make choices not to [stay here], and I
think they are very sensible choices that they are
making...choices I thought about making a hundred
times here.

Even as some women leave because of the difficulty in juggling their demands, some simply can no longer endure their own dishonesty in the façade they feel they must put on each day at work:

I think that's one of the things that made me
leave. It was very hard because you have to sell the
firm. You basically would say, 'This is a very nice
place to work, very friendly place.' I've worked part-
time for nine years and, of course, the inference peo-
ple took from [my saying]: 'I've worked part-time for
nine years, I am an equity partner, I enjoy practicing

*law,' would be: 'This is a great place to work.' And
there were many nights, especially after I had [inter-
viewed] somebody who was really dynamic, who I
really thought would be a great lawyer, I would lay
awake at night and think: 'Oh my God, I am lying. It's
not a great place for women to work.' I mean, it's a
great place if you want to work a billion hours, it's a
great place to work period. But don't be female, you
can be a female but you have to act like a male. If
you're a feminist or you are near and dear to feminist
causes, forget it. You certainly can't be articulating
those things."*

Many women link the cause of high attrition to the difficulty women have
developing their own client base. This becomes a particularly significant issue
when a woman becomes a partner and the firm's business generation expectations of her increase. Women who do not demonstrate solid rainmaking skills
may find their days with the firm limited, as law firms engage in efforts to
prune out partners who do not meet their business generation expectations.
However because this activity is taking place quietly, and often below the
radar screen of even the law firm's own rumor mill, this is one category where
it is difficult to differentiate the voluntary from the involuntary attrition.[35]

In many instances, even where women are not asked to leave, they feel
compelled to take that step on their own. This theme, commonly repeated in
the interviews, was also observed by Reichman and Sterling, in their study of
Colorado practitioners. They noted that women may be deciding to leave their
law firms even before receiving feedback from the firm regarding their long-
term potential.[36] One former partner described the insecurities which drove
her to leave her firm:

*I didn't see how I was going to develop a prac-
tice. The level that you needed to develop it at, to be
competitive, was beyond my understanding of how I
would ever compete in that world. And, since I wasn't
feeling that I had a specialty, and I wasn't feeling like
I had anybody who was going to let me inherit their
practice, it was not a good place for me.*

A former partner of a large firm, whose source of work came primarily through a male senior partner, described the similar insecurities she experienced after she was elected to the partnership:

> So they all decided it was the right thing to do because there had never been a complaint about my work. I got along fine with everyone, and I had done really well in terms of my performance and the quality of the work. I had not been bringing in business at all but that was probably because I was perceived as [name of partner's] helper, and it really was hard to break out of that. Also, I didn't know how to go out and get business....
>
> And so I made partner.... At the time, I was the only woman partner.... I still remember the first time I came in to the partner's meeting.... Part of me was so excited then, to be the first to blaze the trail... But...I always felt like I was there, but I did not belong. And the funny thing, maybe the only thing in life that I've always been confident about, is that my work is of a high quality.
>
> I mean, I'm confident about myself in that regard.... But I just felt like I didn't belong and part of it was that I couldn't prove my value to them in monetary terms other than through [name of partner, with whom she worked most closely]. So it's not like I could sit there and say, 'I've got this independent power source.' It just felt like I had done good work and for that reason I deserved to be a partner, but I didn't feel like they were natural peers.

Another senior partner in a national law firm observed that, in her experience, it was common to see women walk away from their partnership position, afraid that they would not be able to measure up to the expectations others had of them:

> *Most of them were not happy with the compensa-*
> *tion. But even more importantly, I think they just*
> *despaired of the future. By and large, the women*
> *partners...are better than the guys, on average.*
> *Which makes sense when you look at the demograph-*
> *ics, it was much harder for us to get into law school.*
> *[The law schools] proportionately took a much*
> *smaller number and we had to work a lot harder and*
> *be a lot better than the guys. And I think that's still*
> *true...that there is a double standard.*

She expressed particular frustration with the fact that, because women are never honest about the reasons they are leaving, her male colleagues can avoid looking in the mirror for a possible explanation:

> *In the spin that is always put on it, it is that they*
> *made a "life-style" choice. They either wanted to go*
> *in-house, they wanted to become a judge, they wanted*
> *to, whatever, take some other job. And everyone says*
> *that there was a story behind every individual. 'Oh,*
> *we can explain that one. We can explain this one.'*

> *And, obviously, when someone is leaving, no one*
> *wants to burn bridges and really express the dissatis-*
> *faction that they had.*

Other studies corroborate that work/life issues are among the leading causes of attrition. For example, a study of Atlanta-area law firms revealed that most full-time lawyers, both men and women, who recently left a law firm did so to obtain better work schedules, not bigger paychecks.[37]

In their study of Colorado lawyers, Reichman and Sterling observed gender differences in the reasons for career changes reported in their interviews. They found that women were more likely to change careers: "as a result of their dissatisfaction with compensation, a 'dysfunctional' firm, or their interest in an alternative lifestyle. Men tend to characterize changes in their careers as the result of 'new opportunities.'" Women tend to cite family or lifestyle as the reason they are leaving their firms: "rather than express their dissatisfaction and risk closed doors in their future. Similarly, men may find it [gender] inappropriate to cite family or lifestyle as the reason they leave, preferring instead to focus on their new opportunities. Both responses, appropriate from their gender perspective, tend to reinforce the stereotypes of women's commitment to the practice of law."[38]

A former partner at a large Washington-based law firm noted that, when women are not honest about the reasons for leaving, their former law firms can avoid taking any responsibility for the departure:

> *And part of the difficulty is that even those people who do leave never actually say why they are leaving, because you can't burn your bridges. [So whatever reason they give for leaving, the firm believes.]... they believe it... [It's] easier to do that than it is to change. ...[S]ome firms have set up this exit interview thing that is supposed to be anonymous. If you're a woman partner and you leave...it is never going to be anonymous.*

She then emphasized that, even where women leave to take what appears to be a more prestigious position, the reasons for leaving may be deeply rooted in their simmering unhappiness, and becoming a judge or senior government official becomes a socially acceptable way out. She recounted the story of a woman who had left her law firm to become a federal judge:

> *All the guys in the firm were like: 'Oh man, she left to become a federal judge.' And the women were all saying, 'What are they talking about; being a federal judge has never been a career goal of this woman.' But it was a way out, and when I talked to some of her women partners...and said I was really surprised to hear [of her appointment], it turned out that she had finally had it with the law firm, and this opportunity had come up, and it was a legitimate opportunity and she said, 'I'm out of here.' But it was the culmination of a lot of different things that had been happening that made her say she didn't want to stay with the firm any more.*

She also shared her frustration with her male partners' refusal to believe that the departure was related to anything other than a prestigious opportunity:

> *[T]he men would not believe it. It's the status symbol. And she had been pretty cool at the firm when things would happen to her, apparently....So the men thought: 'She loved it here. She loved us. We loved her.' Not a clue.*

A startling aspect of writing this book has been the career transitions of the many women who left their firms subsequent to our interviews. One such woman was a highly regarded senior level associate. During our initial interview, she shared many of her frustrations with the firm's assignment process and the firm's tendency to involve her in significant amounts of non-client billable projects, including matters for institutional clients which the firm chose, as a business matter, to perform on a courtesy basis. At one point, she was asked to undertake such a project for an important client, which was expected to last several months. From the outset, she requested a formal change in her billable-hours target, to ensure that she was not penalized for accepting the assignment. Her request was dismissed, as she was repeatedly told she did not need to worry.

Several months after the project was completed, her mentor informed her that a powerful senior partner in the firm was questioning "why her billable hours were so low." Ironically, as he reported this information, he urged that she not be "defensive" in her response. Her frustration was still palpable as she described the circumstances which ultimately led to her resignation:

> *I am asked by the senior partners to do something. I did it. I did it well. I was commended on my work. I tried to raise this issue before and I was rebuffed....*

> *I thought I gave [him] the factual data that he needed, explaining why they were so low...but then also say, 'Okay. Here we are. [The senior partner has] gone to you, you've come to me, we're sitting here and talking about it. Don't you think there is a better way of approaching this?'*

As she described her feelings following their discussion, she conveyed a sense of being trapped. If she tried to explain her non-client billable time, she was deemed defensive, yet her assignments derived from senior people in the firm who needed the work done, and who were not providing client billable alternatives. The day after their conversation, her mentor left a note on her chair which suggested that their conversation would have been more fruitful had she focused on ways to obtain more billable work, rather than trying to explain the source of the non-billable work she was assigned. He showed no recognition of his impact when he initially approached her, telling her it was at the behest of a key senior partner who was questioning her non-billable work:

> *Actually, during that meeting...I said, 'Well, I am glad to give you that information.'... I had kept track of every non-billable research project [and] partner-assigned pro bono matter where the partner decides to [accept the] pro bono, but I do [the work].*

> *So...my mentor came and talked to me about a concern that had been brought to him. And I think there ought to be some freedom to not present myself to him in that setting as I might to a committee of my firm, or during a review or something like that.... I clearly was frustrated that the question came up because I just tried to address it a month before or two months before...*

> *And here is my boss, and he is a grown man, and he is leaving me a note on my chair.... I think this man is really trying to help.... And he believes that the way...to succeed here, which is to make partner, is not to question, to be a good girl. And I think he thinks: 'Good Girl.'... Keep your nose to the grind stone and...just do your work, and shut everything else out.*

At that point, she felt powerless to respond. She knew that she had been given certain non-billable assignments specifically because of her excellent client relationships and her particular expertise. Frustrated with the constant mixed messages, she decided to leave her law firm and accept a position in a law-related, not-for-profit institution. What amazed her, once she announced her resignation, was the uniform shock of her mentor and others in the firm that she was leaving. She noted, in particular, her mentor's reaction:

> He said, 'I can't believe you are leaving. I didn't want you to go.' It was just so odd. I think: 'This is a man who just clearly lives in a bubble.'...Clearly, he likes me personally and is just telling himself: 'Well, she was really meant to go do this non-profit stuff...She's not really wired for law firm life.'...
>
> When I left, with all of this, he never asked me, 'What could we have done differently?'... No one did. For them, I am not going to a different law firm, I am doing something very different. But I was there for almost seven years, and I got really good performance reviews.... I felt like I left on a very good note, and yet no one, not one partner, asked me the questions: 'What could we have done differently? What did you think? How did we do?' Nothing. So I found that really frustrating.

A former partner in a national law firm also expressed frustration with the failure of her colleagues to probe beyond the superficial reasons women gave for their resignations. She observed that departing women do not voluntarily admit that they are leaving in frustration with the firm; rather, they simply say they need more time with their families:

> I saw so many women not get ahead...and the really good ones would leave.... [W]e did a study that [showed] most of the women that left, the firm wanted to keep. Half of the men that left, the firm didn't want to keep. So there was a very clear correlation that more women were leaving that the firm wanted to keep, versus the men....And most of the women that left were not asked to leave....[A]nd they also found that the number of men going to...other private practices very high and that the women were going into

> *corporate positions or nonprofits or, but there was a lower percentage going back into private practice....[W]ell, I mean the goal is retention of women. And we had, I remember having a few meetings.*

She decried the firm's limited efforts to understand the impact of these attrition statistics, and its poor business judgment in failing to take meaningful steps to address the basic issues driving women out of the law firm. She believed that the firm's findings should have led to a massive effort to help women feel less frenzied at work by creatively implementing ways to diminish the extraordinary time bind in which many working mothers saw themselves. Among the number of suggestions she made to the firm was the recommendation that the firm offer greater assistance around the availability of day care and that it respond creatively to the issues of greatest stress such as offering parking spaces closer to the building for women who have to rush to a day care deadline. However, in her years at the firm, she did not see anyone moving forward on any of these suggestions.

The lack of candor from lawyers who resign impedes the ability to create and track attrition statistics, further enabling firm management to easily hide from the real issues driving the loss. A former senior partner at a large law firm noted:

> *I remember saying to [the Managing Partner], 'One of the things you're facing is that we have this turnover in women here. Look at how many women we hired. Look at how many women have gone.' And he said, 'Well, we have lost a lot of men.'*

> *'But the percentage is way off. We lose 99% of the women we hire, and we lose 50% of the men we hire, and it happens with every single class we bring in.' He still didn't admit we had a problem with keeping women....*

The continued loss of women creates a self-fulfilling prophecy which impacts the hiring process.[39] If women are leaving certain law firms in larger numbers, potential recruits may be less likely to join those firms as they view the small percentage of women attorneys as indicia that their own chances of success are diminished. For example, one partner from a medium-size law firm described the internal problems which contributed to a high rate of attrition among women at the firm. She then expressed dismay that the firm had received very few resumes from women for the senior associate positions which recently became available:

> *I am the co-chair of the Hiring Committee, and I*
> *was really disappointed that so few of the resumes*
> *that we got for the positions that were open were from*
> *women. We ended up hiring three men.*

It was clear from our discussion that the dearth of female resumes was likely due to the firm's reputation for being particularly hard on women attorneys. It was far less clear that anyone in the firm understood that to be the reason.

Ironically, one of the responses of law firms to their growing exodus of lawyers is the creation of "alumni networks" among former attorneys to serve as a business development tool.[40] Since, in many cases, lawyers who leave move to a position where they can refer work or hire their own counsel, law firms are recognizing their alumni pool as a fertile source of future business. Accordingly, an increasing number of firms are holding social events and creating alumni directories as a way to keep connected with their former lawyers. Yet how many women will feel inclined to support a firm with their business if they feel they were, in effect, pushed out the door?

Yet even as women walk out the doors of their law firms, they find themselves looking back at the women remaining, wondering why so few held out a helping hand.

Endnotes for Chapter 11

1. *See, e.g.*, Cunningham, *Father Time: Flexible Work Arrangements and the Law Firm's Failure of the Family*, 53 Stan. L. Rev. 967, 969-70 (Apr. 2001), reporting that law firm attrition is more than double that of other industries. Humorist Sean Carter, writing in the *ABA Journal*, noted: "Once upon a time in legal America, signing onto work for a law firm meant something.... Back in those days, we agreed to stay with our firm through good times and bad until death (or hitting the lottery) did we part. Needless to say, things have changed. Nowadays, the average tenure at a law firm can be measured in hours.... It's come to the point where some lawyers aren't even sure what firm they're currently working for. They simply get up in the morning and drive to the place they went to yesterday, hoping that they haven't somehow changed firms in the interim." Sean Carter, *The Lawyer - Go - Round: Chasing the Moving Target of Attorney Transfers, Mergers and Maneuvers*, at http://www.abanet.org/journal/redesign/home.html (Apr. 8, 2005).

2. See, e.g., the study conducted by the New York State Bar Association which reported that "roughly equal proportions of men and women in in-house counsel and public interest/government work settings (about two-thirds) were very likely to stay in the law for the rest of their careers, and almost all of those in the judiciary thought they would, but only about half of the women in private practice and 72 % of the men indicated they were likely to stay for the rest of their careers." See, e.g., N.Y. St. Bar Assoc. Comm. on Women in L., Gender Equity in the Legal Profession: A Survey, Observations and Recommendations 13 (2001) available at http://www.nysba.org/Content/ContentGroups/News1/Reports3/womeninlawreport-recs.pdf (Dec. 1, 2005). See also Steven Wilmsen, *Law and the Disorder It Can Bring to Family Life*, Boston Globe, June 24, 1999, at D1; See also Paul Frisman, *Toughest Case May Be Family v. Career*, Conn. L. Trib., July 12, 1999, at 16.

3. NALP Found., Keeping the Keepers II: Mobility & Management of Associates 98 (2003). The NALP Foundation and the American Bar Foundation are currently conducting a longitudinal study of 10% of the graduates from law schools in the year 2000. In the first stage of data reported, for the first few years after graduation: more than 50% of the large-firm respondents stated they were planning to change jobs within the next two years. NALP Found. & Am. Bar Found., After the JD: First Results of a National Study of Legal Careers 53 (2004) available at http://www.NALPFoundation.org. The study also noted that more men than women entered private practice: women were likely to work in government, legal services, public defender positions or other public interest or not-for-profit positions. At 57.

4. NALP Found., Keeping the Keepers II: Mobility & Management of Associates 22-23 (2003). This study also reported increased activity in lateral hiring, noting: "[L]ateral associates have evolved from a new generation of law graduates who view their careers differently than any prior generation of lawyers. This thinking has been validated by a new-era economy which promulgates employer-employee relationships that are market-driven, negotiable and (can be) temporary. Long-term, mutual commitments between associates and law firms are not necessarily the norm. Rather, relationships between associates and law firms last only as long as market conditions dictate." At 42. It is important to understand the economic conditions during the time in which this NALP Foundation data was collected: by the year 2000, the economy was in a significant downturn, the technology boom was ending, and then the events of September 11, 2001 further exacerbated already

depressed market conditions. Accordingly, notwithstanding the significant associate movement documented, market conditions were such that many associates who might otherwise have left their firms may have chosen the security of staying. At 17.

5. NALP Found., In Pursuit of Attorney Work-Life Balance: Best Practices in Management, 28 (2005).

6. NALP Found., In Pursuit of Attorney Work-Life Balance: Best Practices in Management, 28 (2005).

7. NALP Found., In Pursuit of Attorney Work-Life Balance: Best Practices in Management, 95 (2005).

8. See, e.g., N.Y. St. Bar Assoc. Comm. on Women in L., Gender Equity in the Legal Profession: A Survey, Observations and Recommendations 6, 42 (2001) available at http://www.nysba.org/Content/ContentGroups/News1/Reports3/womeninlawreport-recs.pdf (Dec. 1, 2005).

9. Debra Baker, *Cash-and-Carry Associates*, 85 ABA J. 40, 41 (May 1999). The article further observed: "No longer willing to submit years of their lives to sweatshop-like schedules, young lawyers are looking at private firm practice with a short-term vision: They want to pay their school debt, earn as much money as quickly as they can, and get out, many leaving the practice for careers that will provide what they are looking for in terms of professional fulfillment and quality of life." At 41. A Boston Globe article attributed rising attorney attrition to: "attorneys questioning whether to stay in a field that no longer offers what they once considered key draws: a chance to help clients and the ability to choose interesting cases over lucrative ones." Ralph Ranalli, *Pleas of Frustration: Lawyers Questioning, Abandoning their Profession*, Boston Globe, Aug. 18, 2003, at A1.

10. Robert MacCrate, *What Women Are Teaching a Male-Dominated Profession*, 57 Fordham L. Rev. 989, 993 (1989), noting that in a span of 10 years, female enrollment in law schools rose from 4% to 40%.

11. Between 1900 and 1985, the percentage of female physicians increased 300% (from 5.6% to 17.2%). The percentage of women teaching in college grew more than 500% (from 6.4% to 35.2%). And the percentage of female lawyers and judges grew from .8% to 18.2%, an increase of more than 2,200%. Charlotte Chiu, *Do Professional Women have Lower Job Satisfaction then Professional Men? Lawyers as a Case Study*, Sex Roles: J. Research (Apr. 1998), available at http://www.findarticles.com/p/articles/mi_m2294/is_n7-8_v38/ai_20914076 (Dec. 7, 2005).

12. Epstein, et al., *Glass Ceilings and Open Doors: Women's Advancement in the Legal Profession*, 64 Fordham L. Rev. 291, 439 (1995 Rpt. to The Assoc. B. City N.Y., Comm. Women Prof.), observing: "Although there is a general crisis of morale among all young lawyers, women do seem to be leaving large firms disproportionately more than men...." See also NALP Found., Keeping the Keepers II: Mobility& Management of Associates 30 (2003), reporting that an analysis of five years of attrition rates from law school graduates of the classes of 1998-2002 revealed that attrition of women was nearly always higher than for men from the same class and time frame. It is important to note that the statistics for women of color are even worse, as nearly two thirds have departed their firms before their fifth year. At 30. See also, N.Y. County Law. Assoc., Report of the Task Force to Increase Diversity in the Legal Profession (2002).

13. See, e.g., Reichman & Sterling, Gender Penalties Revisited 16 (2004). This study of Colorado lawyers reported that of the women who graduated from law school in the 1970s, 31% had retired by the time they were interviewed for this study in 2003; all of the men who graduated from law school during that same time period were still working. The Minority Corporate Counsel Association study reported that 86% of women of color leave their first firm before their seventh year, and that 77.6% of all women leave their law firm prior to being nominated for partner.(generally by their seventh year). See Minority Corp. Counsel Assoc., The Myth of the Meritocracy: A Report on the Bridges and Barriers to Success in Large Law Firms, 2003 MCCA Pathways 24, available at http://www.mcca.com/site/data/researchprograms/PurplePathways/index.html.

14. NALP Found., Keeping the Keepers II: Mobility& Management of Associates 21 (2003). available at http://www.NALPFoundation.org.

15. Aric Press and Susan Beck, *Almost a Revolution*, The American Lawyer, May 2004, at 77, 78.

16. See, e.g., NALP Found., Keeping the Keepers II: Mobility& Management of Associates 111 (2003) available at http://www.NALPFoundation.org. For firms that do closely monitor their numbers, the results can be stark. For example, an article in The American Lawyer reported data from one large law firm which showed that: "Eighty-eight percent of women in an entering class typically leave the firm by their seventh year, as compared to 63% of the men." So even though men and women who are up for partnership are elected in "roughly equal numbers," the total number of women partners remains low because of the high attrition rates. Emily Barker, Engendering Change, The American Lawyer June 2003, at 82.

17. NALP Found., Keeping the Keepers II: Mobility& Management of Associates 22 (2003) available at http://www.NALPFoundation.org.

18. BBA Task Force on Prof. Challenges and Family Needs, Facing the Grail: Confronting the Cost of Work-Family Imbalance, (1999).

19. BBA Task Force on Prof. Challenges and Family Needs, Facing the Grail: Confronting the Cost of Work-Family Imbalance 28-29 (1999). The Report further stated that: "Junior associates' salaries, benefits, and per capita allocated overhead now exceed the billing rate that can be charged for the level of legal work most junior associates can perform, multiplied by the number of hours they can (reasonably or unreasonably) be expected to work." At 28. The Task Force Report noted that a variety of factors impact when a lawyer can finally become profitable for the firm, including, for example, how much of the junior lawyer's time can actually be billed and collected (which can be tied to the lawyer's skill level), the nature of the practice area and work tasks assigned, and the amount of training provided. At 28.

20. Catalyst, Beyond A Reasonable Doubt: Building the Case for Flexibility (2005). In total, 1,439 associates and partners responded to the Catalyst study; the results cited herein are from the first of three reports comprising Catalyst's Flexibility in Canadian Law Firms series. See also, ABA Comm'n Women in the Prof., Options and Obstacles: A Survey of the Studies of the Careers of Women Lawyers 27 (1994) describing the results of a California study in which women ranked "Working too many hours" (56%), "Difficulty balancing personal and professional life" (51%), and "Too little time for family responsibili-

ties" (51%), as significantly more important factors to their dissatisfaction with the legal profession than "Financial conditions" (34%).

21. Catalyst, Beyond A Reasonable Doubt: Building the Case for Flexibility 5 (2005). See also, The State of the Legal Profession: 1990, ABA Young Law. Div. 79, (1991), noting the "impact of the deteriorating workplace environment on law firms and client services." In particular, the survey documented the decreasing stability in the profession which results in a: "change in lawyers' and law firms' mindset from one of long term commitment to one of hard-nosed appraisal of opportunities and mobility." At 79.

22. Catalyst, Beyond A Reasonable Doubt: Building the Case for Flexibility 9-13 (2005). Catalyst reported general consistency among investment and separation costs across the firms analyzed, but did note variability in specific cost items that would affect cost allocations for individual firms. Some firms invest more resources in interviewing larger numbers of candidates and spending on recruitment-related travel, meals, and other services related to hiring; similarly, training costs can vary among firms depending on the amount and use of internal and external training programs. The report also noted that separation costs may be higher for involuntary departures because of severance-related expenses.

23. BBA Task Force on Prof. Challenges and Family Needs, Facing the Grail: Confronting the Cost of Work-Family Imbalance 30 (1999). The Task Force noted how profound the continuing loss of these relationships can be by noting: "The associate who becomes an equity partner in one of the larger firms is likely to have seen 300 other associates come and leave in the seven to 10 years that he or she is an associate." At 30. It is worth noting that this statistic was developed prior to many of the significant law firm mergers that have taken place since the Task Force Report was issued in 1999.

24. Catalyst, Beyond A Reasonable Doubt: Building the Case for Flexibility 17 (2005). Specifically, the Report identified the following intangible costs of turnover: "productivity decreases prior to the departure decision; the potential loss in consistency of client service and client dissatisfaction with disruptions; opportunity costs from repairing relationships; lower morale among those left behind; the loss of intellectual capital and talent; and the potential long-term financial loss of a strong performer who has left the firm." At 17.

25. See, e.g., The State of the Legal Profession: 1990, 1991 ABA Young Law. Div 79, finding: "If a valued lawyer burns out and leaves the firm, the firm has lost its considerable investment of time, money, and knowledge in that individual as well as, potentially, clients who are loyal to that individual and follow him or her."

26. See, e.g., Belkin, The Opt-Out Revolution, N.Y. Times Mag., Oct. 26, 2003, at 6. See also, Jane Bryant Quinn, Revisiting the Mommy Track, Newsweek, July 17, 2000.

27. Louise Story, Many Women at Elite Colleges Set Career Path to Motherhood, N.Y. Times, Sept. 20, 2005, at A1, available at http://www.nytimes.com/2005/09/20/national//20women.html?3i=5070&en=88d5272285b1.

28. Sylvia Ann Hewlett and Carolyn Buck Luce, Off-Ramps and On-Ramps: Keeping Talented Women on the Road to Success, Harv. Bus. Rev., Mar. 2005, at 52.

29. See, e.g., Foster, The Glass Ceiling in the Legal Profession: Why Do Law Firms Still Have So Few Female Partners?, 42 U.C.L.A. L. Rev. 1631, 1657 (1995). According to the NALP Foundation research, "women are leaving or avoiding partnership tracks.... [They] are increasingly rejecting mainstream large-firm practice to work in smaller firms, to serve as

in-house counsel, or to form their own firms." See also ABA Comm'n Women in the Prof., Balanced Lives: Changing the Culture of Legal Practice, 20 (2001).

30. Charlotte Chiu, *Do Professional Women have Lower Job Satisfaction then Professional Men? Lawyers as a Case Study,* Sex Roles: J. Research (Apr. 1998), available at http://www.findarticles.com/p/articles/mi_m2294/is_n7-8_v38/ai_20914076 (Dec. 7, 2005).

31. Ellen R. Auster, *Professional Women's Midcareer Satisfaction: Toward an Explanatory Framework,* Sex Roles: J. Research., (June 2001), available at http://www.findarticles.com/p/articles/mi_m2294/is_2001_June/ai_80805134. (Dec. 8, 2005). Auster noted that the midcareer point is a critical one for many women as it is where: "organizational practices and life responsibilities collide. Whether organizations tailor their organizational practices and support systems to tap the enormous potential of professional women at this midcareer stage will likely have a dramatic impact on whether these professional women stay with their organizations or leave for better opportunities." See also ABA Comm'n Women in the Prof., The Unfinished Agenda: Women and the Legal Profession 7 (2001), noting that women: "typically move to positions with greater flexibility."

32. Foster, *The Glass Ceiling in the Legal Profession: Why Do Law Firms Still Have So Few Female Partners?,* 42 U.C.L.A. L. Rev. 1631, 1657-58 (1995). The author noted that in increasing numbers, women are leaving their law firms or avoiding the firm's partnership track. See also, Nancer H. Ballard, *Equal Engagement: Observation on Career Success and Meaning in the Lives of Women Lawyers,* 292 Wellesley Center Research for Women Working Papers Series 12 (1998): This examination of the ways in which women lawyers define success in their workplaces identified three elements which the author described as a: "Connection-Engagement-Greater Good" pattern. These critical elements that proved central to a meaningful career experience include: positive mutual personal relationships that support a women's engagement in her work; strong engagement with the work project; and the feeling that work-related personal relationships and work engagement will lead to a greater good. See also Reichman & Sterling, Gender Penalties Revisited 24 (2004), reporting that, in their study of Colorado lawyers, women reported significantly less satisfaction with relationships at work than men.

33. Many law firms are satisfied to view this as the "pull" of family life which causes women to leave their firms; this ignores those factors which contribute to "pushing" women out the door because of the firm's inability to address these issues. See, WFD Consulting,"When Talented Women Leave Your Company: Is it Push or Pull?" It's About Time, Winter 2004, available at http://www.wfd.com, nothing that push factors include the: "perception of limited opportunities; lack of role models in senior leadership; unclear career paths; excessive workload due to bureaucratic and management inefficiencies; non-competitive rewards and recognition; and lack of respect for personal life."

34. Fuegen, et al., *Mothers and Fathers in the Workplace: How Gender and Parental Status Influence Judgments of Job-Related Competence,* 60 J. Soc. Issues, 737, 751 (2004).

35. See, e.g., Andrew Longstreth, *Partner in Name Only?,* The American Lawyer, (Mar. 2005), at 65, observing that: "Many firms regularly ask less profitable partners to give up their equity or leave their partnership."

36. Reichman & Sterling, Gender Penalties Revisited 29 (2004).

37. Ga. Assoc. Women L., Atlanta B. Assoc. Women in Prof. Comm., Ga. Comm. Women, It's About Time: Part-Time Policies and Practices in Atlanta Law Firms, (2004), available at http://www.gawl.org/gawl/docs/Its%20About%20TimeFinal.pdf.

38. Reichman & Sterling, Gender Penalties Revisited 24-26 (2004). Importantly, Reichman and Sterling reported that women respondents, when faced with work/life challenges, were more likely to take on new career opportunities outside of private practice, whereas men would tend to reconstitute their practices to get more control over their work: "To what extent these decisions reflected gendered choices (e.g. a woman's willingness to give up higher incomes to engage in something worthwhile) or gendered opportunities (a man's professional network) is hard to determine precisely. Whatever the reason, the impact is to move women away from more lucrative compensation and reinforce gendered expectations about commitment and competence." At 26.

39. The NALP Foundation study also highlights general deficiencies in the legal recruitment process (that affect men as well as women): "[O]ne-page applicant resumes, cursory 20-minute on-campus interviews, brief in-office visits, and summer programs that may or may not provide adequate opportunities for candidates and employers to undertake realistic assessments of each other may have become burdensome accoutrements of the legal recruitment process." NALP Found., Keeping the Keepers II: Mobility& Management of Associates 101 (2003).

40. See, e.g., Jill Schachner Chanen, Home Again: *More Law Firms Create Alumni Programs to Foster Personal, Business Relationships*, 91 ABA J. 32 (June 2005).

PART TWO

CHAPTER 12

FOR WOMEN ONLY

At the outset of this discussion, it is critical to state that clients and, therefore, law firms are fundamentally enriched when their lawyers can offer diversity of individuals, of perspective, of intellectual approach, and of personality. The goal of this book is to identify the opportunities and absolute need for institutional changes that strengthen the connection between new models for success and a thriving workplace.

In a book about women lawyers, it is also critical to emphasize that women do not have a monopoly on the extraordinary challenges facing the profession today. An issue of profound importance is the profession's failure to recruit, retain, and promote lawyers of color, a failure that begins in our nation's law schools and continues in all aspects of the profession.[1] Of note, the ABA Commission on Women in the Profession is focusing on the intersection of race and gender in its critically important Women of Color in the Legal Profession Research Initiative which is developing first-of-its-kind data on the experiences of women lawyers of color. These are challenges which warrant immediate attention. A diverse and inclusive workplace is not only good for all women; rather, it is transformative for the profession as a whole.

In January, 2005, Harvard University President, Lawrence Summers, was caught in a firestorm of criticism for his remarks before a conference sponsored by the National Bureau of Economic Research addressing the under-representation of women holding tenured positions in science and engineering at major universities and research institutions. The speech garnered front-page headlines around the country and severe criticism from scholars, including within his own faculty, for his three hypotheses regarding "...the sources of the very substantial disparities...with respect to the presence of women in high-end scientific professions."[2]

The first of these was the "high-powered job" hypothesis, the notion that the most prestigious positions demand near total commitment to work. The second hypothesis, and the one which ignited the controversy, was based on what President Summers called "different availability of aptitude at the high end," suggesting that innate differences cause men to perform better in these fields. He identified his third hypothesis as "different socialization and patterns of discrimination in a search," which he described as the patterns of discrimination and stereotyping that can take place in the hiring process. Also, he rhetorically questioned whether it was right for society "to have familial arrangements in which women are asked" to make career decisions based on their willingness to have a job "that they think about eighty hours a week," as most prominent jobs require.[3]

The public outcry in response to President Summers's speech focused largely on his suggestion that innate differences between the sexes could be responsible for the under-representation of women in science and engineering facilities.[4] Yet his first hypothesis, that women are not willing to provide the "level of commitment" needed to succeed at the highest levels, raises equally troubling questions that have direct applicability to the legal profession. Acknowledging the significant demands of high-powered jobs in major corporations (e.g., law, medicine, other professional service organizations, and higher education) President Summers stated: "…[T]he most prestigious activities in our society expect of people who are going to rise to leadership positions in their forties, near total commitment to their work. They expect a large number of hours in the office, they expect the flexibility of schedules to respond to contingency, they expect the continuity of effort through the life cycle, and they expect, and this is harder to measure, but they expect that the mind is always working on the problems that are in the job, even when the job is not taking place. And it is a fact about our society that that is a level of commitment that a much higher fraction of married men have been historically prepared to make than of married women."[5]

President Summers's choice of words is instructive. For example, he stated that it is the "most prestigious activities" that "expect" near total commitment, and that married men have been "historically prepared" to make these commitments. Have not married men historically had the luxury to make these commitments because the family's domestic needs were managed and provided by their wives? Since "activities" cannot have expectations, is it not the people involved in these activities who create artificial demands that are not truly integral to getting the job done? In fact, it is not "society" which expects the hours in the office and near total commitment, but rather it is those who make the rules in the workplace who also have the power to change those rules. Are not those "familial arrangements", in which it is typically women who are expected to manage their family's needs more than men, also a cultural artifact that the workplace has the power to change?[6] President Summers's choice of words demonstrate how ingrained the cultural norms of today's professional workplace have become, notwithstanding more than three decades of women in the workforce.

As he discussed his three theories, President Summers promised to address whether society has a right to expect that level of all-consuming effort from people who hold the most prominent jobs, and whether it is fair for society to place the family burdens on women. Unfortunately, he left these most critical questions unanswered and only a public relations nightmare in his wake.[7] However, it is that very question which must be addressed in order to affect change in the workplace. Importantly, President Summers's swift and aggressive responses to the outcry demonstrate that leaders can change these norms, but more on that in Chapter 16.

The experiences of women in law firms are rooted in a culture created by people similar to one another. Yet, as the workplace has changed demographically, the cultural norms and behaviors have remained relatively stagnant.

This chapter addresses the "differences" women have spoken about in their interviews, differences in how they behave, how they are treated, and how they interact with one another. Some of these differences contribute to the tremendous barriers many women face as they strive to succeed. In other instances, the workplace has failed to capitalize on the tremendous positive contributions these differences can make in the life of the firm and its lawyers.[8]

When the ABA conducted its 1990 study of the profession, it reported that almost twice as many women as men in private practice were dissatisfied. In analyzing why, the ABA reported that women experience a far more negative work environment than men. Sources of this dissatisfaction included:[9]

1. lack of confidence in opportunities for advancement;

2. the prevalence of political intrigue and backbiting;

3. a work atmosphere that is impersonal;

4. not having enough time for themselves;

5. not being respected and treated as professional colleagues by their superiors; and

6. lower compensation than their male colleagues.

More than fifteen years later, these same concerns continue to persist. A General Counsel summarized the gender differences she has observed over the years:

> *A woman with an assignment will stay at her desk to finish it, whereas the guy will walk around and talk to people.... Women try to please, so they will eschew networking to complete their project. They won't get out to meet people.... Women are also more risk-averse. Our behaviors are fixed in grammar school, boys are jumping around and girls sit quietly. Women feel like they have to know their topic eight ways to Sunday before they'll speak up. Men are more willing to wing it.*

Many women recalled circumstances where they were treated differently from their male colleagues and, although the intent may have been benevolent, the result was not. For example, a former partner at a large firm recalled observing such situations:

> *[S]omebody would have small children at home and [her male partners] would say, 'You know, we don't really want to put her on this case because then she is going to have to travel.' The outcome is the same because what's going to happen is that the male you put on that case is going to do very well, is going to get better experience than the women who you are not giving the legal responsibility to. I remember I always used to say, 'Ask her! Ask her! Let her make the choice!' And there are times in your life when you have to make different choices. So women have to be given these roles or at least the opportunity to decide about them.*

Others had far more overt examples of behavior that directly undermined women. One associate described her experience working for a prominent male partner:

> *He was just horrifying to work for. I mean so belittling of women, you would walk into his office as a second-year associate and he would look you up and down. Rumors were that he had been sleeping with his secretary for years. So you would go in there and he would tell you in one or two sentences what the problem was for the client, and you would feel like he was trying to intimidate you.*

After describing incidents of overt sexist behavior in the office, she highlighted the Monday morning interrogation she would face from male partners inquiring about her weekend social life. However, in spite of the overtly inappropriate behavior, she struggled to appear unruffled by it:

> *I never really wanted to be thought of as someone who was too offended by it, because I just didn't want that to become part of who I was as a lawyer.*

Even an associate's marriage could lead to awkwardness in the office when male colleagues felt they were losing their control. The same associate noticed that, after she was married, the male partner for whom she did the most work exhibited significant changes in behavior towards her by behaving as though he felt rejected:

> *I remember feeling that I had to reassure him that I was there for him, too.*

Interestingly, this partner exhibited even more possessive behavior when he saw her doing work for another lawyer in the firm. Although he never directly prohibited her from working for another lawyer, he nonetheless expressed his intolerance for any indication of divided loyalty:

> *He would never get stuck saying something [that direct]. What he said was, 'I think you should think carefully about what your opportunities are and I think you should think about the opportunities I've given you, because I've given you a great opportunity to work for this client.'*

A number of women spoke of male partners who treated them in an over-bearing and jealous manner if they spent time on assignments given by others. In addition to such instances of possessive behavior, women described the difficulty of drawing boundaries around social interactions. One former associate described the charged atmosphere in the large Midwest law firm where she had worked:

> *A lot of the male partners were going through divorces.... We didn't want to hang out with them, because, in part, these guys were our supervisors. I'm not suggesting anything inappropriate, but it just didn't feel right. They didn't realize, I don't think, how nervous we were trying to make a good impression and you can't be buddies fully with people that are in a position to evaluate you. And there were rumors that were never confirmed of some of the senior women having affairs with them. And when you hear about that, even if it's not true, you just want to keep your distance.*

> *I remember one weekend we were called in and this was, now looking back, highly unusual. It was almost a 'play well with others' meeting: that the new associates, basically the four women, weren't meshing well in the group. We were doing good work but we weren't partying enough, although they didn't come out and say it that way. And on the one hand, I thought that's really nice, they want to get to know us better, but on the other hand it felt a little claustrophobic.*

These stories paled in comparison to the frustration many interviewees expressed about feeling forced to work competitively, rather than collaboratively, with other female colleagues. Throughout the interviews, a recurring theme that emerged was that women acted too competitively towards one another. One senior associate described her frustration:

> *There is not support. There's not that: 'Let's help bring these women up.' There's none of that.*

A former associate described the qualities of the three men and one woman most likely to be elected as partners in the near future:

> *They fit the profile...and, in fact, every male associate at my firm is married, the wife doesn't work or has a second, smaller income, kids at home, lives in the suburbs, white. I mean that is the profile. [The senior female] is someone who'd step on her mother's back to become a partner, and is just horrible to be around. And I hate not trusting your colleagues.*

In describing this senior woman associate further, the interviewee spoke of an individual who distanced herself from other women, but pretended to be engaged. Her examples were illustrative of the subtle undermining that can occur:

> *Here's a good example. I never talked to her about anything. I recently had a meeting with [well known political figure]...and I was getting ready to go to the meeting and it was exciting for me, as a young woman, to have a meeting with someone of his stature.... [A]nd so she saw me in the ladies' room as I was getting ready to go, and I just mentioned to her where I was going. So I come back from the meeting, I go into [a senior partner's office]... and so we were just talking about things. [The female senior associate] came in. She said, 'Oh, were you telling him about your meeting?' She then said, 'I was really pumping her up for it in the ladies' room!' Very phony. Or...if [a powerful senior partner] is in his office, she'll yell really loudly, 'Thank you, [name of interviewee], you were so helpful!' It's just infuriating. I can't stand that. You know, she's an ex-female.... She's just playing the game.*

She noted the failure of the few senior women partners to support other women in the firm. In one example, she described how a senior partner interacted with a new female associate:

> *She's fabulous, and [name of senior partner] is horrible to her. She'll say, 'This is awful! This is really bad. You need to rewrite this!' She's really harsh. [She does not] respond to [the associate's] inquiries about matters, not give her guidance, but is very quick to criticize, and takes no interest in her whatsoever.*

Finally, she described two other senior women partners who had also been unsupportive to other women:

> *[They are both] glorified associates. They're more fearful of their jobs. I mean, I am in a better position to find work than those other two female partners…. On my way out the door…everyone was so nice to me…. And I would have to say, the people who were either indifferent or maybe not nice were the other two women, so it's really unfortunate. And I just wonder how other women will succeed there. And I feel like I could have stayed there, and I could have succeeded, but I would have been absolutely miserable.*

Many interviewees expressed significant frustration with the failure of senior women partners to support other women. This frustration has also been raised in studies of women's experiences in law firms. For example, a report of the ABA Commission on Women in the Profession observed: "A recurring frustration among younger women lawyers is a perceived lack of understanding and support from some senior women colleagues, particularly on quality of life issues. Whether intended or not, their message seems to be, 'If I had to struggle to make it, so should you;' 'I had to give up a lot, you do it too.'" [10]

In her comprehensive book on marketing for women attorneys, Deborah Graham wrote that: "One of the results of woman-to-woman competition is that women in law firms often have not supported one another by confronting gender bias issues within their law firms. The problem is compounded since senior women in the best positions to bring about the confrontation of gender issues often are the last to do so, either because they are in denial about the existence of these issues or because they are simply scared." [11]

A senior litigation partner in a national law firm described several female colleagues as generally disengaged and unhelpful. She observed a difference between the women in the Litigation Department and in the Corporate Department, suggesting underlying reasons for behavior that tends to be easily dismissed as coming from a "Queen Bee":

> *Some of it is the Queen Bee Syndrome. And I would say that it is driven by [practice] area. Historically, it has been harder for women in the Litigation area. We griped a little bit more. The women in the Corporate area decided that their approach was to play by the guys' rules, 'I'm going to be one of you. I'm going to adopt whatever you say. Look at those whiners down in Litigation.' Even to the extent that you go to the partner meetings and they sit around and they smoke the cigars with the guys. And they participate in the coarse humor...and it's not that I'm a prude, but I'm more likely to say, 'Wait. That's not appropriate at partners' meetings.'*

The "Queen Bee Syndrome" was a recurring theme among the interviewees. In their eyes, these are the women who succeeded under a male model and stayed the course, without looking back. As author Deborah Blum noted: "Women do rise to positions of real power these days, but often only by adopting the traditional values of the men who have come before them. Their success, or lack of it, is measured by the standards of a man's world."[12]

One partner wryly observed that it is often the outspoken women who are responsible for driving the firm's management to include a woman on important firm committees. Yet when management acquiesces, the woman selected is frequently one who has not previously expressed an interest in, nor been outspoken about, the advancement and retention of women in the firm:

> *There is one woman who is on the firm's [Management] Committee who has been completely co-opted by the guys.... And she's not been helpful to the other women at all.... She would actively say, 'There's all these other people, the whiners, the complainers, there is no problem. Look at me. I made it. I'm suc-*

cessful. I'm doing everything I am supposed to do. It's because they are jealous. They didn't make it.'

And I mean even to the point where you brought in your statistics and she kept saying, 'There is no problem.... The women and men are leaving at roughly the same numbers.' And you say, 'Oh yeah? I'm looking around the table.'

She recalled how this woman became a member of the firm's management team:

It was in large part because [of the small number of] women partners.... [We] got together: 'Gee. We think we ought to make a push to get a woman on the Management Committee.' We looked around the room and tried to decide who would be least objectionable to fit in. And that's why she got on the firm committee. It was because the more activist women partners were the ones pushing the idea.

A prominent partner, with substantial roots in government service, expressed frustration with her female colleagues who not only failed to offer support to other women but often judged the female associates more harshly than the male associates. She described the experience of one young associate:

I think she is one of three or four shining stars [in this practice group].... Her writing is terrific. Her legal analytical skills are terrific. Her interpersonal skills are fabulous. I have clients who rave about her. I gave her a rave review. Well, two other [women] partners this time around, gave her, not just mediocre reviews, but early warning signals that she wasn't passing muster.... In both cases, this lawyer was perceived as not pulling her weight under certain circumstances where there was some sort of a crunch. In several cases, I know for a fact there was a matter of miscommunication. ... In both cases, the lawyers who

judged her work as lacking are people who have been
partners for a long time, who will be here at midnight
or one or two in the morning.

This is a young woman who is very efficient, she
does her work, she is often here at eight at night. But
she is getting married in the spring, she has been
planning a wedding, she's been doing some other
things. She has several civic volunteer projects that I
had personally urged her to do to get involved at the
community level...but that kind of thing is not judged
as valuable as it used to be [here], the very law firm
that hired her told her these were valuable things to
do. Now what is valuable is to be here at 3 a.m.. She
wouldn't mind being here at 3 a.m. for a specific
thing, as we would all do under particular circum-
stances. But as a rule, if she feels like the work is fin-
ished, she is not out of here at 5 p.m., she's out of here
at 8 p.m. But she falls into that category of somebody
they don't see hanging around on the weekends....

In both cases, [the women partners] believe they
have set the standard and that no one else can match
up, but I will tell you for a fact that they apply differ-
ent standards to the young men who work for them....

Her conclusion was that these women partners consistently behaved as
Queen Bees, unwilling to help younger women coming through the ranks and
generally holding them to a tougher standard than the male associates who
worked for them. She also noted that, even though the women attorneys in her
firm get together on a regular basis, little is gained by the experience:

[T]he women associates get together regularly,
and what I find is that they come up with a list of
issues and they consistently bring them to women
partners and talk about it with the firm, and then
nothing much happens with it. So I think the firm

> *encourages it because it is a little bit of an outlet so*
> *women can get together and gripe....*

> *And again to the Queen Bee point...the women*
> *who are 40 haven't changed as much.... One women*
> *said recently, 'Well, I should be a role model for*
> *everybody. You know, I've got two children and I*
> *made partner and I worked around the clock.' ... It's*
> *very, very frustrating.*

One Managing Partner of a large firm observed succinctly:

> *I see some older women as pretty tough: 'I had to*
> *suck it up. You should too.'*

Attorney Phyllis Horn Epstein observed this dynamic: "I have also observed women of power who do not see women's advocacy as something that deserves their time and attention. These women believe they are competing in a male profession on men's terms and doing just fine. Because they are successful, discrimination is nonexistent for them, and they feel their efforts on behalf of women at large are not needed. These women distance themselves from the advocacy 'clique' in the way middle-school girls divide into separate cliques based upon clothes, behavior, or friends."[13]

Similarly a social worker who specializes in helping lawyers suffering from depression and other stress-related disorders was blunt in her personal observation:

> *Women don't support each other.*

Throughout the interviews, the term "Queen Bee" came up too frequently to be ignored. So the question arises: What are the possible roots of these perceived behaviors which create the divide between many in the "first generation" of successful women and those younger women behind them?

Perhaps these "Queen Bee" behaviors are, in large part, an adaptive pattern developed by women whose opportunities for success were narrowly constrained by their own abilities to "fit in." In "Queen Bees and Wannabes," author Rosalind Wiseman described the power relationship that can exist among adolescent girls who create sophisticated social structures in order to "navigate the perils and insecurities of adolescence."[14] At the top of this social structure is the "Queen Bee" who: "Through a combination of charisma, force, money, looks, will, and manipulation…reigns supreme over the other girls and weakens their friendships with others, thereby strengthening her own power and influence."[15]

Wiseman's analysis of the teenage Queen Bee personality suggests some interesting commonality with the adult women labeled as Queen Bees within their law firms. Wiseman states that in the process of gaining "power and control over her environment," the Queen Bee "loses herself in the process."[16] A Queen Bee maintains her position at the top of the adolescent pecking order by using her power to remain the center of attention. According to Wiseman, they are at the top of an adolescent clique in which they serve as enforcers of culturally established codes of behavior for females.[17]

Young girls, who are constantly bombarded by media and entertainment images of what constitutes "ideal femininity," learn early to enforce these standards through their peer relationships.[18] However, the price paid is severe and lasting. As Wiseman states: "Clearly, girls are safer and happier when they look out for each other. Paradoxically, during their period of greatest vulnerability, girls' competition with, and judgment of, each other weakens their friendships and effectively isolates all of them."[19]

There are striking parallels between Wiseman's analysis of the Queen Bees and related adolescent behavior and the behaviors of women who have risen to the top of their law firm's hierarchy. For many of these women, the failure to help advance the careers of their female colleagues may be an adaptive behavior whose roots can be traced back to middle school. The older woman partner who finally reached the brass ring of partnership long ago determined that survival and success in her male-dominated world required the exclusion of other women from the top. She felt threatened by those other women trying to join her and intuitively did what she believed she needed to do, perhaps even what she did as an adolescent, to obtain and keep her place in the hierarchy. She did not have the opportunity to learn that her own sense of security could actually be strengthened by a more diverse partnership.

In *A Tale of "O,"* Harvard Business School Professor Rosabeth Moss Kanter uses X's and O's as a metaphor to describe the impact of discrimina tory treatment and unequal representation.[20] In her tale, the O stands out in a workplace full of X's. Never out of the spotlight, the O feels burdened by an obligation to demonstrate continually the same level of competence as the more numerous X's and to set the example of the "good O." The O finds itself under ever-increasing pressure to overachieve as the sole O representative, even as the counterpart X's succeed simply by being average. As the O learns that success is more likely to come through conformity, it develops the qualities that will appeal to the other X's: "The O, of course, is supposed to show its gratitude to the X's for letting it in, by siding with the X's on issues of interest to O's, by adopting the X's point of view, or by taking the lead in criticizing other O's, in putting down O characteristics and sometimes even in outdoing the X's in finding reasons to reject other O's."[21]

Does this sound familiar? Critically, as one of the only O's, the O feels bound to compete to maintain its place: "The O is forced to play a particular part because of the nature of the situation it is in, in this case, being one of very few of its kind among many of another kind."[22]

The path taken by many of the first wave of women partners bears a striking resemblance to the struggles of the O's in their X-filled world. Under scrutiny at all times, these legal pioneers succeeded in a male-dominated environment, often without any peer support or internal safety net. Their adaptive behaviors may be frustrating to their younger colleagues, but it demonstrates how vulnerable these women may feel, notwithstanding the level of success they have achieved. Nonetheless, instead of being able to reach out, the women partners who have resorted to the "Queen Bee" behavior remain in isolation, even as their female colleagues long for their support.

A former partner noted that, although most of the women in her firm felt a bond of camaraderie, they hid their mutual support from a select few other women whom, they felt:

> ...wanted to be viewed as one of the men.

A partner on a reduced-hours schedule summarized her experiences as one of the few women partners in her firm's litigation department:

> *One litigation attorney made partner last year. She had one child and was working full-time. It's tough when you are an attorney with children working part-time and all the other women out there who don't have kids are working around the clock. Or they have one child and are working full time. There was a lot of competition....*

There are other women who are trying to make it part-time and are told they don't have a good work ethic because they are not in the office billing 3,000 hours every year.

She then described how she felt stymied when she tried to discuss her own interest in working part-time with these other women partners:

Another one is in the corporate department with one child. She is incredibly wealthy. She is not an advocate. The other woman who has made partner last year, I initiated conversation with her, I talked to her about going part-time and she feels that it's a cop-out.... She has a baby. She has made it this far. She has succeeded. She basically wants to be seen on a level playing field. She feels like she would be copping out or somehow denigrating herself if she went part-time, even though she cries in her car on the way home because she is afraid she won't get to see her child before her child goes to sleep at night.

As the firm grew, she felt it became even harder for women to communicate openly with one another:

A year or two ago, I organized a couple of luncheons [for women attorneys]. And the group was so big that people just didn't speak.... People didn't feel open to speak. So we would have these luncheons and they were excruciating.... I finally said, 'This is horrible. I am not going to keep organizing these.'

And the question was: 'Should we just have women partners [at these luncheons]?' But it was kind of an odd group.... So unfortunately, our monthly luncheons just fizzled out.

She concluded that the other female partners were afraid to be seen doing anything differently than their male colleagues:

> *They want to be seen in the same playing field,*
> *and they're afraid they won't be.*

But watching what is said around people you do not trust actually pales in comparison to seeing strong women lose their voices entirely. It was hard to reconcile the strong and intelligent women interviewed with their frequent stories about circumstances in which they became silenced when faced with behavior they felt was threatening or which undermined their ability to succeed. Story after story emerged striking this similar theme.

For example, in Chapter Two, a former senior associate recounted the mental and verbal abuse she suffered at the hands of an overbearing partner. Looking back, she was frustrated by her silence as she endured this horrible experience in her life, and angry at the partner who told her he would try to protect her, as long as she did not discuss the matter with anyone else in the firm.

A former partner expressed dismay that her colleagues would not speak out on issues:

> *It wasn't power as much as much as a voice...I*
> *think there are still a lot of issues for women to be*
> *able to stand up and speak [about], and I think the*
> *problem is we don't want to speak about [them].*

How can women who are trained to advocate passionately for others feel inhibited to speak up for themselves? Do the roots of this behavior also begin in adolescence? Wiseman described girls "conditioned to remain silent" in the face of intimidation.[23] In the "Girl World" described by Wiseman, girls who do not speak up fear being thrown out of the clique; in their adolescent experiences, the clique serves as the life raft in which they struggle to remain.

Psychologist Mary Pipher also described the societal influences and pressures which begin to take their toll on strong girls who, by early adolescence, lose their autonomy and self-confidence. She described adolescence as: "an extraordinary time when individual, developmental, and cultural factors combine in ways that shape adulthood. It's a time of marked internal development and massive cultural indoctrination."[24] Dr. Pipher noted the contradiction between the unclear rules for "proper female behavior" and the harsh punishment faced by those who break them.[25] She reported the subtle societal messages that girls internalize and bring with them into adulthood: "Because with boys failure is attributed to external factors and success is attributed to ability, they keep their confidence, even with failure. With girls it's just the opposite.

Because their success is attributed to good luck or hard work and failure to lack of ability, with every failure, girls' confidence is eroded."[26]

Over time, the behaviors learned in adolescence take root and become internalized. Silence becomes the safest alternative in a world of confusing and mixed messages.

Even law school can reinforce the messages which silence women, notwithstanding the constant Socratic dialogue in the classroom. Professor Lani Guinier, who studied the experiences of female law students at the University of Pennsylvania Law School, reported: "The competitive, hierarchical format of the law school's dominant pedagogy is also sometimes used by peers to put down women. Many women who complained that their voices are pushed back and down, suffocated early on by hostile first-year classmates, described how those women who did speak out felt humiliated by male, and some female, contemporaries who silenced those who publicly dared *not* to 'act like gentlemen.'"[27]

A study of women from the Yale Law School class of 1997 also identified experiences of alienation that resulted in disengagement from the classroom experience. The study, based on a series of interviews, noted that: "Women reported diminished confidence regarding all aspects of their academic experiences, including willingness to participate in class, writing skills, and interaction with faculty."[28]

In her study of female design engineers, Joyce Fletcher analyzed the "masculine logic of effectiveness" which suppresses, or causes to "disappear", behavior inconsistent with this mold, even when it better promotes organizational goals than traditionally masculine methods.[29] Fletcher's study looked at "relational theory" which, in essence, is the concept that "growth and development require a context of connection."[30] Fletcher described relational practice as a purposeful set of behaviors that reflect: "a relational logic of effectiveness and requires a number of relational skills such as empathy, mutuality, reciprocity, and a sensitivity to emotional contexts."[31] In other words, relational practice is an intentional behavior to motivate people to achieve their goals more effectively. Fletcher observed, however, that in a workplace culture that values independence and promotion of one's own work, these relational qualities may contribute to a powerlessness and devaluation of effort. Relational practitioners, Fletcher wrote: "are not simply unrewarded but instead are often misunderstood, exploited, or suffer negative career consequences for engaging in these activities."[32]

Fletcher's study of design engineers offered striking comparisons to the law firm workplace. Such similarities were captured by scholar Mona Harrington who wrote of: "male codes of communication that include stereotyped assumptions about women, attitudes at odds with the perception of women as fellow lawyers enjoying equal status in the firms."[33] She also described that, for women, the effects of a law firm's culture can result in: "their effective invisibility and inaudibility in many settings. They are present in the big firms in ever-increasing numbers and, more than in the past, they are becoming partners, but still, in some sense, they are not seen or heard."[34]

Many interviewees spoke of their struggles against what they viewed as external expectations of their silence. One retired partner recalled that, just when she was being considered for partnership, her efforts to speak up for others in the firm, positions she had long supported vocally, became a subject of discussion among her colleagues. A senior colleague who supported her election to the partnership warned her of the impact she was having:

> *And I remember one of the things they told me in my review the year before I made partner.... He said, 'A lot of people say that you're aggressive.'*

Another senior associate echoed the belief that, if you speak up, you become branded:

> *I think it turns them off. I think that then you become the 'troubled person.' You become the thorn in the side and eventually they find reasons to say, 'Well, you know what, you're really not quite working out as well as we said you were for the past seven years.'*

> *I feel what's happening is that I'm becoming more and more invisible. My last review was absolutely horrendous, absolutely horrendous. Why I didn't walk out of here that day, I don't know. It was so horrible...and there was an in-house fight among the partners going on at my review because [a female partner] was expressing things that were not even discussed among the partnership.... It was clearly a 'let's sabotage [name of interviewee]' type issue....*

> *The way she phrased my whole review...it started*
> *out: 'This is very difficult because we really like you*
> *so much.' And I'm like, 'Wait a minute. What are you*
> *saying? Are you saying I should be looking for a new*
> *job?' And she said to me, 'Well, if one comes across*
> *your desk, I think you should take it.' And the two*
> *other partners just went, 'WHAT?' And so I'm damn*
> *near in tears because I'm thinking I just got fired....*

She expressed her frustration that, as a lawyer, she was trained to advocate for other people, yet this experience left her feeling as though she lost the ability to advocate for herself. It was particularly unsettling to her that the partners could not have spent any time preparing for this important evaluation. As a result of the review, she was sent an entirely mixed message and was provided neither an understanding of what she was supposed to have learned nor what she needed to do to succeed.

A younger associate in the same law firm spoke of her own reaction to her colleague's experience:

> *I'm fairly outspoken as well. Actually, very out-*
> *spoken, I think. If I'm being mistreated, then I will tell*
> *someone.... I even told my mentor, 'When I see what*
> *has happened to [name of colleague], it doesn't bode*
> *well with anybody, and I think it is dysfunctional.'*
> *When I used that word, he told me, 'You better not use*
> *that word with anyone other than me.'*

At that point, the younger associate felt she no longer had the option to say what she really believed:

> *One of the things that [they basically told her*
> *colleague] is that if another job opportunity crossed*
> *her desk, she should take it. And the other partners*
> *disagreed with that. If they can't get that together, if*
> *those partners can't figure that out before a review,*
> *that's 'dysfunctional.'*

A junior partner in a midsize law firm admired a former female partner who would always speak up, and then expressed disappointment in her own reticence:

> But I'm not outspoken when it comes to fighting battles or anything. I talk about the issues all the time. It's not that I'm complacent or quiet about it. I talk about it, but I wouldn't stand up in the middle of a partners' meeting and start saying, 'You guys have to straighten things out. Open your eyes. This is not working.' I don't feel I have the position here.

Interestingly, this same young partner recalls once speaking out as an associate, while serving on a committee tasked with recommending whether part-time attorneys should be eligible for partnership:

> The focus of the meeting that month was this part-time issue, and there were plenty of partners in this firm that think that women working part-time shouldn't be up for partnership and shouldn't be made partners. Their view is that: 'We already have part-time partners that don't pull their weight, they don't have good receivables, they don't have clients. We don't need more part-time attorneys. And, moreover, people who work part-time are not committed enough to be lawyers.' Somebody said this at the meeting. I still get my blood pressure up when I think about my kids who didn't bond to me...because I put so much more effort into my job instead of my family, and they tell me that I'm not committed enough to [be their partner]!

The interesting postscript to her outburst at the committee meeting was that, soon after, the firm changed its policy to allow part-time women to become eligible for partnership. Incredibly, she would not give herself credit for spurring this change:

> *And a partner in this office...was [at this meet-*
> *ing] and I talked to him extensively about how I felt.*
> *Lots of emails. And the message got through. It's*
> *something he seemed to pick up, for whatever reason.*
> *He felt that we needed to do something about it. I*
> *don't credit myself with that. It was just that he felt*
> *the timing was right to do something more to support*
> *part-time women because we didn't have enough*
> *women partners.*

So even as she finally spoke up, and there was a direct connection between her involvement in the topic and a change in policy, she did not see herself as having played a significant role in that result.

A former partner of a large firm noted that, once women became partners, they were reticent to express opinions to their male colleagues:

> *So what would happen is that, pretty much, the*
> *only women who would speak out vocally would be*
> *associates who either were very bold, or on their way*
> *into the 'non-accepted' or 'not doing well' category. I*
> *can't remember, there may have been one or two, but*
> *I can't remember anybody who was particularly vocal*
> *about women's issues.*

Deborah Tannen, the noted professor of linguistics, wrote in the Harvard Business Review that: "[W]omen are less likely than men to have learned to blow their own horn. And they are more likely than men to believe that if they do so, they won't be liked."[35] Heim and Murphy described similar behavior, noting: "Women not only diminish their self-esteem through negative self-talk; they also fail to compensate for it by building themselves up when they experience success."[36]

A senior litigator in a national law firm recalled painful experiences in which she felt punished for her outspokenness. For example, she told the firm management that she felt unfairly compensated as a reduced-hours attorney because she worked significantly in excess of her reduced-hours schedule and never received a commensurate bonus or compensation increase:

> *I pointed out that it was unfair.... And I got told I was a 'trouble-maker' and then I started getting punished.*

She described that the "punishment" took the form of significant cuts in her compensation over several years:

> *Once you get that tag, and, again, if you're the only one sitting at the table and you're hearing these asinine comments about associate reviews: 'Well, she doesn't smile enough.'... And you say, 'Excuse me, guys....' And if you are the only woman, you are perceived as a 'troublemaker.' And there were many, many things I didn't raise my hand about and call them on. There was nobody else to say, 'Oh yeah, she's got a point.' And really, for many years, that was the tag line: I was a 'troublemaker' and that was because I was the only one who kept raising the issues. And after a while, there was only so far they could cut my compensation until I was basically paid as a senior associate. And then I realized it gave me a whole lot of freedom...so I started raising a whole lot more issues and people would say, 'Why weren't you fired? Why didn't they force you out? How could you get away with this?'*

Interestingly, she felt that over time, her partners grudgingly came to the conclusion that she was raising valid points.[37] What kept her tied to the firm for so many years was her belief that, even as she was viewed as the "black sheep of the family," she was still recognized by her partners as a good lawyer.

A New York lawyer urged that women speak up more:

> *Women have to be brave enough to ask for an arrangement that would work for them. It's not going to work for every woman. It's got to be a woman who is valued. But for women who are valued, firms will make more accommodations than they are presentably making. But I think women are scared to ask for it....*

However, even in her advice, there was an assumption that women are speaking up to ask for "accommodations," special favors, rather than resolving long-standing impediments to their successful inclusion in the workplace. A former partner of a national law firm expressed concern that few women felt empowered to speak out about issues:

> *I was left on my own to negotiate with [the Managing Partner] on behalf of all of the women, and no other woman wanted to raise a voice or say anything. So it was sort of like I was always the person who had to stick her neck out....*
>
> *[W]omen will not ask for raises. They won't ask for benefits. They won't ask for job enhancements because they are always worried that they are not entitled....*
>
> *I remember saying something at a partners' meeting. Nobody responded to it and then it was the exact same thing that I said was said about three minutes later...and, of course, I was like, 'Didn't I just say that?'... But I think that women are not heard, particularly if you don't say something forcefully. And so I just got into a habit of saying things forcefully that I knew, that people would be like, 'Oh, she's talking.' Because if you don't say things forcefully, you're not heard.*

She spoke at length about why she believed women were so reluctant to speak with confidence in their own voice. As an athlete herself, she believed that the differences in the way girls are socialized to play are very distinct from the way boys play, with life-long repercussions:[38]

> *[Women] don't have the opportunity to use analytical skills or negotiate the way that boys do because girls play with their friends and boys play with people who are not their friends. So there's a negotiation. There's a hierarchy. I might not like you,*

> but I'm going to be on your team because you're bet-
> ter.... [A]nd it's perfect for business. And they are
> well-suited for business because this is how they are
> socialized. Girls don't even want to deal with some-
> body they don't like. And so there is no interaction.
> There's no negotiation.... It's a very different kind of
> dynamic.

> So we grow up, I think, without the kind of skills,
> political skills, and I think the biggest thing is that
> women don't know how to promote themselves. Men
> grow up doing that.... Women, on the other hand, do
> not know how to promote the business they bring in,
> the success they achieve, because they think it is
> bratty and they think it is unladylike. And that's a real
> fine line, how do you become your own PR machine?
> And how do you leak [your success] to your depart-
> ment head?... It was very apparent to me early on
> that if I'm bringing in business, who is going to know
> unless I tell people? So I tried to figure out ways to
> tell people what I was doing in a way that it wouldn't
> look obnoxious.

To accomplish this, she identified specific individuals to whom she would report a particular success, knowing that they would then tell everyone else who mattered in the firm.[39] Emphasizing her successes was critical, she believed, to counter those in the firm who were quick to denigrate the accomplishments of others. She recalled her fury with a female administrator at the law firm who would criticize the women attorneys:

> I remember a comment she made about how the
> women don't work hard.... I remember challenging
> her.... You know, here is a woman who has no kids, no
> husband, no family that she has to tend.... For her to
> tell us that we're not working hard or that the women
> aren't working hard, and she says that to the men!

Many women who believed that, collectively, they could be a more powerful voice felt a sense of loss over the missed opportunities. For example, a former partner in a successful firm attributed the lack of community of women within her large firm to the lack of progress in leveling the playing field for all women:

> *[At this law firm] having a community of women would be very adversely viewed. Even having all the women partners having lunch every month, which we were doing last summer, got people all freaked out because they saw all the women partners marching in. They're reaction was like: 'What's going on in there?'...*

> *There are women partners here who are not content with any notion of a women's community.... It runs counter to the [firm's] culture, which is that: meritocracy is all that matters.*

> *The question that we're asking is, 'We're hiring excellent and effective lawyers, but what is effective? And how does the definition of that affect whom we keep and whom we don't, and whom we encourage and whom we don't? That is, what is the status vis-à-vis women?' Law firms like [ours] hold onto the 'Oh, we are a pure meritocracy' myth, like crazy.... Someone told me that a [male attorney was up for partnership] and that the comment was: 'He doesn't have the strongest technical skills.' Let me tell you something. If someone said that about me, there is no way I'd have been elected partner. They wouldn't allow that for a woman. I have no doubt that technically speaking, the women in this firm are superior to the men because we are judged to a higher standard.*

In their detailed analysis of the ways in which women's reluctance to ask for what they want impedes their opportunities to negotiate for what they deserve, Babcock and Laschever stated: "Women also don't resist gender norm constraints because, in many cases, they are oblivious to their power and believe these norms have no impact on their own behavior."[40] However, by not recognizing their own power, women are losing a valuable opportunity to work collectively to achieve greater gains.

Another partner expressed regret that women failed to maximize their opportunities to exert influence as a group, noting:

> *The women partners get together occasionally, but we are not a monolithic group. We don't always agree, which is too bad because when we agree we are powerful.*

A former large firm associate, now in her own practice, also decried the lack of group support from other women:

> *Women really do have to be much more support-ive...that has not happened.... I think sharing what's worked, what hasn't worked, and supporting each other is really critical. And when somebody finally does make it to the position of partner...they have a duty, a responsibility. You know that mentoring piece, it just doesn't happen. Not just woman to woman.*

Yet, as more fully described in Chapter 14, gender-based stereotypes are breaking down and attitudes are changing in important ways. Moreover, as is discussed in greater detail in Part Three, some firms are successfully imple-menting programs for women, often referred to as Women's Initiatives, and making significant progress developing internal networks among women. One can envision entirely different behaviors than those described by the inter-viewees if the firms were not structured in such a way that only a few women pass above the glass ceiling. Or if the women were supported in finding ways to speak up about their experiences and concerns, for example, provided a coach or mentor with whom they could talk through the challenges they were facing, then the mutual dialogue might have resulted in changes sooner.

Similarly, opportunities abound to remove the perceived threats to the hard-fought position in the firm to which the so-called "Queen Bee" women cling. As Rosalind Barnett and Caryl Rivers wrote: "We are all a product of many interacting forces, including our genes, our personalities, our environ-ment, and chance....In short, we are an ever-changing product of continuous learning and interaction that builds on our genetic heritage."[41] Rivers and Barnett dispel the notion that women are inherently doomed to certain behaviors or personality traits simply because of their gender. Instead, they offer numerous studies to counter the idea that gender-based traits are inherent, as opposed to being the result of one's life circumstances: "The essentialists view the world through the lens of gender, but they ignore a much more important perspective: power. When women use care reasoning, it is because they tend to occupy less powerful positions in society and not because of an innate quality they possess. People in power expect others to listen to them.... Those without power develop a sharp attentiveness to the needs of those with power, often resorting to manipulation and duplicity.... But people who have power don't have to resort to manipulative techniques; they promote the rules because they benefit from them." In other words: "When power shifts, behavior shifts with it."[42]

Ultimately, just like the O's in Rosabeth Moss Kanter's tale, the opportunities for women are remarkably enhanced once they are able to penetrate positions of power and authority in numbers commensurate with their male colleagues. As the balance of power shifts towards equality, women's voices will be heard more clearly and effectively. In the meantime, it is a largely male chorus of the Managing Partners whose words have the greatest impact.

Endnotes for Chapter 12

1. For data relating to minority associates, *see, e.g.,* NALP Found., Keeping the Keepers II: Mobilitiy and Management of Associates (2003) *available at* http://www.NALPFoundation.org. *See also,* Vivia Chen, *Pride and Prejudice,* The American Lawyer, July 2005, at 80, which ranks Am Law 100 firms with the most, and the fewest, minority partners. At 84 and 85. *See also,* NALP Found., *Presence of Women and Attorneys of Color in Large Law Firms Continues to Rise Slowly but Steadily,* (Oct. 3, 2002), at http://www.nalp.org/press/details.php?id=18 (Dec. 6, 2005). For an example of bar association efforts, *see, e.g.,* N.Y. Cty. Law. Assoc., Report of the Task Force to Increase Diversity in the Legal Profession, http://www.nycla.org/publications/taskforce.html (December 19, 2005).

2. Summers, *Remarks at NBER Conference on Diversifying the Science and Engineering Workforce,* Off. President Harv. Univ., at http://www.president.harvard.edu/speeches/2005/nber.html (Jan. 14, 2005).

3. Summers, *Remarks at NBER Conference on Diversifying the Science and Engineering Workforce,* Off. President Harv. Univ., at http://www.president.harvard.edu/speeches/2005/nber.html (Jan. 14, 2005).

4. For a detailed analysis of various studies exploring gender-based differences, *see* Deborah Blum, Sex on the Brain: the Biological Differences Between Men and Women (1997). Author Blum, however, cautioned against relying on biology to explain gender differences, observing: "Science has been used as an effective weapon against women, just as it's been used against a wide array of racial and ethnic groups." She stressed the importance of a complete understanding of the scientific research, including both the "potential and its limits." At 261.

5. Summers, *Remarks at NBER Conference on Diversifying the Science and Engineering Workforce,* Off. President Harv. Univ., at http://www.president.harvard.edu/speeches/2005/nber.html (Jan. 14, 2005).

6. Summers, *Remarks at NBER Conference on Diversifying the Science and Engineering Workforce,* Off. President Harv. Univ., at http://www.president.harvard.edu/speeches/2005/nber.html (Jan. 14, 2005). Specifically, he stated: "Now that begs entirely the normative questions, which I'll get to a little later, of, is our society right to expect that level of effort from people who hold the most prominent jobs? Is our society right to have the familial arrangements in which women are asked to make that choice and asked more to make that choice than men?"

7. *See, e.g.,* Sam Dillon, *Harvard Chief Defends His Talk on Women,* N.Y. Times, Jan. 18, 2005; Daniel McGinn, *The Guy of the Storm,* Newsweek, Jan. 31, 2005, at 38; Barbara Kantrowitz, *Sex and Science,* Newsweek, Jan. 31, 2005, at 36; Marcella Bombardieri, *Summers' Remarks on Women Draw Fire,* Boston Globe, Jan. 17, 2005, at A1.

8. An article in an American Bar Association publication reported that, while a majority of women litigators were defined as "extroverts" in the Myers-Briggs Type Inventory, (and, therefore, more likely to solve problems more collaboratively), 60% of the male litigators were defined as "introverts," (with, therefore, a greater likelihood to resist collaborative problem solving). "The practical effect may be that women are viewed as indecisive and lacking self-confidence," Rebecca Korzec, *Gender Bias: Continuing Challenges and*

Opportunities, 29 ABA Litigation 14, 64-65 (Spring 2003). However, the reality is that law firms could benefit from these differences by placing people in positions which capitalize on specific skill sets.

9.   *The State of the Legal Profession: 1990*, 1991 ABA Young Law. Div 64.

10.   ABA Comm'n Women in the Prof., The Unfinished Agenda: Women and the Legal Profession 32 (2001).

11.   Deborah Graham, Getting Down to Business: Marketing and Women Lawyers 293 (1996).

12.   Deborah Blum, Sex on the Brain, the Biological Differences Between Men and Women 253 (1997). *See also* Reichman & Sterling, Gender Penalties Revisited 30 (2004), noting that: "The women who were the pioneers in law define their early careers in terms of being one of the boys." But even as women adopt masculine behavior, they are held back if they are seen as too aggressive. *See also* Louise Branson, *Reform of the Bully Broads,* Boston Globe, Mar. 17, 2002, (Magazine), at 12, describing a variety of workshops, retreats, and programs to help: "Women who behave like men and still find themselves unable to make it as coworkers recoil in horror." The article reported on programs to address "a third wave of workplace feminism….The third wave, a de facto authenticity revolution, is dedicated to getting women to the heights of corporate America while remaining true to themselves, not as male clones." At 14.

13.   Phyllis Horn Epstein, Women-at-Law: Lessons Learned along the Pathways to Success 59 (2004).

14.   Rosalind Wiseman, Queen Bees and Wannabes: Helping Your Daughter Survive Cliques, Gossip, Boyfriends, and Other Realities of Adolescence 19 (2002).

15.   Wiseman, Queen Bees and Wannabes: Helping Your Daughter Survive Cliques, Gossip, Boyfriends, and Other Realities of Adolescence 25 (2002).

16.   Wiseman, Queen Bees and Wannabes: Helping Your Daughter Survive Cliques, Gossip, Boyfriends, and Other Realities of Adolescence 27 (2002).

17.   Wiseman, Queen Bees and Wannabes: Helping Your Daughter Survive Cliques, Gossip, Boyfriends, and Other Realities of Adolescence 13 (2002). A youth survey conducted by Girls Incorporated and Harris Interactive revealed the continued challenges young girls face: "[T]hree-quarters of the girls surveyed agreed that girls are under pressure to dress the right way; 63% agreed that girls are under pressure to please everyone; and 59% agreed that girls are told not to brag about things they do well." Marcia Brumit Kropf, *Inspiring Girls to Be Strong, Smart, and Bold,* Regional Rev.: 14 Fed. Res. Bank Boston 12, 13 (Q1 2005).

18.   Wiseman, Queen Bees and Wannabes: Helping Your Daughter Survive Cliques, Gossip, Boyfriends, and Other Realities of Adolescence 10 (2002).

19.   Wiseman, Queen Bees and Wannabes: Helping Your Daughter Survive Cliques, Gossip, Boyfriends, and Other Realities of Adolescence 13 (2002).

20.   Rosabeth Moss Kanter with Barry A. Stein, A Tale of "O"-On Being Different in an Organization (1980). *See also,* Rosabeth Moss Kanter, Men and Women of the Corporation, 1977 and 1993.

21. Kanter with Stein, A Tale of "O" - On Being Different in an Organization (1980) 123-124 (1980).

22. Kanter with Stein, A Tale of "O" - On Being Different in an Organization (1980) 204 (1980).

23. Wiseman, Queen Bees and Wannabes: Helping Your Daughter Survive Cliques, Gossip, Boyfriends, and Other Realities of Adolescence 3, 121 (2002). The reluctance of women lawyers to speak up was also identified by Reichman and Sterling in their study of Colorado lawyers. *See* Reichman & Sterling, Gender Penalties Revisited 48 (2004); *see also* Harrington, Women Lawyers: Rewriting the Rules 25 (1995) (1994).

24. Mary Pipher, Ph.D., Reviving Ophelia: Saving the Selves of Adolescent Girls 26 (1994). *See also* Lois P. Frankel, Ph.D., *Introduction to* Nice Girls Don't Get The Corner Office: 101 Unconscious Mistakes Women Make That Sabotage Their Careers xvii, xviii (2004), noting: "Behaviors that were appropriate in girlhood, but not in womanhood, may be contributing to your career's stagnating, plateauing, or even derailing from its career path. Success comes not from acting more like a man, as some might leave you to believe, but by acting more like a *woman* instead of a girl." A national survey of girls in grades 7-12 reported that 28% of the girls believed that "people often or very often decide what they can or cannot do only because they are girls." *Choosing Community: Girls Get Together to be Themselves*, Girls Inc., at http://www.girlsinc.org/ic/page.php?id=2.4.10.

25. Pipher, Reviving Ophelia: Saving the Selves of Adolescent Girls 39 (1994).

26. Pipher, Reviving Ophelia: Saving the Selves of Adolescent Girls 63 (1994). Researches Linda Babcock and Sara Laschever highlighted numerous studies demonstrating significant gender gaps that exist when measuring entitlement. Because women feel unsure about what they deserve, they are not comfortable asking for more than they have. Babcock and Laschever posit: "Two major social forces seem to be responsible for the stubborn persistence of gender-linked norms and beliefs. The first involves the socialization and development of children and the second involves the maintenance of gender roles by adults." Babcock and Laschever, Women Don't Ask: Negotiation and the Gender Divide 67 (2003).

27. Guinier et al., Becoming Gentlemen: Women, Law School and Institutional Change 53 (2002) (1997). Professor Guinier explained that the source of her title is a statement made by a male law professor to his first year class: "To be a good lawyer, behave like a gentleman." In other words, as Professor Guinier noted: "For these women, learning to think like a lawyer means learning to think and act like a man." At 28-29. A clinical psychologist who coaches women lawyers wrote that many of the women with whom she works: "express fears of job loss if they don't 'fly under the radar.' They feel certain that asking to be spoken to respectfully or persistently pursuing the kind of work that interests them will result in career suicide." Ellen Ostrow, *Is Thinking "Like a Lawyer" Holding You Back?*, 28 Beyond the Billable Hour? (2005) at http://lawyerslifecoach.com/newsletters/issue28.html (Dec. 7, 2005).

28. Paula Gaber, *"Just Trying to Be Human In This Place": The Legal Education of Twenty Women*, 10 Yale J. L. & Feminism (1998) at 165, 249.

29. Joyce K. Fletcher, Disappearing Acts: Gender, Power, and Relational Practice at Work 3 (1999).

30. Fletcher, Disappearing Acts: Gender, Power, and Relational Practice at Work 31 (1999).

31. Fletcher, Disappearing Acts: Gender, Power, and Relational Practice at Work 84 (1999).

32. Fletcher, Disappearing Acts: Gender, Power, and Relational Practice at Work 114 (1999).

33. Harrington, Women Lawyers: Rewriting the Rules 124 (1995) (1994).

34. Harrington, Women Lawyers: Rewriting the Rules 124 (1995) (1994).

35. Deborah Tannen, *The Power of Talk: Who Gets Heard and Why*, Harv. Bus. Rev., Sept.-Oct. 1995, at 138.

36. Heim et al., In the Company of Women 37 (2003). In her investigation of low-wage occupations in America, author Barbara Ehrenreich noted a similar psychological toll that occurs when people are treated as inferior over a period of time: "If you are constantly reminded of your lowly position in the social hierarchy, whether by individual managers or by a plethora of impersonal rules, you begin to accept that unfortunate status….But as much as any other social animal, and more so than many, we depend for our self-image on the humans immediately around us, to the point of altering our perceptions of the world so as to fit in with theirs." Barbara Ehrenreich, Nickel and Dimed: On (Not) Getting By in America 210-211 (2002) (2001).

37. Through her ability to communicate her concerns as she performed valued legal skills, she demonstrated her strength and resilience, qualities which are key to retaining one's voice and defining one's boundaries. *See, e.g.*, Wiseman, Queen Bees and Wannabes: Helping Your Daughter Survive Cliques, Gossip, Boyfriends, and Other Realities of Adolescence 150 (2002).

38. In their analysis of a series of studies observing play among young girls and boys, Heim and Murphy reported that boys' games are more competitive, more rule bound, and provide greater opportunities to resolve conflicts, develop organization skills, and function in a hierarchical environments. Girl's play, on the other hand, generally excludes direct competition, keeping the power "dead even" among participants: "Among girls, it is more important to be popular than to win. In fact, boasting about prowess almost guarantees that the gloater will become friendless, isolated from others." Heim et al., In the Company of Women 97 (2003). Linguist Deborah Tannen also observed: "The research of sociologists, anthropologists, and psychologists observing American children at play has shown that, although both boys and girls find ways of creating rapport and negotiating status, girls tend to learn conversational rituals that focus on the rapport dimension of relationships whereas boys tend to learn rituals that focus on the status dimension." She further states that her "research in companies across the United States shows that the lessons learned in childhood carry over into the workplace." Deborah Tannen, *The Power of Talk: Who Gets Heard and Why*, Harv. Bus. Rev., Sept.-Oct. 1995 138, at 140. *See also* Geoffrey Cowell, *Why We Strive for Status*, Newsweek, June 16, 2003, at 67, discussing scientific research demonstrating a man's drive for status as: "a design feature of the male psyche, a biological drive that is rooted in the nervous system and regulated by hormones and brain chemicals."

39. A consultant on leadership urges women to be less modest and self-effacing and learn how to promote themselves more. *See* Diane E. Lewis, *How to Brag, Like a Professional*, Boston Sunday Globe, Sept. 5, 2004, at G1.

40. Babcock and Laschever, Women Don't Ask: Negotiation and the Gender Divide 78 (2003).

41. Rosalind Barnett & Caryl Rivers, Same Difference: How Gender Myths Are Hurting Our Relationships, Our Children, and Our Jobs 12 (2004).

42. Barnett & Rivers, Same Difference: How Gender Myths Are Hurting Our Relationships, Our Children, and Our Jobs 35-36 (2004).

CHAPTER 13

THE MANAGING PARTNERS SPEAK

A significant disconnect exists between those who run law firms and those who work in them.[1] In general, most firm managers seem to preside in a world that is different than the one their associate attorneys inhabit, and would likely be surprised to learn that the frustrations expressed by lawyers interviewed for this book could have come from one of their own. The disconnect is even more pronounced with respect to Managing Partners' understanding of and responses to issues affecting the retention and advancement of women in their firms.

To understand the Managing Partners' views, it is helpful to understand their role in the law firm hierarchy. Managing Partners will generally be the first to point out the irony of having a "management" role in a structure dominated by hundreds of high-powered, driven owners. As one Managing Partner of a national law firm commented:

> *The biggest challenge is the horizontal structure*
> *of the firm. Our law firm has [several hundred] part-*
> *ners and that's [several hundred] bosses. And they*
> *have a more direct impact on the experiences of the*
> *other lawyers they work with than I could ever have.*

Most firms have one Managing Partner (occasionally, it may be a small team of Co-Managing Partners), who is likely maintaining an active client base. As to their management functions, therefore, Managing Partners are, somewhat ironically, working part-time.

Most firms also have an Executive Committee and/or a Policy Committee which supports the Managing Partner and presides over the major policy and economic issues of the firm. In addition, the substantive law groups have their own management structures. Some firms, for example, may have chairs of a small number of major Practice Groups, with additional leadership positions for subspecialties within each group. Others may organize by client or industry groups, and still others have in place a combination of all of these. how ever organized, there is generally a cadre of successful lawyers designated to lead each of these separate groupings.

In addition to the infrastructure supporting each practice group, large firms now have multiple locations which require management. Accordingly, most law firms designate one of more lawyers who are responsible for the management of each branch office.

Even as there are variances in practice group titles, structures, and the number of people involved in any particular management function, nearly all of these managers share one key attribute: they generally are the firm's busiest and most successful lawyers. This reliance on high-performing attorneys to fill key management functions results in a system in which firm management duties are relegated to being addressed in one's "extra" time; that is, in non-client billable time.

However, when you speak to Managing Partners about this issue, most share the perception that only busy and successful attorneys can command the respect necessary to run a practice group, make compensation decisions, or otherwise be involved as senior managers of a law firm. A recently retired Managing Partner used military imagery to explain how practice group leaders are selected by the management committee:

> It's supposed to be someone who has some administrative savvy and has the respect of the troops. Often times they will have one of those two criteria and not the other....

His military imagery moved into full battle mode when asked if he was concerned about a management model in which the manager thinks more frequently about his own clients than the lawyers in his practice group:

> Unfortunately, I still think it is a necessary model. As you know, it is not a good one.... In order to get the respect of the troops, you have to be a troop. You have to be in the battlefield. You can't be back at headquarters. You have to be in the field in the tent with the bombs falling all around you in order to send out your orders and have them obey them.

When pressed why the firm could not identify lawyers with the best management and people skills to serve in these key leadership roles, he emphatically disagreed that it could work:

> *Let's say I bring in $5 million dollars and I ignore what my section manager says. I use the people I want to use, my time sheets are always three days late, my bills are always four days late, but I get the money in at the end of the year and I'm not a bad person. We're going to dock your pay? I don't think so. So if you don't have the power of being able to reward or punish, then you do not have anything but moral suasion. And, for moral suasion, you'd better be the general on the battlefield because then they will respect you. If you're not, you won't have moral suasion, you won't have the power to punish or reward.*

A Managing Partner who was in the midst of integrating a significant merger observed that he works as Managing Partner about half of his time:

> *It's supposed to be 50/50. It's more like 75/75.*

He, too, emphasized that the best management model for law firms is to select department chairs from the ranks of the most successful lawyers:

> *[Y]ou can't, in a professional services organization, lead and manage effectively, if you don't have two things. One is, you have to understand the pressures your folks are under, and if you are not practicing, you don't understand those pressures. The second thing is...you don't have the credibility.... [M]ost of our department chairs are terrific practitioners and leaders, and it's because they have the credibility to say, 'This is the way we need it to be.'*

> *The way the practice moves today, if you are out of it for two years, you really don't understand what people are going through.... [W]hen the corporate*

> *department chair walks into someone's office and*
> *says, 'You mistreated an associate. We're very*
> *unhappy. You can't do it again.' If that person is not*
> *working with the associates under the same time*
> *pressure, there's just no credibility.*

He stressed that, for most firms, the management structure is a function of cultural fit:

> *My view is that law practice management is less*
> *identifying the ideal model and implementing it, and*
> *it's more recognizing what your unique culture is,*
> *and who are your leaders, and what they can do.*
> *And then you build the models to fit your culture and*
> *leadership.*

However a deeper, albeit less frequently articulated, reason for such a management model was alluded to by this Managing Partner's predecessor, who had given up his practice to manage the firm full-time until he retired. He stated that it was self-protective for law firm managers to maintain a busy practice:

> *I was at a stage when I stopped being Managing*
> *Partner, I really sacrificed my practice. I was down to*
> *a handful of clients but I wasn't doing the day-to-day*
> *work. In the last [few] years, I haven't done that*
> *much lawyering, but I've done a lot of client building*
> *and community work. But that was tolerated because*
> *I was at this stage of my career. If I had been 55, it*
> *wouldn't work.*

He observed that the current generation of Managing Partners needs to maintain large practices in order for them to have a long-term future with the firm. He noted other managers who, after relinquishing their client work for management responsibilities, could not then successfully resume their practice when they completed their term as Managing Partners. As a result, most subsequently left to do other things. For himself, however, he saw this split role as unfair to others:

My test was the shower test: What are you think-
ing about when you are in the shower? Are you
thinking about your clients? Are you thinking about
the firm? And so I felt I had to give my thoughts to
the firm.

A management team at another national law firm described their firm's recently reorganized management structure, in which directors of each of the firm's major practice groups were selected for their lawyering skills, rather than any management expertise. These lawyer/managers are expected to devote only 300 to 500 hours a year on their management function, even though their firm duties rival the responsibilities of many full-time chief executives of corporations:

> *Their role is to be responsible for the day-to-day*
> *management of, on average, a $20 million dollar line*
> *of business.... These people are responsible for strat-*
> *egy, growth in a department, opening up other areas*
> *into disciplinary teams, hiring, recruiting, and mak-*
> *ing recommendations with respect to compensation*
> *[for all the attorneys in their group].*

When asked to describe the typical lawyer selected for such an important management responsibility, the response was direct:

> *The best lawyer in the room, and I think, the*
> *highest quality people we have. It isn't the person*
> *whose practice has sort of faded and made time for*
> *management responsibilities. It is the opposite. It is*
> *the people with the most potential and the highest*
> *quality people. It is a real management job....*

What is stunning about this description of these high-powered manage-ment roles is that the managers were expected to undertake the complex and sophisticated job of managing a $20 million dollar line of business in, essen-tially, less than two hours a day. As startling, the current Co-Managing Part-ners were expecting to bill 1,800 hours a year for client work and hoping to limit the time they spent running this national law firm to about 600 hours annually. When challenged as to why lawyers, who would be aghast if their own clients tried to run major businesses on a part-time basis, accept such a business model for themselves, the response reiterated that the highest-quality lawyers must serve as the standard-bearer for other attorneys in the firm:

> *We went through [an extensive] succession planning [process].... It was a major debate over whether we ought to have people in management who didn't have a lot to do right now, who were viewed as good administrative and skilled people, but they really weren't practice leaders. Ultimately, we decided to stick with the model...in that it takes our hardest working and best lawyers and uses them.*

Similarly, the recently retired Managing Partner of another national law firm stated:

> *It would be difficult for the firm and the people we've picked as managers to move to a more corporate structure. The people we pick as managers, one of the reasons we pick them is, they are first-rate lawyers. If they weren't, they wouldn't have the credibility with their partners that's necessary to manage. So if we took them out of the role of practicing law, we would be, by definition, taking some of our best talent away from our business. And they would be unhappy about it....*

> *I think that you have to have credibility with the people you are to manage. In a law firm at least, proven ability as a lawyer/rainmaker isn't so important here, but proven ability as a lawyer is paramount in terms of getting and gaining that credibility.*

One Managing Partner acknowledged the contradiction between the mantra of most law firms that: "we've got to be run like a business," and the fact that they are a business that is managed on a part-time basis:

So let's examine why that is. First, when lawyers say they want to run like a business, what they really mean is, they want everyone else in the firm run like a business, and they want to run the way they want to run. So that's part of the cultural change that we're undergoing, trying to shift that out. Second,...we have high, fixed costs businesses, and where that has an impact is, every time you take somebody off the line, it's really money right off the bottom.... [A]nd I would add that lawyers are extraordinarily, in terms of billable hours, extraordinarily short-sighted.

And you're stuck with the unusual situation that, most of the people that you want to manage the firm are among the more productive people. And so you always look at it and say, 'Gee, it'd be great if I had this guy working full time with all the practice groups.' And then all of a sudden, you're saying, 'Well, gee, he's got a million-dollar practice, and who's going to take that?'

And he does a lot of the work himself, so all of a sudden you find yourself saying to yourself: "For me to put this guy on the line as a full-time manager, he's got to make a million dollar-plus difference to the bottom line, and I've still got to pay him something to do it, and you've got to convince him that there's a real career path. Because if he gives up his clients and doesn't like it after two years, he's toast."

So these are all the forces that are pushing us to profitability. They are also holding us back from really trying to manage this thing, so we're struggling with it. We really are. Every firm is trying to find a balance between controlling people and still letting them run wild. Having said all this, our greatest asset as organizations is that we've got this large pool of

> *very smart and very motivated, very ambitious people*
> *who are out there trying to find business and trying to*
> *keep stuff going. So the last thing we really want to do*
> *is create a bureaucracy to slow them down. It's just a*
> *constant struggle.*

One Managing Partner of a national law firm, who gave up his practice to manage full-time, disputed the notion that a Managing Partner must also maintain a successful, busy practice. He stopped short, however, of agreeing that leaders of large practice groups should be other than full-time practicing lawyers. With respect to his own firm, in which all other managers have busy law practices, he described the structure succinctly:

> *I like to say we are managed pragmatically. That*
> *is the word I've used.*

He recognized the inherently conflicting obligations that successful lawyers face in their dual roles when they are also trying to manage large practice groups. In the end, however, the part-time model trumped:

> *To really be a leader of the firm, you've got to*
> *have the respect of your partners and the entire insti-*
> *tution. And I think it is the rare case, if there is a case,*
> *that you can achieve that respect without people*
> *respecting you as a lawyer first.... Our most precious*
> *commodity is leadership. We have too little of it, and I*
> *don't know of a law firm that's got any excessive lead-*
> *ership. Lawyers, for whatever reasons, tend not to be*
> *all that strong.... But to be a leader in the type of*
> *organization we are, with the type of people we have,*
> *requires a variety of very special skills. There are not*
> *that many people who have them.*

The Managing Partner of a mid-size regional law firm similarly saw no alternative to a part-time practice management model:

> *Our groups range in size from 10 to 20. So a 10-*
> *person group may not take a lot of time, but it would*

take, I would guess, 150 to 300 hours a year, if they do it right, [to manage a larger group].

When it was noted that 150 to 300 hours is barely an hour a day of management time, his response indicated a comfort level with that allocation of time for management responsibilities:

But, you know, there are always issues. There are placement issues. There are workload allocation issues.... Hopefully, a lot of it is client development issues, professional growth issues. I mean you're really kind of like a parent or big brother/sister to those in your group. You're looking to cheer them on, encourage them, admonish them...do all those things and you don't do that by giving them a half an hour a week of your time.

He added that, when designating lawyers to serve as Practice Group Leaders, he looks for someone who has nurturing qualities and who will help enhance the skills of others. Ironically, even as managers extol the importance of and need for strong leadership skills, and decry their scarcity in law firms, they are reluctant to consider the opportunities that could arise by identifying and implementing a different management model.

In a management hierarchy that promotes its leaders from the ranks of its major rainmakers, the opportunities for women have been few. One Managing Partner, seemingly oblivious to the steady stream of women attorneys who have exited his firm in the last few years, commented generally on women in leadership in the firm:

I can recall when we did not have a woman on the Policy Committee and were soliciting ideas for replacements. Partners raised the question of, 'Wouldn't it be a good idea to have a woman on the Policy Committee?' But all kinds of questions like this get raised. Wouldn't it be a good idea to have somebody from a small department on the Policy Committee? Wouldn't it be a good idea to have a black on the Policy Committee?... [The issue of

women's advancement] doesn't appear to be a prob-
lem we need to solve, but sensitivity sometimes avoids
problems.

He further stated that within his firm, the lack of women in leadership roles has not emerged as a problem to be solved because no one has raised it to the management level. His comments displayed no recognition of the number of women who have left his firm in their despair that there would be no meaningful future role for them if they stayed. Nor did he seem aware that women in his firm had given up speaking out, because past efforts to address these issues went nowhere.

Managing Partners clearly view their role as complex and demanding. As managers, they view their top priority as ensuring the economic health of the firm. In the highly pressured environment they oversee, this economic outlook tends to the short-term, rather than the longer view. One major goal of their focus is to keep partners from leaving for firms offering more money, and to attract associates by offering highly competitive salary packages.

Most Managing Partners worked extraordinarily hard to achieve their current success. It is, therefore, expected that they would see the future through the prism of their past. However, this is also the prism through which they evaluate lawyers in their firm and which inevitably causes them to compare the contributions of others to their past selves. One long-time Managing Partner, when asked how he defines success, stated:

A successful partner is somebody who first and
foremost has a very successful law practice measured
both in terms of his/her productivity, billable hours,
something above 2,000, in most cases. There are
some practices where to get to 2,000 hours would be
very difficult. There are some where you can get to
2,700 hours without enormous difficulty. But some-
thing about 2,000, generally speaking.... On top of
that, a significant contribution to the firm of some-
thing we value but do not bill for, such as manage-
ment, training, associate mentoring. We expect that
out of every partner and in different degrees.

Another Managing Partner, describing his vision of a successful lawyer, emphasized that high-quality work was the "entry ticket":

> *[W]e need to be honest about who we are and who we are not. And in the hiring process, it may hurt us, but it helps us longer-term if we're honest with people and say, 'We do work pretty hard here.' We always have, we always will. We do work much harder than our competitors.... And we produce very high-quality work.*

For some Managing Partners, financial success is a prerequisite to everything else, such as community engagement and opportunities to participate in non-client activities. In other words, first bill enough hours to keep the firm economically healthy, and then think about community involvement:

> *[B]ut the one thing I continue to tell people is that one of the reasons we are able to do as much good as we are in the community...because the platform is successful. As you know, the first thing you've got to worry about is putting food on the table and earning a nice living.... Once you get beyond that, once you feel comfortable in your platform, then all these other things will follow very naturally.*

Another Managing Partner whose firm expects 2,500 total hours for its partners stated that section managers are responsible for an average number of billable hours for each of the lawyers. Accordingly:

> *They have some people that get reduced hours because of leadership roles or because of significant business development responsibilities or whatever, and then other partners take on more billable hours.*

In general, the world of the Managing Partner is gender neutral. Whether speaking about assignments, billable hours, marketing, or compensation, they view law firms as pure meritocracies where the best will succeed and flourish.

Those that fail are simply not as good. This contributes to a "hands off" management style that exacerbates the challenges described in this book.

For example, when Managing Partners describe the work assignment process, most express an intellectual appreciation for the inherent link between the nature and quality of work assignments and the successful retention of a diverse talent pool. However, probe further into whether their firm has in place a system to ensure equity and oversight in the assignment process, and the response generally hovers around the notion that billable hours are the best development tool for success. Simply put, they see high hours as the optimal work allocation model by exposing attorneys to a variety of partners and work assignments. One Managing Partner described the dynamic:

> *It's how you give work to associates because that's how they develop, that's how they prove their worth to the organization, that's how they get promoted. And work allocation can't be just [working for a particular partner who likes the quality of your work].... An even better approach is [to ensure the associates are] exposed to different kinds of deals.*

Even as Managing Partners recognize the importance of the work assignment process in theoretical terms, some seemed aloof from knowing whether, in fact, their own firm has procedures in place to ensure a level playing field. The result is a further disconnect between the management roles lawyers assume in a law firm, and the successful execution of their obligations as managers.

The Managing Partner of a regional law firm acknowledged the informality of his mid-sized firm's assignment process, and noted the need for change:

> *[O]ne of the things that we are trying to do is to formalize, within practice groups, assignments. Because a lot of time a file will come into a lawyer and, say, if it comes into a senior employment lawyer, that lawyer might have two or three associates that he or she would work with and the file might tend to go in those directions. And while the firm might want to cross-pollinate those relations a little bit more, we are all creatures of habit and we tend to go to the*

force of least resistance. So we're asking Practice
Group Leaders to try to get more involved in some of
those informal assignments and at least know who is
getting what, from whom, so we can make sure that it
is a good balance and folks are getting to work across
or within practice groups, and not just with the same
associate, or two, or three.

When Managing Partners speak about their definition of a successful law-yer, the conversation inevitably turns to the importance of a lawyer's time commitment. The management team of one national law firm described their firm's formula for success:

[T]hree things will make you successful here:
contributions to revenue, teamwork, and intensity of
effort. It is those three things. The first one is, there is
a number that is different for me as a part-time per-
son and you as a full-time person, perhaps. But the
second and third thing are 100%. We are all operat-
ing as team players here or we are not. And that's not
part-time. We are all having the same intensity of
effort or we are not.

With respect to the articulation of specific billable-hour expectations, the response of Managing Partners varies. One long-time Managing Partner con-curred with a management consultant's theory that successful professional careers should be viewed as a 2,500 hour-per-year commitment which includes billable hours, charitable activities, and time spent networking and attending events:

You might spend 1,800 or 1,900 [of those 2,500
hours] billing, but how you spend the other 600 is
equally important.... To be a full-time, full-engaged
professional...[it's all] that time you spend market-
ing, writing speeches, going to the Chamber of Com-
merce breakfast, and the charitable chicken dinner
for all these organizations. When you throw that in, I
think you find that most of us spend that.

A Managing Partner of a national law firm explained his firm's reluctance to establish a specific billable-hour target. He explained that associates are provided quarterly information that allows them to measure where they stand against the rest of the firm. The measures include both client billable time as well as a category for pro bono and other non-revenue generating activities. When asked what he tells new attorneys who inquire as to the firm's target billable hours, he stated:

> *We give them the averages, and we say, 'We ask people to carry their fair share of the load.' ... And we give you the information that lets you know how you stack up against others. And we also tell them that the workload can vary by practice group, and that they should work with their assignment partners to be sure that they are carrying their fair share.*

He acknowledged his answer frustrates those who simply want to be given a specific target to meet, and responds by telling associates:

> *It's the average. We tell them what the average is. I would not want to see big deviations from the average in either direction.*

When pressed in the interview for specific numbers, he stated that lawyers in the firm average close to 2,300 hours per year of combined client-billable and other time.

Some managers will state that any articulated standard is unnecessary. One former Managing Partner observed:

> *We don't have a target. But I think associates know what the average is.*

But do they? The key question, of course, is whether that Managing Partner knew that, by having no articulated expectation, lawyers at the firm felt pushed into achieving increasingly competitive results. When he was asked whether an attorney could be considered to be working too hard, his response was revealing:

If somebody over a period of two to three years were billing 2,600 to 2,700 hours, we'd at least take a look and see whether we think [it is a problem].... If somebody were billing 2,600 or 2,700 hours and not, a newly-minted partner we'd look at it pretty hard and say, 'Is this fair to our partners and fair to our clients?' Those can't be 100% efficient hours at 2,700. You begin to worry about that.

A Managing Partner of a multi-state regional law firm distinguished between minimum standards for billable hours, which his firm does not have, and "expectations," which he distinguishes by the fact that "there's no real penalty" if the "expectations" are not met. Another spoke of a "theoretical expectation of 1,925 billable hours" as a way to give people a "benchmark." A former Managing Partner of a large national firm referred to a "range" for bonus eligibility purposes:

1,900 to 2,250 is what we say is the range for bonus compensation for associates. So at the 2,250, you can expect the highest level bonus. At 1,900, you are just eligible for a bonus.

However the true meaning of this "range" became clearer as he spoke in greater detail about the importance of "passion" as a critical attribute of success. Individuals with passion for what they do, he observed:

They are billing 2,100, 2,200, 2,300, 2,400 hours a year. They are solid.

The Managing Partner of a national firm reported what he tells their associates:

For associates, we basically say that unless somebody is on our part-time program, we really expect about 2,000 hours, and then we expect some time on top of that....Normally 300 or 400 hours...for practice development, marketing, firm citizenship, all kinds of things.

When he was asked whether lawyers concerned about meeting their family obligations can vary that expectation by working less and offering to earn less, he responded negatively:

> *We have some people who made choices.... Some work a little less and make less. But you can't have too many of those. It's the marketplace, so that's what we're competing with.... We've got to maintain enough of the organization operating at the level our competitors operate at.... It's the dilemma that we all face.*

Not all Managing Partners will concede that there is a difference in the work demands of a modern law firm, compared to their own early experiences several decades ago. A recently retired Managing Partner of a national law firm, recalling his hard-charging days as a rising star associate, stressed that he worked as many hours as any associate in today's firms:

> *I think this idea that we're working harder now than we used to is a little strange.... I mean, I put in a lot of all-nighters...and a lot of weekends.... It puts a strain on a family.*

The difference between then and now, he acknowledged, was in the increased stress and time pressures brought about by modern technology. Interestingly, his successor viewed the past somewhat differently. When he began practicing two decades earlier, he recalled that:

> *The expected number of hours for a senior partner was 1,700. And for [an older] senior partner, the expected number was 1,250. [Today you] have the productivity expectation coming from firms being run as businesses and the profession having created greater pressure. The second thing is that email, voicemail, BlackBerries, all have created another set of pressures. In 1976, if I went home at seven at night and answered every call, nothing could happen before eight the next morning. There wasn't even a switchboard operator. Now, you get home at seven*

*and you get in at seven and there are five faxes. While
the productivity expectation has increased, the working day and working week has increased. For some
firms like ours and some other folks.... [W]e're practicing at a different level than we were 20 years ago.*

He further noted that each of the firm's lawyers are required to prepare
annual individual practice goals. He reported that all of the attorneys projected working between 1,800 and 2,400 hours annually.

Even as lawyers are expected to work long hours, firms are always considering the frequency with which they may raise their hourly rates. One recently
retired Managing Partner described how his firm stayed abreast of billing rate
opportunities:

*We're pretty aggressive about our rates, and I'm
constantly surprised to find out that somebody else is
charging more than we are. I think that what we've
learned about rates is to stay away from, to the extent
you can, commodity work and to try and do things for
clients where they are not sensitive to rates.*

*Now, some clients always talk about it or raise it,
but even if they complain about it, we find them coming back to you the next time they have a similar
problem.... They didn't really mean it. We try not to
price ourselves above the high end of the market, but
try to be at the high end of the market.... We do go up
annually. We sometimes have made a mid-year
adjustment, if we found that we really missed the
market.*

There is a profound connection between the high billable rates that law
firms charge for their services, the compensation demands of many lawyers,
and the increasingly stressful pace and pressured existence that lawyers lead.
Observed one member of a national firm's management team:

*The difference between the billable rates and the
compensation has really upped the ante.... How many*

> *clients are willing to pay you $600 an hour? You bet-*
> *ter be the best at whatever advice you are giving, it*
> *better be really good, the gold standard. I think that*
> *has just turned up the heat.*

The high rates have an enormously negative impact on associates' careers, as clients and law firms exhibit less patience with anything other than extraordinary performance:

> *I don't think associates realize what a bargain*
> *with the devil their high billing rates are. It pushes up*
> *the bar for partnership, makes the firm much quicker*
> *on the trigger in the downturn and a lot of other real*
> *detriments.*

Many of the Managing Partners noted that clients still seem to be relatively passive about trying to change a system in which inefficiency in handling client matters is, arguably, rewarded. Stated one Managing Partner who has tried to convince clients to consider alternate billing arrangements:

> *It's a bit of a sale, ironically.... [Clients] can see*
> *that there is a misalignment in billable-hours' mea-*
> *surement to their bottom-line results. They talk a*
> *game, but at the end of the day, a lot of the General*
> *Counsel are used to managing a lot of billable hours,*
> *so there is some resistance.*

Even as Managing Partners judge their attorneys by the hours they bill and the hourly rates they can charge, another critical criterion for future success is whether aspiring partners are viewed as demonstrating a capacity to develop business. As in other critical areas in which law firm managers judge their attorneys, there is little uniformity in the business generation expectations imposed on aspiring partners. Concrete opportunities for law firm managers to judge that ability earlier in an associate's career are quite limited: most young lawyers are working too hard on existing work to take the time required to cultivate new clients. Few senior associates are likely to have a peer network that can pay the high hourly rates of most large law firms. As a result, when it comes time to assess the business development skills of associates, firm managers do so from an internal lens:

This isn't a law firm where your clients come from your golfing buddies, that sort of thing. Business development is something that presents itself not typically to a very young partner, but it's usually a partner who's developed a reputation in a particular field, who's presenting the opportunity on the basis of recommendations, observations by boards of directors who are investment bankers or auditors.

The key to business development in a law firm like this, is developing a reputation first among your partners, and then among your clients and others who are providing first-rate legal services in whatever your area of specialty is. Business development also requires, and here is something that can be learned, you aren't born with it, an aptitude for presenting yourself to prospective clients in a way which projects self-confidence and makes them think: 'This is somebody I would like to work with.'

Most Managing Partners see business development as a gender-neutral issue. Of course, this means there is never a problem to fix. One recently retired Managing Partner discussed the advice he gave to his new associates:

I always told them that the way to succeed...is to become an excellent lawyer and to market internally to partners. And over a period of four or five years, you will begin to get client assignments where you begin to manage the client relationship and then that client will begin to call you instead of the grey-haired guy. You can become partner just by taking existing firm clients and growing them.

This advice sounds like a disarmingly simple formula for success. In addressing some of the business-generation challenges women face, Managing Partners concur that a large national law firm offers multiple routes to business development success. Those who do not feel comfortable directly asking clients for business can still be successful by focusing on the "internal market" of the hundreds of lawyers in the firm who need help with their existing client base. However, the Managing Partners will also acknowledge that, to reach the level of equity partner in these law firms, an attorney is expected to be primarily responsible for, or have brought into the firm, at least a million dollars' worth of business. Even that number, like billable hours themselves, seems to be a continually evolving target.

One former Managing Partner observed that partners should be able to support themselves and at least two other lawyers, either through new work that they bring in directly, or by managing a large workload from existing clients. He admitted that, in large firms in particular, there could be a bias in favor of men, since a lawyer can be viewed as a successful rainmaker by working on matters for, and ultimately inheriting, important firm clients:

> *It's all about getting business.... Women don't have as much time because they are dealing with the home life as well as they are doing the work, so that element of marketing suffers.... [With respect to senior male partners who pass their work down to make protégés], I would think it would be more, 'Well, she is part-time. Or, even worse, she is going to have kids and go part-time. And, therefore, I'm better off with John who will be there for my client whenever my client needs him.' It's not because it is a woman.... It's been a long time since I've seen anything that I thought was gender-bias as opposed to part-time bias.*

This failure to acknowledge "part-time bias" as a distinct form of gender bias leaves unaddressed a major impediment to success and a significant cause of attrition.

For the Managing Partners, one of the least enviable tasks is the setting of compensation. As described earlier, in many firms, the process and the formula are steeped in firm history and culture; therefore, any effort to change the process proves difficult and traumatic. Notwithstanding the size and sophistication of many of these institutions, law firm managers acknowledge that compensation is still a firm-by-firm struggle to create a system that aligns incentives and ensures that people are working in the best interests of the institution, as opposed to their own individual salary increases. Whether a firm's system is strictly objective (that is, set in accordance with a formula that generally measures some combination of billable hours and fee receipts) or whether it is a subjective formula allowing for the analysis of both statistical and non-statistical measures, most systems are fraught with opportunities for second-guessing and mixed messages.

Managing Partners are the first to bear the brunt of these criticisms. One recently retired Managing Partner reflected in depth on his experiences as a key player in setting compensation. Based on his own role in his firm, he came to the conclusion that, just as successful lawyers will thrive under any system, there is no such thing as a compensation formula without flaws:

> *People who produce, will produce. They will get credit for it, and it will all work out. If you're not [producing], a lot of it is excuses, a lot of it is rationalizations. Why are you not being rewarded? A lot of it is the firm itself is not profitable enough and, therefore, your overall compensation at the end of the year isn't what you expected. But if the firm was making twice as much money and you earned twice as much, you wouldn't be so worried about how they allocate the credit. It is your relative positioning compared to everyone else in the firm and your absolute dollar amounts, not the way you get there. We have all sorts of formulas, none of them are accurate.*

> *Let's say you go to a totally subjective [system]. The Compensation Committee gets in a room, thinks about who has done what they were supposed to have done, been cooperative, teamwork, and all those things. In addition to working the hours, how do I know what someone in [the office of another state] has done? I have no idea. How do I know what somebody in [a different practice group] has done? I have no idea.*

> *So you are going to have a lot of...stories told and whoever tells the best story for their person, they're going to get the reward. On the other hand, it gives you the opportunity to be flexible, not get into a fight*

over: 'Did you produce that client? Did I produce that client? I know you met them at the cocktail party, but then I saw them at the ball game.' It enables the firm to say, 'Look, this is a great, new client. We want you to work on it. Rather than going to produce your own $50,000 client, we would rather you work on this $2 million dollar client because you are a fabulous lawyer. We need you to build that client, and we'll reward you more than if you take in this $50,000 client.'

The objective of a real formula is you will get what you 'deserve.' If the formula says you get 10% of what you bring in and 40% of your hours, whatever. Make up any formula you want, it doesn't matter, they're all coming to the same thing. No one can screw you; it's on the numbers. It's not about personality, it's not about whose favorite you are, whose coat tails you ride, it's objective. It's how you do.

It's a meritocracy. [But it never is.]... And so that's the theory, it protects against decisions that are arbitrary and it gives you control over your destiny. You know the rules and if you play by those rules and win by those rules, you go around the Monopoly Board, you Pass Go, and you get what you expected, so there are no surprises.... It wasn't some committee saying, 'You stink!' It's the numbers.

All of these have benefits, none of them work. None of them work. The reason everybody is always unhappy is because I can come up with the reasons that they don't work. Because lawyers are, if nothing else, argumentative and logical and can see the flaws in anything. So since there isn't an ideal system...if they're not happy with their compensation or they're not happy with the way they are performing or they're nervous that they can't do what is being asked of them, then they will complain about all this stuff.

He then spoke of his firm's preeminent senior partner as the prototype example of why he believes that the particular characteristics of any compensation formula do not matter:

You put [partner's name] on any formula; I don't care what you call it, objective, subjective, the size of your desk, it doesn't matter, he will win that game. He will win that game. So personally...I get nauseous when people come in and complain about the formula. It will happen. It will be obvious. If you're that good, it will happen. And if not, look at the end of the year with your fitness scale. Does it look about right? Are you within 10% of where you think you should be?

Another Managing Partner, describing his own key role in his firm's subjective compensation process, extolled its virtues because of the flexibility it allows. The difficulty, he observed, is the highly competitive nature of lawyers:

You're not looking at [compensation] in a vacuum. Because you're looking at it vis-à-vis your competition.... We're all making more money than we ever thought we'd make in the practice of law.

Some Managing Partners described efforts to develop compensation formulas that would promote greater teamwork among the firm's lawyers. However the relentless drive for more money often overshadows these efforts. When Managing Partners were asked if they felt pressure to increase attorney compensation each year, the responses were remarkably similar. Every year has to be better than the year before:

The partners want to make more money. Everybody wants to make a little more every year. We always ascribe to achieve at least a 5% increase in per partner profits.

Another resorted again to his military terminology:

> *We have high overhead and people expect to earn a lot of money. And we have to, partly to keep up with the Joneses. I'm very happy and I think if you ask each of the partners individually right now, they would say they are very happy with the economics of the firm today. But if you say, 'Well, [named competitors] are probably going to report a million dollars a partner-how do we attract our next laterals? How do we retain our best people so we can pay significantly more?' So as a competitive matter, we have to work harder, we have to charge more, we have to collect more because the arms' race continues. So we're caught in it and we can't deny it if we want to get the best people.*

In most law firms, information about each partner's compensation is shared among all partners, exacerbating competitive behaviors. In a small number of law firms, however, individual partner compensation is not disclosed, in order to remove these competitive tensions. One former Managing Partner lauded the benefits of his firm's closely-held compensation results. He stated simply:

> *It makes it a lot easier to run the place with that off the table.*

With respect to partnership elections, Managing Partners continue to see their world as a gender-neutral meritocracy which results in partnership for high-quality lawyers of either gender. However here, too, the Managing Partners' view of reality can be quite different than the actual circumstances within the firm. When asked about their percentage of female partners, it was not uncommon for the Managing Partners to guess a number higher than the actual statistic. For example, when the Managing Partner of a multi-office law firm was asked about the firm's percentage of women partners, his first guess was that women comprised between 20% and 25% of the partnership. When he then calculated the actual number, however, the result was slightly below the national average of 16.5%. This phenomenon of Managing Partners over-estimating their total percentage of female partners does not seem to be a purposeful effort to misrepresent their statistics. Rather, it is more likely due to a rose-colored vision of the firm that sees only the successes, and not the lost opportunities that never even make their radar screen.

One former Managing Partner attributed his firm's low ratio of female partners solely to voluntary attrition:

> *For the women who stick it out through the part-*
> *nership track period, which is nine years here, pro-*
> *motion to partnership is about as certain as it is for*
> *males who stick it out.... I would say every woman*
> *who has gone to the ninth year here has become a*
> *partner.... But the problem for women's progression*
> *in a law firm occurs before the time is right for the*
> *promotion to partnership.*

However where he saw a straight-forward progression for women who stayed, he described a process where less likely prospects are weeded out long before their ninth year:

> *It really begins in the seventh year. In some cases,*
> *it begins earlier than that because we, at least inter-*
> *nally, decide that somebody is either a dud or a star.*
> *But most people are neither and about the end of the*
> *seventh year, we begin to say, 'Is this person capable*
> *of representing us as a partner?' We look at the busi-*
> *ness case for adding partners to the associate's prac-*
> *tice specialty.... [B]ut if somebody's clearly not going*
> *to become a partner, we'll at the end of seven years,*
> *hopefully, tell that person it is unlikely that he or she*
> *is going to become a partner.*

Even as he stated that women who remained until the ninth year would become partner, his perception of his firm as a gender-neutral institution which was a victim of voluntary attrition was at odds with reality. The Managing Partner did not see that his firm forced attrition before that time by weeding out those senior associates identified as having no partnership prospects. The firm's position was that it would not be "good for morale" if they remained at the firm knowing that partnership would not be available to them and, therefore, recommended that they find other opportunities. So, while it was true that if associates made it to the ninth year they were elected, it was because the firm essentially terminated those who would not succeed prior to that time. However, in the eyes of the Managing Partner, if associates could just "hang in" until their ninth year, success was virtually assured.

The problem, however, is that for those associates not viewed as partnership material, there was no effort to address gender bias and diversity issues in the critical years leading up to these final partnership decisions. When asked whether there was anything he thought the firm could be doing to help more women achieve partnership, he answered in the negative. Rather, he seemed pleased to observe that, based on the number of women currently in the pipeline, the firm would reach approximately 20% women partners over the next 10 years. He did not express any recognition of the fact that, based on the number of women in the pipeline for the past two decades, his 20% target should already have been achieved and exceeded.

A highly respected Managing Partner at a national law firm observed the connection between billable-hour demands and partnership decisions. He also noted the difficulty of trying to develop an alternative model for partnership election and criteria:

> I think that in any profession where time is money, where the unit of productivity is the hour, that effects how people think about the value of others in ways that are very antithetical to work/life balance. And no matter how you try to cut it, it is just so pervasive in the thinking, that 'more time means more commitment, and more money for everybody.'

> And I see that coming from people where I wouldn't expect to see it, people who seem to be genuinely committed to work/life balance. But when it comes to how they assess candidates for a promotion, for example, I see an attitude creeping in there. That sometimes gets expressed directly, sometimes not. The billable hour is responsible for a lot of bad things in the profession, and this is one of them.

For some Managing Partners, there is a simplistic acceptance of a double standard in viewing the gendered paths to success. A recently retired Managing Partner, reflecting on those successful women who have become equity partners in his national law firm over the years, observed that:

> *There will always be that selection process that is so subtle and has so many intangible features to it that you can't formularize it. But you know it when you see it. I'm also thinking that there is an ingredient that we haven't talked about and that is for women to be successful, they have to have a very understanding and supportive husband, if they have a husband, or have no husband at all. That is a generality, but as I think of some of the ones I know, that's been the case. Whereas, for a man...it is helpful to have a supportive wife, obviously, but I don't think it is as essential for a man to have a supportive wife, or no wife, as it is for a woman to have a supportive husband or no husband.*

In law firms which have multiple tiers of partnership, the junior partner level is generally distinguished from the equity, or ownership, tier by a lawyer's business development success. A recently retired Managing Partner noted:

> *The initial tier is: you have the promise of [business development] and you are a fine lawyer that we're comfortable with. We've seen you relatively fully engaged and you are in an area that we believe is one that will continue and be a good service. That is the standard for the first level of partnership. Once you get to the next level, it's really a difference of economics, for the most part, not one of skill. Sometimes they go together.*

The management team at a national law firm recognized the gender differentiation that exists between the two tiers:

> *Associates become non-equity partners first, and then equity partners. It is a minimum of three years before you are considered for equity partner.... [The non-equity tier] is the category where we have a lot of part-time women....*

To them, the non-equity level of partnership serves as a place of opportunity for many women working on a reduced-hours schedule, because it bestowed the distinction of being a partner, even if it were only at the first tier of the partnership track. Yet the firm's own statistics did not support the assertion that non-equity partnership was a place where more women thrived, as only approximately 13% of their non-equity partners were women, a number even lower than the national average. So, notwithstanding their perception, the non-equity level of partnership was not increasing the retention and promotion of talented women.

One Managing Partner defended his firm's "up-or-out" junior-to-equity partnership track by emphasizing that the road to success was not based on the independent generation of clients. Rather, it was one's reputation as an extremely high-quality lawyer who services existing firm clients and develops strong internal relationships within the firm:

> *[Our junior partner category is:] if you are an associate who is doing Okay, you make junior partner. It's just a status change.... If you don't make equity partner in three to four years, you have to leave.... By the time people are eight to nine years here, the people who are going to become partners, it's pretty clear.*

However the reality is that even terrific candidates may not get elected, for reasons entirely out of their control. Firms become particularly cautious about electing new partners in a weak economy or if the candidate's practice group is not sufficiently profitable. The Managing Partner of a national law firm, when asked about his firm's partnership election criteria, confirmed that even highly qualified candidates are subject to economic conditions beyond their control:

> *It is a combination of factors. Quality of work being absolutely critical, but it also depends on the*

> *economics of their practice and of the firm. And*
> *someone may do great work, but if the nature of the*
> *work load and the area where they practice is such*
> *that we can't support another partner, it will be very*
> *difficult to make partner.*

If the language of law firm management is critical to firm culture and, concomitantly, the success of the women within it, then there is perhaps no word used more frequently and fraught with potential damage to women's careers than the word "accommodation." Law firm partners and senior management constantly use the word to address work-family issues. However the word itself highlights the chasm that exists between those who see a need to alter the structure of the workplace to promote the retention of good lawyers, and those firm managers who proudly tout their "accommodations" to help women address the needs of their young children. In this world view, family obligations diminish by the time children are through their toddler years, ignoring the even greater demands of raising teenagers, or even dealing with the needs of aging parents.

This failure to incorporate into the structure of a law firm the basic reality, that family responsibilities last for decades, is an enormous impediment to fundamental change. If managers see no need for their institutions to do anything but briefly "accommodate" lawyers with very young children, then the pipeline will always remain clogged. A retired Managing Partner of a large firm unwittingly highlighted this concern when he stated:

> *It's clear that family-oriented issues and the pace*
> *at which we practice law are the two principal factors*
> *that cause women to leave here and do something*
> *else.... We talk at the management level with our*
> *partners and our associates about the pressure that*
> *working here involves, career alternatives, how we*
> *can make things easier for people who are in the*
> *early stages of family rearing. We try to be accommo-*
> *dating through part-time arrangements.*

The perception that flexible hours policies are an "accommodation" for women, as opposed to a focused effort by the firm to retain talent, manifests itself in a casual approach to the success of reduced-hours arrangements. Recall the interview with an associate at a large firm, whose Monday through

Thursday schedule was more illusion than reality, and who was advised by a female senior partner never to openly discuss family issues, and listen to the words of the Managing Partner of that same firm as he revealed his own negative views of flexible schedules:

> *At the end of the day, I think part-time requests are worked out in a way which, hopefully, will work for the firm and seem satisfactory, at least at the outset, to the associate.... I would observe that part-time has not been a great success for us. There are several reasons, one is that an associate wants to work part-time and let's say it is litigation or a transactional corporate practice. It's very hard to make that work. Maybe she can do a piece of the whole. But if she's a sixth-year associate, that's when we expect associates to run the whole thing.... Unless she's working a fairly full schedule or more and is flexible with respect to client service requirements, it's going to be very hard for her to progress.... The department head or the partner who has ultimate responsibility is going to be unwilling to entrust an important client matter to her because she is not going to be able to cover all the bases. So it doesn't mean we won't try to keep her busy, but it isn't going to be challenging new things that are what her peers who are working full-time are getting the opportunity to experience.*

To him, part-time lawyers were not fully-integrated members of the firm, but rather people to be "kept busy." When he was asked about management's responsibility to intervene if a reduced-hours attorney was consistently undermined by those who managed her assignments, his explanation revealed his own lack of engagement as Managing Partner in the implementation of these issues:

> *Certainly the department heads and practice group leaders, I think, are very good about [these scheduling issues] and in making sure the partner of the senior associate who is responsible understands*

what the ground rules are and will not stand for part-
ners or the senior associate putting pressure on the
part-time associate to rearrange what had been
agreed to or bad-mouthing her.

Now individual partners...they are on the front
line and I wouldn't want to generalize how individual
partners react to being confronted with something
where they may have to pick up and do something or
find somebody else to do something. But nothing is
ever going to change that, I don't think....

[Junior-level associates] are, relatively speaking,
easier to manage than the fifth-, sixth-, seventh-year
associate who is running a deal or litigation. These
people can do it, but they have to, vis-à-vis the client,
make it transparent, but that is a more difficult propo-
sition for the part-time associate and for the firm and
the clients. Because that person is no longer just
doing a piece of something, she is responsible for the
whole thing. That's what makes the law firm profit-
able, because the partner may have three projects
going on and the mid-senior level associate should
just have one major thing going on, but it's hers to do.
So her, not her absence, but her unavailability, is very
difficult for the partner to get along with...that we
find is harder from a management perspective than a
third-, fourth-, or early fifth-year associate.

His choice of words make clear that the associate, particularly a senior
associate, is solely obligated to make the schedule work for the firm; there is
no recognition of this as a firm-wide responsibility. His final quotes on the
topic demonstrate how deep-seated the resistance to change can be:

I don't think the law firm model in the near to
immediate term is going to change a lot.... So I think
what we need to figure out is incremental ways we
can make it more likely that women will want to prac-

tice in the large law firm environment and incremental ways in which we can make it easier to accommodate their practicing law in this environment and their other interests....

I should tell you I'm really not a fan of part-time...and that is based on our experience with it.... It has not been a vehicle or a method of working that has kept talented women challenged and developing. It is sort of a holding pattern. It's valuable because these are people with whom we have an important investment, and working part-time for two or three years allows them to fulfill their obligations to the development of their family and to stay associated with us. That's a positive.

In essence, he viewed his firm's role in assisting a lawyer's effort to address her family responsibilities as a benign, and even begrudging, willingness to allow a two- to three-year bump in a career, as opposed to a multi-decade commitment. He concluded that any other option would likely fail:

I think this would be a very difficult career path at this [large law firm]. If you didn't have really first-rate child care support, I can't imagine.... You have to have really superb child care support.

Another recently retired Managing Partner was also blunt in his assessment of the impact of part-time hours on a woman's career:

The fact is that the people who put in the hours have the breadth of experiences that those hours give them, and they develop faster and better.... So, if you've got that as a given, to try to do this profession on any less than a full-throttle basis is going to mean you are positioned differently.... After five years of that kind of less-than-full throttle, by definition you are going to have less closings, less cases, and, there-

fore, perhaps be less prepared as a lawyer. You just can't have it both ways.

When asked whether that meant it would just take longer for a part-time lawyer to develop enough experience to become a partner, he stated that the impact was broader:

> *It not only takes longer to be a partner, but I think the end quality of the lawyer will be somewhat different because you wouldn't have had the breadth of exposure on as many cases and you can't make that up.*

The Managing Partner of a large regional law firm was candid in stating his assessment that these arrangements are amorphous, at best:

> *Our experience is that there are a couple of practice areas where it works very well and then there a couple of other practice areas where it's terrible. The other functional problem is the nature of the child care that the woman has at home. If there is no flexibility, it is really problematic. If there is flexibility, it can work. If there's no flexibility, it can't.... Institutionally, you will find firms making more accommodations for the really smart woman than they will for an average performer. And I think there's a much harder burden on an average-performing lawyer who's trying to make these balances.*
>
> *When I look at the people who have got goofy schedules, they are all people who are really good. Everybody is happy to put out to keep this person balanced, because you want them here for the long-term. Then you get to someone who is just average. In many respects, they get viewed as blockers, because they are taking up routine work that could be done by a lot of different people. If you don't see them going somewhere long-term, it's harder to accommodate them.*

It is no wonder that attorneys in law firms perceive mixed messages regarding the acceptance of a reduced-hours schedule, as many Managing Partners see them as a detriment, rather than as a viable option for retaining, and even energizing, attorneys. Since Managing Partners have an instrumental role in the culture of their firms, the ambivalence cascades throughout the firm, becoming a self-fulfilling prophecy of failure. Every Managing Partner has his own anecdotes about failed efforts to "accommodate" the schedules of certain valued women attorneys, who ended up leaving the firm anyway. With each such anecdote, the opportunity to say the system is unworkable grows. One Managing Partner summarized the ambivalence he has observed:

> *There are...lawyers involved at the senior level who don't respect the part-time nature of a particular lawyer's commitment. They say, 'Look, the work has to be done. She wants to be on these matters, then she's got to do just what I do. I worked that sixth day. I didn't go on vacation, or I left my kids at Disneyland and came home, because I had to. That's what we do. If you're going to be a lawyer, you have to do that.'*

However, it would be expected that lawyers in his firm would express these attitudes, in light of his own negativity:

> *Part-time pay is a bad deal for the women and a bad deal for the firm because you still have a full-time office, you still have a secretary, you still have overhead. If we really, really, really were going to equitable pay, you wouldn't get 60% of the 60% pay, you would get 40% of the 60% pay. You have to look at the economics of that of the firm.... Your overhead is still at 100%. You still have an office....You still have a secretary. You still have malpractice insurance. You still have all the things that cost the firm money.... So, it's not a good deal for the firm. It's not a good deal for the lawyers either because they actually work more hours. Unless it is significantly more, they don't get paid.*

His assessment was even gloomier with respect to part-time litigators:

> *If you want to be a litigator, you are asking for it...a little bit of masochism. Because juries don't care, judges don't care. You are going to be on trial and that's the way it is. There is nothing I can say or do about it: part-time doesn't work. Now what you can do, once you are done with that trial, you want to take a week off to recoup and to do the laundry and to do everything you didn't get to, I should be able to give you that opportunity without you feeling guilty about it or me feeling angry about it. I should give you a computer at home, I should give you a Black-Berry, I should give you all the tools so you don't have to be here any longer than necessary so that you can do your work at home. You can prepare for a witness after dinner, after you put the kids to bed. I should help you in ways that I can, and I think we do those things. But ultimately, think about the choices, don't blame me because you decided to be a litigator. Going in, I will tell you if you ask me, it is almost impossible.*

Managers at one national firm described the detailed process they used to "accommodate" those seeking to work a reduced schedule, culminating in a policy which left enormous discretion to the firm and an unstated, but clear, message for those seeking a more flexible schedule:

> *If the business needs of the organization can be met by making this accommodation, we will make the accommodation.... In the past, our policy was to say, 'Yes,' and we didn't really know against what criteria we would be saying 'no' to.... So what we have done is to say that the [practice area leaders are] responsible for all the resource issues within their department and this is a resource issue. When a request is made, they will initially and at least annually make an*

assessment using many factors about whether or not they can make this accommodation.

These factors included the power of the Practice Group Chair to refuse a lawyer's request for a reduced-hours schedule if the Chair thought that an upcoming project would be important to the lawyer's professional development. In addition, a request could be denied if a department was too busy or if the individual's profitability warranted a need to work full-time. They further reported that, when they began their internal task force, a leading law firm consultant told the firm that allowing anything less than an 80% part-time schedule does not work, because the individual is not demonstrating sufficient "commitment" and "passion" for the job. Ultimately, the firm agreed that a lawyer could choose to remove herself from the partnership track by working at a less than 80% schedule. This particular manager felt that his past experiences actually warranted a more stringent approach:

> *[For decades] we have bent over backwards to try to make this work and I think we ought to just go in the opposite direction and say: "80% except in rare, short-term circumstances." People have to have a passion to practice law and if they don't have the passion, then they really ought to do a lot of other things.*

Ultimately, the percentages of reduced-hours allowed in the firm's policy are likely to matter little in light of the substantial commitment that is expected under any circumstances:

> *We say to someone, 'Your intensity of effort, your commitment to our clients is 24/7. That's 24/7 for you at 60%, for you at 80%, and for you at 100%. Your commitment to our clients is 24/7. As long as you agree and we agree that those are the rules of engagement, we can talk about a part-time arrangement. If you are a 60% person, that is what we pay you for, so your numbers are 60% of the standards that I apply to everyone else.' That does not translate into a less intensity of effort.*

*Here is how the backlash happens. I am a 60%
person, so I don't work Mondays and Fridays, 'So
don't call me on Mondays and Fridays.' Well in what
profession is that ever going to work? For the professional level person, that is a silly way to write the
rules. What we say is 60%, 'I'm available all the
time.'...You can't say, 'I'm not working Fridays.' You
can say, 'I anticipate that the way I will work my flexible work arrangement is, Friday is the day I'm going
to try to take off, but you can't guarantee it.'*

In essence, many Managing Partners seemed united in their ambivalence
about implementing firm-wide, reduced-hours arrangements. At its best, most
saw it as an opportunity to hold onto star performers:

*Again, let's be perfectly honest. You're only going
to do it for your stars. It's not worth it for somebody
else. It's just not. So for our stars, like anything else,
you make the accommodation....*

However even as the Managing Partners discuss the costs of reduced-
hours arrangements or some other flexible compensation system which allows
a diminished workload, they show remarkably little knowledge about the cost
to the firm every time a woman leaves. One Managing Partner's words articulated both the challenge and the opportunity that exists for the law firm that is
ready to create a structure that truly allows talent to thrive:

*[T]here are no easy solutions. You know, if any-
body thinks it's easy, forget it, it's not easy...it's about
the right thing to do, but it's also good business.
...You know, whenever firms can crack the code here,
you have a tremendous advantage.*

Managing Partners have every opportunity to "crack the code," and
understanding the "tremendous advantage" that can be gained by doing so is a
good first step. Fortunately, the code can be easily interpreted by any committed law firm leader. The one that moves aggressively will be guaranteed a dedicated, highly competent talent pool and the promise of reduced attrition.

Endnotes for Chapter 13

1. This discrepancy among perspectives was also identified by the Boston Bar Association's Task Force on Professional Challenges and Family Needs. See BBA Task Force on Prof. Challenges and Family Needs, Facing the Grail: Confronting the Cost of Work-Family Imbalance (1999).

PART THREE

CHAPTER 14

ENDING THE GAUNTLET

The explosive growth and rapid changes that have transpired in law firms over the past three decades have resulted in an unsustainable business model. The health of the profession requires a commitment to bold initiatives and the development of a strategic vision that sees a future filled with more than increased billable hours and higher hourly rates. We know that major changes in the profession are possible; the fact that law firm dress codes changed literally overnight and associate salaries skyrocketed in a matter of weeks demonstrate that where firms have the will, they find the way.

The business case for change is compelling, as studies demonstrate the increased morale and concomitant gains in productivity and retention resulting from workers who feel they can be active parents and valued employees.[1] By raising morale, law firms will improve their productivity. The importance of employee morale as a factor in the bottom line has been understood by the corporate sector for years. Statistical surveys demonstrate a strong correlation between happy employees and successful business units.[2] In fact, the positive relationship between worker morale and productivity has influenced many major corporations to implement changes that result in increased employee morale and an improved bottom line.[3] Law firms cannot continue to ignore the clear messages from their own current and future workforce.

Moreover, the growing shift in attitudes among more recent graduates is palpable. Increasingly, surveys and social science studies demonstrate that men and women endorse more egalitarian attitudes as well as the availability of more family-friendly work schedules.[4] Business publications and related media coverage of workplace issues are replete with articles documenting that the post-baby boom generations, so called generations X and Y, expect to blend their professional aspirations with the needs of their family. In doing so, they have no intentions of having their family responsibilities take second place to their work.[5]

More than a decade ago, an ABA study of the state of the profession identified signs of these generational changes. In its 1990 data on levels of career satisfaction, 19% of all lawyers in private practice reported being dissatisfied. This percentage increased to 31% for those lawyers who graduated after 1967.[6] In comparing its data to a similar study undertaken in 1984, the ABA identified an important change in the cause of dissatisfaction in the workplace: where the 1984 study reported a direct correlation between job satisfaction and the existence of intellectual challenge, by 1990, other factors were eroding the level of satisfaction that lawyers reported and were contributing to a negative work environment. The five factors highly correlated to overall job satisfaction identified by the American Bar Association included:[7]

1. social environmental (for example: advancement determined by quality of work; respect by superiors; lack of firm politics and backbiting; and a warm atmosphere);

2. challenge/involvement (for example: control over case selection; input into management decisions; intellectual challenge; opportunity for professional development; and the encouragement of involvement in pro bono work);

3. support/reward (for example: extent of support staff; financial rewards; and opportunity to advance);

4. pressure (for example: time for family and self; level of tension at work; pressure from clients); and

5. training (for example: involvement of superiors in both training and feedback; and a sense that skills learned in law school are useful).

Still another ABA research project confirmed that work/life issues are no longer gender specific. In its detailed qualitative study analyzing the needs of the legal profession, the ABA reported: "Interestingly, while the work-life balance seemed especially relevant to women two years ago, the importance and relevance of the issue is now noticeable among men as well. Some are foregoing partnership track in order to ensure they can spend more time with their children."[8] The identification of work/family issues was also highlighted by the NALP Foundation as a critical component of associate retention: "Regardless of gender or seniority, associates were unanimous in noting that balance is essential to their professional lives. Many associates indicated that they are willing to change employers again and again or leave the profession entirely to achieve this goal, noting that it isn't just about billable hours, but also about the acceptability of taking time off to attend to family needs and participate in children's school and community events."[9]

One of the more comprehensive analyses of the generational distinctions between generations X and Y and their predecessors was conducted by the Families and Work Institute for the American Business Collaboration. The study found that fewer employees of both genders are interested in moving into positions of greater responsibility, and are rejecting the work-centric nature of today's workplace. This change in the workforce has critical future implications. As the report noted: "Although a lot has been written about the 'Opt-Out Revolution,' defined as employed women leaving the workforce when they have very young children, we see this downtrend in career ambitions as the real revolution, where very sizable numbers of women and men are working hard, but not wanting the trade-offs they would have to make by advancing into jobs with more responsibility."[10] Observing these generational differences, Dr. Sheila M. Statlender, a former career counselor at Harvard Law School, told Massachusetts Lawyer's Weekly that students are both marrying and having children younger than their parents' generation.[11]

A study of Washington, D.C. law firms noted that the economic necessity of two-income earners means that few families have the luxury of only one spouse working outside the home. The author noted that, as the number of two-earner families is increasing, research indicates that men are: "willing to trade half of their salaries for more time with their families."[12] This necessitates that law firms analyze their own recruitment strategies: "New law firm recruits are passing up lucrative jobs with firms having a 'sweatshop' reputation for firms promising a higher quality of life. Firms that address the concerns of this generation of lawyers will likely become the firm of choice for new recruits."[13]

A highly respected specialist in the attorney placement field confirmed that she has seen these generational changes in the course of her recruitment work:

> *Yet the entry-level associates are really not taking it like 10 years ago in terms of time. I mean, they want a life.... If they persist in asserting themselves in that area, then there's going to have to be some impact on the law firms.*

Similar observations were echoed by a number of interviewees. For example, a prominent partner from the Midwest stated:

> *Particularly the younger generation that is coming into law firms now would take a [pay] cut in return for knowing they didn't have to do 2,200 to 2,300 hours.... I think you [could] hire, retain, and attract higher level women and men, too, because I see the younger generation of men being not that interested. They are contributing to families more and they want different lives,...they aren't really all that interested in working until midnight seven days a week to get it, other than the student loan issue.*

A young partner who formerly chaired her firm's committee for the evaluation and promotion of associates echoed these concerns:

> *I must have heard a million times: 'I don't want to make any more money. I'd rather work less and make less.'*

However, not everyone attributes these generational differences simply to an altered work ethic. Some have defined this generational difference as the logical result of recognizing that the opportunities for partnership are small and, therefore, the relationship with their law firm employers will be of diminished duration: "These recruits no longer have aspirations of making partner, and join firms planning to leave in two years."[14]

A Managing Partner of a national law firm suggested a very different explanation for why Generations X and Y may approach work differently than their predecessor generations:

> *There is something going on out there, but I think that one of the explanations is that they don't see an awful lot of loyalty from their employers to them.... The percentage of people making partner, at least equity partner in a law firm, I think, is going down. And I think that the explanation is that if you go to a firm and do good work, it isn't a reality any more. And*

that is going to affect...any kind of relationship. You are going to protect yourself and keep a little distance when you don't think that your loyalty and commitment is going to be reciprocated.

Understanding this generational change is critically important to the future strategic planning of any law firm. Equally significant is recognizing that this is not solely a gender-based distinction. For example, the study conducted for The Association of the Bar of the City of New York reported that younger associates were expressing concern that long hours and an unpredictable schedule comprised the norm of law firm life: "[I]n recent years, younger associates have mounted a more concerted attack on the prevailing norms, creating a generation gap at these firms."[15] The Study also noted the link between the generation gap and the gender gap due to the impact of the increasing number of women in the associate ranks: "Since these women now comprise a substantial proportion of entering associates, and since their ability to 'stay the course,' as one partner phrased it, is routinely threatened by the requirement that work take precedence over personal life, the firms must now seriously consider revisions in the previously inviolable work ethic."[16]

To discern the causes of both satisfaction and dissatisfaction within the legal profession, and to identify changes that could help lawyers find greater fulfillment in the law, the Boston Bar Association created the Task Force on Professional Fulfillment. The Task Force conducted sector-specific analyses (e.g., large law firm partners, large law firm associates, solo practitioners and small firms, in-house counsel, etc.), and reported several critical themes that emerged from all of the groups studied. Among the issues of concern identified were: [17]

1. the difficult balance among work, home, and community service;
2. the increasing measurement of and pressures for greater productivity;
3. the increasing commercialization and commoditization of the practice of law;
4. the increasing trend towards clients seeking lawyers to function as technicians, rather than counselors;
5. a growing sense of isolation;
6. lack of effective training and mentoring; and
7. the increasing debt burden which graduating law students carry with them into the profession.

All law firm managers should pay close attention to what these survey responses reveal: the top reasons which associates said would drive them to leave are wholly different from the retention strategies on which most law firms focus. So as law firms recruit on the basis of their competitive compensation and opportunities for upward mobility, associates are seeking greater control over their work schedules and a more family-friendly environment. Law firms can gain a tremendous competitive advantage by matching their retention strategies with these specific articulated concerns of associates.[18]

The simple fact is that law firms must realign to attract a new generation of lawyers who are unwilling to sacrifice their family responsibilities for their work. At the same time, firms must embrace proven and reliable business practices, such as: focusing on the development of a strong workforce; creating a sound management structure; and implementing policies and procedures that attract and retain a talented and diverse pool of attorneys.

Moreover, law firms must focus specifically on the significant gender gaps that exist in leadership positions, compensation, and the overall retention and advancement of women. Each firm has an obligation to develop clear strategies to remove the barriers that continue to thwart careers. In proposing a new metaphor for the more subtle and systemic discrimination that occurs today, authors Debra Meyerson and Joyce Fletcher state that: "It's not the ceiling that's holding women back; it's the whole structure of the organizations in which we work: the foundation, the beams, the walls, the very air."[19] In response, Meyerson and Fletcher propose a strategy of incremental changes that can be put into action quickly and are likely to lead to other changes that can: "…add up to a whole new system."[20]

For some firms, the "small wins" which Meyerson and Fletcher describe may be the only way to begin to address some of the more subtle forms of gender bias. However, for most law firms, incremental changes may be too slow an approach to spark the significant changes that are needed. In the competitive world of law firms, where behavior is easily emulated, meaningful change is more likely to be achieved by a courageous law firm which steps forward with a bold visionary agenda that will be a model for restructuring and re-energizing the profession.

The Managing Partner who noted the competitive advantage to be gained by the firm which "cracks the code" was correct in his assessment. Only, in reality, the code has already been cracked. The challenge for the profession is to translate the code by walking away from a centuries' old model of doing business and implementing the dramatic changes needed to lead the profession into the future.

Endnotes for Chapter 14

1. *See, e.g.*, Catalyst, Beyond A Reasonable Doubt: Building the Case for Flexibility 4 (2005), observing that: "[M]en and women associates with more positive perceptions of their firms' work-life culture (i.e., the observed norms, practices, and behaviours within the firm work environment that enhance or diminish associates' sense of support for work-life balance) intend to stay longer with their firms. This finding suggests that law firms that proactively address the work-life balance concerns of associates are capitalizing on a powerful lever for retention."

2. *See, e.g., It's the Manager, Stupid,* The Economist, (Aug. 8, 1998) at 54 *available at* 2005 TG A21000938.

3. *See, e.g.,* Sue Shellenbarger, *Companies are Finding It Really Pays to Be Nice to Employees,* Wall St. J., July 22, 1997, at B1. *See also* Diane E. Lewis, *Happy Right Here,* Boston Sunday Globe, July 17, 2005, at G1.

4. *See, e.g.*, Rosalind Chait Barnett, *Preface: Women and Work: Where Are We, Where Did We Come From, and Where Are We Going?*, 60 J. Soc. Issues 667 (2004).

5. *See, e.g.*, Penelope Trunk, *A New Generation Puts the Focus on Family,* Boston Globe, Apr. 17, 2005, at G1. *See also* Cunningham, *Father Time: Flexible Work Arrangements and the Law Firm's Failure of the Family,* 53 Stan. L. Rev. 967, 970 (Apr. 2001), which noted: "Faced with the stark view of what life in the law firm holds for them, many of today's law school graduates make employment decisions based not only on salary but also on quality-of-life considerations, such as a firm's personnel policies and work atmosphere. ... The old notion that associates must 'eat, breathe, and sleep' their work might not be as palatable to the new recruits as the old guard would like." *See also* Patricia Wen, *GenX Dad,* Boston Globe, Jan. 16, 2005, (Magazine), at 21.

6. *The State of the Legal Profession: 1990,* 1991 ABA Young Law. Div 55.

7. *The State of the Legal Profession: 1990,* 1991 ABA Young Law. Div 57. Also of interest, in a survey of associates conducted by *The American Lawyer,* even though 85% reported satisfaction with their compensation: "[O]nly about 27% of respondents said they expected to be at their current firms, either as a partner or associate, in five years." In this survey, interesting work and treatment by partners ranked as more important factors than compensation. Karen Hall, *Take the Money and Run,* The American Lawyer, (Oct. 2000), at 11-12.

8. C&R Research, *Pulse 2002: The State of the Legal Profession* 2002 ABA 21. This qualitative study was conducted as the result of a partnership between the ABA and C&R Research.

9. NALP Found., Keeping the Keepers II: Mobility& Management of Associates 16 (2003).

10. Generation & Gender in the Workplace, an issue brief by Families and Work Institute, American Business Collaboration, 5. (October, 2004). See also, Kathleen Dreessen, *The Work/Life Challenge: Not Just A Women's Issue,* (pts. 1 & 2), Diversity & The Bar, (Minority Corp. Couns. Assoc.), July/Aug. 2005; Diversity & The Bar, (Minority Corp. Couns. Assoc.), Sept./Oct. 2005.

11. *See* Paul D. Boynton, *Balancing Work & Family,* Mass. Law. Wkly., July 12, 1999. *See also* Carter, *A New Breed,* 87 ABA J. 37, 39 (Mar. 2001) which noted: "On the coasts and in the

middle of the country, law firms are dealing with accommodating the new lawyer, from salary increases to demands for training programs and alternative work arrangements geared to lifestyle."

12. Linda Bray Chanow, *Results of* Lawyers, Work & Family: A Study of Alternative Schedule Programs at Law Firms in the District of Columbia (2000), Women's Bar Assoc. D.C., Women's Bar Assoc. Found. D.C., and Am. U. Wash. Coll. of Law, Gender, Work and Family Proj. 9 (2000). *See also,* Williams, Unbending Gender: Why Family and Work Conflict and What to Do About It 273 (2000), noting that, unlike the earlier generation of successful women who: "had to act just like the men if they were to have any glimmer of a chance to succeed in 'a man's job,' many younger women feel a sense of entitlement to good jobs on their own terms." Williams further observed that both younger men and women: "want to put limits on work time in order to leave time for family life."

13. Chanow, *Results of* Lawyers, Work & Family: A Study of Alternative Schedule Programs at Law Firms in the District of Columbia (2000), Women's Bar Assoc. D.C., Women's Bar Assoc. Found. D.C., and Am. U. Wash. Coll. of Law, Gender, Work and Family Proj. 10 (2000).

14. *See* Chanow, *Results of* Lawyers, Work & Family: A Study of Alternative Schedule Programs at Law Firms in the District of Columbia (2000), Women's Bar Assoc. D.C., Women's Bar Assoc. Found. D.C., and Am. U. Wash. Coll. of Law, Gender, Work and Family Proj. 10 (2000).

15. Epstein, et al., *Glass Ceilings and Open Doors: Women's Advancement in the Legal Profession,* 64 Fordham L. Rev. 291, 389 (1995 Rpt. to The Assoc. B. City N.Y., Comm. Women Prof.). *See also* Nancy R. Baldiga, *Promoting Your Talent: A Guidebook for Women and Their Firms,* 2003 Am. Inst. Cert. Pub. Acct. 17, which noted: "No longer can firms argue that the desire for work/life balance is simply a women's issue or even a family issue. In fact, the search for balance is an issue for all professionals."

16. Epstein, et al., *Glass Ceilings and Open Doors: Women's Advancement in the Legal Profession,* 64 Fordham L. Rev. 291, 389-390 (1995 Rpt. to The Assoc. B. City N.Y., Comm. Women Prof.).

17. *See* BBA Task Force on Professional Fulfillment, Expectations, Reality And Recommendations For Change 4 (1997).

18. *See, e.g.,* Catalyst, Beyond A Reasonable Doubt: Building the Case for Flexibility (2005), noting: "But in an environment in which pay and advancement opportunities vary only marginally between one firm and another, policies that support associates' personal commitments and offer more control over their work may contribute to retaining top talent." At 6.

19. Debra E. Meyerson & Joyce K. Fletcher, *A Modest Manifesto for Shattering the Glass Ceiling,* Harv. Bus. Rev., Jan.-Feb. 2000, at 126, 136.

20. *See* Meyerson & Fletcher, *A Modest Manifesto for Shattering the Glass Ceiling,* Harv. Bus. Rev., Jan.-Feb. 2000, at 126, 136.

CHAPTER 15

"CRACKING THE CODE" BY CHANGING THE CULTURE

Few things matter more to the day-to-day life within a law firm than its culture. Each law firm has its own distinct culture which dramatically impacts the way that it conducts business and the lives of the lawyers who work there each day. A firm's culture can be as palpable as the unique, distinct atmosphere that exists on different college campuses: it is a feeling that can be seen from the way people talk about the institution and the way they treat each other.

A management consultant to law firms wrote: "A firm's culture may be its greatest strength for determining and achieving its immediate and longer-term objectives. However, that culture may be its greatest weakness if it is bound to (1) outdated traditions ('because we've always done it this way'), (2) management styles that are dysfunctional and inconsistent with the desires and expectations of a majority of the partners and with the needs and priorities of the firm, or (3) outdated philosophies of senior or even departed partners that are inconsistent with the marketing and compensation programs required to compete aggressively with other financially successful, proactive law firms."[1]

Many of the practitioners interviewed for this book emphasized that the profession needs more than incremental changes. Rather, they advocated for changes in firm culture that would lead to a new institutional model. A prominent attorney who left private practice summarized the feeling of many when she stated:

> *The saddest thing is that nothing has changed. So what do you change? I don't think you can make change under the current model.*

The model cannot change unless the culture changes first. To do so successfully requires that the partners of the firm look within and "[r]each a consensus ...about the kind of culture that they want for the firm. Then, develop a plan detailing how to achieve these goals, with partner responsibility for putting practical components of the plan into action, along with designated dates for status reports and implementation."[2]

A senior partner of a large Western law firm spoke passionately about his law firm's extraordinary efforts to maintain a culture of teamwork and mutual support:

> *A culture is the DNA of any firm. Too many businesses, law firms, corporate industries, whatever, don't realize the incredible significance of a culture....*

> *And you don't walk in one day and declare what a culture is. It's the value system of the people in the business. And that's what creates the culture: when you create value systems that appreciate a nice place to work, strong work ethic, no egos, no jerks. And that permeates the system when you hire people.... We always tell people when they come to work for us, "It's got to feel like a place that's comfortable for you."*

An East Coast Managing Partner spoke of his law firm's culture as "the glue" which binds the firm together through good and bad times:

> *Any firm is going to have good times and less good times.... There are certain cycles to it under any circumstances; you're at the mercy of forces that are larger than you are. Under the best of circumstances, unless you've got something that's holding you together in the tougher times, you are not a firm. You are not a partnership. You're an economic unit.*

> *We attract these very, very talented people who want to practice law in a certain way, and there's a self-selection.*

In a study of alternative partnership structures, an American Bar Association report noted the importance of culture: "A growing understanding of organizational cultures has important implications for organizing and managing law firms."[3] Of importance, culture is transmitted in a variety of subtle way. The Boston Bar Association Task Force on Professional Challenges and Family Needs observed: "Much of a firm's culture and values are transmitted in casual conversations during which partners and associates characterize themselves or the firm relative to other lawyers and firms."[4]

Accordingly, if a firm wants to begin to change its culture, it needs to look carefully at its own internal language. For example, the BBA Task Force noted that firms frequently describe themselves as a "meritocracy," yet it is a term which can actually have a negative impact on a firm's culture.[5] When a firm describes itself as a meritocracy, its real message is that lawyers succeed by working exceptionally long hours to demonstrate dedication and commitment to the firm. A law firm which speaks with pride of its "culture of meritocracy," generally does not recognize dedication to the needs of one's family as part of that culture.[6]

Law firms committed to changing their culture will carefully examine the language they use, whether it's in their own marketing materials, in casual conversations, or in internal meetings, as it is those self-descriptions which reveal the culture of the firm and what it values most. As noted experts on work-life issues stated: "Transformation of the corporate culture seems to be a prerequisite for success on the work-life front."[7]

Because each firm's culture pervades the atmosphere within the workplace and impacts individual behavior, any effort to introduce structural change without addressing the underlying culture will fail. However, once such changes are introduced at the highest levels, the results can be dramatic. Deloitte's Initiative for the Retention and Advancement of Women is an impressive example of how a change in culture revolutionized the firm's opportunities for women. As one of the largest professional services firms in the world, Deloitte understood that results can only be achieved if progress is measured. In the early 1990s, the company identified and then began to address two challenges which posed significant, measurable costs (1) women were leaving the firm at a much faster rate than men; and (2) the company projected that, by the year 2000, women would comprise approximately 60% of new accountants entering the profession.[8] In other words, the changing demographics posed a threat to the future of the company. If addressed, however, the company faced great opportunity.

In response, the then Chief Executive Officer and Chairman of Deloitte & Touche, LLP, Mike Cook, initiated a dramatic program to reverse the attrition trend and to develop opportunities to advance women. The effort began with a methodical investigation and data collection process, followed by two-day workshops for the company's approximately 5,000 management professionals to supplement the hard data with a more direct analysis of the impact of gender attitudes on Deloitte's workplace environment. From there, the company developed a system of accountability by which changes could be measured.[9] With a clear focus, strong commitment and leadership from the highest levels of the organization, Deloitte's Initiative for the Retention and Advancement of Women has become a national model of how a professional services organization can revolutionize its workplace.

The Deloitte experience teaches that cultural change must start at the highest levels of the organization, and its goals must then be inculcated into every employee's day-to-day operations. Deloitte succeeds by creating a culture of firm-wide accountability.[10] As important, the company does not allow itself to become complacent. When progress in one area seems stalled, it unveils a new initiative to address it.[11] A former partner of a large law firm spoke admiringly of the very public and specific commitments the accounting firm has made, particularly with respect to its articulated goals and established milestones to increase the percentage of women partners:

> *That's a very public commitment.... [W]hen they did their full-page ad in the New York Times tribute to their departing chairman, they noted his leadership on many fronts. One of the things that they noted was his leadership on the advancement of women, which said to me that the advancement of women has been inculcated into the value system of Deloitte. If the marketing people knew to put it in the ad copy, that said a lot to me. If I were an accountant, I would be working at Deloitte.*

A senior partner, whose firm prides itself on its commitment to maintaining a strong culture of teamwork, stated:

> *We have a range of people that basically have a bottom-line commitment to the culture of the firm. I think that we've seen other firms fail, you know, the extreme, where it's personality-driven and eat-what-you-kill.... Conversely, those that have a strong culture, where there is a congenial working atmosphere,*

have tended to hold [together]. Even in some cases
where the economics have not been great.

She added that laterals coming to her firm from other law firms sometimes take two to three years before they fully acclimate to their culture of
teamwork and collegiality.

For many law firms, a fruitful way to begin the process of changing the
firm's culture is through a strategic planning process. At its best, strategic
planning can be a tool to obtain attorney support and consensus for a set of
core values and a firm mission that can set the law firm's course for the next
three to five years. An important component of such a process should be the
implementation of a firm-wide effort to recruit and promote women, ensuring
a "critical mass" at all levels of the organization. This means including
women in the highest levels of management who are willing to use their
authority to secure cultural changes that will make a difference for future generations.[12]

The ABA Commission on Women in the Profession stressed the importance of law firms creating: "a strategic plan that ensures that women attorneys are recruited, trained, retained, and promoted at the same rate as their
male colleagues."[13] In fact, the Commission suggests that firms develop a
mission statement on inclusivity, distribute that statement throughout the firm,
and include it on the firm's intranet and internet websites. Further, the Commission recommended the creation of a strategic plan on gender inclusivity,
articulating time frames, goals, objectives, and measurements, and providing
a budget allocation for implementation.[14]

On the other hand, strategic planning can be a recipe for disaster if it is
simply presented to the partners as the result of the labors of a small group,
rather than a more complex process which involves the entire firm in its development. In today's competitive marketplace, each law firm should be able to
articulate its core values, its vision for the future, and its goals. The difficulty,
of course, is reconciling the many varying perspectives that will be expressed
in a strategic planning process, and bringing them together into a cohesive
plan. A good plan can provide opportunities for lawyer flexibility and individual growth; a great plan will motivate and excite the entire firm.

However, it is critical to distinguish between thoughtful strategic growth
and the competitive decisions that are driven by external factors. For example,
for more than two decades, there has been a dramatic increase in media coverage of law firms, in which the primary focus is the firm's economic success
and competitive rankings. The question must be asked: To what extent are law

firms driven by publicized rankings or other artificially created measures which rely on profits-per-partner as the crucial criteria?

Years ago, if there was any coverage of lawyers or law firms, it was generally incidental to more in-depth articles about their clients. Today, lawyers are the story and their firm activities are often reported as though they were sporting events. Recently, a major publication for the legal profession reported that a particular law firm "hasn't yet made the major leagues" with respect to "the world of big-ticket M&A" deals, because the firm ranked *only* "seventy-fourth based on value of deals, with a total of $4.75 billion."[15] This type of reporting creates an artificial competition, driving the firm to increase the value of its deals, with wide-ranging ramifications. The story also reported that, in its strategic planning process, the firm included as one of its "fundamentals" the importance of "[b]ecoming more explicit about the expectation that partners log 2,400 hours a year, with 1,900 hours of that billable time."[16]

Ultimately, law firms will need to become smarter about the way they integrate their strategic thinking with their competitive positioning. It is not a sustainable long-term strategy, and it makes for an unbearable culture, to increase revenue through hourly rates and increased hours alone. In observing that professional services firms lack sophistication regarding "the notion of aligning competitive strategies with a firm's culture," marketing expert Suzanne Lowe urges firms to manage their culture to "achieve a strategic, market-focused goal."[17] This means looking inward as well as outward to ensure compatibility between what a firm is and what it ultimately wants to be.

However, part of the focus requires a strategic planning process which reconciles a growth strategy consistent with a workplace that values individual contributions. Culture is the place where strategic planning, workforce development, and law firm economics meet. Firms cannot achieve a more diverse workforce and continue to attract top law students through a culture that demands a uniform billable-hour contribution from everyone. The recognition of individual contributions is a management challenge which, if met, will reap tremendous dividends, and ultimately will help law firms achieve their strategic vision through the more effective utilization of multiple talents.

Of course, the critical question is whether today's large law firms are capable of changing their culture. When the Managing Partner of a firm known for its teamwork was asked that question, he responded by noting that:

> *The thing you cannot do is, you cannot walk into*
> *a room full of 300 people and say, 'By the way, we*
> *have a new culture.' This is not what causes culture.*

It's the value system of people.... [To change culture]
takes a long, long time.

His point is critical to any firm willing to take the steps that will result in cultural change: a firm's heart and soul can be found in its value system and that is how its culture will be defined. All law firms value economic success. However, do they also value their employees? Do leaders in the firm have an interest in how the lawyers feel about coming to work each day and the atmosphere in which they are practicing? Do law firm managers promote a system of teamwork that operates not only to bring in new business but also to support the entire legal staff once the work is in the door?

Clearly, each day and in countless ways, law firms reinforce their own internal culture. In order to change, law firm leaders must recognize the messages they send and then check whether these messages conform to the cultural ideal they want to create. Then comes the really hard part: changing the messages and the behaviors to develop, over time, a new model.

Endnotes for Chapter 15

1. Joel A. Rose, *Is Your Firm's Culture an Asset or a Liability?*, Of Counsel, April 2005, at 5. Lawyer/author Walter Bennett observed: "It may well be that one key to envisioning a new profession for the twenty-first century is for lawyers, men and women, to begin to see their lives and work in a less linear mode and more open to change and *in*direction." Walter Bennett, The Lawyer's Myth: Reviving Ideals in the Legal Profession 167 (2001).

2. Joel A. Rose, *Is Your Firm's Culture an Asset or a Liability?*, Of Counsel, April 2005, at 6.

3. ABA Sec. Econ. L. Prac, Two-tier Partnerships and Other Alternatives: Five Approaches, 59 (1986).

4. BBA Task Force on Prof. Challenges and Family Needs, Facing the Grail: Confronting the Cost of Work-Family Imbalance 36 (1999). The Task Force noted, for example, that the words firms choose to define themselves, (*e.g.*, such as "entrepreneurial" or "tough and aggressive") help create the firm's identity.

5. BBA Task Force on Prof. Challenges and Family Needs, Facing the Grail: Confronting the Cost of Work-Family Imbalance 36 (1999).

6. BBA Task Force on Prof. Challenges and Family Needs, Facing the Grail: Confronting the Cost of Work-Family Imbalance 36-37 (1999).

7. Hewlett and Lyce, *Off-Ramps and On-Ramps: Keeping Talented Women on the Road to Success*, Harv. Bus. Rev., Mar. 2005, at 52.

8. *See The Year in Review,* Deloitte & Touche Team Bull., May, 1994, at 7.

9. *See,* Douglas M. McCracken, *Winning the Talent War for Women: Sometimes it Takes a Revolution,* Harv. Bus. Rev., (Reprint R00611) (Nov./Dec. 2000). The article highlighted key lessons from Deloitte's Women's Initiative: Make sure senior management is front and center; make an airtight business case for cultural change; let the world watch you; begin with dialogue as the platform for change; use a flexible system of accountability, and promote work-life balance for men and women. At 7. For more in-depth information regarding Deloitte's efforts, see, Rosabeth Moss Kanter & Jane Roessner, *Deloitte & Touche (A): A Hole in the Pipeline,* Harv. U. Bus. Sch. 9-300-012, (May 2, 2003) and *Deloitte & Touche (B): Changing the Workplace 9-300-013,* (May 2, 2003).

10. An article in *Workforce* captures Deloitte's internal mechanisms for success: "The performance management system links mentoring, counseling, performance feedback, and career planning so that individuals realize that hosting and participating in mentoring is staunchly supported throughout the company. Finally, the firm emphasizes accountability. Each practice and region completes a Women's Initiative Plan annually. This has firm-wide goals and benchmarks for measuring progress against such statistics as female headcount, turnover, gender gap, female promotions, percentage of flexible work arrangements, and women partners in leadership positions." Charlen Marmer Solomon, *Cracks in the Glass Ceiling,* Workforce, Sept. 2000, at 87, 89 *available at* http://condor.depaul.edu/~mwilson/extra/discover/glassceil.html (Oct. 2, 2003).

11. For example, when Deloitte saw that, despite its success in admitting new women partners, women were not achieving leadership roles at the same rate as men, the company created a week-long program for those women partners identified as future leaders. Within a year

after their first program, 65% of the participants were promoted to a leadership position in the firm. Charlen Marmer Solomon, *Cracks in the Glass Ceiling*, Workforce, Sept. 2000, at 87, 90 *available at* http://condor.depaul.edu/~mwilson/extra/discover/glassceil.html (Oct. 2, 2003).

12. ABA Comm'n Women in the Prof., Empowerment and Leadership: Tried and True Methods for Women Lawyers 13 (2003).

13. ABA Comm'n Women in the Prof., Walking the Talk - Creating a Law Firm Culture Where Women Succeed 5 (2004).

14. ABA Comm'n Women in the Prof., Walking the Talk - Creating a Law Firm Culture Where Women Succeed 13-14 (2004). Strategic Planning should also assist associates in planning their careers, a tool which could be particularly helpful in stemming unwanted attrition by creating a culture which supports individual growth and development. See, e.g., Amy Sladczyk Hancock and Cordell Parvin, *What Firms Can Do to Help Associates Take Responsibility for Their Careers*, NALP Bull., Nov. 2004, noting that firms should provide: "an alignment of leadership, purposes, strategy, core values, culture, and systems that includes goal setting." At 6.

15. Susan Beck, *3 Arrows and a Diagram*, The American Lawyer, Mar. 2005, at 105. Of interest, an ABA Task Force noted that historically, and until well into the 1960s: "A salient feature of law practice, large or small, in this period was the professional sensibility for keeping to one's self not only a client's confidences, but also firm information as to finances, billing, income, relations with clients, or firm operations. Discreetness was the rule." ABA Sec. Legal Educ. and Adm. Bar, Legal Education and Professional Development - An Educational Continuum, Report of The Task Force on Law Schools and the Profession: Narrowing the Gap 77 (1992).

16. *See, e.g.*, Beck, *Three Arrows and a Diagram*, The American Lawyer, Mar. 2005, at 102.

17. Suzanne C. Lowe, Marketplace Masters: How Professional Service Firms Compete to Win 11 (2004).

CHAPTER 16

LEADERSHIP MATTERS

Leadership and culture are inextricably entwined. A great leader can dramatically improve culture, just as a poor leader can drain energy and enthusiasm from the firm. Jim Collins wrote that every "good-to-great" company he studied had the benefit of a "Level 5" leader, that is, someone at the helm who was building: "enduring greatness through a paradoxical blend of personal humility and professional will."[1] Critically important to his description of these key individuals is the way they lead with a combination of fierce will, yet humble modesty. As Collins noted, their ambition is not directed toward themselves, but at building a great institution. In a profession with a long history of individual, rather than team, emphasis, this is a critical transition for law firm managers to make.

An ABA report on alternative partnership models referred to law firm leadership as the critical foundation on which a positive culture can be built.[2] Similarly, a New York State Bar Association official wrote: "One of the key factors differentiating present and future leaders promises to be the firms' ability to adopt approaches to change that differ profoundly from the way they have managed the practice in the past. This approach challenges the most prevalent law firm management culture that relies on management by consensus...."[3]

Invariably, when interviewees were asked about changes that could make a significant difference for them in their law firm, they described a desire for open communication with leaders who were engaged in the business of management. Communications expert Suzanne Bates noted that: "Leading is all about communicating. The leader's job is generally not to *do*; it is to communicate what is to be done. People must see, hear, feel, and believe in the vision. They must see, hear, and believe in *you*. You are the message and the message is you."[4]

An *ABA Journal* article linked one firm's dramatic success to, in part, its enhanced internal communications established by the leadership of the firm's female Managing Partner. The article noted that by increasing internal communications via emails, memos, and meetings, all lawyers had equal access to key information: "Besides generally being a smart way to run an operation, it is less likely to leave women out of the loop, so that they can better position themselves for leadership roles should they so choose."[5]

In its detailed report analyzing the barriers to success in large law firms, the Minority Corporate Counsel Association stated that law firms must do a better job managing people. The report specifically noted: "Those who lead departments and manage the performance evaluation process must be particularly vigilant about encouraging inclusive workplaces and ensuring that exclusionary tactics do not occur."[6]

Management experts Patrick McKenna and David Maister emphasize that professional service managers must take an interest in the members of their group, and recommend that leaders informally "check in" with their people. They urge the importance of understanding when personal issues may be causing distractions, noting that: "[Y]ou cannot build a successful business enterprise if everyone always stays in role and deals with everyone else solely on a functional, logical, rational basis....The reality is that you cannot separate the human being from the performer."[7]

McKenna and Maister further state: "Group leaders, as player-coaches, must give up some portion of the client or production work they were trained to do, are certainly skilled at, and probably find deeply satisfying. For what? The chance to deal with the emotions of their colleagues. The responsibility to be the one to let people know they could do better. The obligation to resolve conflicts and crises. All of which requires skills that no one ever trained you for."[8] But, they add, the benefits are significant: "There is also the comfort and satisfaction that comes from knowing that you have made a difference in people's lives. That you have helped them accomplish more than they ever dreamed that they could. That you helped people understand themselves more deeply and more accurately, and helped them find a path in professional life that would play to their special strengths."[9]

Several interviewees offered examples of good management which resulted in an improved culture in their law firms. For example, one retired partner distinguished her firm's current Managing Partner from his indecisive predecessor:

> *He is decisive. He will listen and he makes a decision. It may not be a decision you like, but at least it is a decision. His predecessor was not a good decision-maker. Things dragged and he wouldn't think about it, and then he would make a decision and*

somebody said, 'I don't like that.' Then he would reconsider it. It was just terrible.

Another former associate spoke with admiration of the Managing Partner at the firm where she had worked:

When he was Managing Partner, he would walk the halls, I don't know if he was on his way some- where, or if he just did that, but he would look in your office and say hello. He was just so easy going and friendly. He knew your name, where you went to school. He always made a connection....

Just as Managing Partners have a critical role in contributing to the cul- ture of a law firm, Practice Group Managers similarly are critical to the effec- tive implementation of the firm's overall goals and strategic vision. Experts at Hildebrandt International, Inc. wrote that the modern job description for today's Practice Group Leader includes:[10]

1. overall leadership and direction for the group, including strategic planning;
2. work load management and attorney utilization;
3. quality control;
4. training and professional development;
5. forms, systems, and procedures;
6. financial management;
7. knowledge management; and
8. business development.

A senior litigator effusively described the management qualities of one of her firm's Practice Group Leaders:

[He] is an exquisite manager. He is great.... He brings in the business and makes sure that the other guys who are on his team, this one gets client X, this one gets client B, so there is no competition. [Part- ners in his practice group] felt there was a future, they felt that he was behind them. He was. He made

sure that when it's compensation time, he looks at the relative seniority, he looks at the relative book of business, and they by and large feel like they are treated pretty fairly. And I think they are, too. He also took a very active role in saying when these people are in the partnership lineup, when he can have another partner in the group, whose turn is it. And that is very unusual. In other groups, whoever the team leader is, he is just trying to grab every case for himself, not trying to spread things around. Not thinking about succession issues, for example, which I think is a serious issue.

Many interviewees craved direct communications about their own career progress. The former senior associate, whose mentor wrote her a note to reprimand her for being too "defensive" during their discussion, spoke of conversations she longed to have had at her law firm:

I think I would have said that there needs to be more of an open dialogue between partners and associates. There needs to be more communication, meaningful [communication]. If people have a desire to make things better, or a concern, there ought to be a safe place to air those concerns.... The message I was sent was: 'By questioning how things are here, you are being disloyal and you don't realize how good you have it.' I think, in fact, the opposite is true ... I think [name of law firm] is a great law firm.... I think the quality of law practiced by the bulk of the people there is excellent. I think they're very good to their clients (most people, not all, most), and it's because I believe it can be a better place that I would bother to speak up.

So when someone is speaking up, it's not to vent. It's not to be a thorn in your side, but it's really a sign of loyalty, a sign of caring, and a sign of being invested in a place. And I guess that would be the overarching message that I would want them to hear.

And then there are all kinds of specifics about departmental jobs or how associates are trained which is: associates aren't really trained, they're just kind of run into the fire. And that can be made better.

As analyzed in Chapter 3, a significant example of a leadership void in most law firms can be found in the way legal work is assigned. Law firm managers must ensure that assignments are fairly distributed and that women are provided opportunities to do high-profile work. The ABA Commission on Women in the Profession noted that, because assigning attorneys play a critical role in determining the career paths of lawyers, they should be held accountable through the compensation structure. The implementation of a formal work assignment system which designates partners to assume leadership in and oversight of the process significantly enhances the opportunities for greater equity in the nature of the work which women are assigned.[11]

The link between strong law firm management and a successful firm is always important, but it is particularly crucial if the firm is about to implement significant changes.[12] In the decentralized world of law firm partners, law firm leaders must take special care to open lines of communication as they attempt to move the firm in a new direction. As Rosabeth Moss Kanter stated: "Leaders must sense what the content will handle and then pick the rhythm of change that appears right for their organization."[13]

In reality, the dilemma women have faced for the last several decades is that their advancement has been limited by their exclusion from the internal sources of power. As the former president of Barnard College observed: "The overall situation for women and the limits on their advancement will not be satisfactorily resolved until women are admitted to the inner circles of power. In law firms, that means that women not only need to be made partners, and in greater numbers than is the case now, but, of equal importance, women need to be placed on the executive and management committees of their firms. It is also important for women to head various practice groups at their firms."[14]

This perspective was recently echoed by the President of the District of Columbia Bar Association. He noted that women leaders are critical to the successful recruitment of other women lawyers: "...it is important to be able to demonstrate that hard work brings promotion and achievement, and that is best demonstrated by showing every newly hired woman that other women are already occupying important management positions."[15]

As the chair of the Defense Research Institute's Task Force On Women Who Try Cases wrote: "Once promoted to partnership, women attorneys also should be given the opportunity...to assume positions on their management committees."[16] She added that women should be involved in all levels of: "leadership positions that are substantive, not just stereotypical (such as serving on the recruiting committee)."[17] The Managing Partner of a Western law firm recognized that a firm which operates under the corporate model needs better criteria for selecting managers then to simply appoint key rainmakers:

> *We have a Board of Directors. We call it a Board by design to make it sound like corporate America. We believe in centralized management. We have long ago made the decision that we do not appoint people who are the most senior or the most powerful, if I can use that word, in business development as managers. We don't care what color you are or what gender you are, what age you are. If you are a great manager, that is who we are going to put in the position.*
>
> *So we have some fantastic women leaders, okay? They evolve up even though they are much younger. They have tremendous power in their roles. We have young men too...who may lead key positions.... You've got to ferret out the best managers. And we move people around through committees by design to let people observe them.*

He then highlighted the critical distinguishing features of good leaders:

> *Leaders are picked by the people. And they are picked because they trust them as being fair. They don't think they have big egos. They think they have great business judgment, and they are unselfish. And if you're selfish, and you have a big ego and you are not good at management, you are never going to be a leader.*

A senior partner, who has been with the same major law firm throughout his four decades of legal practice, expressed a compatible vision:

> *Over the years I've observed that the approach of the most successful people is: "If anything goes wrong, it's my fault; and if it goes right, it's the people who are working for me."*

Strong firm leadership plays a critical role in addressing bias, the longer the history of commitment, the better the firm's results. As noted in an article in *The American Lawyer:* "A firm's success in promoting diversity today typically correlates with having had a leader with vision years ago."[18] Among those interviewed for this book, the perception was universal that, unless firm leaders take an active, day-to-day role in improving opportunities for the retention and advancement of women, then the profession will be poorly equipped to address the challenges posed by the changing demographics within law schools and the workforce.[19]

The ABA Commission on Women in the Profession stated that it is important to examine an organization's leadership selection systems and criteria to ensure a democratic and participatory process, maximizing opportunities for women to serve in a leadership role.[20] As Heim and Murphy reported: "Study after study find that women outscore men in most management categories. According to one investigation of about 6,400 managers of which nearly 2,000 were female, researchers found that the women did better than the men on 28 of 30 management skill areas including problem solving, planning, controlling, managing relationships, leading, and communicating."[21]

The in-depth study of gender, racial, and ethnic bias in the federal courts of the First Circuit, undertaken by Task Forces of the First Circuit United States Court of Appeals, offers recommendations for ensuring fair treatment and promoting gender, racial, and ethnic equality in the courts. These recommendations are instructive for a strong management team willing to implement parallel approaches to address issues of bias in a law firm.[22] Extrapolating from the recommendations in the First Circuit's report, Managing Partners could:

1. encourage intervention of firm leadership when inappropriate remarks are made or other examples of gender inequality are observed;

2. educate all firm personnel to raise awareness of the issues (for example, respectful workplace training programs for mentors, diversity programs, etc.);

3. Institute a formal grievance procedure to investigate aggressively complaints of bias or misconduct;

4. develop a system to periodically monitor and to check for indicia of bias;

5. adjust compensation for those who have acted inappropriately; and

6. explicitly commit to increasing the number of women in the partnership and in leadership positions.

Ultimately, law firm leadership requires accountability: managers must be held accountable for defined goals around the recruitment, retention, and promotion of women and their ability to achieve those goals. As Susan Estrich noted: "How do companies change? Very simply. People with power use that power to demand better; they insist on results, and they get them."[23]

The importance of a strategic program that measures the success of each law firm leader's efforts to recruit, train, retain, and promote women cannot be overstated. A recent publication of the American Bar Association Commission on Women in the Profession emphasized: "Progress is accelerated if partners 'own' the success of a gender equity plan in ways that can be tracked. Systems that create partner accountability for the success of the plan through either compensation or evaluation reviews are proven tools for ensuring appropriate leadership on the effort as well as a consistent message on the importance of the plan."[24] Current compensation models present a distorted picture by, for example, measuring revenue generation without looking at each partner's role in costs relating to attrition. As the study of alternative scheduling in the District of Columbia observed: "[P]artners should be held accountable for their role in promoting a supportive atmosphere."[25]

An interviewee in the attorney placement industry highlighted the importance of implementing management incentives to encourage change:

> *In corporate America, people are incentivized for hiring women and minorities. They see it in their bottom line. They see it in their compensation. There's no reason why, in law firms, people couldn't be incentivized to do better in terms of retention and in terms of trying to make things work for a group of people.*

It is also critical that good leaders think about their own succession. Building great leadership in any organization is a long-term process and needs to be an ongoing part of the firm's leadership development culture. A manager of a large law firm explained their system for identifying future leaders: the senior management in the firm conducts annual interviews with all of the firm's partners as part of the compensation process. A number of years ago, he noted, they added an unusual question:

> *What would you do if you walked in on Monday morning and were told that [the senior leadership of the firm] were all killed...and we've got to replace the Executive Committee because the banks want to know, the clients want to know, the staff wants to know, and the lawyers want to know. Who are those people?*

He added that most attempted to defer the question until they had an opportunity to think further, but the senior leaders were insistent on getting each partner's gut reaction. Based on the names most frequently mentioned, they developed a list and began to assign those top individuals to different positions, in order to test their leadership skills. By the next time that question was again posed to all the partners a number of years later, the list had nearly doubled, providing a fertile pool from which to develop future key leaders, including a number of women.

A leader should also be able to apologize for mistakes and then correct them. When Lawrence Summers was under attack in the media and by members of the Harvard faculty for his speech suggesting that the shortage of female scientists might, in part, be attributed to innate differences between men and women, he moved quickly and decisively to atone, and more importantly, make a change. He appointed not one, but two task forces to focus on ways in which the University could improve its recruitment of women and support careers of female scholars, particularly in the areas of science and engineering. He also announced plans to create a senior position to focus on the recruitment and advancement of women on the faculty. When the two task forces released their reports, he then pledged $50 million dollars over a 10-year period for the implementation of the recommendations. He even appointed a long-time critic as the new Dean of the Graduate School of Arts and Sciences.[26] His dogged and visible efforts ultimately resulted in a turning point, ending the wave of negative publicity.[27]

The fact is, Summers turned his disaster into a "teachable moment."[28] The moment extended to the numerous articles which followed, offering informed debate about the basis for observed differences between men and women. Critically, other leaders also stepped up to address the issue. For example, the presidents of three major research universities wrote of the need to create a culture, as well as policies, to help working mothers "strike a sustainable balance between the workplace and home."[29] The lesson to be learned is that leadership can include a willingness to demonstrate publicly that you have learned from your mistakes, providing an important opportunity for reflection and teaching.

Finally, and probably most significantly, leaders should inspire confidence, which is the fundamental underpinning of success. Harvard Business School Professor Rosabeth Moss Kanter emphasized the importance of confidence and its influence on positive outcomes: "The fundamental task of leaders is to develop confidence in advance of victory, in order to attract the investments that make victory possible: money, talent, support, loyalty, attention, effort, or people's best thinking."[30]

Perhaps there can be no more crucial role for a law firm leader than to demonstrate confidence in the entire firm's ability to invest in each other's success in a way that "creates positive momentum" for everyone. If confidence can positively influence how we invest our time and energy, then law firm leaders can have a major impact by creating a culture of support for women that will have a positive reverberation throughout the firm.

These are but some of the critical elements of effective leadership. Law firms, however, have an additional set of hurdles to overcome. Law firm partners must relinquish the mixed messages to, and impossible demands made upon, those entrusted with the management of the firm. That means accepting certain realities of today's law practice.

Those with significant responsibilities for firm management must be compensated for their labors. The successful management of a group of people requires both appropriate compensation and an allotment of time to perform the duties of the role, not as an adjunct to other responsibilities, but as a key element of one's day.

Critically, in today's complex economy and sophisticated legal environment, managing a law firm is a full-time job. It takes time for leaders to grow into their positions. The frequent rotation of senior partners through key management roles ensures a caretaker position, at best, rather than the bold visionary leadership that emerges from someone expected to produce in that position over a significant period of time.

In essence, law firms must leave behind their ad hoc ways of management. In its place, they need to develop leadership models for the future of which a critical component is an unwavering commitment to the retention and promotion of women into key positions throughout the firm.

Endnotes for Chapter 16

1.   Jim Collins, Good to Great 20 (2001).

2.   Heintz and Markham-Bugbee, *Two-tier Partnerships and Other Alternatives: Five Approaches*, 1986 ABA Sec. Econ. L. Prac. 59. *See also* ABA Comm'n Women in the Prof., Empowerment and Leadership: Tried and True Methods for Women Lawyers 13 (2003): "An organization's workplace environment is largely shaped by the policies and practices that the partnership or CEO endorses. These practices - both formal and informal - have a critical impact on the organization's overall culture."

3.   Stephen P. Gallagher, *Family v. Career: More Lawyers Caught in the Middle*, N.Y.St. Bar Assoc., State Bar News, July/Aug. 1999, 14.

4.   Suzanne Bates, Speak Like a CEO: Secrets for Commanding Attention and Getting Results 4 (2005).

5.   Carter, *Paths Need Paving*, 86 ABA J. 34, 39 (Sept. 2000).

6.   Minority Corp. Counsel Assoc., The Myth of the Meritocracy: A Report on the Bridges and Barriers to Success in Large Law Firms, 2003 MCCA Pathways 48, *available at* http://www.mcca.com/site/data/researchprograms/PurplePathways/index.html.

7.   McKenna & Maister, FIrst Among Equals 52 (2002).

8.   McKenna & Maister, FIrst Among Equals 259 (2002).

9.   McKenna & Maister, FIrst Among Equals 261 (2002).

10.   Susan Raridon Lambreth & Amanda J.Yanuklis, *Practice Groups - Selecting the Most Effective Partners as Leaders*, Hildebrant Int'l, at http://www.hildebrandt.com/Documents.aspx?Doc_ID=1062 (Dec. 8, 2005). This article further noted that ideal qualities for today's practice group leader include: credibility; integrity; organizational skills; the ability to build teams; flexibility; strong interpersonal and communication skills; the ability to motivate; commitment; and business acumen.

11.   ABA Comm'n Women in the Prof., Empowerment and Leadership: Tried and True Methods for Women Lawyers 34-35 (2003).

12.   *See, e.g.*, Heintz and Markham-Bugbee, *Two-tier Partnerships and Other Alternatives: Five Approaches*, 1986 ABA Sec. Econ. L. Prac. 74: "Leadership within a firm is of utmost importance during a significant change. If a firm's leaders are positive and consistent during a change, others will eventually give support."

13.   Rosabeth Moss Kanter, *The Rhythm of Change*, Women's Bus., Apr. 2001, at 16, 17 as excerpt from Rosabeth Moss Konter, eVolve! Succeeding in the Digital Culture of Tomorrow (2001).

14.   Ellen V. Futter, *Women Professionals: The Slow Rise to The Top*, 57 Fordham L. Rev. 965, 965 (1989). *See also* Bailyn et al., Work-Family Policy Network, MIT Sch. Mgmt., Integrating Work and Family Life: A Holistic Approach 50 (2001): "The fastest way of elevating the priorities assigned to work and family issues is for corporate leaders to reflect the demographic profile of their staff."

15. John C. Cruden, *The Case for More Women Leaders in the Profession,* Washington Lawyer, November 2005, 7 *available at* http://www.dcbar.org/for_lawyers/washington_lawyer/november_2005/president.cfm.

16. Shelley Hammond Provosty, *DRI Task Force Examines the Status of Women Litigators at Law Firms,* Of Counsel, July 2005 at 7.

17. Shelley Hammond Provosty, *DRI Task Force Examines the Status of Women Litigators at Law Firms,* Of Counsel, July 2005 at 7.

18. Vivia Chen, *Cracks in the Ceiling,* The American Lawyer, June 2003, at 76, 77-78.

19. In a book detailing the rise of Skadden, Arps, Slate, Meagher & Flom, prominent partner Joseph Flom, on the occasion of the law firm's 40th anniversary, was quoted as saying: "We must remember that the history of major institutions is that they are not permanent. The only permanence comes from what you make of it, or what the institution makes of itself. If it becomes a dinosaur, it will disappear." Lincoln Caplan, Skadden: Power, Money, and the Rise of a Legal Empire 13 (1993).

20. ABA Comm'n Women in the Prof., The Unfinished Agenda: Women and the Legal Profession 34 (2001), further cautioning that selection criteria for key decision-making positions should not give undo weight to business development as a criteria: "Both women and firms can benefit from adequate consideration of other leadership capabilities, particularly interpersonal skills."

21. Heim et al., In the Company of Women 250 (2003).

22. U.S. Ct. App., 1st Cir., Report of the First Circuit Gender, Race and Ethnic Bias Task Forces (1999). The report's specific recommendations for promoting gender equality in the courts were: "(1) Encourage judges to intervene when inappropriate remarks are made; (2) Educate judges and court personnel/raise awareness of the problem; (3) Institute a formal grievance procedure for complaints of bias or misconduct; (4) Develop a system to periodically monitor court cases to check for bias; (5) Punish/fine people who violate others' rights because of their gender; (6) Increase the number of female court employees; and (7) Monitor whether members of the jury reflect the gender of litigants." At 129.

23. Estrich, Sex & Power 142 (2000).

24. ABA Comm'n Women in the Prof., Walking the Talk - Creating a Law Firm Culture Where Women Succeed 8 (2004). The report recommends that baseline measurements be created as an essential tool in judging success and includes a model self assessment questionnaire which firms can customize and use as a starting point in their internal analyses. At 61-83.

25. Chanow, Results of Lawyers, Work & Family: A Study of Alternative Schedule Programs at Law Firms in the District of Columbia (2000), Women's Bar Assoc. D.C., Women's Bar Assoc. Found. D.C., and Am. U. Wash. Coll. of Law, Gender, Work and Family Proj. 25 (2000).

26. For further discussions of the aftermath of the Summers speech, *see, e.g.,* Marcella Bombardieri, *Harvard Aims to Spur Advancement of Women,* Boston Globe, Feb. 4, 2005, at A1; Marcella Bombardieri, *A Woman's Place in the Lab,* Boston Sunday Globe, May 1, 2005, at A1; Marcella Bombardieri, *Summers Sets $50m Women's Initiative,* Boston

Globe, May 17, 2005, at A1; Marcella Bombardieri, *Summers Critic Gets Harvard Post*, Boston Globe, June 4, 2005, at A1.

27. *See, e.g.,* Marcella Bombardieri, *Summers Displays New Understanding of Women's Careers*, Boston Globe, Apr. 8, 2005, at B3. *See also,* Marcella Bombardieri, *Harvard Improves on Tenure Offers to Women*, Boston Globe, Aug. 1, 2005, at B1. Notwithstanding his substantial efforts in response to this particular crisis in his leadership of Harvard, Lawrence Summers notified the Harvard Corporation that he would resign as President of the University as of June 30, 2006, noting in his resignation letter that: "...the rifts between me and segments of the Arts and Sciences faculty make it infeasible for me to advance the agenda of renewal that I see as crucial to Harvard's future." See Letter to the Harvard community by President Lawrence H. Summers, February 21, 2006, available at http://www.president.harvard.edu/speeches/2006/0221_summers.html.

28. *See* Goodman, *Summers' Teachable Moment*, Boston Globe, Feb. 24, 2005, at A11. Goodman observed: "His opponents are suspicious of this deathbed conversion, and his supporters are sure that he's bowing to the neo-Stalinists. But he has surrounded himself with the retaining walls of task forces and made promises to put the status of women high on his list."

29. Hennessey, et al., *Women and Science: The Real Issue*, Boston Globe, Feb. 12, 2005, at A13.

30. Rosabeth Moss Kanter, Confidence: How Winning Streaks & Losing Streaks Begin & End 19 (2004).

CHAPTER 17

MEASURING SUCCESS

Law firms that are truly committed to the retention and advancement of women attorneys will create an evaluation process that effectively measures performance in a gender-neutral way. Moreover, to ensure firm-wide commitment to its implementation, the evaluation process must be seen as an integral component of the law firm's overall goals and strategic plan.[1] As one Managing Partner of a national law firm stated:

> *I do think that it is critical to have somewhat objective results or measurements of how well women are doing in various parts of the firm so that managers are accountable for the success of the diversity program in their businesses. A lot of that then translates to the back of your managers to figure out how to do it well. Then you give them a lot of good ideas about best practices and how things work, and if you truly make diversity as one of the accountable goals, you start to see changes.*

> *You can also manage people that are doing it less well by saying, 'None of the excuses you're throwing up about work/life and everything else works because...[in] other parts of our firm people are doing very well with this.' I think that is one key thing, and that's clearly one of the objectives and set of goals that need to come from the top, with buy-in by the partners. If you don't have that, it's going to be tough to be successful.*

> *You measure the results and it's one of the statistical measures you use for your section perfor-*

mance. Section leaders are compensated based on how well their section does against their objectives, and one of them is diversity...promotion, how well the women are doing in their business development, leadership positions?

There may have been resistance to the process initially, but over time the partners realized that the effort worked and, accordingly, the resistance was diminished.

Babcock and Laschever emphasized the importance of an evaluation process that is vigilant to hidden biases and committed to the promotion of talented women: "Managers, in particular, need to recognize that stereotypes can influence how they evaluate people without their knowing it. They need to take strong steps to prevent this from happening when women are performing jobs that have traditionally been performed by men or when the proportion of women doing a particular job is very small. They need to establish transparent evaluation processes and criteria that minimize the impact of subjective responses in performance evaluations. By teaching themselves to react differently to women who assert themselves, and consistently applying fixed and well-known standards to the work of everyone they supervise, male or female, managers will free women to promote their own interest without censure or blame."[2] The authors further noted the connection between the establishment of a gender-neutral evaluation process and the opportunity to retain valued employees.

In 1997, the American Bar Association's Commission on Women in the Profession published a comprehensive set of recommendations for creating a gender-neutral evaluation process.[3] The report emphasized the need to develop evaluation standards which: "account for, and approve of, diverse models of successful attorney performance."[4] The Commission also stressed the importance of senior management commitment to developing a gender-neutral evaluation system.

The Commission highlighted eight steps that are indispensable to a gender-neutral evaluation process. These include: [5]

1. developing multiple definitions of success that encourage varied communication styles and other differences;

2. instituting a mutual evaluation process which allows junior attorneys to evaluate their superiors;

3. designing an evaluation form that clearly sets out performance criteria, includes a rating scale that allows the evaluated attorney to understand how her performance compares with the performance of others, and narrative comments to capture factors not conducive to a rating scale;

4. conducting evaluation interviews that provide an opportunity for feedback in both directions, as well as an opportunity to establish an action plan to assist the attorney's professional growth;

5. holding goal-setting sessions to capture, early in the process, the associate's professional goals (this could include client relations, training, and other skills development);

6. establishing an educational program for everyone participating in the evaluation process to understand the importance of valuing diversity and to be aware of the potential for bias;

7. including women in all aspects of the evaluation process, including on any teams or committees;[6] and

8. periodically reviewing the effectiveness of the process.

The recommendation that opportunities be provided for feedback in both directions is particularly important if a firm is serious about accountability. The Boston Bar Association Task Force on Professional Challenges and Family Needs noted that some law firms were beginning to institutionalize "360" or "bottom-up" evaluations by which associates confidentially review supervising attorneys on such criteria as supervision, training, feedback, and mentoring. The BBA Task Force also reported the recommendation of several associates with whom it spoke, urging that support for work-family balance within the law firm become an explicit part of the review criteria.[7] As one interviewee observed, such "upstream evaluations" can be powerful tools if used effectively in compensation formulas, but are otherwise meaningless if not used to incentivize a change in unwanted behavior, or reward model behavior.

These evaluations can only be truly effective in changing behavior, however, if their results are able to influence compensation. Performance reviews that feature rigorous, detailed criteria, and that are regularly scheduled, taken seriously, and conspicuously tied to compensation and advancement are a critically important factor for easing gender bias. As summarized in one analysis of gender issues in the legal profession: "Linking results to compensation is the fail/safe method for encouraging compliance. People often complain that intangibles such as professional abilities are difficult to break down into categories and measure. But corporate America has had great success in measuring even abstruse qualities, by thinking deeply about what skills, traits, and attitudes contribute to a top-flight environment."[8]

Finally, law firms should pay close attention to the link between evaluating performance and actual accountability for results. Law firm leaders, particularly those in charge of practice groups, play a key role in their firm's ultimate ability to retain and promote women. When Deloitte & Touche began to address the institutional impediments to success women faced at the firm, one of the first steps it took was to require all local offices to statistically measure whether women were receiving their proportionate share of top assignments. The results clearly measured where women were failing to receive assignments that offered high visibility or contact with important clients. After operational changes were made to facilitate better results, managers then became accountable for specific goals and objectives, the results of which were circulated throughout management. As the former CEO of Deloitte Consulting LLP wrote of these efforts: "Today partners know that they will not become leaders of this organization if they have not demonstrated their commitment to the Women's Initiative."[9]

It is instructive that other areas of the legal profession have learned that opportunities to participate in important and varied work experiences provide a critical evaluation tool. For example, a United States District Court Judge wrote that female prosecutors have historically had greater success advancing in their field because it is an area in which "talent and dedication" are the key measurement variables: "The speed and frequency with which young assistants find themselves on trial makes it possible to judge new prosecutors based on one criteria: pure ability....A young prosecutor gets that chance to prove herself quickly and repeatedly. Talent, regardless of gender, thus is soon discovered not only by unit chiefs with supervisory responsibilities, but by judges, court personnel, and the defense bar, all of whom spread the word effectively."[10]

The bottom line is that success requires access to the opportunities that allow talent to flourish. An effective evaluation process provides the level playing field which ensures equal access to challenging work assignments. The foundation for gender-neutral opportunities to demonstrate excellence is a gender-neutral evaluation process.

Endnotes for Chapter 17

1. It is interesting to note that respondents participating in the *After the JD* study, when asked to rate their level of satisfaction on 16 job-related measures, reported that they were least satisfied with their performance evaluation process. NALP Found. & Am. Bar Found., After the JD: First Results of a National Study of Legal Careers 47 (2004) *available at* http://www.NALPFoundation.org.

2. Babcock and Laschever, Women Don't Ask: Negotiation and the Gender Divide 110 (2003).

3. ABA Comm'n Women in the Prof., Fair Measure: Toward Effective Attorney Evaluations (1997).

4. ABA Comm'n Women in the Prof., Fair Measure: Toward Effective Attorney Evaluations 20 (1997). In addressing this point, the Commission added: "The importance of this last issue cannot be overstated. Rigid standards for acceptable styles will skew ratings, unfairly downgrading performance which, although different from the 'norm' is satisfactory." At 20.

5. ABA Comm'n Women in the Prof., Fair Measure: Toward Effective Attorney Evaluations 21-24 (1997).

6. Importantly, the Commission noted: "If there are not enough senior women attorneys for these tasks, consider using more junior women attorneys, and provide meaningful credit for the time devoted to such administrative service." ABA Comm'n Women in the Prof., Fair Measure: Toward Effective Attorney Evaluations 24 (1997).

7. BBA Task Force on Prof. Challenges and Family Needs, Facing the Grail: Confronting the Cost of Work-Family Imbalance 37 (1999).

8. Holly English, Gender on Trial: Sexual Stereotypes and Work/Life Balance in the Legal Workplace 308-309 (2003).

9. Douglas M. McCracken, *Winning the Talent War for Women: Sometimes it Takes a Revolution*, Harv. Bus. Rev., (Reprint R00611) (Nov./Dec. 2000), at 7.

10. Reena Raggi, *Prosecutors' Offices: Where Gender is Irrelevant*, 57 Fordham L. Rev. 975, 977 (1989). Judge Raggi noted that successful government prosecutors themselves are rainmakers when other members of the law enforcement community bring them cases directly. At 977. It is also interesting to note that public sector experience is increasingly being recognized as a stepping-stone to prestigious general counsel positions. Corporations seeking to create greater diversity in their ranks are casting a wider net in identifying talent outside of the traditional route of looking for potential candidates in law firms. See, e.g., Eichbaum, *Becoming a General Counsel: The New Track to the Top*, Diversity & The Bar, Sept./Oct. 2005 at 51-61.

CHAPTER 18

TRIUMPH OVER TYRANNY—THE ROAD AWAY FROM BILLABLE HOURS

One of the single biggest challenges facing the profession today is its economic dependence on an inefficient method of payment for services rendered that is not in the best interests of either the lawyer or the client. Moreover, the profession must heed the warnings which permeate the surveys and other data showing that many lawyers would happily decrease their compensation in exchange for more time with their families. This perspective was succinctly summarized by a former partner who gave up her law firm income for a high-level government position:

> *I think a whole lot of us would have given up the income. If you could have figured out how to trade the hours for a [lower] salary, people would do it.*

A recently retired senior litigator recalled urging his associates to speak against his firm's proposed pay increase:

> *I said repeatedly, 'It is not in your best interest.'...*
> *The near uniform answer was, 'You see, we've already made the pact with the devil. We already knew coming in here we were going to work those kind of hours. So what we think is, if we are going to have to work those kinds of hours, we may as well get some money for it. If we really, really, really believe there is a choice, we would be interested...but we don't really believe that.'*

So in an endless vicious circle, associates assume they will have to work hard to justify their high salaries, and then finding themselves working even harder, they seek ever increased compensation.

Imagine if you will, a law firm which determines it is going to be flexible enough to develop alternative compensation structures to allow for a variance in billable hours among the lawyers. With the right management tools in place, a law firm could, through careful planning and data development, ultimately develop a structure flexible enough to allow lawyers to meet both their work and family responsibilities.

It is critical to commence any challenge to the billable-hours model by dispelling a misguided notion: changing the culture with respect to billable hours does not mean that everyone works less. Managers of law firms should not decline opportunities to innovate out of fear that they are opening a "Pandora's Box" that will negatively impact the work ethic of the entire profession. The profession has a long and deep history of attracting people who thrive on hard work and exceeding expectations. In fact, changes in the profession are likely to create an even more loyal and dedicated workforce.

However lawyers do need firms to clarify expectations and to remove the guesswork from their firms' definition of success.[1] A healthy culture should articulate clear expectations, providing a roadmap to success rather than a path shrouded in mystery.

For example, firms need to be honest and direct about billable-hour requirements. The Boston Bar Association Task Force on Professional Challenges and Family Needs noted: "In workplaces where long hours are the norm, and people strive to exceed the norm, associates place pressure upon themselves (acting on what are perceived to be the implied messages in the workplace) that is unhealthy for them, and leads to attrition."[2] The BBA Task Force also suggested that law firms clearly tell their associates when and how to limit their work lives without adverse affect. This could include, for example, articulated expectations with respect to working on weekends, acceptable times for leaving work at the end of the day, when firm intervention can be sought to resolve problems, and other ways in which law firms can demystify their culture of success.[3]

It is not enough, however, simply to demystify the ways in which a law firm defines success. It is also critical to expand the definition of what it means to be a successful lawyer. A senior partner spoke of her efforts to reassure other women in the firm that, even if they did not always hit the billable-hour targets, they are not in danger of losing their jobs, as long as they do high-quality work:

> *But what came up was that these are all people*
> *who are accustomed to making A's. They are*

accustomed to succeeding. They are accustomed to what the job is and doing it. And they are very unhappy going along on a continuing basis where they are not doing what they think the job is.

Her point is critical: by the time most people graduate law school, they are used to performing at a very high level and are deeply motivated by a need to succeed. By creating a more expansive definition of success, law firms have an opportunity to capitalize on this motivation.

Such motivation can be further enhanced by greater sensitivity to schedules and clearer communications about expectations. One partner spoke of a conversation she once had with a senior partner who consistently promised his clients a work product on Monday whenever he received a late Friday afternoon telephone call. She suggested to him that he could do a better job differentiating between when it was necessary to make somebody work over the weekend and when it might not be:

> *And I remember we talked about that: 'You know, if the client doesn't have to have it Monday morning, I understand the desire, but let's think about that. And maybe we can say, '... [W]ould it be okay if we got that to you midweek?" Ninety-nine percent of the time, that is fine. You know when it's a crisis and when it's not, so as a manager, [don't] over promise. [For example,] as a manager of young working moms, [don't] schedule early morning meetings. You know, there are a lot of things you can do. I've talked to judges who are sensitive about it and might not schedule early morning hearings.*

Even more transformative change can be achieved, however, if firms could reduce their dependency on the billable hour as the primary source of revenue and measure of success. Even if law firms are reluctant to alter the traditional billable-hour model, clients may force the transition. Client dismay over book-length bills that detail enormous amounts of time spent on various tasks are driving some changes. For example, some are experimenting with blended hourly rates and contingency fee combinations, or other forms of alternative billing.[4]

In its report, the ABA Commission on Billable Hours offered a variety of suggestions for the pricing and delivery of legal services as alternatives to the billable-hour model. These included: fixed fees; discounted rates (for example, for high-volume referral clients); blended billing rates (where firms bill at the same set hourly rate for all lawyers working on that client's matters); contingent fees; outcome-based billing; or some combination of these alternatives.[5]

The Commission's report emphasized that the development of these alternatives requires careful attention to how work will be managed and services delivered. Accordingly, the Commission recommended key questions that should be asked when analyzing an alternative billing approach:[6]

1. how much should this cost?

2. what has it cost to do this type of work previously?

3. what is the value to the client?

4. what is the benchmark cost?

5. what is the cost estimate based on the use of full-time equivalents?

6. what other methodologies should be analyzed (for example, from the client's industry or elsewhere)?

Finally, the Commission encouraged lawyers to see their value in terms of a range of skills that include wisdom and expertise, rather than viewing themselves as selling hours.[7] With that as a foundation, firms can then create alternative fee budget models to begin the process of moving away from billable hours as the primary means of fee generation and as the measure of individual performance.[8]

Even within the billable-hour system, however, firms could implement "best practices" to minimize some of the more negative impacts. The ABA Commission compiled examples of such "best practices" in its report. First, it recommended that any analysis of a lawyer's productivity as measured by billable hours also be coupled with an evaluation of quality factors for purposes of determining compensation and bonuses. Another suggested best practice is to establish a billable-hours ceiling; once that ceiling is reached, no additional compensation would be paid, no matter how high the hours. The Commission also recommended several best practices which would provide credit towards a billable-hour requirement for time spent on pro bono matters. For example, the Commission highlighted one firm's establishment of a separate bonus program to reward excellence in pro bono activities, and the implementation of a "Model Citizens" bonus program to honor distinguished service to the law firm.[9]

To balance the aspirational goals of an alternative system with the current pervasiveness of the billable-hours model, the Commission proposed a Model Firm Policy Regarding Billable Hours which includes a mix of billable and non-billable activities.

Elements of the Model Policy included:[10]

1. A statement that lawyers are expected to be "scrupulously honest" in recording their time, with an admonition that violators who deliberately inflate the time expended, or the nature of the work done, will be terminated.

2. A mix of target hours that includes client billable, pro bono, firm services, professional development, and client development. With respect to such targets, the Report offered the following model expectations:

Billable Client Work	Pro Bono Work	Service to the Firm	Client Development	Training and Professional Development	Service to the Profession
Target Hours	Target Hours	Target Hours	Target Hours	Target Hours	Target Hours
1,900	100	100	75	75	50

It is laudable that the Commission recommended that firms recognize the variety of important functions which lawyers undertake, in addition to their client-billable work. It is troubling, however, that the Commission recommended a total commitment of 2,300 hours a year to the full-time practice of law. Although the Commission described the Model Policy as allowing for a "reasonable" 50-hour work week with time for vacations, it only arrives at that calculation by assuming that 100% of one's time can be productively billed. However as discussed in Chapter 4, it takes more than 1,900 hours of actual work to legitimately bill 1,900 hours to clients. As a result, the targeted goals would result in much more than a 50-hour work week in order to produce the total Model Policy goals of 2,300 total hours, of which 1,900 hours would be client-billable.

Moreover, in providing the 1,900-hour *expectation*, the Model Policy stated that it did not propose: "hard-and-fast minimum levels."[11] However by failing to recommend a *maximum* target, the Model Policy does not help to alleviate the intense competition that exists to ratchet up billable hours.

As a practical matter, many firms today set a billable-hour "expectation" of 1900 hours. Associates hoping to achieve partnership, however, know that it is critical to exceed that target. The Model Policy could exacerbate the pressure associates feel by creating an expectation that, in addition to the escalating race for client billable time, an additional 400 hours must be devoted to pro bono, firm service, client development, training, professional development, and service to the profession.

Ultimately, far more is needed than a redesign of the billable-hour model. Both law firms and clients must develop fair and equitable alternative-fee arrangements. As one writer noted: "The essence of alternative billing is risk shifting....Accepting more risk will entail a basic shift in the relationship between lawyers and clients."[12]

This notion of risk acceptance need not be so daunting, particularly with the billable-hour model serving as the point of comparison. Law firms could begin immediately to collect the information needed in order to develop a data-base that provides a better understanding of alternate ways to price services fairly. The flaws in the billable-hour model and the opportunities for mutual gain suggest that other alternatives can, with some degree of effort and collaboration, offer mutually rewarding alternatives that will have a demonstrably positive impact upon the profession.

Endnotes for Chapter 18

1. *See, e.g.,* BBA Task Force on Prof. Challenges and Family Needs, Facing the Grail: Confronting the Cost of Work-Family Imbalance 37 (1999). See also Ward, Billing Basics: Associates Need to Learn Nuances of Billing Before Starting Big Projects, 90 ABA J. 42, 42 (Oct. 2004), suggesting that, at the outset of an assignment, associates should ask the supervising lawyer his or her expectations regarding the anticipated amount of time the assignment should take.

2. BBA Task Force on Prof. Challenges and Family Needs, Facing the Grail: Confronting the Cost of Work-Family Imbalance 37 (1999).

3. BBA Task Force on Prof. Challenges and Family Needs, Facing the Grail: Confronting the Cost of Work-Family Imbalance 37 (1999).

4. *See, e.g.,* Jarrett Banks, *General Counsel Experiment With Full Contingency Fees,* Corp. Legal Times, June 2005, at 32. Of interest, some law firms are recognizing the marketing significance they can derive from advertising alternatives to the traditional hourly rate structure of billing. *See* Ameet Sachdev, *Hourly Legal Fees under Attack,* Chi. Trib., Apr. 18, 2005, at B1 *available at* http://pqasb.pqarchiver.com/chicagotribune/advanced-search.html (April 28, 2005).

5. ABA Comm'n on Billable Hours, ABA Commission on Billable Hours Report: 2001-2002 16-18 (2002) available at http://www.abanet.org/careercounsel/billable/toolkit/bhcomplete.pdf (Dec. 13, 2005) See also Griffith, Creative Billing: Is The Reign Of The Almighty Billable Hour Over?, Lawcrossing, available at http://www.lawcrossing.com. One alternative fee arrangement described in the article is where a firm bills monthly on a fixed-fee basis; the client holds back 10-20% which is paid when the case is successfully concluded. The firm may benefit from a bonus, such as a multiple of the hold back if the outcome is favorable.

6. ABA Comm'n on Billable Hours, ABA Commission on Billable Hours Report: 2001-2002 20-22 (2002) available at http://www.abanet.org/careercounsel/billable/toolkit/bhcomplete.pdf (Dec. 13, 2005).

7. ABA Comm'n on Billable Hours, ABA Commission on Billable Hours Report: 2001-2002 23 (2002) available at http://www.abanet.org/careercounsel/billable/toolkit/bhcomplete.pdf (Dec. 13, 2005).

8. ABA Comm'n on Billable Hours, ABA Commission on Billable Hours Report: 2001-2002 27 (2002) available at http://www.abanet.org/careercounsel/billable/toolkit/bhcomplete.pdf (Dec. 13, 2005).

9. ABA Comm'n on Billable Hours, ABA Commission on Billable Hours Report: 2001-2002 47 (2002) available at http://www.abanet.org/careercounsel/billable/toolkit/bhcomplete.pdf (Dec. 13, 2005).

10. ABA Comm'n on Billable Hours, ABA Commission on Billable Hours Report: 2001-2002 49-51 (2002) available at http://www.abanet.org/careercounsel/billable/toolkit/bhcomplete.pdf (Dec. 13, 2005).

11. ABA Comm'n on Billable Hours, ABA Commission on Billable Hours Report: 2001-2002 50 (2002) available at http://www.abanet.org/careercounsel/billable/toolkit/bhcomplete.pdf (Dec. 13, 2005).

12. Douglas McCollam, *The Future of Time*, Litigation 2005, (Suppl. Am.Law. & Corp.Couns.), 2005, at 72.

CHAPTER 19

FROM PUDDLES TO POURING— EXERCISING POWER OVER BUSINESS GENERATION

The opportunities for women to advance are immeasurably enhanced by their ability to generate business for their law firm. As a former partner in a large firm stated:

> *We have to figure out a way to find the economic answer for women. I think that is the next frontier, finding the economic answer. Because I think it is when women have the ability in greater numbers to walk with their business, that is going to make the institutions that are larger have to listen. At [her old law firm], I always felt like, well, I look at them and how they evaluate equity partners who are thinking of leaving. And those that they really, really hold onto tightly are the ones with the large group of clients, large money makers. And they never were women.... I think we will begin to be listened to much more carefully when we have some of that.*

A senior partner located in the New York office of a national law firm commented on her own instincts over the years to focus on business development, even at the expense of billable hours, in order to develop greater independence as an attorney:

> *I am a firm believer that it is not enough to work hard and be smart.*
>
> *Unless you learn how to market yourself, you will never be independent in this profession. And women*

> *seem to have a particularly difficult time marketing themselves.*

She noted the continual tension she feels about her firm's pressures to maximize billable hours, even as she follows her own instincts to maximize her opportunities to be independent:

> *As far as the firm supporting it, I am sure they would rather I had just put in the time to billable matters.... I have almost always spent a minimum of 500 hours a year, sometimes it's close to 1000, on client development. I happen to have a very large book of business, which is wonderful, but those hours took away from other things I could be doing. And, in fact, they took away from billable hours when I was younger.... I always had acceptable billable hours, but I certainly never had the highest. I made a conscious decision that the marketing was really important because I wanted to be able to be independent. But a lot of people aren't going to make that choice.... My priority was being independent and knowing that if I didn't like what was going on in the firm, I could pick up and go. And the only way you can do that is if you have a significant enough book of business.*

Her experiences offer a valuable lesson for women struggling with the demands of their firm to increase billable hours and their own recognition of the importance of spending more time on business generation. The reality is, the price for the temporary job security that high billable hours offers is the lost opportunity to develop one's own book of business and, thereby, achieve greater long-term security. In the law firm environment that exists today, only the latter offers true economic independence, as business development will always play a critical role in an attorney's success. New business is critical to the long-term success of every law firm, and the ability to bring it into the firm provides the business generator with a significant degree of economic stability.

Even new associates can begin developing rainmaking prowess because, at the most basic level, good business development begins with demonstrating excellence and reliability to the client. Attorney and author Heidi Brown offered a number of suggestions for nascent business generators, recognizing that true rainmaking requires a multi-year investment of time. She recommended, for example, that junior practitioners spend: "even just one or two hours a week to brainstorm about opportunities."[1] She also urged associates to seek out: "high-level rainmakers at the firm as mentors, and volunteer to help them grow the firm's client base."[2]

Also, the amount of that weekly investment of time should increase with experience. Business coach and consultant, Lois Frankel, urged women to focus on the importance of creating networks and relationships to foster one's career growth. She stresses the importance of devoting daily time to this effort: "If you're not spending 5% of your day building relationships, you're doing something wrong."[3]

However, truly successful business development comes in many forms. For some, it is the act of introducing new clients to the firm. For others, it means recognizing and acknowledging the new assignments that follow from a client's confidence in the work done to date. Both have enormous value.

Smart law firm managers understand that not everyone brings the identical talents and skills to the tasks of business development, and will develop ways for appropriately rewarding the full range of efforts. Some lawyers may excel at generating new work from existing clients simply through the high quality of their work product. Others may thrive in an atmosphere where they can meet potential new clients through organizations or Board activities. The sophisticated law firm should identify who has these various abilities and then recognize that it is in the firm's best interest to help each lawyer be successful.

In some instances, this will warrant a reorientation of priorities. For example, if a lawyer excels as a potential business generator and helps raise the profile of the firm, then the firm ought to provide the tools and encouragement for those efforts to continue, including the reduction of billable-hour demands. It is unrealistic to expect all members of a professional workforce to be uniform in the hours billed to clients and the time spent on new business generation.

Along with their male colleagues, women are ready and eager to build their rainmaking skills. However as described in Chapter 5, women are finding themselves trying to make up for lost time as a result of their exclusion from the informal networking and mentoring that has long been a component of successful business generation. Consequently, law firms need to create a broad panoply of skill-building opportunities.

Fortunately, where law firms have been slower to recognize the need for such skill-building, others have jumped in to fill the void. For example, the Law Practice Management Section of the American Bar Association established a Women's Rainmaking Committee which offers programs on business development skills, as well as an opportunity for women to develop national networks. National and state bar associations are also filling the void, as are local and specialty bar associations which have created committees and programming focused on developing rainmaking skills for women. The popularity of many of these efforts demonstrates the important need they are fulfilling.[4]

Law firms are also beginning to implement creative ways to enhance the business generation skills of women. Many of the interviewees who objected to the more gender-based forms of marketing (for example, through golf or sports events), suggested alternatives that would be a better fit. For example, one equity partner observed:

> *There are plenty of other kinds of marketing that you can do that can be way more comfortable. I don't do any of those sort of traditional marketing things that were more popular, I guess, when guys were controlling the profession. We tried to do things like 'spa days,' so that the women who participate feel more comfortable doing something with women clients...that would be enjoyable. Now, at the end of the year when we do gifts for clients, one of the gifts the marketing department was willing to do to help you develop new clients is to give a basket of hand creams and soaps, which was a really nice addition to the corporate [gift] list. It just suggests that there are powerful women in our client base we need to cater to.*

The bottom line is that each woman needs to find the business development style that feels most comfortable. One marketing specialist drew a direct link between the skills needed for marketing and the successful service of clients: "The fact is that the communications skills that apply when profession als market themselves are the same skills that must be used to successfully serve client needs....In litigation, or during crises, clients' critical interests demand an ability on the part of their representatives to communicate in the court of public opinion."[5]

In her book on business generation for women lawyers, Silvia Coulter noted the correlation between the attributes of a good rainmaker and a good lawyer. Fortunately, there is sufficient overlap. A good lawyer can transfer the very qualities that helped her excel in the law into qualities that can help her excel as a rainmaker.[6] Both Coulter and networking expert Diane Darling emphasize that truly effective networking is about the ability to develop and sustain relationships which, at their best, are mutually beneficial and reinforcing.[7] The key for each individual is to create a plan and get started.

As women excel in their own business-generation skills, firms will see even greater results by instituting a comprehensive, team-based culture that recognizes new business development as well as rewards those who support and nurture client relationships through excellence in work quality. A leader in a Western law firm emphasized that the way to help lawyers strengthen their business generation abilities is to assist them in developing outstanding legal skills:

> *First of all, you have got to be a great lawyer. Anybody who thinks they can develop business at the country club, forget it. That is not true in this millennium. You have got to be good at what you do. So we tell all of our people, 'Learn to be a great, great lawyer. And we are going to teach you business development skills.'...We are not going to do anything with them for three to four years because we are saying, 'You worry about being a great lawyer.' Then we are going to start giving them an expense allowance to take people to lunch. ...*

> *Be known for your expertise. Be an expert in your specialty, be known for your expertise and be a good sales person. Be a member of a referral club. That is a key one.... If you go look at the source of most of your business, I will be willing to bet that 80% of your*

work was from other lawyers, and here is who it comes from....

> *We tell people, 'We want you to go through your class that was ahead of you in law school, your own class and the class behind you. And we want you to track those people over time, because they move around the country and one day they [may need something done in your city]. 'They are going to refer to somebody they know, right? We have a rule: if you ever go to another city on business or whatever, don't leave the city if it has any of your law school classmates or friends without calling them and telling them what you are doing. Because that is where your referrals come from, other lawyers.... So we tell people you have got to network with the lawyers who are your peers because they will be ultimate major sources of referrals. So that is what the lawyer referral club means.*

> *And then be a great service provider. You have to answer the phone.... You have got to be relationship driven. You have got to be involved in your community. You have got to be focused in executing your business development plan.... You have to be a cross seller. You have to learn how I can sell you 10 times better than I can sell myself. And then you have to be a conveyor. That means, as I move along up, when I get a client I hand it off to somebody immediately....*

> *So our older partners are always asked, 'What are you doing to move the younger partners into that work so they can have it.' We work on that.*

Another Managing Partner similarly emphasized the team-centered approach at his firm:

We try to discourage internal competition and encourage external competition.... The greatest compliment that you can give someone is that they handed a client off to someone else, either to a young lawyer passing a client down, or a file came in that maybe was outside your area of expertise but they got it in and handed it off to someone else. Those sort of things that show you are really looking after the client's interest first, and you are putting your own interest behind the client and the firm.

The reality is, each woman lawyer must determine for herself how to juggle the increasingly daunting billable-hour demands with the added challenge of trying to generate business for the firm. Law firms will be acting in their self-interest when they structure themselves to support fully the optimal mix of activities that maximizes each lawyer's opportunity for success. The paths to rainmaking are many and varied, but they all intersect at one key place, and that is where passion, talent, teamwork, and good firm management meet.

Endnotes for Chapter 19

1. Heidi K. Brown, Fundamentnals of Federal Litigation 583 (2004).

2. Brown, Fundamentals Of Federal Litigation (2004). Brown offers cautionary advice, however, to associates before they engage in direct client contact, observing: "[S]ome law firm partners are extraordinarily protective of their client relationships and have strict preferences regarding direct communications with clients by associates." At 585.

3. Frankel, Ph.D., Nice Girls Don't Get The Corner Office: 101 Unconscious Mistakes Women Make That Sabotage Their Careers 25 (2004). Frankel further noted that: "People aren't hired and promoted simply because they work hard. It happens because the decision maker knows the *character* of the person and feels confident about his or her ability not only to do the job, but also to do it in a way that promotes collegial team relationships." At 24-25.

4. For example, *Massachusetts Lawyers Weekly*, reporting on a sold-out business development program, noted: "Judging from the size of the crowd at the first business development seminar of the Women's Bar Association, there is a flood of interest in the subject of rainmaking." See, *Reigning Women,* 32 M. L.W. 1342, Feb. 23, 2004, at B2. *See also,* David E. Frank, *Networking: Golf's No Longer the Only Game in Town*, Mass. Law. Wkly., Oct. 3, 2005, *available at* http://www.masslawyersweekly.com/subscriber/archives_FTS.cfm.

5. Larry Smith, *Publicity Equals Communications Equals Case Management*, 24 NO. 5 Of Counsel 5, May 2005 http://www.westlaw.com.

6. Coulter, The Woman Lawyer's Rainmaking Game: How To Build A Successful Law Practice 1-4 (2004). In her listing of the important attributes of a successful rainmaker, Coulter ranks among the top three: (1) the ability to listen, (2) confidence, and (3) negotiation acumen. At 1-5. See also, Deborah Graham, Getting Down to Business: Marketing and Women Lawyers 666 (1996): "Increasingly, women are developing a variety of marketing models and proving that marketing is not a man's game which can only be played by men or by women who 'act like a man.' Effecting the changes that may be necessary to market effectively does not mean ignoring gender differences or adopting a different gender style, but rather taking who you are and what you have and intelligently making the most of it." See also, Jenny B. Davis, *Distinction with a Difference*, ABA J. (April 2003), available at http://www.abanet.org/careercounsel/abajournalarchives/distinctionwithadifference.html.

7. See Diane Darling, The Networking Survival Guide: Get the Success You Want by Tapping into the People You Know (2003). In stressing the importance of relationships to professional and personal success, author Keith Ferrazzi states: "Connecting is that rare thing that lets us have our cake and eat it, too. We end up serving the interests of both our work and our life, ourselves and others." Keith Ferrazzi with Tahl Raz, Never Eat Alone and Other Secrets to Success, One Relationship at a Time 289 (2005).

CHAPTER 20

WHERE CULTURE IS TESTED— CLARITY AND THE COMPENSATION PROCESS

If there is one critical piece of advice that anyone interviewing with a law firm should heed, it is to ask the firm to describe its compensation model. Awkward? Not if asked properly. The answer may provide the most important information of the interview.

In an environment in which compensation drives behavior, the daily work environment for most lawyers is significantly impacted by how the lawyers perceive that they are rewarded. What can be more important, therefore, than to learn what the firm values and rewards through compensation? The challenge is to ask the question in a way that demonstrates not only the job candidate's best intentions, but his or her own strengths as well. For example: "As a lawyer, I care about working as part of a team on behalf of clients. Can you please explain how your compensation system encourages lawyers to work together?"

Then listen closely to the answer. The interviewer will always put the law firm in its best light, but pay attention to the emphasis. Does the answer describe a competitive environment or a collaborative one? Is the firm focusing on ways to reward individual behavior or team behavior? Is the system rigid and formulaic, or are subjective factors included? Does it sound like associates are a welcome part of the team? Are those lawyers who service existing clients valued, or is it only those who bring in new business from new clients?

Law firm managers make a variety of assumptions when developing a compensation system, but most have one underlying premise: compensation has to be high, and it must increase yearly. However, if studies support that money is not the most important driving factor for the vast majority of lawyers, is it not time to redesign the model and its flawed assumptions?[1]

A senior partner in a New York City branch of a mid-sized national law firm noted that she could command substantially increased compensation if she took her book of business to a larger New York firm. However, she remained loyal to her firm because they shared a similar philosophy regarding the practice of law and their approach to caring for clients:

> *I could leave here and be better compensated...but I have great loyalty to this firm because I think this firm has a lot of things the other firms don't have.... First of all, they think the way I think.... I am not academic. You have go to be smart to be here, but I just want to get the deal done. I just want to get whatever the client wants. If I have to say no, I want to say, 'Well you can't do it that way, but here are two other ways.' And this is a firm that thinks that way, so I am very much at home here.*

In other words, because her firm culture was not driven solely by compensation, she felt that she was able to appreciate the commonality she shared with her colleagues in the firm's underlying law practice philosophy. She also expressed the importance of a compensation system which recognizes the variety of contributions that women make, in addition to their client billable time:

> *Women tend to end up on the committees for recruitment and mentoring and training and all those things, and a lot of times they waste their time doing those things....Women get put into these positions because it sounds good to be on all these different committees, and they think it's important and shows they're a team player and that they finally have arrived.... But, in fact, if it's not compensated for, it takes them away from those things that would help them build their careers and is often a mistake.... The compensation system should reward them for running recruitment or the summer program, or whatever, because it would finally recognize that these are really important contributions.*

She noted that if firms adequately recognized and compensated those interested in devoting time to these important roles, and if firms saw such work as an alternative to client-billable time, more women might choose to stay in the profession.

Law firms have a tremendous opportunity to use compensation as a tool for change. As Peter Drucker noted: "people in organizations tend to be influenced by the ways they see others being rewarded."[2] In fact, firms have the greatest opportunity to change their culture by developing a compensation system focused on rewarding teamwork rather than individual results. One indicia of whether a firm actually has implemented a more team-based approach is to analyze the compensation difference between the highest paid partner and the lowest. As *The American Lawyer* observed: "Partner compensation spreads are a handy metric for assessing firms' business models and cultures."[3]

Firms have much to gain by analyzing and incorporating aspects of compensation systems that have evolved in law firms in which culture and collegiality are highly valued. It is interesting to note that history offers an instructive example. Earlier in the 20th century, one of New York City's most prestigious law firms deviated from the standard method for determining associate compensation by implementing its own innovations: first, the firm treated clients as firm clients, rather than "belonging" to a particular lawyer for compensation purposes. Second, the firm became the first to share profits with associates by implementing an annual bonus system. What is particularly sobering about this example is that the leaders most instrumental in developing these innovations were succeeded by three partners who insisted on receiving more of the firm's profits because of their greater business generation. In accomplishing their own goals, the culture of the firm changed so significantly that it led to the departure of a group of partners who went on to found Cleary, Gottlieb, Friendly & Cox, now one of the nation's largest law firms. Still other lawyers passed over for partnership at the changed firm left to become the founding partners of Skadden, Arps, Slate, Meagher & Flom.[4]

Today, no differently than a century ago, leaders drive the firm's culture, and culture drives everything else that matters in the law firm, including compensation. A senior partner described her firm's compensation model as a modified lock-step system based on the primary goals of facilitating teamwork and removing the economic impediments to involving others in direct client generation and contact. She stressed that the compensation system is entirely devoted to maintaining a culture in which all the attorneys work for the success of the enterprise, not their individual statistics:

> *We do no origination, so it's not all tied to that.*
> *It's not tied to billables. It's tied to overall effort and*
> *participation, looking at everything you would nor-*
> *mally look at. How do you contribute to the firm?*
> *How are you doing visibly out in the community*
> *doing things? Are you bringing work in? Are you*
> *supervising? Are you training? Are you recruiting?*
> *They look at a whole host of factors....*

She further noted that members of the Compensation Committee meet with individual partners to provide each partner with an opportunity to speak not only about themselves but to share information about other partners:

> *Just what that means is you're thinking of people*
> *who have just given way above and beyond, or people*
> *that really drop the ball. But the really important*
> *thing to keep in mind is that we don't do it based on*
> *what happened in one single year. It has to be over a*
> *period of time.*

In essence she described a system which accentuates teamwork.[5] The Managing Partner of her firm noted another important contributing factor to the overall economic health of the firm: by retaining 5% of income each year, the firm avoids carrying debt. As a result, the firm has been able to survive economic downturns without significant employee layoffs or major declines in compensation. His fundamental theory is that culture drives compensation, and the firm institutionalizes that belief by aligning the entire law firm around a system that supports and recognizes teamwork:

> *We don't give credits. We do not track business*
> *development.... [T]eam culture...is so much more*
> *powerful in business development than development*
> *of individual fiefdoms....*

> *None of us individually is as good as all of us*
> *working together. As a result, as far as market-*
> *ing...this is the strongest marketing group because we*
> *never work against each other. We share resources.*

> *We help each other because your compensation is*
> *built largely on how the whole firm does.*

He eschewed the common practice of designing compensation systems around the top echelon of lawyers:

> *Ten percent of your partners are unbelievable.*
> *They are what we all refer to as 'superstars.' They are*
> *incredible business developers, they are incredible*
> *lawyers, they are incredible managers, they are*
> *incredible recruiters. They just far out-perform every-*
> *body. Then there is 10% who quit working, but forgot*
> *to tell you about it.... Now, in the middle is 80%....*
> *Now most people design their system to take care of*
> *the 10% at the top. And where is your core of stability*
> *and strength? Its your 80%. And your 10% can never*
> *be great without the 80% supporting them.*
>
> *Our view is that the 10% have to leave something*
> *on the table and take out less money.... And if they*
> *take out less money then they could arguably get*
> *somewhere else, the 80% know that. But because the*
> *80% know that, they don't raise a ruckus about their*
> *own compensation. So the people sitting on the*
> *money at the top, are leaving money on the table....*
>
> *You want to create a law firm that is internally*
> *noncompetitive, but extremely competitive externally*
> *because you work together as a team helping each*
> *other. So today I might get a call from [another office]*
> *that says, 'We've got a big potential client down here*
> *we have a good chance of getting. Would you fly down*
> *here tomorrow and help?' I will fly down tomorrow*
> *and spend all day, and may never work on it.... That is*
> *just the way we work. Tackle everything as a team.*

Yet efforts to promote teamwork are frequently overshadowed by other considerations. The fear of many firms, for example, that major business producers will leave if not highly rewarded has generally led to compensation systems which favor the firm's "stars." In its article noting the significant variance between the top and lowest paid partner in many firms, *The American Lawyer* recently observed that: "the threat of cherry-picking is really the main driver behind increasing compensation spreads...."[6]

It is time, however, for this deeply-held belief to be tested. For example, perhaps these so-called "stars" are leaving because of the lack of any meaningful reason to stay in one firm, other than the amount they earn. As billable-hour tension continues to rise, and opportunities to participate in collegial activities diminish, what else is there other than the scorecard of compensation? However maybe more of these "stars" would be content to stay in a firm that offers something more than money as the measure of value.[7]

Significantly, recent research suggests that star performers generally disappoint when hired by a new company. This analysis of the change in circumstances of "stars" who were lured from their corporate organizations for apparently greater income or opportunities is instructive to law firms. In addition to a drop in performance and a decline in the functioning of the team with whom the star worked, the star also tended not to stay with the new organization for long.[8]

An *ABA Journal* article noted that the use of compensation as a way to retain star business generators has: "driven most large law firms to two-tier partnerships as well as to more subjective compensation systems with committees looking behind the numbers to determine where credit is due." The article also noted a shift towards collaboration in an effort to eschew the so-called "eat-what-you-kill" system which results in the most lucrative compensation going to those who generate the most business: "[T]he recent trend is toward collaboration, with some stars getting more when they work their magic in areas the firm deems strategic, which would be part of the behind-the-numbers subjectivity."[9] In other words, some firms are providing for greater compensation for those partners whose business generation is in identified areas of strategic growth.

The Managing Partner of a firm known for its culture of teamwork stressed the important role compensation can play in facilitating teamwork:

> There are no huge variances [between the highest and lowers paid partners].... The spreads are pretty reasonable and pretty evenly distributed.

He also emphasized the Compensation Committee's attention to determining each partner's contribution to the overall goals of the firm:

> *Two members of the Compensation Committee meet with each [partner] and one of the things they do in that interview is talk about other people.... How do you think he did? Was he a significant contributor? So the whole process is one of listening to information about others.*

The Managing Partner of a mid-sized firm in another part of the country also stressed the value of a Compensation Committee which analyzes a variety of factors:

> *So when we evaluate each others' numbers, we don't look at any hard economic data. We don't look at group production data. We don't track origination credits. We take a one-firm approach that everyone we get will contribute in each person's unique way to the betterment of the firm. And we evaluate each other.*

> *Every partner evaluates every other partner. We have a Compensation Committee that interviews each partner and gets feedback about each partner, and then comes together on an annual basis to distill all of that and make recommendations....*

Ironically, even as many law firms struggle to recognize teamwork in their compensation systems, clients want and value legal relationships which demonstrate a comprehensive, team-based effort to understand and respond to the needs of their business. As David Maister and his colleagues wrote: "If a professional firm wishes to develop an institutional relationship with a major client, it requires more than a single member of the firm (the relationship manager) focusing his or her attention on a few key decision makers."[10] Rather, they stated that the successful relationship: "requires the full participation of a large number of people who service or deal with the client. Everyone who participates in serving the client can, and does, affect the relationship. Multiple contacts must be established, and a *consistency* of service and attentiveness must be attained. It's no good if each provider behaves in different ways, since a firm-wide reputation is built only if each person can be trusted and relied upon to operate to the same standards."[11]

Critically, Maister and his colleagues advocated the importance of relationship managers for clients, distinguishing between managing the relationship and simply maintaining it: "He or she must be active in creating opportunities for other members of the professional firm's team to meet with additional client executives and begin new trust relationships."[12] A key challenge of this function, as they noted, is engaging other members of the team to nurture the relationship and serve other team members by providing them opportunities to become involved in highly visible activities and obtain valuable client exposure. At the essence of their advice is the importance of managers committed to teamwork. Without a compensation system that encourages and recognizes this key management role, the impact is felt by all attorneys in the law firm and is likely to impact client service as well.

An equity partner in a Western law firm praised her firm's compensation system because it offered multiple ways to credit lawyers for their various client roles. For example, where she might have Billing Partner credits for bringing a client to the firm, others may be designated as Supervising Partner for their working contributions to the client. She was blunt in describing what happens when lawyers fail to recognize the firm's efforts to foster teamwork:

> We have had some people who have told other people they would not work on a matter unless they got part of the billing credits. Those people don't usually last very long here, because that really isn't the way we work.

A former partner in a large law firm criticized the profession's failure to recognize that it takes a variety of talents and skills to create a successful law firm. She offered her own advice for changes that would recognize each lawyer's individual talents:

> I would put people into: you're either a scrivener, you're generating work, or you're administrative/project manager. You're one of those three and you're going to be compensated on the value that you bring to that job....

She questioned, for example, why firms fail to formally recognize the contributions of managers for big institutional projects whose skills can be critical to achieving a successful client result. She recalled a $500 million transaction that required lawyers in her former firm to work in teams, and the unheralded Project Managers who successfully fulfilled their assigned responsibility for the successful outcome of their team's tasks. In her vision of a well-functioning law firm, attorneys who excel in project leadership positions would be recognized and encouraged to maintain those positions, rather than required to assume other functions less suited to their skills.

Ultimately, firms need to devise systems that appropriately compensate the entire range of skills and talents that individual lawyers bring, whether it is excellence in lawyering or contribution to firm management, or participation in key roles such as mentoring. As part of such systems, firms should clarify and expand opportunities to share credits for business development activities, whether for new or existing clients. Only by instituting such measures can firms then begin to confront the inevitable gender gaps they will find in their compensation at all levels where discretionary factors are considered.

As described in Chapter 6, the compensation gaps between male and female attorneys are real and must be eliminated. Confronting systemic inequality, as Evelyn Murphy reported, requires careful attention to data collection, a commitment to instituting measurable change, and a willingness to monitor the results continually.[13] The collection of useful data is critical, and particularly complicated in a law firm setting. The data collected should include relative comparisons of raw earnings numbers, as well as an underlying analysis of performance records, evaluations, and the variety of criteria that may be used in a firm's compensation system.

To ensure that pay equity issues are successfully addressed, senior management involvement is a fundamental prerequisite for change: "Without commitment from the top, nothing will change. When there *is* commitment from the top, that priority gets accomplished."[14]

That priority is far more likely to be accomplished, however, when those at the top include a critical mass of women who are committed to the implementation of a law firm compensation model that eliminates gender gaps at all levels. Accordingly, Compensation Committees must include women who can assist in the fair assessment of their female colleagues during the compensation review process.[15]

Of course, whenever compensation is the subject of discussion, there must be recognition of a fundamental underlying truth: no one ever thinks they are paid what they are worth. Accordingly, one Managing Partner described how he responds to individual complaints in order to discern whether the Compensation Committee did its job effectively:

> *To me, at the end of the day, my description of the process is that it works if, when you see the numbers, you think everybody else is compensated fairly, not yourself.*

Endnotes for Chapter 20

1. *See, e.g., The State of the Legal Profession: 1990*, 1991 ABA Young Law. Div. 58, reporting that in 1984, only 12% of the respondents rated compensation as the most important factor affecting job satisfaction; by 1990, that number dwindled to 9%.

2. Peter F. Drucker, The Essential Drucker: The Best of Sixty Years of Peter Drucker's Essential Writings on Management 134 (2004).

3. Nathan Koppel, *The High-Priced Spread*, Am. Law, July 2005, at 98.

4. Lincoln Caplan, Skadden: Power, Money, and the Rise of a Legal Empire 18-19 (1993).

5. As the trend for teamwork grows, however, Deborah Tannen cautions that it may create complications for performance evaluations: "When ideas are generated and work is accomplished in the privacy of the team, the outcome of the team's effort may become associated with the person most vocal about reporting results. There are many women and men - but probably relatively more women - who are reluctant to put themselves forward in this way and to consequently risk not getting credit for their contributions." Deborah Tannen, *The Power Of Talk: Who Gets Heard And Why*, Harv. Bus. Rev., Sept.-Oct. 1995, at 138, 141-142.

6. Koppel, *The High-Priced Spread*, Am. Law, July 2005, at 98.

7. The fact is, the legal services industry is performing remarkably well from an economic perspective. *The American Lawyer* reported that among the top 100 law firms, 2004 profits per partner were up 9% from 2003. *Figuratively Speaking*, The Am. Law., July 2005, at 106, 107.

8. Boris Groysberg, Ashish Nanda & Nitin Nohria, *The Risky Business Of Hiring Stars*, Harv. Bus. Rev., May 2004, at 93, 94.

9. Carter, *A Delicate Balance*, ABA J., Mar. 2005, at 28.

10. David H. Maister, Charles H. Green & Robert M. Galford, The Trusted Advisor 181 (2000).

11. Maister et al., The Trusted Advisor 181-82 (2000).

12. Maister et al., The Trusted Advisor 182 (2000).

13. Murphy with Graff, Getting Even: Why Women Don't Get Paid Like Men and What to Do About It 234 (2005).

14. Murphy with Graff, Getting Even: Why Women Don't Get Paid Like Men and What to Do About It 236 (2005).

15. ABA Comm'n Women in the Prof., Empowerment and Leadership: Tried and True Methods for Women Lawyers 41 (2003).

CHAPTER 21

MENTORING MODELS

The importance of a meaningful mentoring relationship to long-term career success cannot be overstated. The preliminary results of the longitudinal study of approximately 5,000 lawyers who graduated in the year 2000 noted that: "informal mentoring in law firm settings, however difficult to measure, is central in the careers of new lawyers. Well over a third (and as high as half) of respondents in these settings identify informal mentors as the first most important source of assistance for learning office protocols/customs and for having a personal advocate in the firm."[1]

Nor does all mentoring require intensive, one-on-one relationships. Sometimes it can be part of a team approach to management. A company president, who serves in the dual role as general counsel noted: "Taking the time to explain the reasons for a particular approach to a legal issue, soliciting input…and showing a genuine interest in your team will directly benefit work relationships and the projects at hand."[2]

As we have already seen, these informal mentoring relationships tend to elude many women. Even as the inability of women to find mentors is identified as one of the key causes of attrition, effective mentoring remains elusive. It is, therefore, necessary for firms to provide formal mentoring programs to ensure the benefits that can be derived from these relationships.

A senior partner described how her mentor contributed to the development of the skills she needed to progress along her career path.

> *I had the fortunate experience of having a great mentor at my firm. …who took an interest in me from day one. He was a partner who did a pretty broad mix of things. He made sure I took depositions my first year, and we tried some cases together, so I had a lot of experience [by the time I started] my fourth year.*

Excellent resources currently exist for law firms and individuals to help in developing sustainable and effective mentoring relationships and formal programs. Two of the leaders in this effort, the NALP Foundation and the Minority Corporate Counsel Association, joined together to study how women and lawyers of color enter into successful mentoring relationships. One important finding from this study is that, even though informal mentoring is a preferred model: "90% of participants who were matched in formal mentoring programs were satisfied with their mentoring experience."[3]

A strong mentoring program should train the participants to ensure they have access to resources that can teach them mentoring skills, and that they begin with a common baseline which addresses all the elements needed for a strong relationship. As one attorney wrote regarding the potential pitfalls and benefits of the mentoring relationship: "Some individuals are born mentors. For others, it is an acquired skill. Either way, all mentors benefit from training that is focused on interpersonal skills that are critical to the mentoring relationship. For example, the best mentors know they cannot shape their mentees in their own image. To the contrary, gifted mentors try to cultivate a mentee's own gifts, no matter how different they may be from their own."[4]

The former chair of the Boston Bar Association's Mentoring Committee offered recommendations for both mentors and their mentees. Some of his suggestions included:[5]

1. mentors need to listen to the junior lawyer, making sure to answer the questions he or she wants addressed;

2. mentors should make sure the Mentee is comfortable asking questions by creating a non-threatening atmosphere;

3. mentors should broaden mentoring topics beyond legal questions to cover a wide range of issues a young lawyer may face;

4. mentees should pay attention to the timing of their inquiries to ensure the mentor has the opportunity to focus and is not distracted;

5. mentees should ask concrete rather than hypothetical questions as a way to get more specific advice; and

6. since no one senior lawyer has all the answers, mentees should seek out more than one mentor.

Ideally, a formal mentoring program would assign both a partner mentor and a senior associate mentor to each new lawyer. A junior mentor can offer frank advice and answer questions that a young associate may not feel comfortable asking a senior partner, even one in a mentor role. A junior mentor may also be better at anticipating and responding to the types of questions and insecurities that senior attorneys would not even have on their radar screens.[6]

In a formal mentoring program, careful attention must be paid to how mentors and mentees are paired. As Arin Reeves, a noted diversity expert, wrote: "For a mentoring program to be successful, the mentor matching process has to effectively match the strengths of the mentors with the needs of the mentees. Effective matching facilitates the interactive mentoring process and provides the infrastructure necessary to sustain a successful mentoring program."[7]

A mentoring program should also include opportunities to report regularly to firm management on both the effectiveness of the formal mentoring program as well as the effectiveness of the informal mentoring which takes place within practice groups.[8] Consistent monitoring and management review are critical to successful implementation. For example, the firm's human resources manager could periodically evaluate the firm's mentoring relationships by speaking individually with the parties involved to detect whether there are problems that need addressing, and, if so, whether a new mentor should be assigned.[9]

Of critical importance, law firm management must analyze ways to provide appropriate incentives to ensure partner involvement in mentoring and related professional development activities. The best incentive, of course, is a compensation system which recognizes the collective responsibility to support the growth and development of junior lawyers. The firm may also develop other creative ways to encourage involvement, for example, by developing educational programs that involve junior lawyers and are open to clients, and by creating internal systems to recognize openly model mentoring behavior.[10]

Mentoring expert, Ida Abbott, wrote that the cornerstone of mentoring success is for mentors to begin by caring about the mentee's learning and development.[11] She also urges the mentees to honor their own mentors by "passing along" the "wonderful gift" of mentoring by becoming mentors themselves.[12]

Effective mentoring is the gift that keeps on giving by developing skills, loyalty, and confidence. Mentoring provides the personal touch that can be transformative for someone's career. Fortunately, there are a plethora of ways to pass on the experience and wisdom that is at the heart of every mentoring connection.

Endnotes for Chapter 21

1. NALP Found. & Am. Bar Found., After the JD: First Results of a National Study of Legal Careers 80 (2004) *available at* http://www.NALPFoundation.org. The importance of informal mentoring was noted by the Chief Executive Officer of the Beth Israel Deaconess Medical Center who wrote: "Mentoring works best when it happens informally with the person who happens to be standing next to you when you need it. A work environment that encourages risk-taking, discourages criticism, and supports social relationships will allow and encourage women to develop their skills and achieve high-level satisfying careers." Paul F. Levy, *Teamwork on the Field & at Work*, 14 Regional Rev.: Fed. Res. Bank Boston 15, 15 (Q1 2005).

2. Roger Marks, *Has Mentoring Become a Forgotten Ritual?*, Corp. Legal Times, Jan. 2005, at 7.

3. Ida O. Abbott & Rita S. Boags, *Mentoring for Women and Minority Lawyers: Making It Succeed in Your Firm*, NALP Bull., Feb. 2004, at 1, 1-14. This article highlighted key aspects of their research study which is titled Mentoring Across Differences: A Guide to Cross-Gender and Cross-Race Mentoring, Minority Corp. Couns. Assoc., *available at* http://www.mcca.com/site/data/researchprograms/GoldPathways/index.shtml (Dec. 1, 2005).

4. Jonathan A. Segal, *Mirror-Image Mentoring*, HR Mag., Mar. 2000 *available at* http://www.shrm.org/hrmagazine/2000index/0300/0300segal.asp. Interestingly, the author also noted that misperceived attention and misunderstood comments may create a potential for harassment or discrimination claims; Segal recommended cautionary measures that can be taken to preserve the positive benefits of mentor/mentee relationships and minimize the risks.

5. Richard J. Yurko, *Mentoring: A Guide for Both Sides*, B. Bar J., Nov./Dec. 2003, at 16-17.

6. *See, e.g.*, Stephanie Francis Ward, *Coming of Age: When it Comes to Mentoring, Younger is Sometimes Better*, 90 ABA J. 27, 27, Jan. 2004.

7. Arin N. Reeves, *Five Principles for Creating Diversity in Law Firms,* Practical Lawyer, Oct. 2002 at 46.

8. ABA Comm'n Women in the Prof., Walking the Talk - Creating a Law Firm Culture Where Women Succeed 18 (2004).

9. *See*, Jonathan A. Segal, *Mirror-Image Mentoring*, HR Mag., Mar. 2000 *available at* http://www.shrm.org/hrmagazine/2000index/0300/0300segal.asp.

10. *See, e.g.*, Caren Ulrich Stacy, *Incentivizing Partner Participation in Professional Development*, NALP Bull., Aug. 2004, at 6.

11. Ida O. Abbott, Being an Effective Mentor: 101 Practical Strategies for Success (2001). At 3.

12. Ida O. Abbott, Working with a Mentor: 50 Practical Suggestions for Success, #50 (2001).

CHAPTER 22

THE FUTURE STARTS NOW

Law firms should create comprehensive economic models that include and analyze all costs associated with recruitment retention and attrition. A model that captures the full range of costs is likely to provide a compelling rationale for change and an even more compelling rationale for flexibility.

Firms should start by recognizing that clients have an investment in the lawyers with whom they work. Each time a lawyer leaves the firm, it is disruptive to the client relationship. Ironically, even as law firms ponder the perceived trade-off between reduced-hours schedules and commitment to client service, clients are seeking law firm relationships that are stable and where the work is performed by an engaged lawyer, one who has an interest in the client and who can build a base of institutional knowledge that can serve the client well into the future.[1]

The NALP Foundation urged law firms to develop detailed accounting systems that document associate hiring and departure patterns. In referring to a study by Watson Wyatt Worldwide, the NALP Foundation stated: "[T]here is now a new perspective proposing that improvement of recruitment activities must become an essential focus of top-performing organizations. A 2002 Watson Wyatt study of human capital management practices suggests that systematic, detailed accounting of hiring and attrition is no longer an optional activity, it is a requirement for optimal profitability. The Watson Wyatt Study stated that knowing with considerable accuracy the key skills and characteristics being hired, developed, and lost through unwanted attrition, as well as the attending costs of all these interactions, is imperative in a time of economic, business, and market change."[2]

The NALP Foundation also recommends specific strategies which law firms should consider to improve their associate retention rate. They include, for example: [3]

1. examining the associate work assignment and utilization systems to improve training and advancement opportunities;

2. aligning the evaluation program with the training and work distribution process to ensure that associates are fairly evaluated on work assignments which they have been trained to undertake;

3. treating associates with professional respect;

4. improving two-way communications between associates and the firm;

5. clarifying expectations around advancement to partnership and other criteria for success, and clearly articulating these to the associates;

6. investing in associate mentoring and related training programs;

7. answering questions honestly about the firm's culture which are raised during the recruitment process, and developing marketing materials that honestly reflect and communicate the culture of the firm;

8. facilitating the development of relationships between junior female and minority associates with role models; and

9. assessing the firm's support for family friendly policies and providing flexibility for childcare, elder care, or related obligations.

More frequently, associates are clearly expressing a lack of confidence in their future opportunities. For example, *The American Lawyer's* survey of associate satisfaction revealed that today's mid-level associates are highly pessimistic about their future partnership opportunities.[4] Importantly, in that same survey, approximately two-thirds of the associates agreed that creating alternatives to the partnership track were important.[5]

Law firms would be wise to heed these concerns. The fact that such a high proportion of both male and female associates believe that alternative models are needed corroborates that the current system is not working.

The Boston Bar Association Task Force on Professional Challenges and Family Needs reported that associates are growing: "increasingly sophisticated and skeptical about life in large law firms. They recognize that the prospects of partnership are speculative at best, and many feel that the life of a law firm partner is not compatible with their own life goals."[6] The challenge, therefore, is for law firms to develop organizational models that allow valued lawyers to thrive. As the BBA Report further noted: "[F]irms benefit from experienced lawyers who can provide valuable long-term contributions in the form of legal experience, relationship continuity, and profitability."[7] Law firms which see success for the firm and its attorneys as a broadly-defined vision, will create: "first-class opportunities to do challenging work, offer true family-work flexibility, and carry respect within the firm…."[8]

What does real flexibility look like? Many attorneys would happily work full-time as long as they had the flexibility they needed to tend to family obligations. A recent NALP Foundation study reported that the implementation of flexible work hours, as distinct from reduced-hours, is an initiative which would substantially benefit efforts to address work-life issues.[9] For one senior partner, the answer was simple:

> *I would create lots of flexibility for all kinds of different issues...and give the people the option to make less.*

She, and many others interviewed, strongly disputed the argument that invariably follows any discussion of reduced-hours or flexible arrangements: that law firms would economically suffer if the workplace allowed for greater flexibility in both work practices and compensation models. The Study for The Association for the Bar of the City of New York identified this concern as a common barrier to implementing changes: "Frequently, as most attorneys indicated, the conflict between serving clients and attending to personal interests or commitments is posed as a stand-off requiring the sacrifice of the latter."[10]

In its 1986 study, the ABA Section of Economics of Law Practice recognized the importance of flexibility in order for a partnership structure to respond as economic conditions change.[11] The study identified important trends in the legal profession that ought to affect significantly organizational structures, trends as relevant today as they were 20 years ago, even as too few firms have availed themselves of the alternative models described. Some of the challenges facing the profession that the study identified included:[12]

1. impacts of competition;
2. pressure on partner earnings (as particularly impacted by escalating operating costs);
3. market demand for specialties;
4. need for business generation;
5. new approaches to service delivery that involve varying roles for partners, associates, and other support personnel;
6. revival of the entrepreneurial spirit in which partners expect to be rewarded for their successful business development and entrepreneurial skills;
7. segmentation of partner rewards;[13]

8. need for associate development and motivation, recognizing that voluntary attrition is highly costly;

9. changing expectations of partners and associates;[14] and

10. evolution of governance from more democratic structures to greater centralized management.

To meet these tremendous challenges successfully requires a redesigned workplace. The Report of the Sloan Work-Family Policy Network noted: "The problem should be framed not as how organizations can design high-performance work systems, but how work practices can be redesigned to achieve both high performance at work and a more satisfying personal and family life."[15]

One attorney described her vision of a law firm capable of seamlessly integrating work/life issues:

> *The firm needs to recognize itself as part of somebody's life, not just as being a business, even though your primary goal is the business. So, all those issues about childcare, family care, elder care, people with substance abuse issues, interim stress issues where they need a leave of absence or sabbatical, people need to take time off just to do something completely different. They need to be more open to that.*

The problem is, however, that developing greater opportunities for meaningful flexibility is at odds with the associate-to-partner model that currently exists. Maybe this is the fundamental change whose time has finally come.

It would be difficult to develop much of a fan club for the current model. Younger lawyers frequently do not see partnership as an achievable goal, and even question whether it would be worth the high price to get there. For example, the study conducted for The Association of the Bar of the City of New York reported that partnership was not every attorney's goal.[16]

Critically, the very definition of what it actually means to be a partner is up for debate. As firms have grown larger, opportunities for meaningful partner involvement in firm decisions have diminished. As a result, in many law firms it is no longer clear whether partnership carries any responsibilities or opportunities beyond higher compensation.

This definitional issue of what it means to be a partner has significant ramifications for the entire profession, as the result of a lawsuit filed by the

United States Equal Employment Opportunity Commission against the law firm of Sidley Austin Brown & Wood. The suit alleges that the firm violated the Age Discrimination in Employment Act by expelling or involuntarily retiring partners on the basis of age.[17] The legal question raised by the lawsuit is whether, prior to their demotion, these partners were, in effect, law firm employees and, therefore, subject to the federal government's anti-discrimination laws. In a press-release issued when the lawsuit was filed, an EEOC Regional Attorney stated: "Whatever titles Sidley had decided to give these lawyers...our investigation indicated that they had no voice or control in governance of the firm and that they could be and were fired just like any other employees without notice and without the vote or consent of their fellow attorneys. A small self-perpetuating group of managers at the top ran everything...."[18]

As noted by one legal writer, the legal answer to the question of whether these partners were, in fact, a protected class of employees: "is intertwined with cultural changes that have taken place in the legal profession over the last few decades."[19] The lawsuit is a cautionary tale for those law firms which continue to expand significantly in size, while consolidating policy and management decisions to fewer lawyers, thereby diminishing, and even eliminating, the involvement and decision-making of the majority of those who have the title of "partner."

However the underlying questions raised in this lawsuit are fundamental to a rethinking of the professional structure of today's law firms. If partnership is merely a title, and not a designation which carries with it a set of responsibilities, then it has far less substantive meaning as an aspirational goal. If that is the case, then the entire institutional framework of the associate-to-partner structure currently rests upon a false set of assumptions about what it means to achieve partnership. It seems that even as opportunities to achieve partnership are diminishing, so, too, has the value of reaching that position.

What messages can firms give to their new associates to keep them engaged and excited about working in an environment where there is little opportunity for advancement to partnership? A Managing Partner offered this observation:

> *I think they should look at it as an opportunity to acquire skills that will stand them in good stead wherever they end up. That they are building their professional credentials and experience. And wherever the road brings them, they are going to be a bet-*

ter lawyer and better equipped for the future than they were before.

And I think that is the commitment that a law firm has to make to everybody.... [W]hether we have a long-term place for you or not, you are going to get first rate professional development here. You are going to acquire a skill set that will stand you in good stead for the rest of your life. And I think that is something, from what I have read and observed, that is actually of interest to Gen X and Gen Y people. The conventional wisdom is that they don't expect to spend their careers with a single employer.

He then highlighted the importance of offering alternative pathways, for example, "counsel" positions for those valued attorneys who may not become a partner but should not be part of the "up or out" structure of most firms:

Often people who are Counsel will have specialized expertise in areas where we need the expertise as a service offering, even if the economics of the person are not such as to support their being a partner.

He stressed the need to pay such counsel positions fairly, noting that in his own firm, an attorney slotted as Counsel could make as much as or more than a partner. However, he added that law firms must take great care to assure that the establishment of alternative pathways does not result in a group of people who are marginalized within the firm:[20]

It can create an underclass of people who are not very happy, who feel underappreciated, second-class. Even in firms where they have partner tiers, and someone's partner status is not apparent to the outside world, my experience is that people value how they are perceived internally, and that is at least as important as how they are perceived externally. And even if the outside world thinks that they look just like this other partner, and they are not, if everybody

inside the firm knows that they are not an equity part-
ner, that doesn't make people feel good. And it isn't
that much consolation to them day-to-day that the
outside world is oblivious to the distinction.... Every-
one wants to feel valued and appreciated, and doesn't
want to feel less valued or less appreciated than
somebody else.

These important observations should be part of any strategy to redesign the traditional partnership model. The fact is, there are a myriad of ways to develop and retain valued employees. Just as corporations have multiple roles and opportunities to use diverse talents, so, too, should law firms. Most management functions do not need to be filled by equity partners with extraordinary practices, nor should they. Management expert Peter Drucker emphasized that there is a "high risk in picking managers in professional organizations...." He stresses that there is no correlation, except for a negative one, between the success of a professional in the "operations" function and that person's subsequent success in a "staff" role as a manager.[21] As law firms move away from a centuries-old organizational structure, they would be wise to draw from the experts and implement alternative management models that emphasize, and reward, leadership skills.

Ultimately, the way to solve the structural dilemma is, first, to speak truth to the current power of most firms. The reality is that for today's crop of law school graduates, equity partnership in most medium to large firms may be an unrealistic goal for all but a very few lawyers. Being a successful lawyer, however, is both realistic and achievable. Modern law firms can join in widening the paths to a successful career by paying attention to the specific and unique talents of the lawyers that walk through their doors, and then putting those talents to their best use in the myriad of roles and functions required to run a first-class law firm in the 21st century.

Endnotes for Chapter 22

1. For an in-depth discussion of the critical connection between the business case for a reduced-hours program and the client's interest in retention, *see* James J. Sandman, *The Business Case for Effective Part-Time Programs*, Women Law. J., Winter 2003, at 16-18.

2. NALP Found., Keeping the Keepers II: Mobility& Management of Associates 111 (2003).

3. NALP Found., Keeping the Keepers II: Mobility& Management of Associates 102-104 (2003).

4. Amy Kolz, *Can You Hear Me Now?*, The Am. Law., Oct. 2005, at 105.

5. *Associates Talk Back*, The Am. Law., Oct. 2005, at 119.

6. BBA Task Force on Prof. Challenges and Family Needs, Facing the Grail: Confronting the Cost of Work-Family Imbalance 31 (1999).

7. BBA Task Force on Prof. Challenges and Family Needs, Facing the Grail: Confronting the Cost of Work-Family Imbalance 36 (1999).

8. BBA Task Force on Prof. Challenges and Family Needs, Facing the Grail: Confronting the Cost of Work-Family Imbalance 36 (1999). One commentator wrote about the use of Sunday as a "spare day for work" to make-up for time spent during the regular work day on family or personal responsibilities. Angela Lin, *Sunday Offers a Good Time to Get Work Done*, Boston Sunday Globe, Sept. 12, 2004, at G9.

9. NALP Found., In Pursuit of Attorney Work-Life Balance: Best Practices in Management, 43 (2005).

10. Epstein, et al., *Glass Ceilings and Open Doors: Women's Advancement in the Legal Profession*, 64 Fordham L. Rev. 291, 388 (1995 Rpt. to The Assoc. B. City N.Y., Comm. Women Prof.). The Study further reported a hypothetical conversation that could take place between a lawyer and a client that would simply allow the opportunity for both to explore a mutually acceptable time to talk without having to sacrifice a family commitment.

11. Bruce D. Heintz & Nancy Markham-Bugbee, Two-tier Partnerships and Other Alternatives: Five Approaches, 1986 ABA Sec. Econ. L. Prac.: "For firms to grow and thrive financially, partnership structures should be flexible enough to respond to changing economic conditions. Our thesis is that for an increasing number of firms, the 'up - or - out' structure does not provide this flexibility." At 10.

12. Heintz & Markham-Bugbee, Two-tier Partnerships and Other Alternatives: Five Approaches, 1986 ABA Sec. Econ. L. Prac.13-23. In identifying these challenges, the report refers to a rise in the "quality-of-output expectation" as a significant challenge. Interestingly, this observation was made prior to the advent of email as a tool which has raised client expectations exponentially. At 14.

13. Heintz & Markham-Bugbee, Two-tier Partnerships and Other Alternatives: Five Approaches, 1986 ABA Sec. Econ. L. Prac.; the report noted that: "Partner rewards can be separated into individual elements such as monetary compensation, equity participation, voting, policy-making rights, autonomy from close supervision, and can include such benefits as office size, level of secretarial support, and so on. Firms should use the various ele

ments of partner rewards to differentiate contribution based not only on the traditional definitions of partnership where excellent performance is required in all criteria, but also in definitions of partnership which allow different kinds of partners to exercise different skills and play different roles in the firm." At 20.

14. Heintz & Markham-Bugbee, Two-tier Partnerships and Other Alternatives: Five Approaches, 1986 ABA Sec. Econ. L. Prac.; The report recognized that these changing expectations not only include issues around the demands of the legal profession on one's family life, but the expectation that communication within the firm will be well-managed and associates informed, and, sometimes, even consulted, about important firm matters. "Lack of communication tends to hurt morale and loyalty." At 22.

15. Bailyn et al., Work-Family Policy Network, MIT Sch. Mgmt., Integrating Work and Family Life: A Holistic Approach 50 (2001). A colleague of Professor Bailyn highlighted the critical link between work/family issues and gender inequality in the workplace: "New models of work organization, work schedules, and careers will be effective tools for resolving work/family conflict only if women's roles in the family and the workplace also change." Ann Bookman, Starting in Our Own Backyards: How Working Families Can Build Community and Survive the New Economy 24 (2004). The founder of Catalyst wrote: "The high-performing career-and-family woman can be a major player in any company. She may switch gears in mid-life and re-enter the competition for the top. The price of retaining these women is threefold: The company must plan for and manage maternity, must provide the flexibility that will allow these women to be maximally productive and must take an active role in helping to make family supports and high-quality, affordable child care available to all of its employees." Felice N. Schwartz, *It Costs to Employ Women, but Pays a Talent Dividend*, L.A. Times, Mar. 17, 1989 at 7.

16. Epstein, et al., *Glass Ceilings and Open Doors: Women's Advancement in the Legal Profession*, 64 Fordham L. Rev. 291, 359 (1995 Rpt. to The Assoc. B. City N.Y., Comm. Women Prof.). "When Associates were asked whether they aspired to partnership, responses were mixed."

17. Press Release, U.S. EEOC, EEOC Charges Sidley & Austin With Age Discrimination (Jan. 13, 2005) at http://www.eeoc.gov/press/1-13-05.html (Dec. 8, 2005).

18. Press Release, U.S. EEOC, EEOC Charges Sidley & Austin With Age Discrimination (Jan. 13, 2005) at http://www.eeoc.gov/press/1-13-05.html (Dec. 8, 2005).

19. Neil, *Who is a Partner?* 91 ABA J. 34, 37 (June 2005).

20. This issue was also identified by a task force of the Boston Bar Association which noted that associates would be more interested in "off-track positions" if, by serving in such roles, the attorneys were not viewed as "second class citizens" who would be assigned "less sophisticated work." BBA Task Force on Professional Fulfillment, Expectations, Reality And Recommendations For Change 9 (1997).

21. Drucker, The Essential Drucker: The Best of Sixty Years of Peter Drucker's Essential Writings on Management 132-133 (2004).

CHAPTER 23

FAMILY AND FLEXIBILITY—THE IMPORTANCE OF THE "F" WORDS

It is imperative to the retention of valued personnel that law firms develop policies and practices that assist families. Law firms which want to "crack the code" to successfully retain and advance women will focus on one key word: flexibility. Reduced-hours policies, as a critical component of flexibility, should be viewed as one essential element of a comprehensive retention policy that addresses the unique demands of the legal profession. The law firm that implements a panoply of truly flexible ways in which attorneys can meet all of their client and family obligations will find itself a magnet for the top talent in the country.

Clients have clearly recognized the business case for effective reduced-hours programs as a way to stem attrition. In its analysis of work/life issues and attitudes in corporate law departments, the Project for Attorney Retention reported that: "A key reason in-house counsel generally support part-time work for their outside counsel is the fact that effective part-time programs cut attrition at law firms. In-house counsel repeatedly noted the negative effects of high law firm attrition, including the costs of repeatedly training and building relationships with new counsel and the loss of valuable institutional knowledge."[1]

As one Boston lawyer wrote: "Lawyers and firms must embrace a fundamental change in the way they establish priorities....Working together, sharing burdens and responsibilities, the attorneys in the firm can attend appropriately to time-sensitive client needs while at the same time safeguarding their personal time and commitments."[2] Indeed, in the law, as in society, generally, work/family issues can only be solved when all stakeholders work together to develop solutions.[3]

However, each proposal must be carefully vetted to ensure it is genuinely family friendly in both its intent and its results. Too often, law firms measure their commitment to families by offering expanded day care services which allow parents to spend even longer hours at work. The Report of the Sloan Work-Family Policy Network noted the critical differentiation: "We divide corporate work-family policies into two types: those that allow employees to more closely match the ideal worker norm, and those that seek to provide employees with flexibility so they can better manage their own work-life integration. Concierge services such as on-site meals, doctors, dentists, and laundry, as well as back-up childcare and sick-child care services serve as examples of the first type. Quite differently, options around parental leave, flexible work arrangements, and telecommuting provide employees with more control and flexibility in their work and family arrangements."[4] In other words, initiatives which provide day care for sick children or which offer weekend child care with the expectation that the service will be used end up being a disservice to families.

An article recognizing the 20th anniversary of *Working Mother* magazine and the changes that have taken place in the two decades since its inception observed: "Companies that had valued 'face time' above all else now have programs that include part-time work, job sharing and four-day work weeks. Workers who were once tied to the office now work from home with the help of computers, faxes, e-mail, and video conferencing."[5] The article noted, however, that these advances tell only part of the story since, despite these gains, the need for greater workplace flexibility that enables both working parents to address their family obligations is still a significant hurdle that negatively affects careers.

It is surprising that, as sophisticated and creative as attorneys can be, few law firms have figured out how to accomplish what so many other businesses now achieve: the successful implementation of a reduced-hours policy. The irony, however, is that for those few interviewees who described positive experiences, the basis for their success seemed remarkably simple.

Essentially, success was achieved in those instances where the firm was fully committed to ensuring that a lawyer working a reduced-hour schedule was afforded full opportunities to succeed in the law firm. These are the firms that have realized it is in their own economic interest to retain women in whom they have invested years of training and development, women who know the law firm, who have been introduced to and worked with important firm clients, and who have served the firm well in all other respects. As the Boston Bar Association Task Force on Professional Challenges and Family Needs observed, a mutual commitment to a reduced-hours schedule and flexibility by both the law firm and the attorney are key ingredients for success.[6]

One senior associate noted the mutually reinforcing behavior that arises when law firms are respectful of reduced-hours schedules:

For me, the fact that [my Practice Group Leader]
and others in my department are now generally so
sensitive to my flexible schedule...make me that much
more willing to be available to them when client
needs arrive.

They are good to me in that respect, so I feel that
much more willing to return the favor. It is people
whose schedules are often ignored that I believe are
more militant about trying to safeguard their time
away from the office.

Firms who respond by saying they cannot afford to embrace flexible work options for anyone other than their superstar performers are ignoring the fact that their approach is economically unsound. The economic cost of someone working a reduced-hours schedule cannot be adequately calculated without also factoring in the additional financial burden and resource drain imposed by the constantly revolving door of attrition.[7] As the study for the Women's Bar Association of Massachusetts observed: "The results of this study refute the notion that limiting part-time work opportunities or making them relatively undesirable will bring about a more profitable work force. In the absence of a supportive environment, attorneys leave, they do not become long-term, full-time attorneys."[8]

The study also identified critical components of a successful reduced-hours policy. Key recommendations included: allowing reduced-hours attorneys to be both eligible for partnership and for firm management positions; ensuring that reduced-hour attorneys have the same access to professional development as their full-time colleagues; clear management support which includes intolerance of disrespectful comments and behaviors; and fair compensation.[9] As an example of a more flexible approach to reduced-hours scheduling, some law firms focus on an annual billable-hour commitment, rather than on a schedule defined by weekly hours in the office.[10]

In essence, numerous studies and reports have emphasized that a reduced-hours policy will succeed if firm management creates a culture of mutual commitment to the success of its attorneys on a flexible schedule.[11] Of particular note, among the considerable body of research that now exists on this topic is the work of the Project for Attorney Retention at The American University Washington College of Law's Program on Gender, Work & Family. In fact, many of the comments and recommendations made by interviewees for this book echoed the recommendations of the Project for Attorney Retention. To measure how usable and effective a firm's reduced-hours policy is, the Project has delineated the "PAR Usability Test."[12] This six-pronged analysis focuses on the following as key measurements of success:

1. the policy's rate of usage by men as well as by women;[13]

2. median number of hours worked and duration of the balanced hours schedule;[14]

3. schedule creep;[15]

4. the assignments given to attorneys on a balanced hours schedule, as compared to assignments given before and after the reduced-hours schedule went into effect;[16]

5. the elevation rates of attorneys on balanced-hours schedules as compared to their colleagues on a standard schedule; and[17]

6. the attrition rates of attorneys working a reduced-hours schedule as compared to those working a standard schedule.[18]

Implementing a test to determine the usability and effectiveness of the policy is one important measure. Ensuring, however, that best practices are in place to support the existing policy is equally critical. Here, the Project for Attorney Retention specifically recommended key practices (1) the "Principal of Proportionality" to ensure proportional pay, proportional benefits, and proportional advancement, (2) flexible and fair policies, and (3) effective implementation.[19]

The "Principal of Proportionality" simply states that attorneys working a reduced-hours schedule should receive proportional compensation, including benefits and eligibility for bonuses, as well as proportional opportunities for advancement. Moreover, reduced-hours attorneys should be eligible to receive credit for pro-bono work and other non-client billable time that attorneys on standard schedules are able to track. Specifically: "The best practice is for firms and attorneys to recognize from the outset that non-billable work has to be planned and scheduled. It should be part of the written agreement, and the hours worked should be recorded."[20]

The importance of a flexible and fair policy is to ensure universal accessibility and applicability, but neither requires that everyone be on the same schedule, nor ignores the reality of individual personal needs. As the Project for Attorney Retention noted: "Creating a policy that is universally applicable does not mean creating a policy that is one-size-fits-all."[21] In fact, there are a variety of ways in which people can structure their time that would be acceptable to the firm, whether it be a schedule which addresses the number of hours each day an individual will work, or whether it accounts for time on a weekly or annualized basis. It is also important that firms refrain from setting deadlines by when balanced hours attorneys must return to a standard schedule. Concomitantly, the firm should also be flexible enough to allow lawyers to move between balanced hours schedules and standard hours at the firm.

Effective implementation requires a number of specific actions to take place. Most critical is support from the leadership of the law firm. The Project for Attorney Retention also urged firms to communicate support for the policy, and to implement training programs to ensure that all attorneys understand their role in making the reduced-hours policy a success. A prime ingredient of such training is to ensure that partners fully understand the connection between a successful policy and lower attrition.[22]

Similarly, it is important that partners in the firm "model" behavior which articulates a clear message of welcome to individuals working a reduced-hours schedule. Modeling such behavior would mean that partners allow themselves to take vacation time, be open about family care commitments, and otherwise act in a way that allows people to be comfortable about expressing their family circumstances.[23]

Finally, the Project for Attorney Retention identified detailed recommendations for ways in which a reduced-hours attorney and the law firm should address their respective roles, to ensure smooth implementation. Of critical importance is the recommendation that practice group managers be held accountable for the successful implementation of the policy. For example, by measuring attrition, law firms can monitor whether disproportionate attrition rates exist in certain practice groups over others.[24] Practice group leaders who have disproportionate attrition rates would be held accountable, just as those who show ongoing progress would be recognized.

In fact, the Project for Attorney Retention noted that firms err by failing to factor the costs of attrition into their cost-effectiveness analysis. The Project rejected the common practice of applying the same overhead calculation used for full-time attorneys to each of the reduced-hours attorneys: "In that context, the high cost of attrition dramatically inflates the overhead figure and makes balanced hours look costly, despite the fact that a usable part-time policy, by reducing attrition, would reduce overhead."[25] Instead, the Project recommended that actual individual expenses be included in the calculation, as is similarly done in the corporate model. The Project further noted that reduced-hours attorneys impose only marginal costs, compared with the costs of partners with larger offices and higher expenses related to use of resources, staffing needs, business development, and other costs.[26]

The bottom line calculation, according to the Project, is to alter the way of analyzing reduced-hours opportunities: "The reality is that law firms can't afford *not* to offer balanced hour policies that are both usable and effective. To keep the keepers in an era when half or more of law students are women, and in a society where the younger generation has become more insistent on work/life balance, law firms need to offer balance without career penalties. Those that do so become 'employers of choice,' able to attract and retain legal talent better than their competitors."[27]

Many of PAR's concepts can be found in those firms which have successfully implemented a flexible hours program. For example, a partner highlighted the key elements of her successful experience:

> *I can honestly say that I was never treated any differently when I was a woman associate here without kids, and then once I had my kids. There was never a feeling that I was getting less complex cases as an associate than people who were working full-time, or people who didn't have the same family commitments....*

> *Because I [was] on a reduced-time schedule as an associate, there was an effort made to limit the number of cases that I had. Since I had fewer cases, people tended to give me the very big cases, the complex cases, because it's easier to focus on a big case than 50 smaller ones. And I think that worked to my advantage in terms of the experience I got and the quality of work. I was running very big cases on my own as a senior associate, and at least from what I understand now of the discussions around my partnership, that was a big factor. I had already shown myself to be capable of running a big case and getting a big case ready to try. So that actually worked to my favor in some respects.*

Her appreciation for the significant opportunities she received, notwith-standing her reduced-hours schedule, caused her to fashion her own family responsibilities as flexibly as possible.

Many interviewees noted with irony the fact that their clients tended to be far more supportive of their reduced-hours arrangements then the partners who feared the same clients' reaction. Here, too, direct communication can resolve most concerns. One Managing Partner hypothesized a conversation that could take place between a lawyer and her client to ensure a continuum of flexibility:

> *When a lawyer has been working with a client for some time and can say, 'I am here for you. I am available. I am willing to be flexible, but I have other things going on in my life. Here's the schedule that I keep. You can call me at home on the days that I am not in my office, but I just ask that you do it when it is an emergency. I will be there for you.' Under circumstances like that, the client often sees that it is in their self-interest to help make the relationship work. Because the client will see that the alternative is not that the lawyer is not going to work part-time. The lawyer is going to leave. And they understand implicitly, if it doesn't get stated explicitly, that they are far better off having whatever percent of the lawyer they would be getting, than not having any of the lawyer at all.*

> *Too many of these conversations that I hear in the law firm context go on with no client involvement at all. And I think they are leaving, in a service profession, a key component out to try to address these issues without in some way involving the client.*

He also stressed the importance of appointing an institutional advocate to assist people who are struggling with work-life balance issues within the law firm, noting that the power dynamics that exist make it uncomfortable for people to raise these issues "with an intimidating senior partner." He described the responsibilities of his own firm's Part-Time Coordinator:

She does everything from meeting with people before they go part-time, to talking about the kind of part-time schedule that might be most effective. Or she meets for lunch regularly with the part-time lawyers, to talk about issues and get a sense of where there might be problems. She is available to counsel people one-on-one where problems come up. And they do. They are going to come up in any law firm. If anybody tells you otherwise they are not being honest.

Associates who are on a reduced-hours schedule should be allowed to remain on a partnership track. This is not doing someone a favor, rather, it is an important client-relations decision. In a system that divides lawyers into essentially two classes, clients expect that the associates assigned to their matters have the requisite skills and standing within the firm to be promoted to partner at the appropriate time. When years pass and the associate's status remains unchanged, and as her colleagues are promoted around her, what message is being conveyed to the client? In essence, the clients are left believing that their work must be viewed as unimportant because it is assigned to someone whom the firm seems disinclined to elect as its partner. It also inhibits that associate's ability to generate further business from the client, or the client's contacts, because of her continued diminished stature.

It is critical that law firms recognize and address the message sent to clients when reduced-hours attorneys are not promoted.[28] All clients have a right to expect that their work is being done by well-respected lawyers with a bright future at the firm. An equity partner in a national law firm who works a reduced-hour schedule stressed the importance of a partnership track that allows individual lawyers to develop a full range of skills:

> *I always encourage everyone to step back and not
> be in a hurry. The longer you are here before you're
> considered, the stronger candidate you'll be as com-
> pared to others. That if you've taken 10 depositions
> and everyone else has only taken four, chances are
> you're going to be in a better place. And I think that
> people get that. I think people understand it's to their
> advantage to wait. It's a gift. It's an opportunity to be
> that much better....It's not fair for [someone working
> a reduced-hours schedule] to be judged against peo-
> ple who are working gang busters....*

A former associate in a mid-size firm recommends that lawyers approach a request to work a reduced-hours schedule as a negotiation in which they are arguing from a position of strength. She described her own request at a firm which had never allowed such an arrangement:

> *'I'm only going to work part-time.' 'Well, we don't
> have part-time.' 'I know, but I'm only going to work
> part-time.' 'Yeah. But we have no policy.' 'I know, but
> I'm only going to work part-time, so we'll try this as
> an experiment.'*

> *But their willingness to try that as an experiment
> was the best thing that happened to me and to them,
> because it continued for other women afterwards....*

> *It's a negotiation process. 'Here's what I need,
> but here's what I can give to you in exchange for that.'
> So really analyze what is it that you have that's valu-
> able to them.... And [that can be] the trade-off for
> what you need personally.*

However, it is important that reduced-hours be offered as one of many tools. For many, all that may be needed is more progressive, flexible schedul-ing options, rather than working reduced-hours. A world of difference in cul-ture and morale could be accomplished simply by allowing people to make decisions about when they need to adjust their schedule.[29] This is also where technology offers opportunities to work remotely, allowing individuals greater flexibility, for example, to attend children's school and sporting events.[30]

A senior partner summarized the importance of schedule flexibility:

> *Well, to some extent, I think that all law should be flex time. We should all have the right, if we can, to get to the basketball game or the recital or whatever. I read very early on, really, like over 30 years ago, something in some magazine that said that the key for a working mom to have a degree of satisfaction is flexibility. That's not just a law issue.*

Perhaps the true hallmark of a successful flexible schedule policy will be the willingness of men to utilize these opportunities. One commentator noted: "Arguably, the most significant factor in making flexible working arrangements and maternity leave schemes successful at law firms is having applications from both male and female lawyers. If men don't take advantage of these arrangements, concern for life/work balance remains labeled a 'woman's issue,' and ambitious female lawyers will not therefore regard it as a real option."[31]

The Managing Partner of a major law firm wrote about the personal impact of a six-month sabbatical he took shortly after the birth of his son: "there are few things more effective in improving work/life balance for working mothers than to permit and encourage working fathers to spend more time on parenting."[32] He noted that the most significant change is likely to emerge from those firms whose senior managers are willing to lead by example, thereby demonstrating that it is fully acceptable for a male attorney to use a firm's family-friendly policies in his own personal life. If fathers could do so without fear of being perceived as less committed to success than their male colleagues, then more dads could take steps to be full participants in the life of their family.

Interestingly, the generational shift to more equal roles in parenting may hasten the opportunities for gender-neutral participation in flexible workplace options. Catalyst reported that in its 1998 study of dual-career marriages, nearly 50% of the male respondents stated that they would choose a formal flexible schedule with a new employer.[33]

In a New York Times article describing Gen-Xers' desires to avoid the frenetic pace of those who entered the workforce even half a generation before them, the writer suggested that the added commitment of the Gen-X Dad could help change the workplace: "If Gen-Xers don't succeed in forcing a shift in the very concept of a 'career,' the balance between work and family we desire will remain out of our reach. Instead of the traditional corporate ladder, which emphasizes stamina, we must seek a model of career progress that resembles mountain climbing, which requires flexibility, lateral moves, and lengthy rests at base camp."[34] In other words, the generation which is insisting on gender-neutral family structures in the home is more likely to transform the workplace and remove the barriers which prevent both parents from participating in their children's lives. For the time being, however, the imagery of the mountain climb is an appropriate metaphor for the difficulty of the task, even as it offers a plan for attempting to reach the summit.

Of critical importance to the recruiting goals of law firms, this generational shift is also taking place in the law schools, impacting even those elite domains at the top of every law firm recruiter's list. Harvard Law Professor Mary Ann Glendon, commenting on this important change, has noted: "Law schools were strongholds of feminism in the late '70s when women were a minority. But now that women make up nearly half the student body…I hear much more concern about how you can have a decent family life without suffering excessive career disadvantages. And, most significant of all…is that this worry seems to be bothering the young men almost as much as it concerns the women."[35] Professor Glendon further stated: "In the world of work, men as well as women are increasingly chaffing under pressures to put the demands of the job ahead of the needs of their families."[36]

New concepts are emerging in the effective management of work/life issues. A *Harvard Business Review* article identified three "mutually reinforcing principles" that managers have used effectively. The first principle is to clarify to the employee the business priorities, and understand from the employee his or her personal priorities. The second principle is the management recognition of and support for the employees' roles outside the office: "These managers understand that skills and knowledge can be transferred from one role to another and also that boundaries, where these roles overlap and where they must be kept separate, need to be established."[37] The third principle integrates the first two by continually experimenting in ways that benefit both the organization's need for performance and the personal needs of the employees. In their study of dozens of companies which have successfully addressed work/life issues, the authors emphasized the importance of mutual commitment and honest exchanges which, at their essence, allow individuals greater autonomy over ways to achieve their company's goals.[38]

The importance of this integrative communication cannot be overstated. Lawyers lament that, even where a firm may offer what appears to be family-friendly policies, professionals are reluctant to take advantage of them for fear it will damage their opportunities for advancement. The NALP Foundation found that: "Supervised attorneys opined that more attorneys might take advantage of work-life balance options if employers clarified and communicated the consequences of using the initiatives."[39] This observation underscores the fact that more than 46% of the law firm respondents reported that the work-life initiative in which they had the greatest interest was the creation of a committee to address quality of life and/or retention issues.[40] The NALP Foundation suggested that, among other functions, such a committee could include the development of programs to assist attorneys in addressing their own work-life challenges.

Ultimately, law firms will implement effective flexible working arrangements because they must. Law firms will learn, just as the corporate world has, that the demographics demand it. As Catalyst reported, by 1999 women comprised more than 45% of workers employed in executive, administrative, and managerial occupations, and each of the companies recognized in *Working Mother* magazine's "100 Best Companies for Working Mothers" all offered at least one flexible-work option, and most also offered others.[41] The results of the Catalyst longitudinal study of flexible work arrangements in the corporate sector demonstrate the long-term benefits: only one of the women followed has left the workforce, and half no longer work flexible schedules and have returned to full-time work.[42] Most still work for the same company and all hold senior level positions.[43] Importantly, Catalyst reported that the women in their study: "think about their professional and personal lives as integrated, not separated."[44]

In addition to the valuable research and related tools available to assist firms with these issues, there is also a need for a more personal and direct connection. For example, in the interviews, many senior women reported that their more junior colleagues frequently ask them for advice. One of the most frequently asked questions is: How should family planning considerations be factored into one's career decisions? For many young attorneys, the timing of a first child is fraught with concern over whether and how it will impact their opportunities for advancement. Most senior lawyers, when asked this question, try to convey that professional considerations cannot drive such a personal decision.

One senior partner in a large firm emphasized that she always urges women to separate family decisions from their career goals. Another former large firm partner poignantly illustrated that point by describing advice she had been given:

> *Toward the end of my associate run, [I said to my Managing Partner], 'Gee, I don't know whether I should wait to have kids until I make partner or whether I should have them as an associate. What do you think?' And he said to me, 'You can never let your professional advancement make that decision. That is a decision you have to make.' And that was very good advice; that was excellent advice. Because I think that is true. I think there are many women out there who feel that they postpone that decision and they end up unhappy in all different ways...that was actually our experience. Actually, I was waiting, and then we said, 'The heck with it. We'll just try.' And then we found out that we couldn't have kids.*

The fact is, just as it is difficult to create sharp distinctions between the professional and the personal in today's technology-based world, so, too, are flexibility and retention inextricably bound within the corridors of every law firm. As the Catalyst study observed: "What stands out as common to all participants is how flexibility plays into retention."[45] These words were essentially echoed in the NALP Foundation's study which found that: "A successful work-life program requires educating all attorneys on the mutually dependant relationship between the financial bottom line and work-life balance."[46] This mutually dependant relationship has the ability to be transformative for those law firms smart enough to recognize the connection.

A woman who left her large firm to establish her own practice recited the advice she always gives other women:

> *My advice would be to maintain who you are. And to keep sight of the fact that you do not need to become like a man practicing law. There really is a difference, whether you have children or whether you don't have children, a sort of mental processes of managing a household and thinking about the details...caring for elder parents, caring for friends,*

> *making social arrangements, caring for the house,*
> *planning vacation even. So that sort of extra work*
> *details of life...belong to the women.*

The bottom line is that the ultimate retention tool for any law firm is the agility to allow lawyers to integrate flexibility into their daily work lives. This is not about "making an accommodation." It is a necessary tool to retain talent.[47]

Endnotes for Chapter 23

1. Am. U. Wash. Corp. Council Proj. Atty Retention, Better on Balance? The Corporate Counsel Work/Life Report, (Final 2003) at 51, *available at* http://www.pardc.org.

2. Michael Rader, *Building a Fence Around the Law*, Boston Bar J., Nov./Dec. 2004, at 16, 17.

3. *See, e.g.*, Stephanie Davolos-Harden, Judith Presser, & Marta T. Rosathe, *Who Cares?: Building Cross-Sector Partnerships for Family Care*, (presentation summary from spring 2004 program), MIT Workplace Center, MIT Sloan Sch. Mgmt., (Susan C. Cass ed., 2005).

4. Bailyn et al., Work-Family Policy Network, MIT Sch. Mgmt., Integrating Work and Family Life: A Holistic Approach 18 (2001). The Executive Director of the MIT Workplace Center at the Sloan School of Management wrote compellingly of the need for corporations to integrate work/family policies with their responsibility to the community, a recommendation which has direct applicability to law firms. *See* Bookman, Starting in Our Own Backyards: How Working Families Can Build Community and Survive the New Economy 230 (2004): "Employers need to address community on several levels: to assess and respond to the needs of the community (or communities) in which their offices and plants are located; to make investments in the family support services on which their employees rely, usually located where employees live; and to encourage employee involvement in community volunteer work."

5. Diane E. Lewis, *A Look Back, and Forward*, Boston Sunday Globe, May 30, 1999, at F4. An article pointing to successful and expanding family-friendly policies in many European countries noted that the policies may have a revitalizing impact on the workforce: "[A] half-dozen European countries, including France and Germany, now rival U.S. productivity output per hour, even while workers put in 150 to 500 fewer hours a year than the average American, according to data released...by the Organization for Economic Cooperation and Development. Meanwhile, Europe's work-family programs have expanded." Maggie Jackson, *Family-Friendly Europe Offers a Model for Redefining U.S. Workplace Policies*, Boston Sunday Globe, Nov. 21, 2004, *available at* http://bostonworks.boston.com/globe/archives/112104.shtml.

6. BBA Task Force on Prof. Challenges and Family Needs, Facing the Grail: Confronting the Cost of Work-Family Imbalance 35-36 (1999). "The attorneys most satisfied with their reduced hours arrangements felt that their flexibility was matched by the firm's commitment to honor their arrangement. When there is mutual commitment to reduced hours career paths, flexibility naturally evolved." At 36. *See also* Ward, *Part-Time Possibilities*, 90 ABA J. 36, 36 (Apr. 2004), describing a successful compensation policy for reduced-hours attorneys which specifies that those who work in excess of the agreed amount are compensated for that time. That clarity is particularly important to reduced-hours attorneys who are frequently subject to "schedule creep."

7. *See, e.g.*, The study for The Association of the Bar of the City of New York which observed: "An economic argument can be made in favor of altering the traditional assumptions about the absolute priority of work. The basic question is whether or not the investment firms make in training associates is wasted if a large number of women at this level, or men, for that matter, find it impossible to balance work and other commitments."

Epstein, et al., *Glass Ceilings and Open Doors: Women's Advancement in the Legal Profession*, 64 Fordham L. Rev. 291, 413 (1995 Rpt. to The Assoc. B. City N.Y., Comm. Women Prof.).

8.   Women's Bar Assoc. Mass., Employment Issues Comm., *More than Part-Time: The Effect of Reduced- Hours Arrangements on the Retention, Recruitment and Success of Women Attorneys in Law Firms* 42 (2000). *See also* Melissa Nann Burke, *Flexing Their Muscles*, Legal Intelligencer, Nov. 11, 2004, at YL3.

9.   For the full list of recommendations, *see* Women's Bar Assoc. Mass., Employment Issues Comm., *More than Part-Time: The Effect of Reduced- Hours Arrangements on the Retention, Recruitment and Success of Women Attorneys in Law Firms* 42-49 (2000).

10.   *See* Martha Neil, *Working 9-5, or 10-3, or 1-4?*, ABA J., Dec. 2003, at 62.

11.   *See, e.g.*, ABA Comm'n Women in the Prof., The Unfinished Agenda: Women and the Legal Profession 34 (2001) noting: "Although the details of effective policies will vary across organizations, the key factors are mutual commitment and flexibility. Both the individual and the institution have to be willing to make adjustments that are fair for all concerned." *See also,* Catalyst, A New Approach to Flexibility: Managing the Work/Time Equation 77 (1997), observing in its comprehensive study of part-time work arrangements that leadership support will follow a clear articulation of the business rationale, in light of the significant benefits that derive from creating more flexible work places: "[T]he organization that will succeed with flexible arrangements is one that clearly relates their importance to the bottom line." At 77. For an interesting discussion of a Department of Labor program that provides mentoring assistance to female business owners interested in creating flexible work arrangements, *see* Maggie Jackson, *Flex Time, Mentoring for Women Help Create a New Business Culture*, Boston Globe, Oct. 24, 2004, at G1.

12.   Williams & Calvert, Balanced Hours: Effective Part-Time Policies for Washington Law Firms, Am. U. Wash. Coll. L., Project Att'y Retention 16 (2001). For an analysis of the potential to create a body of discrimination law to gain legal protections for workers with family responsibilities, *see* Joan C. Williams and Holly Cohen Cooper, *The Public Policy of Motherhood*, 60 J. Soc. Issues 849 (2004). For an analysis of the development of maternity leave policies between 1955 and 1985, including the role of sex discrimination law in the rise of these policies, *see* Erin Kelly & Frank Dobbin, *Civil Rights Law Work: Sex Discrimination and the Rise of Maternity Leave Policies,* 105 Am. J. Soc., 455, 455-492 (1999).

13.   The Project for Attorney Retention states that: "A low usage rate is a strong signal that a firm's culture makes the use of hours options undesirable, either because of schedule creep, or because of adverse career consequences perceived to accompany a decision to reduce hours, or both." Williams & Calvert, Balanced Hours: Effective Part-Time Policies for Washington Law Firms, Am. U. Wash. Coll. L., Project Att'y Retention 17 (Final, 2nd ed. 2001).

14.   The Project for Attorney Retention noted that a typical 80% "part-time" schedule can translate into a work week consisting of 40 to 48 hours. PAR recommends tracking the median number of hours worked and the median duration of balanced-hours schedules: "If firms find the median hours of balanced hours attorneys are in a range that would be considered full-time or overtime by non-law firm standards, their policies are not effective and

usable." Williams & Calvert, Balanced Hours: Effective Part-Time Policies for Washington Law Firms, Am. U. Wash. Coll. L., Project Att'y Retention 17 (Final, 2nd ed. 2001).

15. According to the Project for Attorney Retention: "If the comparison shows that attorneys on non-standard schedules are consistently working more hours than their balanced hours agreements call for them to work, then schedule creep is undermining the effectiveness and usability of the policy." Williams & Calvert, Balanced Hours: Effective Part-Time Policies for Washington Law Firms, Am. U. Wash. Coll. L., Project Att'y Retention 18 (Final, 2nd ed. 2001).

16. The Project for Attorney Retention noted the practice in certain major accounting firms to track: "whether those on alternative schedules are receiving high quality assignments by assessing whether they are assigned to work with the firm's largest and most valuable clients." In addition, PAR cautions that the type and quality of such assignments also be monitored. Williams & Calvert, Balanced Hours: Effective Part-Time Policies for Washington Law Firms, Am. U. Wash. Coll. L., Project Att'y Retention 18 (Final, 2nd ed. 2001).

17. The Project for Attorney Retention stated that it is important to compare promotion rates of attorneys working reduced-hours schedules with those on the firm's standard schedules: "While the promotion rate will not necessarily be identical for these two groups, a persistent imbalance in favor of standard hours attorneys may well indicate that balanced hours attorneys are being penalized in terms of promotions." Williams & Calvert, Balanced Hours: Effective Part-Time Policies for Washington Law Firms, Am. U. Wash. Coll. L., Project Att'y Retention 19 (Final, 2nd ed. 2001).

18. The Project for Attorney Retention urged firms to compare attrition rates among: men working full-time; women working full-time; men working part-time; and women working part-time to ensure that the attrition rates for attorneys working reduced hours is not significantly higher than for the other groups. Williams & Calvert, Balanced Hours: Effective Part-Time Policies for Washington Law Firms, Am. U. Wash. Coll. L., Project Att'y Retention 19 (Final, 2nd ed. 2001).

19. Williams & Calvert, Balanced Hours: Effective Part-Time Policies for Washington Law Firms, Am. U. Wash. Coll. L., Project Att'y Retention 20 (Final, 2nd ed. 2001).

20. Williams & Calvert, Balanced Hours: Effective Part-Time Policies for Washington Law Firms, Am. U. Wash. Coll. L., Project Att'y Retention 25 (Final, 2nd ed. 2001).

21. Williams & Calvert, Balanced Hours: Effective Part-Time Policies for Washington Law Firms, Am. U. Wash. Coll. L., Project Att'y Retention 28 (Final, 2nd ed. 2001).

22. The Project for Attorney Retention emphasized two important components of training. The first is providing specific information on how to implement all aspects of the program, including how to supervise an attorney on a balanced-hours schedule. The second is ensuring all attorneys understand the importance of the business case, to create a culture that avoids resentment. Williams & Calvert, Balanced Hours: Effective Part-Time Policies for Washington Law Firms, Am. U. Wash. Coll. L., Project Att'y Retention 31-32 (Final, 2nd ed. 2001).

23. Williams & Calvert, Balanced Hours: Effective Part-Time Policies for Washington Law Firms, Am. U. Wash. Coll. L., Project Att'y Retention 30 (Final, 2nd ed. 2001).

24. Williams & Calvert, Balanced Hours: Effective Part-Time Policies for Washington Law Firms, Am. U. Wash. Coll. L., Project Att'y Retention 37 (Final, 2nd ed. 2001).

25. Williams & Calvert, Balanced Hours: Effective Part-Time Policies for Washington Law Firms, Am. U. Wash. Coll. L., Project Att'y Retention 42 (Final, 2nd ed. 2001).

26. Williams & Calvert, Balanced Hours: Effective Part-Time Policies for Washington Law Firms, Am. U. Wash. Coll. L., Project Att'y Retention 42-43 (Final, 2nd ed. 2001).

27. Williams & Calvert, Balanced Hours: Effective Part-Time Policies for Washington Law Firms, Am. U. Wash. Coll. L., Project Att'y Retention 52 (Final, 2nd ed. 2001).

28. *See, e.g.*, Henry, *The Case for Flex-Time and Part-Time Lawyering*, 23 Penn. Law. 42, 46 (2001). *See also,* the Study of the Women's Bar Association of Massachusetts which recommends that attorneys on a reduced-hours schedule be eligible for partnership and considered for firm management positions. Employment Issues Comm., Women's Bar Assoc. Mass., More than Part-Time: The Effect of Reduced- Hours Arrangements on the Retention, Recruitment and Success of Women Attorneys in Law Firms 43 (2000).

29. It is important to add that flexibility reinforces the opportunities for successful reduced-hours arrangements in any practice group: "The practice area in which an alternative-schedule attorney works impacts the degree of effort needed to make the schedule satisfactory to both the attorney and the firm....Litigation attorneys report that although it may be difficult to be a part-time litigator, both the firm and the attorney can benefit from the arrangement. The participants make it work by being extremely flexible, having full-time day care, and aggressively seeking more challenging assignments. Part-time for these attorneys does not mean rigid three-days-a-week work schedules. Firm management, on the other hand, are respectful of a part-time attorney's skill and commitment. The assigning partners are also sensitive to the attorney's scheduling needs, i.e. providing advance notice for traveling when possible, assigning fewer cases, and respecting the attorney's decision to use down time to handle family work." Women's Bar Assoc. & Found. DC and Am. U. Gender, Work & Family Proj., Results of Lawyers, Work & Family: A Study of Alternative Schedule Programs at Law Firms in the District of Columbia 19 (2000).

30. A cautionary note should be sounded, however, regarding the potential for technology to exacerbate, rather than solve, the problem. In addition to the already-discussed concern of technology as a further tether to work, there is also the possibility that women who use technology to telecommute are further marginalized: "Sociologists have documented numerous examples of how potentially liberating new technologies end up being adapted to, and governed by, preexisting gender hierarchies in the workplace." Michelle A. Travis, *Equality in the Virtual Workplace*, 24 Berkeley J. Emp. & Lab. L. 283, 309 (2003).

31. *The Crucial Next Phase: Facilitating the Success of Women in Private Practice*, 2003, Levick Strategic Communications, & NorthStar Conf. (unpublished material on file with Levick Strategic Communications, LLC).

32. Jim Sandman, *What a Difference a Dad Makes*, Remarks at the Working Mother WorkLife Congress, (Oct. 1, 2003).

33. Catalyst, Flexible Work Arrangements III: A Ten-Year Retrospective of Part-Time Arrangements for Managers and Professionals 38 (2000).

34. Elizabeth McGuire, *Still Seeking a Perfect Balance*, N.Y. Times, Op-Ed, Aug. 11, 1998, at A19.

35. Mary Ann Glendon, Feminism & the Family: An Indissoluble Marriage, Commonweal, (Feb. 14, 1997) at 11, 12.

36. Mary Ann Glendon, Feminism & the Family: An Indissoluble Marriage, Commonweal, (Feb. 14, 1997) at 11, 13.

37. Stewart D. Friedman, Perry Christensen, and Jessica DeGroot, *Work and Life: The End of the Zero-Sum Game*, Harv. Bus. Rev, (Reprint No. 98605) (Nov./Dec. 1998) at 120. For an interesting article highlighting some of the tools and training opportunities that some businesses are making available to help managers address work-life challenges in the workplace, see Maggie Jackson, *Work-life Issues Can Test Managers*, Boston Sunday Globe, Aug. 28, 2005, at G1.

38. Friedman, et al., *Work and Life: The End of the Zero-Sum Game*, Harv. Bus. Rev, (Reprint No. 98605) (Nov./Dec. 1998) at 121.

39. NALP Found., In Pursuit of Attorney Work-Life Balance: Best Practices in Management, 41 (2005).

40. NALP Found., In Pursuit of Attorney Work-Life Balance: Best Practices in Management, 42 (2005).

41. Catalyst, Flexible Work Arrangements III: A Ten-Year Retrospective of Part-Time Arrangements for Managers and Professionals 15-16 (2000).

42. Catalyst, Flexible Work Arrangements III: A Ten-Year Retrospective of Part-Time Arrangements for Managers and Professionals 4 (2000).

43. Catalyst, Flexible Work Arrangements III: A Ten-Year Retrospective of Part-Time Arrangements for Managers and Professionals 9 (2000).

44. Catalyst, Flexible Work Arrangements III: A Ten-Year Retrospective of Part-Time Arrangements for Managers and Professionals 4 (2000).

45. Catalyst, Flexible Work Arrangements III: A Ten-Year Retrospective of Part-Time Arrangements for Managers and Professionals 6 (2000).

46. NALP Found., In Pursuit of Attorney Work-Life Balance: Best Practices in Management 70 (2005).

47. See, e.g., the study of the Women's Bar Association of Massachusetts, which found that over 90% of its Respondents reported that the availability of a reduced-hours schedule affected their decision to join or to stay at their firm. Employment Issues Comm., Women's Bar Assoc. Mass., More than Part-Time: The Effect of Reduced-Hours Arrangements on the Retention, Recruitment and Success of Women Attorneys in Law Firms 36 (2000).

CHAPTER 24

WOMAN TO WOMAN

A woman who breaks down the barriers she has erected against other women is likely to find that, by contributing to another's success, she is enhancing her own. Professor Eleanor Fox wrote that she always urges her female students and students of color to be open about sharing their experiences: "Sharing of negative experience is hard to do, but the reason it is hard to do is the reason it should be done, each individual's painful experience, if isolated, tends to reflect negatively on her own merits. But by sharing experience, patterns, if they exist, can be observed. If patterns are observed, the meritocracy story may be impeached; and if the meritocracy story is impeached, or even ruffled at the fringes, the person who once felt herself devalued may gain a clearer view of reality and of the possibilities for both adjustment and change."[1]

Professor Fox's advice is critically important to eliminating the isolation so many women feel in their own law firms. By finding opportunities to work together, learn from each other, and share experiences, women create a collective path to their individual success.

This is the essential wisdom found at the conclusion of *A Tale of "O,"* where Professor Rosabeth Moss Kanter noted that the things "O's" can do include: "Talk with other O's about O-ness; share coping strategies and support."[2] She also urges X's to ensure that everyone has equal access to the resources, skills, and information needed to succeed in the organization. In the world of X's and O's, life improves considerably when more O's are brought into the world of X's and provided opportunities to succeed.[3]

This message easily translates into a law firm environment. As O's, that is, women partners, support each other and the other women trying to succeed, they will enhance their own opportunities. In doing so, they can step away from the spotlight which requires a constant need to prove oneself and join with their fellow O's on equal footing with the X's.

Many firms are beginning to support that journey through the creation of Women's Initiatives designed to provide women with the tools they need to succeed. Although they range tremendously in scope and sophistication, these initiatives offer skill-building and related training opportunities, the development of business networks, and provide a safe environment for women to discuss issues of concern. Even as these initiatives are a product of the energy and involvement of a firm's female lawyers, they cannot succeed without clear and visible senior management support. As the former CEO of Deloitte Consulting LLP stated about its own efforts: "[T]he Women's Initiative was always driven by the managing partners....[F]rom the start, senior management signaled that the initiative would be led by the partners." In doing so, and in appointing a woman partner viewed as a star performer to lead the effort, Deloitte made clear that this initiative represented a cultural change driven by firm leaders. [4]

Such initiatives should be developed to maximize the involvement of women attorneys throughout the firm. For example, some women attorneys may, at the outset, feel a certain degree of discomfort with the idea of meeting "separately," and may express concern about how this may be viewed by their male colleagues. Most women who have been involved with the implementation of successful initiatives reassure reticent colleagues, and explain to questioning male attorneys, that as long as women constitute small minorities of equity partnership and leadership positions, the need exists to seize every opportunity to develop skills and networks that can lead to greater success.

It is also critical to ensure that the activities of the initiative are the product of significant input. Some of the most successful women's initiatives began by bringing in speakers of interest to meet with the women attorneys on a variety of topics ranging from client development, media relations, negotiation skills, gender issues in the courts, and even such issues as dressing for success.

After the initiative has taken root and a critical mass of the firm's women are engaged, then the firm can develop programs that provide business development and related networking opportunities directly with women clients. Models range from panel discussions which are open to clients and business contacts, to retreats or even "spa days" for key clients.

At their best, these initiatives serve to build a stronger internal network of women who will advocate for institutional changes and serve to support the external business development activities of women lawyers.[5] One partner in a national law firm described her firm's Women's Initiative:

> *We do some coaching and training of the women*
> *in the office at every-other-month meetings. Some-*
> *times we bring in outsiders. Sometimes we have*

people from inside, and talk about everything from
public speaking to networking...

And then we do things with outside organiza-
tions.... And then we try to vet opportunities for
women out there in the community and act as a
resource.... Or try to figure out which of the different
charities are good to be involved with...the whole
purpose of it is to help women become more econom-
ically successful.

She noted that their firm's Women's Initiative now has a National Coordi-nator to implement activities at the firm's many branch offices, including opportunities to bring the women partners together. The sophistication of this firm's efforts is being matched across the country, as law firms become increasingly adept at creating the internal and external networks to help women in firms get to know each other and bring women business leaders together with women attorneys.[6]

Those involved in establishing Women's Initiatives, however, must resist efforts to "measure" the success of the Initiative by tracking new clients or new business directly attributable to these efforts. This is a false measure-ment and would only undermine the reason for establishing such an Initiative in the first place, which is, to assist the firm's efforts in the retention and pro-motion of women attorneys. Accordingly, to the extent a firm seeks to mea-sure the success of its Women's Initiative, it should track the number of women it has retained, and how many are elevated to partnership and firm leadership positions.

This point is critical to the underlying value and importance of these efforts. The purpose of a Women's Initiative is to focus on ways women can succeed in the firm. Accordingly, even though management support is a cru-cial component, it is women who must drive the agenda and identify the mea-sures of success. As Mona Harrington bluntly stated: "[W]omen need to learn not how to conform but how to refuse to conform.... They need to talk, to pro-test, to dissent, to resist, to organize new structures to accommodate their val-ues and visions. And to do this, they need a voice. In spite of their increasing numbers, they do not have a sufficient voice in the profession to make their common interests heard. They need to speak their interests and values, not hide them."[7]

Author Blum observed the positive impacts of women helping other women in the workplace: "The most heartening part of seeing women rise in the power structure is not seeing them perform like powerful men, but like powerful women."[8] She noted that as women's voices have been heard in the workplace, the result has been an increased emphasis on day care, flexible schedules, and the importance of addressing work-family issues.

In other words, critical mass matters. Toward that goal, women are becoming effective at joining forces to accelerate a change in demographics. For example, the San Francisco Bar Association established a "No Glass Ceiling" initiative in which signatory law firms agreed to a goal of 25% women partners by the year 2004.[9] Results reported in July, 2005 revealed that significant progress had been made by a majority of the participating firms.[10]

The Chicago Bar Association's Alliance for Women initiated a "Call to Action" to Chicago law firms. The Call to Action proposes a variety of initiatives that signatories are asked to implement relating to the retention, advancement, and fair compensation of women, including proportional representation in key management roles.[11]

In addition to the developing initiatives to promote the elevation of women to partner and their inclusion in key roles on client teams, one key organization has taken the path of promoting certain law firms which are owned by women or minorities. The National Association of Minority and Women Owned Law Firms ("NAMWOLF"), founded in 2001, was created to advocate for the use of minority and women-owned law firms by major corporations and public entities.[12] NAMWOLF, through its selective application criteria and certification process, offers clients an important option for achieving their own diversity requirements. Law firms would be wise to heed the lessons offered by NAMWOLF and its commitment to the success of its member law firms.

Throughout their careers, women will have difficult decisions to make as they seek to address their myriad responsibilities. Harvard Law School Professor Alan Dershowitz offered an important context for framing these decisions: "Every decision has consequences and few are entirely reversible, but there is a considerable difference between those kinds of decisions that lead to a point of no return and those that simply slow down progress toward one goal in the interest of another."[13] He stressed the importance of individuals finding their own way, knowing that each experience and decision offers a learning opportunity that helps inform the next decision point.

Fortunately, these decisions do not have to be made without guidance. Throughout the interviews, women offered advice for one another. Even in a context in which the fundamental concept is that the institutions must change, interviewees shared their tips and advice with other women to help them succeed in the current environment.

One highly successful female partner urged women to ignore the external impediments to their success, and instead charge forward with their own plan:

> *The one thing that I think is the most important thing to do to improve the lot of women in law firms is, I think that women themselves have got to own the issue. To the extent that women, and I don't care how young they are in the firm, define what is impeding them as somebody's attitude towards them, I think the game is over right there. And I think it is very important to work with women to get them to realize that the cultural bias is as much in their head as it is in the eyes of the male majority. And I don't mean to say that it isn't real, it is absolutely real. But you have got to wake up to it in your own head before you can deal with it.*

> *And by that I mean, women have a lot of times got unconscious beliefs that they can't do something or that they will be stopped. They never explore it. They just don't go there. So I think every woman has got to go within and figure out what they really want to do, not what they think they can have, but what they really want to do and then look in their own minds for their beliefs about why they can't do it. And then go for it anyway. Because you find that a lot of the stuff just melts away once you have stopped empowering it in your own consciousness.*

She then described how she applied this lesson to herself to enhance her opportunities as a rainmaker and a law firm leader. She attributed her success to something greater than her own self-confidence:

It also had a lot to do with the choices I made day-to-day. If there was no limitation out there, I might choose A instead of B. If there was a limitation, I might never get to A. I think it made a lot of difference in my choices. So I was exuding confidence, but I also think it was what I did with my time....

I wanted to be a player.... I realized in my own head I had a lot of beliefs about how women could not do that; there were certainly no role models out there for me. So I started picturing in my head what stood in my way of achieving this. And I saw CEOs that wouldn't give women a break, and I saw large firms that just wouldn't put me in the right position to meet the clients. I had a lot of things in my head, and until I got conscious about them, I didn't realize how much I would avoid cognitive dissonance by not bringing these topics up with the senior leadership of the firm. Or I would avoid going to community events where I'd be intermixing with a lot of male CEOs that might make me nervous. Once I got onto this, then I started making a lot of different choices. And I would talk to the partners that could help me with my aspirations. And I would go to networking events where I would meet people out there that would be useful. And I was also very consciously pursuing women General Counsels that I knew could give me a break with less cultural blinders. So I just did some things differently than if I hadn't been as aware of what I was scared of internally....

I realized that I actually did not talk to some people because I made assumptions about how they would react to me, and what they might be willing to do for me, based on my attitude about what males thought. And instead I...[became] a much better

> *mentee...and I would go in there with some new*
> *ideas [about how they could help me].*

She recommended that women take matters into their own hands when confronted with a problem they want solved, by forging ahead on their own:

> *What they need to focus on is what they want to*
> *get done. And just go and get it done. It puts you in a*
> *very different posture in the firm. And it leads to very*
> *different consequences. I have spent many years in*
> *this firm trying to solve the problems, and then I just*
> *decided I was going to go for what I wanted. I was*
> *much happier.*

Other advice offered by women ranged from the general to the specific. Several women observed that some of their colleagues moved too quickly to a reduced-hours schedule, even where they were, in reality, maintaining a relatively full-time work load. One partner recalled her conversation with another woman in the firm who was planning to work one less day a week:

> *I advised against it.... I advised her...not to vol-*
> *untarily take less. Because if you look around, you*
> *will have men at any given time who are not doing*
> *that much. And there is no reason to take a step down.*
> *No one will really say anything to you, unless you*
> *voluntarily go and do that. Because sometimes I think*
> *women are more conscientious that way, they think*
> *they are not giving their all. But if you look around*
> *there are some men associates who are doing a lot*
> *more than them, but most of them aren't. They don't*
> *ever say, 'Oh I am slow. Dock my salary.'*

Other suggestions ranged from the importance of developing a self-confident demeanor to tips on style and presentation. A number of women interviewed stressed the power of exuding self-confidence. One former partner stated bluntly:

> *Promote yourself. That's really the biggest piece [of advice] is to promote yourself, promote yourself, promote yourself. And the other piece is to be entitled…. I mean there is this lack of confidence…. I remember [a colleague] saying to me that women operate on merit. And you know what? That's not right. You can't operate on merit. You can be the best lawyer you can be, but you're not going to get promoted just because you're a good lawyer…that only gets you to square one. That doesn't get you to home, you know? And I think there is real surprise when women…come into this setting, [thinking] that things are fair….*

> *And again, I think it's how we are socialized. Men are socialized so differently from women…and men are taught to be political animals so early on. Whether it's promoting themselves or how they relate to each other or how they speak or how they put themselves in this hierarchy, and women are really uncomfortable with hierarchy.*

Almost without exception, the advice women offered for each other was to develop a self-confident style and recognize the importance of relationships. Again, the former partner minced few words in her own analysis of why she succeeded:

> *I've always been the kind of person where I think proactively. Who am I going to hook up to help with so-and-so and how am I going to get this person to succeed? If they succeed, then they'll owe me a chip later. Even as a kid, I've always thought politically. I think that's the best. And not necessarily selfish. But maybe if I can help them, that person might like me better….*

> *I think that women don't think strategically. Whether it's political relationships, whether it's help-*

> *ing people, connecting people, I mean I try to find*
> *people all the time. I hook people up because it helps*
> *them....I'm like, okay, I did something good for that*
> *person. I can call them up if a crises hits or if I need*
> *them, or it's sort of you're accumulating goodwill.*
> *You're storing up goodwill.*

She summarized by saying that star performers think strategically in their relationships. The power of relationships was also highlighted by a New York partner who succinctly summarized the advice she would give to other women:

> *I think that making friends, keeping connec-*
> *tions, being loyal to people, just developing a posi-*
> *tive network of people is probably the most positive*
> *thing you can do.*

Many of the women interviewed approached issues of style and presentation with trepidation, but believed it hard to ignore the importance of appearance in making an impression. As the study conducted for The Association of the Bar of the City of New York noted: "The higher one goes up the professional and managerial ladder, the more subjective assessments are employed to evaluate individuals."[14] These subjective evaluations are an inherent part of most professional interactions, and they are not gender-based. Associates, in particular, are always under scrutiny for factors beyond the quality of the work product: "The hardest qualities to assess are those of personal manner and style, but these are certainly regarded as important in the partnership decision."[15]

Several of the women interviewed expressed their concern that women need to take additional measures to ensure a professional appearance. For example, a senior partner spoke of her efforts to help the younger women understand that the way in which they present themselves has an impact on how well they are heard by others:

> *We actually sat down with the women and said,*
> *'Look, casual days haven't done you any big favors. It*
> *is one thing to want to be casual, but you don't dress*
> *as well as the secretaries. How do you expect you are*
> *going to get ahead? How are people going to take you*

> *seriously? Go get a hair cut. Wear some makeup. Put some jewelry on. You know, you don't have to be dolled up. That's not what we are saying. You dress the part. You have to look professional…. If you're going to make a good impression on the client, going to make a good impression on the judge, or a partner, you need to look professional and appropriate. People need to start thinking of you in that context.'*

> *There are some of the women associates who giggle a lot. And I mean, these are hard things; they are awkward things to tell somebody, but you have to do it.*

She added that, because it is difficult for younger lawyers to hear their own partners critiquing their appearance, an outside consultant may be useful in these types of discussions. She then spoke of other behaviors where women undermine their own success and urged that they find a greater confidence level:

> *I personally see a big difference in the way the male associates interact with me, and this is one of the other things we are telling the women associates, 'You never come by my office and just schmooze. When you report, a lot of times it is very impersonal. You do it by voicemail; you do it by an email. You are very efficient.' And they say, 'But I'm assuming I don't want to waste your time. You're a partner. You're important.' And I say, 'I know why you are doing that.' On the other hand, here is this young associate, he's a guy, he's in my office, he is enthusiastic. He is talking about this case: 'I've got this issue.' The image I have is, he cares. He takes his job seriously.*

Her fundamental message was that women could make tremendous gains simply by "showing up," getting out from behind their computer screens and finding opportunities for greater direct interaction with their senior colleagues. Finally, she urged that, in those interactions, women exude a greater degree of self-confidence:

> *In terms of group dynamics, women associates frequently will come in and say, 'Well, gee, I don't know. Maybe I'm all wet about this.' You never hear the men come in and preface something like that.*

Through their advice and attention, these women offer themselves as genuine role models, a critical relationship for younger lawyers. Professor Lani Guinier noted their importance: "As a catalyst for progressive change, genuine role models have responsibilities, not just privileges. To be a role model in this sense is a responsibility to those who come after us, and to those whom we follow. Role models should be people with whom members of the outgroup identify who are then held accountable to other outsider aspirants. Especially to the extent that they are seen as representatives or agents for others, role models need to nurture their roots not just model their roles."[16]

Perhaps, then, once the role model designation begins to feel more comfortable, women can take note of their own power and work together to implement significant change. Importantly, even a small band of committed compatriots can begin to effect change. As Susan Estrich wrote: "Three female partners, three tenured women, three female directors or trustees or senior officers - one you can ignore, but three today could be more tomorrow, and even if it's only three, they'll get attention."[17]

Finally, women must let go of the illusion of perfection. Most women feel an incredible obligation to be perfect, at work and at home.

However, it is really the illusion of perfection they are chasing, since no one actually attains this elusive status. The study conducted for The Association of the Bar of the City of New York identified the problems which develop when women receive "multiple messages" that lead them to believe they are doing nothing well. These are messages, however, which can be altered: "But women do succeed when the evaluations of what they are doing are positive rather than negative, when they have support from their husbands and in the firm from their colleagues; when they have enough child care of good quality and dependability; and to some extent, when they are insulated from cultural norms regarding one 'correct' way to be a mother."[18]

A partner in a law firm described her struggle to "let go" of this need for perfection:

> *I think women tend to want to do things, or like doing things, but that at a certain point you have to say to yourself, 'I like doing this. I want to do this. But I can't do it by myself, so I'm going to let my husband do some of this.' So I've made a deliberate effort to make him buy 50% of the birthday presents and make 50% of the play dates.*

Perfection, Anna Quindlen observed: "torments…both those who are trying to attain it and those who feel they never can."[19] By sharing experiences, and imperfections, it may be possible to tear down the isolation and unrealistic striving towards goals that may not, in truth, be desired.

Endnotes for Chapter 24

1. Eleanor M. Fox, *Being a Woman, Being a Lawyer and Being a Human Being - Woman and Change*, 57 Fordham L. Rev. 955, 963 (1989). Similarly, Professor Lani Guinier highlights the importance of students sharing their experiences by working together in teams in law schools: "To reach women and people of color in particular, I encourage all students to prepare for class in teams, to talk through their ideas first in less formal settings. Students who have otherwise been silent are often more likely to share their points of view openly with their classmates in such a context. And many women and men of all colors thrive once they have a chance to hear themselves think aloud, alone with their peers." Guinier et al., Becoming Gentlemen: Women, Law School and Institutional Change 91-92 (2002) (1997).

2. Kanter with Stein, A Tale of O 216 (1980). It is important to note that women in the American workforce have a significant history of joining together to create social networks that served also to advance their interests in the workforce. *See, e.g.*, Priscilla Murolo, The Common Ground of Womanhood: Class, Gender, and Working Girls' Clubs, 1884-1928 (1997). As Susan Estrich wrote: "Getting more women to the table almost always builds the power of women in general, and the ones who got them there in particular." Estrich, Sex & Power 155 (2000).

3. *See, e.g.*, Kristin Eliasberg, *Tapping on the Glass,* Law Firm Inc., (October, 2005) at 36.

4. Douglas M. McCracken, *Winning the Talent War for Women: Sometimes it Takes a Revolution*, Harv. Bus. Rev., (Reprint R00611) (Nov./Dec. 2000) at 4.

5. The ABA Commission on Women in the Profession highlighted four key areas of focus for internal women's groups: (1) increasing opportunities for business development; (2) working to resolve work/life balance issues within the firm; (3) developing formal mentoring programs and coaching opportunities that can offer practical advice as women try to succeed to the partnership ranks; and (4) helping to get women promoted to leadership positions within the firm. ABA Comm'n Women in the Prof., Empowerment and Leadership: Tried and True Methods for Women Lawyers 24-25 (2003). For examples of media coverage of law firm efforts to target women clients through organized initiatives and the related impact of women's growing business influence; *see, e.g.*, Sheri Qualters, *Going Where Business Is: Law Firms Target Women*, Boston Bus. Journal, July 19, 2002, at 23; Robert Weisman, *Hear Women Roar as Technology, Business Force*, Boston Sunday Globe, Nov. 2, 2003, at C2; Joann S. Lublin, *Women Aspire to be Chief as Much as Men Do*, Wall St. J., June 23, 2004, at D2; Mary K. Pratt, *Her Place at the Table*, Boston Bus. Journal., June 11-17, 2004, at 53; Sheri Qualters, *Women Lawyers Hone Rainmaking Skills*, Boston Bus. Journal., Aug. 1, 2005, *available at* http://boston.bizjournals.com/boston/stories/2005/08/01/focus3.html (Dec. 7, 2005).

6. *See, e.g.*, Leslie A. Gordon, *Women Mean Business*, ABA J. (Aug. 22, 2005).

7. Harrington, Women Lawyers: Rewriting the Rules 203 (1995) (1994). *See also*, Arlie Russell Hochschild, The Time Bind: When Work Becomes Home and Home Becomes Work 245 (1997), noting: "A more daunting yet ultimately more promising approach to unknotting the time bind requires collective - rather than individual - action: workers must directly challenge the organization, and the organizers, of the American workplace."

8. Blum, Sex on the Brain, the Biological Differences Between Men and Women 283 (1997). In writing about the importance of women learning to work collaboratively together, author Leora Tanenbaum wrote that: "We can see that competition between women serves only the status quo. And the status quo keeps us from gaining more power over our lives, our work, and our relationships." Leora Tanenbaum, Catfight: Rivalries Among Women - From Diets to Dating, From the Boardroom to the Delivery Room 303 (2003) (2002).

9. *See, e.g.,* B. Assoc. San Fran., *Fifty Firms Commit to No Glass Ceiling for Women,* at http://www.sfbar.org/about/newfiftynoglass.html (Sept. 9. 2003).

10. *See, e.g.,* B. Assoc. San Fran., *BASF's No Glass Ceiling Initiative Results in Huge Strides for Bay Area Women Attorneys, available at* http://www.sfbar.org/about/releases/no-glass_ceiling_results.htm (July 28, 2005).

11. *See* Chicago B. Assoc., CBA Alliance for Women, *Call to Action: Focus on Diversity, available at* http://chicagobar.org/calltoaction/default.htm.

12. *See* The National Association of Minority and Women Owned Law Firms at http://www.namwolf.org.

13. Alan Dershowitz, Letters to a Young Lawyer 28 (2001).

14. Epstein, et al., *Glass Ceilings and Open Doors: Women's Advancement in the Legal Profession,* 64 Fordham L. Rev. 291, 365 (1995 Rpt. to The Assoc. B. City N.Y., Comm. Women Prof.).

15. Epstein, et al., *Glass Ceilings and Open Doors: Women's Advancement in the Legal Profession,* 64 Fordham L. Rev. 291, 365 (1995 Rpt. to The Assoc. B. City N.Y., Comm. Women Prof.).

16. Guinier et al., Becoming Gentlemen: Women, Law School and Institutional Change 94 (2002) (1997).

17. Estrich, Sex & Power 149 (2000).

18. Epstein, et al., *Glass Ceilings and Open Doors: Women's Advancement in the Legal Profession,* 64 Fordham L. Rev. 291, 438 (1995 Rpt. to The Assoc. B. City N.Y., Comm. Women Prof.).

19. Anna Quindlen, Being Perfect 32 (2005).

CHAPTER 25

THE POWER OF CLIENTS

Clients represent an awesome force. When they speak, their lawyers listen. If they used their collective voice to seek changes in the profession, the results would be immediate and compelling. The specialist in the attorney placement field, who previously commented upon the generational differences she has observed, concurred:

> *The only change that can occur, in my view, is*
> *that which is driven by the clients of the law firm....*
> *You've got to incentivize people to do it differently.*

For the profession as a whole, the growth in General Counsel's offices has been significant. By the turn of the 21st century, corporate law departments had grown significantly, accounting for approximately 10% of all lawyers.[1] American Bar Association statistics report that approximately 12.5% of men and 10% of women work in the corporate sector.[2] Also, according to a recent poll, 44% of corporate law departments have added lawyers to their payrolls in the past three years and 37% expect to add additional attorneys within the next year.[3] As these corporate law departments have expanded, the numbers of women who have become in-house counsel has also increased.[4]

The influence of women clients on career patterns in law firms was recently demonstrated in a study analyzing whether women-led corporate clients had an impact on the number of women who became partners at their law firm. The results demonstrated that "law firms that have corporate clients with women as CEO or legal counsel have higher growth rates for women partners."[5] The authors observe that a key finding of their study is that: "direct interaction with women and the visibility of prominent women in the corporate client influence the law firm."[6] The implications of this study are significant because it links growth in the number of women partners with the presence of women clients in high-level positions (CEO and General Counsel).

A Managing Partner of a national law firm emphasized his view of "the business case" for client involvement, stating that nothing will change a law firm's culture faster than hearing from clients that work/family balance issues should be a priority because it is in the clients' own economic self-interest. Once clients articulate this concern, he believed that his partners would understand that attorney retention was a client-driven problem to solve:

> *I think that the best pitch, ultimately, is a client service pitch, and not the high cost of attrition. I say that because I saw a few years ago, when the economy was down, the cost-of-attrition argument was still being made by advocates, not realizing that many firms were hoping for attrition. And they weren't aware of the fact that such an argument works well when a firm is growing rapidly and needs to recruit, and can't afford to lose people, but it falls on deaf ears and worse when the economy is down. [Then] you are hoping to shed people.*

> *The one argument that endures through the ups and downs of the economic cycle is client service. Turnover and loss of people is not in the interest of your client. At least not your good people.*

> *Clients are very aware of the effects of attrition. When they have an investment in a person who has learned their business, and their legal problems, not only do they not want to pay to get somebody new up to speed, they just don't want to have to go through the trauma of getting to know a new person and having a new person get to know them. And where I have seen work/life balance issues addressed most effectively is when a client is part of the solution and the client is involved in almost advocating for the lawyer working to achieve work/life balance.*

He further observed that as important as it is for clients to take a more active role in working with lawyers and their schedules, it was also important that clients become more involved in finding alternatives to the billable-hour model. He noted the importance of client engagement in firm operations, and how the current lack of interest has allowed complacency to continue:

> *For all the talk about it, I don't see all that much client interest. They want to do something on a fixed fee basis, where the firm bears all the risk. For all its problems, the billable hour is something that people have gotten used to and are relatively comfortable with.*

He felt confident that law firms will have to change because women comprise half of the talent pool:

> *The change will be forced because it just won't work in the long term, as a matter of client service and as a matter of economics, for firms to be unable to retain and attract a significant portion of the talent pool.*

To accelerate that change, he stated that clients should ask detailed questions that would force firms to focus on the issues that drive attrition rates higher, including detailed questions about work/life concerns.[7] The reality is, clients lose when valued lawyers leave their team. And they benefit from law firms which understand the strengths of perspective offered by a diverse team.

Interestingly, Harvard Law School Professor David Wilkins cautioned against complete reliance on advocating the "business case" for diversity from the client's perspective, absent an analysis that recognizes both its importance to the bar itself and an underlying social justice vision, such as that which produced the body of legal cases resulting in the defeat of segregated practices in American society. He noted that the business case, or, as he described it, demand-side initiatives, are vulnerable: "to the changing winds of corporate self-interest."[8]

Rather, Professor Wilkins stated that the clients themselves have duties that arise out of the increased leverage they yield with their law firms. In contrast to the "agency model of the attorney-client relationship" which presumed that lawyers use their own professional judgment in employing their skills on behalf of a client: "Clients now routinely exercise decision-making authority over virtually every aspect of a law firm's staffing decisions." He noted that, although this involvement was originally an effort to reduce costs: "it is also part of a general move by corporate clients to assert control over an increasing array of tactical decisions about how their cases will be handled."[9] The altered dynamic between lawyer and client has resulted in a relationship in which: "two independent entities...have decided to temporarily join forces to achieve a common objective."[10] Accordingly, the parties look more like joint venturers and, as such, issues of trust and control, as well as ethical duties, have become reciprocal.

What this means, according to Professor Wilkins' analysis, is that corporate clients have ethical obligations to address law firm diversity because of their own role in creating: "the economic conditions that adversely affect the career opportunities of minority lawyers. The contemporary structure of elite law firms, including high wages, a growing associate to partner ratio, and diminished training opportunities, disproportionately disadvantages minority lawyers. Corporate clients bear important, although by no means sole, responsibility for these institutional practices."[11] Moreover, Professor Wilkins stated that these corporate clients are generally themselves lawyers and, therefore: "have a direct stake in the long-term legitimacy of the legal profession."[12] In essence, Professor Wilkins posited that: "ethics is about more than enforcement. It is about recognizing power and acknowledging responsibility....The agency model of legal ethics was created in a time when lawyers held sway over their clients. If we are to build an account of legal ethics that takes account of the contemporary realities of the lawyer/client relationship, we must recognize that both parties have ethical obligations to each other and to their joint cause."[13]

Professor Wilkins' considerable body of work is based on his research and analysis of issues with respect to lawyers of color. The principals are also applicable to the issues and experiences of women attorneys and have tremendous relevance to any analysis of the client's responsibilities and obligations to the profession.

The bottom line is, clients should choose to become actively engaged in these issues because it is in their own and the profession's best interests. Much of a law firm's corporate legal work derives from outside counsel who have a stake in the profession and a concomitant duty to use their power to encourage fundamental fairness. Lawyer and lawyer-client, therefore, should mutually reinforce these obligations and opportunities. Fortunately, several major corporations have taken leadership roles in requiring meaningful diversity within their own law offices and in the law firms they hire.

Even if ethics and business alone cannot change the result, then certainly demographics should drive behavioral changes. Increasingly, women are joining in-house law departments, nearly all of which are purchasers of legal services. Accordingly, the greatest opportunity for clients to spur meaningful change may be in the hands of women in-house counsel, many of whom have left positions in private practice, to use their purchasing power to alter the face of the private law firms that they have left behind.

The rise of women in key corporate positions will invariably have a positive impact on the progress of women in law firms. As Deborah Graham noted: "Seeing women in senior spots on the client side may do more than anything else to affect both the ways in which women lawyers in private practice see themselves, and the ways in which they are seen by men-and to promote the belief, among both female and male lawyers, that women lawyers can and will be important players in the business side of legal practice."[14]

By ensuring that women lawyers are included in the competition for their business, women in-house counsel offer their former colleagues critical client generation opportunities. Each time a client hires a women attorney as outside counsel, she is helping to eliminate the barriers that women have faced for decades, and gaining a very loyal attorney in response.

In-house lawyers have much to consider when hiring outside counsel. They are being relied upon to use their judgment, expertise, and legal relationships to select an attorney in private practice who can achieve a great result as economically as possible. There is little room for error.

The path of least resistance, therefore, has been to turn to the "name" firm or the "go-to" lawyer for outside help. Frequently, however, this will narrow the selection to male senior partners who have had ample opportunities to develop a reputation in a particular area. One woman General Counsel stated succinctly:

> *When I choose a law firm or a lawyer my Board*
> *has never heard of, the results had better be great or I*
> *am the one that bears the consequences.*

Some in-house counsel expressed concern about using anyone but the known name for the "bet-the-company" types of cases. However, statistics show that, in a typical year, less than 5% of the legal market is truly focused on "bet-the-company" cases.[15]

Moreover, there are ample due diligence opportunities to expand the list of those who may be considered the "go-to" lawyer. For example, in-house counsel can develop a simple tracking system of attorneys identified in trial court opinions issued in the areas of expertise for which outside counsel is being sought. Various tracking services and online court decisions allow easy access to this information. Keeping a database of such details as the names of the lawyers, the subject matter of the cases, and the prevailing party can later be the basis for compelling statistics that will greatly expand the pool of "go-to" lawyers.

There are also many ways to expand the pool of those experienced practitioners capable of handling even the most critical matters. For example, a fruitful source of referral possibilities is the decisions of a state's Supreme Court or the Federal Court of Appeals which identify the attorneys involved.[16] As the first woman president of the Pennsylvania Bar Association noted: "The number of women trying and winning major verdicts has jumped exponentially in the last two decades. Women attorneys are winning cases, at trial and on appeal, in every area of law...."[17] Attorneys with demonstrated success before these courts are highly likely to be excellent choices that even the most difficult Board of Directors could approve.

Many in-house counsel indicated that they consult with other in-house lawyers for recommendations. That process itself can be flawed if there is no system behind it. For example, do the other lawyers consulted have their own system for developing a more diverse pool of talent? Is the inquiry casual, or do in-house counsel consult at least three to five other colleagues for suggestions, and know the criteria on which the recommendations are based? If referrals are sought in a systematic way, it can ensure a bountiful source of new information, and not simply a perpetuation of the same well-known names.[18]

With clear systems in place to identify, hire, and evaluate outside law firms, in-house counsel can make tremendous strides in diversifying their selection of attorneys. As former ABA president, Robert MacCrate, stated: "[T]he quest for gender equality must become a central objective of the legal profession if we are to be faithful to the professional ideal of opposing all forms of discrimination, and if we are to achieve full integration and equal participation of women."[19]

In addition to the power that women in-house counsel hold, women-owned businesses represent a critical demographic that should catch the eye of all law firm marketers. Women have been starting their own businesses at twice the rate of men.[20] The Center for Women's Business Research provides compelling statistics that show the demographic force of entrepreneurial women if they use their clout in the purchase of legal services:

- 10.6 million privately held businesses are 50% or more women-owned

- these businesses generate $2.5 trillion in sales and employ more than 19.1 million people

- women-owned enterprises are estimated to expend $103 billion dollars annually on information technology, telecommunications, human resources services, and shipping

- between 1997 and 2004, the estimated growth rate in the number of women-owned firms was nearly twice that of all firms, and employment expanded at twice the rate of all firms[21]

In its Annual Report on Women's Clout in Business, the Committee of 200 noted that: "Even though parity with men is still far off into the future, the world of entrepreneurship has proven to be a haven for businesswomen - often a welcome alternative or antidote to the glass ceiling in corporate America."[22]

Some corporate counsel clients, including those led by men, are beginning to use their economic clout in a meaningful way to promote change in the diversity of the law firms they hire. As reported by the American Bar Association Commission on Women in the Profession, some of the more successful efforts include General Motors Corporation's statement to outside counsel of its expectation that the diversity of the corporation's legal service providers match that of GM's law department. The Sarah Lee Corporation conducted a baseline assessment of its outside legal providers and created three tiers; the company then sent a clear message to the lower ranking law firms that they risked losing Sarah Lee business if their commitment to diversity did not improve. DuPont links its women legal providers nationwide, encouraging cross referrals among these select firms who meet DuPont's strict diversity requirements.[23]

Corporate general counsel have also joined together to express their mutual commitment to diversity. For example, hundreds of corporations have endorsed as signatories a commitment to diversity in the legal profession entitled *Diversity in the Workplace - A Statement of Principle.*[24]

Efforts like these send clear messages to law firms: the power of clients is pervasive because law firms cannot exist without them. As more clients become serious about diversity, the change in the profession could be dramatic.

Endnotes for Chapter 25

1. Epstein et al., The Part-Time Paradox: Time Norms, Professional Lives, Family, and Gender 13 (1999).

2. ABA Comm'n Women in Prof., A Current Glance at Women in the Law (2005) at http://www.abanet.org/women/womenstatistics.html.

3. Cathleen Flahardy, *The Hire Power: Legal Departments Add Lawyers to the Payroll*, Corp. Legal Times, May 2005, at 45.

4. By 1991, for example, women held approximately 20% of all positions in general counsel offices and, in 1992, were estimated to hold 4.2% of positions as the top legal officers positions in the 250 largest corporations in the country. *See* Epstein et al., The Part-Time Paradox: Time Norms, Professional Lives, Family, and Gender 13 (1999). A 2001 report issued by the ABA Commission on Women in the Profession noted the significant growth of women in corporate counsel positions in just a five-year period: "up from about a quarter in the mid 1990s to over a third at the turn of the century." ABA Comm'n Women in the Prof., The Unfinished Agenda: Women and the Legal Profession 25 (2001). Among Fortune 500 companies, the number of women general counsel increased to 15% in 2004, up from 8.4% in 2000. ABA Comm'n Women in the Prof., Walking the Talk - Creating a Law Firm Culture Where Women Succeed 3 (2004).

5. Christine M. Beckman and Damon J. Phillips, *Interorganizational Determinants of Promotion: Client Leadership and the Attainment of Women Attorneys*, 70 Am. Soc. Rev. 678, 687 (Aug. 2005).

6. Christine M. Beckman and Damon J. Phillips, *Interorganizational Determinants of Promotion: Client Leadership and the Attainment of Women Attorneys*, 70 Am. Soc. Rev. 678, 687-688 (Aug. 2005).

7. Mere questionnaires, however, without aggressive follow-up activities are insufficient. For example, Harvard Law Professor David B. Wilkins eschewed the perfunctory approach of corporations which: "do little more than send the same form letter to their outside [law] firms 'requesting information' about the number of minorities working at the firm and dole out small projects that are below the pricing structure of many large firms." David B. Wilkins, *Do Clients have Ethical Obligations to Lawyers? Some Lessons from the Diversity Wars*, 11 Geo. J. Legal Ethics 855, 864 (1998).

8. David B. Wilkins, *Do Clients have Ethical Obligations to Lawyers? Some Lessons from the Diversity Wars*, 11 Geo. J. Legal Ethics 855, 866 (1998). Professor Wilkins stated that: "Greater diversity along the legally-projected dimensions of race, sex, religion, national origin, age, disability, and veteran status may produce the diversity of views, cultural competence, attitudes, and lifestyles that are beneficial to organizations in a global economy. But when the construct of diversity is broadened to encompass these attributes, along with others such as geographic diversity, rank in the organization, and even taste in food, chattiness, and fondness for certain sports, then efforts to achieve diversity will have that much less impact on socially disenfranchised groups. Resources put into achieving diversity on non-legal dimensions will do less to improve the position of women and minorities. And as white males claim rights based on their diverse likes and dislikes, the language of diversity will be that much less likely to empower women and minorities to make rights-based claims to equality within organizations."

9. David B. Wilkins, *Do Clients have Ethical Obligations to Lawyers? Some Lessons from the Diversity Wars*, 11 Geo. J. Legal Ethics 855, 876 (1998).

10. David B. Wilkins, *Do Clients have Ethical Obligations to Lawyers? Some Lessons from the Diversity Wars*, 11 Geo. J. Legal Ethics 855, 887 (1998).

11. David B. Wilkins, *Do Clients have Ethical Obligations to Lawyers? Some Lessons from the Diversity Wars*, 11 Geo. J. Legal Ethics 855, 892 (1998).

12. David B. Wilkins, *Do Clients have Ethical Obligations to Lawyers? Some Lessons from the Diversity Wars*, 11 Geo. J. Legal Ethics 855, 892 (1998).

13. David B. Wilkins, *Do Clients have Ethical Obligations to Lawyers? Some Lessons from the Diversity Wars*, 11 Geo. J. Legal Ethics 855, 899 (1998).

14. Graham, Getting Down to Business: Marketing and Women Lawyers 396 (1996).

15. Statistics presented by Susan Raridon Lambreth at a September 2002, program sponsored by the Hildebrant Institute. Within the 5%, Ms. Lambreth includes the following categories of cases: major IP litigation, catastrophic litigation, and major bankruptcies. Address at the Developing Women Leaders in the Legal Profession Conference, (June 10, 2005) sponsored by the Hildebrandt Institute, (unpublished; on file with the author).

16. For example, in addition to reported decisions, Massachusetts Lawyers Weekly annually summarizes all decisions issued by the Commonwealth's Supreme Judicial Court. This compilation summarizes the decision, sorted by subject matter, and includes the names of the attorneys involved.

17. Leslie Anne Miller, *Special Report on Women and Minorities in the Profession: Women in the Legal Profession: Where Are We Now?*, The Pennsylvania Lawyer, Jan/Feb 2003, at 20.

18. Many of these recommendations with respect to the power of in-house counsel first appeared in the following: Lauren Stiller Rikleen, *Female In-House Counsel Can Wield Economic Power to Level Playing Field in Hiring Outside Lawyers*, New Eng. In-House, Feb. 3, 2004 *available at* http://www.newenglandinhouse.com.

19. Robert MacCrate, *What Women Are Teaching a Male-Dominated Profession*, 57 Fordham L. Rev. 989, 990 (1989).

20. Dianne Hales, Just Like a Woman: How Gender Science is Redefining What Makes Us Female 332 (Bantam 2000) (1999).

21. Center for Women's Bus. Res., 2004 *Key Facts About Women-Owned Businesses*, (Pamphlet; 2005 update *available at* http://www.womensbusinessresearch.org/researchstudies.html, last visited on December 8, 2005).

22. Michael Llewellyn-Williams, *The C200 Business Leadership Index 2004: Annual Report on Women's Clout in Business*, 2004 Commission of 200, at 9.

23. ABA Comm'n Women in the Prof., Walking the Talk - Creating a Law Firm Culture Where Women Succeed 11 (2004). These types of efforts have also been the subject of media coverage. *See, e.g.*, John Share, *Big Clients Pressuring Firms on Diversity*, The Minn./St. Paul Bus. J. (Minn./St. Paul) (Oct. 17, 2003) *available at* http://twincities.bizjournals.com/twincities/stories/2003/10/20/story3.html.

24. *See*, http://www.cloCallToAction.com.

CHAPTER 26

THE POWER OF LAW STUDENTS AND THE OBLIGATION OF LAW SCHOOLS

Law schools may achieve excellence in fulfilling their mission of teaching about substantive law topics, but there is also a growing need for law schools to undertake a broader role. Specifically, today's law students need a sufficient understanding of the varied career paths available, and the inherent sacrifices and rewards associated with each choice.

In general, once students leave the relative security of their academic environment and enter the work force, they are unprepared for the sense of disillusionment with the profession that may follow. The initial results from the study of law school graduates of the year 2000 indicated that law schools need to do a better job preparing their students for the transition to practice.[1] More than a decade ago, author Richard Moll observed: "The current, standard curriculum of law schools is questionable as an appropriate and effective introduction to serving the common good as a lawyer."[2]

Moreover, just as law firms have not kept pace with the corporate sector in the training and development of their leaders, law schools are trailing their business school counterparts in addressing the very real career challenges of work/life issues. For example, several leading business schools have added to their curriculum courses that address work/life issues. These courses can prove invaluable for employees heading out into a demanding work environment.[3]

Law schools should also be helping their students learn about the business of law. It is no longer tenable to send graduating students off into a highly competitive, business-oriented work environment without any training as to the myriad of issues in which they will be expected to excel in order to succeed. Author and law firm consultant Larry Smith decried the failure of law schools to develop a curriculum that can teach: "business, sales, market research, advertising, public relations, and marketing strategy classes specifically designed for the lawyer."[4]

The fact that law schools do not adequately prepare students for the practical difficulties of the profession is exacerbated by summer associate programs for law students where opportunities to attend baseball games and social events can occur with far greater frequency than actual work assignments. Most national law firms are locked in a competitive effort to reap high scores in such public measure as *The American Lawyers'* annual summer associate survey. As a result, these summer experiences resemble high end summer camps far more than they accurately depict law firm life.

The American Bar Association has expressed concern about the legal community's failure to prepare law students for what their life will be like once they enter into the profession. For example, more than a decade ago, a report of the ABA Commission on Women in the Profession noted that: "[T]he very institutions which should be preparing students for practice are contributing to the wide-ranging dissatisfaction within the profession."[5] Subsequently, the Commission published two additional reports focusing on women in legal education which recommended that law schools both undertake gender studies and create committees to address gender issues. Yet, when the Diversity Committee of the American Bar Association polled law schools to determine whether they had taken steps to implement the recommendations of these reports, only 11 of the 177 law school respondents had undertaken gender studies. Similarly, only 10 of the 177 respondents created an ad hoc or a standing committee on gender.[6]

In addition to the lack of opportunities to learn in law school about the professional challenges ahead, an increasing number of law students are graduating having incurred extraordinary debt to pay for their education. A Report of an ABA Commission stated that today's law students are graduating with greater debt than ever before.[7] According to the Commission, between 1992 and 2002, the cost of living rose 28%, yet public law school tuition increased between 100% and 134%, and private law school tuition rose by 76%. Also, to finance their legal education, more law students than ever are borrowing money. Today, most students are graduating with cumulative undergraduate and law school debt in excess of $80,000.[8]

This debt significantly impacts the career options of young lawyers and diminishes their flexibility during the years when they must pay back their student loans.[9] The ABA Commission recommends a number of steps law schools can take to help students reduce their debt burden. These steps include, for example, increased financial aid, greater funding of loan repayment assistance programs, and the development of closer relationships with bar associations, foundations, and others to increase and coordinate programs which can assist in the reduction of law school debt.[10]

Law schools and law students must also recognize their own unique opportunities to transform the profession. Law schools, for example, should reevaluate their curriculum to provide instruction that can facilitate the transition into the profession. Also, law students must recognize their own power as potential recruits in a highly competitive market.[11]

The NALP Foundation detailed an action plan that law schools could implement to assist students in their career paths. The recommendations highlighted the importance of providing practical opportunities to law students so they have the tools to make intelligent choices in their career decisions. For example, the NALP Foundation recommended that law schools and career service programs: [12]

1. develop mandatory programs to continually help students understand the implications of law school debt;

2. consider a requirement that all students participate in career counseling programs;

3. provide students with the tools and resources needed to analyze employer characteristics, to assist in identifying employers most likely to be compatible with their own career goals;

4. help students learn how to use the interview process and related fact-finding to gather credible and useful information on prospective employers; and

5. encourage students to participate in clinical programs or other opportunities to develop important lawyering skills that can serve as a foundation for future success.

The NALP Foundation also offered an action plan to help students and associates choose a prospective law-firm employer: [13]

1. partake in the full range of career counseling and job search assistance that law schools provide;

2. be aggressive in gathering intelligence on a prospective employer. It is important to note that this includes direct inquiry to different points of contact within the firm;

3. realistically assess the trade-offs that excelling in a private practice environment may involve; and

4. use the interview process as a tool to get the job that is the best fit possible.

In its detailed analysis of the relationship between the legal education community and the profession itself, a Task Force of the American Bar Association proposed a "Statement of Fundamental Lawyering Skills and Professional Values" to assist law students in preparing for private practice.[14] Specifically, the purpose of the Statement is to help law students: "begin their legal education with a clearer sense of the importance of acquiring skills and values in the course of professional development."[15]

The Statement offers a significant opportunity to serve as a tool for curriculum development in law schools. The ABA noted that, at its essence: "the Statement of Skills and Values identifies, as a fundamental professional value, the need to 'promote justice, fairness, and morality.' Law school deans, professors, administrators, and staff must not only promote these values by words, but must so conduct themselves as to convey to students that these values are essential ingredients of our profession."[16] The ABA stressed the importance of a law school's commitment to these values, particularly because the Socratic method itself can promote: "the impression that wit, sharp responses, and dazzling performance are more important than the personal moral values that lawyers must possess and that the profession must espouse."[17]

The need for a closer connection between the profession and those who train lawyers is critical. Law schools must play a more aggressive role in preparing students for the profound challenges they face once they graduate and take their place in the profession. As Suffolk University Law School Professor and former Boston Bar Association President Renée Landers wrote: "[M]y colleagues in the academy must fulfill their obligation to participate in the work of the profession."[18]

Law schools have a unique opportunity to help their students enter the modern workforce with a more sophisticated understanding of the challenges ahead. By doing so, they would be making an important contribution to the legal profession.

Endnotes for Chapter 26

1. NALP Found. & Am. B. Found., After the JD: First Results of a National Study of Legal Careers 79 (2004) *available at* http://www.NALPFoundation.org. Noted Harvard Law School Professor Alan Dershowitz observed of law schools: "Their graduates are not adequately trained to confront the real-life temptations they are likely to encounter in the competitive world of law firms and clients." Alan Dershowitz, Letters to a Young Lawyer 90 (2001).

2. Richard W. Moll, The Lure of the Law: Why People Become Lawyers, and What the Profession Does to Them, 218 (1991).

3. *See, e.g.*, Tatsha Robertson, *Between Work and Life There's Balance: But Do You Have to Sacrifice Career Goals to Get It?*, Boston Sunday Globe, June 19, 2005, at E1.

4. Larry Smith, Inside/Outside: How Businesses Buy Legal Services, v, (2001).

5. ABA Comm'n Women in the Prof., Options and Obstacles: A Survey of the Studies of the Careers of Women Lawyers 11-12 (1994).

6. *See*, ABA, *Report of the Diversity Committee, 1999-2000* at http://www.abanet.org/ legaled/committees/diversity.html (Aug. 8, 2004).

7. ABA Comm'n on Loan Repayment and Forgiveness, Lifting the Burden: Law Student Debt as a Barrier to Public Service 10 (2003).

8. ABA Comm'n on Loan Repayment and Forgiveness, Lifting the Burden: Law Student Debt as a Barrier to Public Service, 9 (2003). *See also*, NALP Found. & Am. Bar Found., After the JD: First Results of a National Study of Legal Careers 71 (2004) *available at* http://www.NALPFoundation.org. This study reported similarly high debt for graduating law students with median education debt of $70,000.

9. *See,* Margaret Graham Tebo, *The Debt Conundrum*, 87 ABA J. 42 (Mar. 2001). The NALP Foundation recommends that law schools offer mandatory training to students to help them understand the impact of law school debt on their career choices. *See* NALP Found., Keeping the Keepers II: Mobility& Management of Associates 105 (2003).

10. ABA Comm'n on Loan Repayment and Forgiveness, Lifting the Burden: Law Student Debt as a Barrier to Public Service, 48-51 (2003).

11. See, e.g., Ronald J. Gilson and Robert H. Mnookin, *Coming Of Age In A Corporate Law Firm: The Economics Of Associate Career Patterns*, 41 Stan. L.Rev. 567, 590 (1988), noting that major firms were said to be hiring only those law students graduating in the top half of their class from the top 20 law schools. As the article noted, however, the math reveals the competitive difficulties: a 1986 analysis of a group of top 20 law schools found that approximately 3,000 students graduated in the top half of the class, nearly 1,800 less than the number of new associates hired by the top 250 law firms. Nearly two decades later, the competition for law school graduates has intensified as a result of tremendous growth in the size of law firms.

12. NALP Found., Keeping the Keepers II: Mobility& Management of Associates 105-106 (2003).

13. NALP Found., Keeping the Keepers II: Mobility& Management of Associates 107 (2003). Importantly, the report urges: "Interview knowing that job satisfaction may be dependent on workplace culture and environment as much as on the work itself." At 107.

14. ABA Sec. Legal Educ. and Adm. Bar, Legal Education and Professional Development - An Educational Continuum, Report of The Task Force on Law Schools and the Profession: Narrowing the Gap 77 (1992). For a detailed overview of the Statement, see Chapter 5, pages 135-221. The Statement first sets forth a set of fundamental skills which should serve as the foundation for all aspects of practicing law (for example, the key skill of problem solving), and then proposes professional values that move beyond specific obligations and accountability (such as striving to promote justice, fairness, and morality).

15. ABA Sec. Legal Educ. and Adm. Bar, Legal Education and Professional Development - An Educational Continuum, Report of The Task Force on Law Schools and the Profession: Narrowing the Gap 127(1992).

16. ABA Sec. Legal Educ. and Adm. Bar, Legal Education and Professional Development - An Educational Continuum, Report of The Task Force on Law Schools and the Profession: Narrowing the Gap 236 (1992).

17. ABA Sec. Legal Educ. and Adm. Bar, Legal Education and Professional Development - An Educational Continuum, Report of The Task Force on Law Schools and the Profession: Narrowing the Gap 77(1992).

18. Renée Landers, *A Profession of Students, Practitioners, Professors, and Judges*, Boston Bar J. Nov./Dec. 2003, at 2.

CHAPTER 27

TRANSITION AND TRANSPARENCY

Even though most law firm partners have been out of school for many years, they have never really been able to escape getting a report card. From first grade through law school, aspiring lawyers would find themselves altering their behavior based on their response to five letters of the alphabet. Once law school ended, the quest for the "A" turned into the goal of working at a well-respected law firm. When that job came, the new report card came in the form of compensation and elevation decisions. The grading always continued; it was just the system that changed.

Perhaps it is time to develop and implement a grading system that looks closely at how law firms manage themselves to promote inclusive workplaces. If law firms are routinely subject to a variety of rankings relating to their profitability and size, why not the same with respect to their retention and promotion of women? There are a myriad of ways that could be developed to recognize positive changes and to identify where further improvements are necessary.

It is important to note at the outset, however, that report cards are meant to recognize progress and to sound an alarm when problems exist. In a law firm, internal measures can serve as a foundation for decisions relating to compensation, advancement to partnership, and leadership opportunities. This is different from the external systems created to measure certain criteria. In fact, there are pitfalls to public recognition programs. In striving for the great report card, there may be a temptation to present an altered view of reality.

For example, in 2001, the law firm of Brobeck, Phleger & Harrison was named by *Fortune* magazine as one of the top 100 places to work in the country. Yet a few months later, the firm was cutting staff and laying off more than 200 associates.[1] By the end of January 2003, the firm had dissolved.[2] So even as the firm may have had attributes sufficient to be deemed successful by some measures, it was certainly not a secure institution in which its lawyers had a long-term future.

Brobeck is but one example of a firm that failed to live up to its public persona. Wall Street Journal columnist Sue Shellenbarger has noted that even as "Best Places to Work" lists grow in influence, opportunities exist for employers to "cook the books" via the data they provide, and for unhappy employees to challenge the basis for their company's recognition.[3]

Moreover, public rankings that recognize positive attributes of an organization may not be fully reflective of the firm's culture. A firm may be recognized for certain laudable activities, but may still be lacking in its ability to advance and retain women.

One example of an outside effort to "grade" law firms on a variety of measures is *The American Lawyers'* "A List." The "A-List" consists of 20 law firms, which is 10% of the AM Law 200, deemed to be "the best of the best among the nation's top law firms," as measured by four criteria: (1) financial performance, (2) pro bono commitment (which includes both the number of firm hours devoted to pro bono activities and the number of lawyers participating), (3) associate morale, and (4) diversity.[4] The criteria capture important aspirational elements for a law firm. However, by creating a formula which doubles the points allotted to the categories for Revenue per Lawyer (RPL) and Pro bono commitment, the other criteria, associate satisfaction and diversity, have far less impact on the ultimate ranking.[5]

All this simply points to the fact that, although outside grading systems can be important, their susceptibility to manipulation or the weighing of information that can alter the overall data analysis suggests that these systems cannot replace internal mechanisms for monitoring progress. Such internal mechanisms should include the institutionalized collection of information that allows firms to grade themselves, and use the results to promote continued improvements.

Catalyst further observed that: "Every organization desiring to improve women's advancement should always take the time to collect the facts that underlie its unique situation... ."[6] This requires collecting baseline information against which future progress is measured.

Here is where transparency matters. All lawyers need to understand where their firm is, and where it is heading. Senior management support and involvement creates the culture that communicates the importance of the endeavor. Then everyone is held accountable for the implementation of identified best practices to help the firm achieve its goals. Catalyst observed that: "Before embarking on a change initiative, a company should identify a clear problem to solve or goal to achieve; should be able to articulate the business rationale for understanding change; have a commitment from the company's leadership to play an active, visible role; make extensive efforts to communicate the importance of the initiative, and decide who will be accountable for implementing and tracking the progress of the initiative. These steps create the conditions that make implementing best practices possible."[7]

For lawyers, this means transitioning towards a law firm culture that consciously and conscientiously seeks to retain and advance women to all levels of the firm, and is willing to measure the success of these efforts. It also requires a willingness to focus on more than the practical difficulties of implementing change; rather, it means maintaining a clear vision about why change is important, and allowing that vision to propel needed activities to achieve the desired outcomes.[8]

Change can and must happen from all directions. Successful change requires a stated willingness to face long-held assumptions about care-giving responsibilities in our society. Toward that goal, Mona Harrington urges women lawyers to eschew the "either/or choice" between professional equality and the humane values associated with care-giving roles. A program for change, she observed, requires a recognition that: "the big issue for women is not intentionally discriminatory inequality but *structurally* discriminatory inequality."[9]

There remains an inextricable link between structure and culture. Just as Mona Harrington argued that women cannot allow care and equality to be "de-linked," it is clear that success requires a new structure to emerge. This new structure must be built on the willingness to eliminate the inherently discriminating impact of a workplace that insists on the false choice between care-giving and professionalism.

Endnotes for Chapter 27

1. *See, e.g.,* Brenda Sandburg, *Brobeck Cuts Paralegal Supervisors,* at http://www.Law.com (Mar. 15, 2002). *See also* Levty, *Law of Gravity Pulls Down Brobeck,* S.F. Bus. Times, at http://www.bizjournals.com/sanfrancisco/(May 13, 2002).

2. Young, *Silicon Valley Law Giant to Dissolve,* S.F. Bus. Times, Jan. 27, 2003.

3. Sue Shellenbarger, *Those Lists Ranking Best Place to Work are Rising in Influence,* Wall St. J., Aug. 26, 1998, at B1.

4. *The A-List,* The Am. Law. (September, 2005) at 106.

5. Carlyn Kolker, *Keeping Score,* The Am. Law., (Sept. 2005) at 112, 115.

6. Catalyst, Advancing Women in Business - The Catalyst Guide: Best Practices from the Corporate Leaders 4 (1998).

7. Catalyst, Advancing Women in Business - The Catalyst Guide: Best Practices from the Corporate Leaders 18 (1998).

8. A physicist interviewed about the critical need to address the clear danger posed by climate change observed that on issues of such magnitude, asking about the practicability of change is the wrong question. Rather, the real focus should be on *caring* enough to change, because then change will happen. Elizabeth Kolbert, *The Climate of Man - III: What Can Be Done?,* The New Yorker, (May 9, 2005) at 56.

9. Mona Harrington, *Is Time-Out for Family Unprofessional?,* Trial, (Feb. 1997) at 71.

EPILOGUE

For many of today's Managing Partners, the air is rarified and the outlook is rosy. Profits are up beyond anyone's expectations. Work continues to flow in, keeping many lawyers too busy to develop new business. After years of envying the high income of their business clients, now it all seems attainable.

Equally impressive, law firm managers are presiding over firms that are exploding in size. For some, the growth is driven by strategic mergers, as part of an aggressive plan for expansion. For others, the growth is a reluctant and defensive teaming created to ward off the feared designation of "midsize." Regardless of the reasons behind the growth, these mergers take place with an expectation that increased size equates to higher billing rates and higher billable hours per lawyer.

For other firms, however, the changed climate has been fatal. Many have closed their doors, unable to respond quickly enough to the buffeting winds of change. Some were venerable names who could not hold together their core culture and keep their top rainmakers. Some simply had no core, which complicated the parting with fierce disputes in addition to the sadness.

Then there are the firms that have remained immobile. Many of these have that "deer in the headlights" sense of fear, knowing that staying still is dangerous, but not quite sure which way to run. For them, inaction may lead to an action no one wants to face.

However, with all the frenetic activity, there is still a nagging sense of whether these significant changes are sustainable. Can billing rates really exceed $1,000 per hour, as some predict? Will clients continue to pay the ever-increasing rates?

Also, how can firms continue to expand without a concurrent change in their management structure? How can hundreds of lawyers function in the best interests of an institution without a sophisticated group of leaders who can devote significant time to the variety of tasks needed to promote both individual growth and strong teamwork? As critical, how can a partnership model survive as the substantive responsibilities of being a partner diminish? What does it really mean to be someone's partner if the essence of the relationship is disagreements over "credit" for clients and one's "share" of compensation?

The case for change is clear and compelling. Law firms must listen to their partners, associates, and their clients, and develop a blueprint for the future. They can no longer rely on antiquated business models and the ineffective leadership structures of the past. Also, the total devotion to billable hours as a measure of success is unsustainable and anathema to the ideal of law as a profession, an ideal which every lawyer should insist on perpetuating. Professor Wilkins argued: "If the American legal profession hopes to maintain its current prominence on the global stage, it must find ways to attract and support lawyers who aspire to be social engineers for something other than the narrow concerns of global capital. If the financial scandals of the first few years of the 21st century have taught us anything, it is that a world in which professionals are encouraged to bleach themselves of every commitment save the ruthless pursuit of profit is a prescription for disaster of near-biblical proportions."[1]

The leadership model for the future will require a recognition of gender-based practices and assumptions that for too long have negatively impacted women's careers as well as the workplace in general. As Joyce Fletcher observed: "The issue of gender equity in organizational theory is most often studied through an analysis of the glass ceiling, that is, an analysis of the factors in organizations that are problematic for the professional progress of women. However, the disappearing of relational practice suggests that the factors inhibiting women's progress in organizations are not only problematic for women: they are problematic for organizational effectiveness as well."[2] Importantly, as Fletcher observed, the issues raised by the study of relational practice are not about men versus women. Rather, they provide an understanding of: "how the masculine logic underlying organizational practices shapes the experience and understanding of what is seen as important work in organizations, with potentially negative consequences for women, men, and the organization."[3]

The insistence that the profession stand for something other than a race to be ranked highest in profits per partner must be considered along with our societal obligations to our families. Professor Glendon observed that, for those trying to combine their work and family life, the question is not whether one can have it all: "The grown-up question is not can all our dreams come true? The real question is whether we can do better than we're doing now. Is it possible to harmonize women's and men's roles in social and economic life with their desires (and their children's needs) for a decent family life?"[4] The answer to this question, she observed, requires a societal recognition of the importance of our family obligations. Society as a whole must be prepared to recognize the crucial importance of raising children well: "Governments, private employers, and fellow citizens would all have to recognize that we all owe an enormous debt to parents who do a good job raising their children under today's difficult conditions. There's something heroic about the everyday sacrifices that people have to make these days just to do the right thing by their nearest and dearest."[5]

We can begin by recognizing that this is not a debate about work/family "balance." Balance is elusive and, in most cases, not achievable. This is really about how we can all function along a work/family *continuum* that is flexible enough to adjust to the ebb and flow of our work demands and our families' needs.

In addition to letting go of the concept of balance, we also must eliminate the word "accommodation" from the discussion. The word itself implies that we are doing someone a favor - by "accommodating" an individual's need for a schedule adjustment, we have temporarily "helped" her over a brief hurdle. However, nothing about the issues being raised should be viewed as an accommodation to anyone. The frequent use of this word only perpetuates an imbalance of power that has impeded the retention and advancement of women in the profession.[6]

Those who have succeeded to the top of this profession must acknowledge that their success was likely owed to something more than their considerable skills. To succeed at that level frequently requires a support network that resembles the proverbial village, tending to most of the day-to-day needs of one's family. However, there are a lot of talented lawyers who cannot afford, and may not choose, to delegate the tasks of daily life to others. Yet they have a hunger and a capacity to work hard and succeed.

It is, therefore, time to redefine what it means to be successful in the legal profession. Along the work/life *continuum*, there is a place for serving clients well, raising healthy children, caring for elderly parents, and participating in our communities.

Authors Laura Nash and Howard Stevenson write that enduring and sustainable success is not about "having more, being more, doing more," but requires a combination of happiness, achievement, significance, and legacy. They note: "To get to more wins on the various important measures that make up your notion of the good life, success has to rest on a paradigm of limitation in any one activity for the sake of the whole. Or...'on the reasoned pursuit of just enough'."[7]

As we all strive for professional success that is enduring, it is worth taking a brief moment to imagine the unthinkable, the autumn of our lives. How do we truly choose to be remembered, once the hustle and hassle of our extensive commitments have ebbed? As we reflect, we should also acknowledge that, at the end of it all, our legacy will last far longer than our careers.

ndnotes for Epilogue

David B. Wilkins, *Symposium: Brown at Fifty: From "Separate is Inherently Unequal" to "Diversity is Good for Business": The Rise of Market-Based Diversity Arguments and the Fate of the Black Corporate Bar*, 117 Harv. L. Rev. 1548, 1614 (March 2004).

Fletcher, Disappearing Acts: Gender, Power, and Relational Practice at Work 138-39 (1999).

Fletcher, Disappearing Acts: Gender, Power, and Relational Practice at Work 117 (1999).

Mary Ann Glendon, *Feminism & the Family: An Indissoluble Marriage*, Commonweal, (Feb. 14, 1997) at 11, 14. Professor Joan Williams observed that "[C]hildren need parental guidance and companionship throughout their youth in order to learn the skills required to find their own way in our complex and intensely individualistic society. This does not mean that one adult need stay home with them 24 hours a day? The alternative is to end the system of providing for children's care by marginalizing their caregivers." Williams, Unbending Gender: Why Family and Work Conflict and What to Do About It 273-274 (2000).

Mary Ann Glendon, *Feminism & the Family: An Indissoluble Marriage*, Commonweal, (Feb. 14, 1997) at 11, 14.

For a thoughtful discussion of rights and reform efforts, *see* Martha Minow, Making All the Difference: Inclusion, Exclusion, and American Law (1990). Professor Minow observed: "Absent opportunities to challenge the inequality of the helper and the one to be helped, the act of helping may unleash attitudes of domination, superiority, and denigration of the other." At 264.

Laura Nash and Howard Stevenson, *Success that Lasts*, Harv. Bus. Rev., Feb. 2004, at 102. Nash and Stevenson observe that: "Many of today's weak business ethics and performance problems can be traced to a failure to adopt the skills of enduring success." This ultimately can lead to "costly success pathologies such as greed, lack of loyalty or commitment, burnout, insensitivity, and the demoralization of knowing that your work isn't making a positive contribution to society." At 108. *See also*, Laura Nash and Howard Stevenson, Just Enough, (2004).

BIBLIOGRAPHY

Abbott, Ida O., Being an Effective Mentor: 101 Practical Strategies For Success, NALP: Washington, DC (2001).

Abbott, Ida O., Working with a Mentor: 50 Practical Suggestions For Success, NALP: Washington, DC(2001).

Abbott, Ida O. And Boags, Rita S., *Creating Pathways to Diversity?®: Mentoring Across Differences*, Minority Corporate Counsel Association, *available at* http://www.mcca.com/site/data/research-programs/goldpathways/index.shtml.

Abbott, Ida O. And Boags, Rita S., *Mentoring for Women and Minority Lawyers: Making It Succeed In Your Firm*, NALP Bulletin, February 2004.

Amer, Mildred L., CRS Report For Congress, *Membership Of The 109th Congress: A Profile*, Congressional Research Service, The Library Of Congress, Order Code RS22007, Updated October 25, 2005.

American Bar Association Commission on Billable Hours, ABA Commission on Billable Hours Report: 2001-2002 (2002).

American Bar Association Commission on Loan Repayment and Forgiveness, Lifting the Burden: Law Student Debt as a Barrier to Public Service (2003).

American Bar Association Commission on Women in the Profession, Balanced Lives: Changing the Culture of Legal Practice (2001).

American Bar Association Commission on Women in the Profession, Basic Facts from Women in the Law: A Look at the Numbers (1995).

American Bar Association Commission on Women in the Profession, A Current Glance at Women in the Law (2005), *available at* http://www.abanet.org/women/womenstatistics.html.

American Bar Association Commission on Women in the Profession, Empowerment and Leadership: Tried and True Methods for Women Lawyers (2003).

American Bar Association Commission on Women in the Profession, Fair Measure: Toward Effective Attorney Evaluations (1997).

American Bar Association Commission on Women in the Profession, Options and Obstacles: A Survey of the Studies of the Careers of Women (1994).

American Bar Association Commission on Women in the Profession, The Unfinished Agenda: Women and the Legal Profession (2001).

American Bar Association Commission on Women in the Profession, Unfinished Business: Overcoming the Sisyphus Factor (1995).

American Bar Association Commission on Women in the Profession, Walking the Talk - Creating a Law Firm Culture Where Women Succeed (2004).

American Bar Association, Diversity Committee, Report of the Diversity Committee, 1999-2000.

American Bar Association Network, *First Year Enrollment In ABA Approved Law Schools 1947-2002 (Percentage Of Women) at* http://www.abanet.org/legaled/statistics/femstats.html.

American Bar Association Prepared By C&R Research, Pulse 2002: The State of the Legal Profession (2002).

American Bar Association Section of Law Practice, Two-Tier Partnerships and Other Alternatives: Five Approaches (1986).

American Bar Association, Section on Legal Education and Admissions to the Bar, Legal Education and Professional Development - An Educational Continuum, Report of the Task Force on Law Schools and the Profession: Narrowing the Gap, (1992).

American Bar Association, Young Lawyers Division, The State of the Legal Profession 1990 (1991).

American Bar Foundation, *Growth And Gender Diversity: A Statistical Profile Of The Legal Profession In 2000*, 16 Researching Law: An ABF Update (Winter 2005).

American University Washington Corporate Council Project for Attorney Retention, Better on Balance? The Corporate Counsel Work/Life Report (Final 2003), *available at* http://www.pardc.org.

Archambeault, Bill, *MBA Survey Reflects Income, Gender Trends*, Massachusetts Bar Association Lawyer's Journal, October 2005.

Associates Talk Back, The American Lawyer, October 2005.

Auster, Ellen R., *Professional Women's Midcareer Satisfaction: Toward an Explanatory Framework*, Sex Roles: A Journal of Research (June 2001) *available at* http://www.findarticles.com/cf_0/m2294/mag.jhtml?issue=1.

Babcock, Linda and Laschever, Sara, Women Don't Ask: Negotiation and the Gender Divide, Princeton University Press: New Jersey (2003).

Bailyn, Lotte; Drago, Robert and Kochan, Thomas A., Integrating Work and Family Life: A Holistic Approach, A Report of the Sloan Work-Family Policy Network, Massachusetts Institute Of Technology Sloan School Of Management, (2001).

Baker, Debra, *Cash-and-Carry Associates*, 85 ABA Journal, May 1999.

Baldiga, Nancy R., Promoting Your Talent: A Guidebook for Women and Their Firms: American Institute of Certified Public Accountants: New York (2003).

Ballard, Nancer H., Equal Engagement: Observation on Career Success and Meaning In the Lives of Women Lawyers, 292 Wellesley College Center for Research on Women, Working Papers Series: Massachusetts (1998).

Banks, Jarrett, *General Counsel Experiment with Full Contingency Fees*, Corporate Legal Times, June 2005.

Bar Association of San Francisco, *Fifty Firms Commit to No Glass Ceiling for Women*, at http://www.sfbar.org/about/newfiftynoglass.html.

Bar Association of San Francisco, *BASF's No Glass Ceiling Initiative Results In Huge Strides for Bay Area Women Attorneys, available at* http://www.sfbar.org/about/releases/noglass_ceiling_results.htm.

Barker, Emily, *Engendering Change*, The American Lawyer, June 2003.

Barnett, Rosalind Chait, *Preface: Women And Work: Where Are We, Where Did We Come From, And Where Are We Going?*, 60 Journal of Social Issues, 2004.

Barnett, Rosalind and Rivers, Caryl, Same Difference: How Gender Myths are Hurting Our Relationships, Our Children, and Our Jobs, Basic Books: New York (2004).

Bates, Suzanne, Speak Like a CEO: Secrets for Commanding Attention and Getting Results, McGraw-Hill: New York (2005).

Beck, Susan, *3 Arrows And A Diagram*, The American Lawyer, March 2005.

Beckman, Christine M., and Phillips, Damon J., *Interorganizational Determinants of Promotion: Client Leadership and the Attainment of Women Attorneys*, 70 American Sociological Review, August 2005.

Belkin, Lisa, *The Opt-Out Revolution*, New York Times Magazine, October 26, 2003.

Bennett, Walter, The Lawyer's Myth: Reviving Ideals In the Legal Profession, University of Chicago Press: Illinois (2001).

Bennis, Warren and Nanus, Burt, Leaders: The Strategies for Taking Charge, Harper Row Publishers, Inc.: New York (1985).

Blanton, Kimberly *Associates' Bonuses Up at Top Hub Law Firms*, Boston Globe, December 22, 2004.

Blum, Deborah, Sex On the Brain, The Biological Differences Between Men and Women, Viking Penguin Group: New York (1997).

Blum, Deborah, *Solving For XX*, Boston Sunday Globe, January 23, 2005.

Bogus, Carl T., *The Death of an Honorable Profession*, 71 Indiana Law Journal, Fall 1996.

Bombardieri, Marcella, *A Woman's Place In the Lab*, Boston Sunday Globe, May 1, 2005.

Bombardieri, Marcella, *Harvard Aims to Spur Advancement of Women*, Boston Globe, February 4, 2005.

Bombardieri, Marcella, *Summers Critic Gets Harvard Post*, Boston Globe, June 4, 2005.

Bombardieri, Marcella, *Summers Displays New Understanding of Women's Careers*, Boston Globe, April 8, 2005.

Bombardieri, Marcella, *Summers' Remarks on Women Draw Fire*, Boston Globe, January 17, 2005.

Bombardieri, Marcella, *Summers Sets $50m Women's Initiative*, Boston Globe, May 17, 2005.

Bombardieri, Marcella, *Harvard Improves on Tenure Offers to Women*, Boston Globe, August 1, 2005.

Bookman, Ann, Starting In Our Own Backyards: How Working Families Can Build Community and Survive the New Economy, Routledge: New York and London (2004).

Boston Bar Association, Committee on Gender and the Practice of Law, Preliminary Report of the Boston Bar Association Study of the Role of Gender In the Practice of Law, Litigation Sciences, Inc. (1988).

Boston Bar Association, Task Force on Professional Challenges and Family Needs, Facing the Grail: Confronting the Cost of Work-Family Imbalance (1999).

Boston Bar Association, Task Force on Professional Fulfillment, Expectations, Reality and Recommendations for Change (1997).

Boynton, Paul D., *Balancing Work & Family*, 28 Massachusetts Lawyers Weekly, September 27, 1999.

Bradwell v State Of Illinois, 83 U.S. 130 (1873).

Branson, Louise, *Reform of the Bully Broads*, Boston Globe Magazine, March 17, 2002.

Brown, Heidi K., Fundamentals of Federal Litigation, Thomson West: Minnesota (2004).

Burke, Melissa Nann, *Flexing Their Muscles*, Legal Intelligencer, November 11, 2004.

Burke, Ronald J., *Workaholism In Organizations: Gender Differences*, 41

Sex Roles: A Journal of Research, September 1999, *available at* http://www.findarticles.com/cf_0/m2294/mag.jhtml?issue=1.

C&R Research, Prepared for the American Bar Association, Pulse 2002: The State of the Legal Profession (2002).

Caplan, Lincoln, Skadden - Power, Money, and the Rise of a Legal Empire, The Noonday Press: New York (1993).

Carter, Sean, *The Lawyer - Go - Round: Chasing the Moving Target of Attorney Transfers, Mergers and Maneuvers*, ABA Journal, *at* http://www.abanet.org/journal/redesign/home.html, April 8, 2005.

Carter, Terry, *A Delicate Balance*, 91 ABA Journal, March 2005.

Carter, Terry, *A New Breed*, 87 ABA Journal, March 2001.

Carter, Terry, *Homegrown vs. Lateral*, 91 ABA Journal, August 2005.

Carter, Terry, *Paths Need Paving*, 86 ABA Journal, September 2000.

Catalyst, A New Approach to Flexibility: Managing the Work/Time Equation, Catalyst: New York (2000).

Catalyst, Advancing Women In Business - The Catalyst Guide: Best Practices From the Corporate Leaders, Jossey-Bass Publishers: California (1998).

Catalyst, Beyond a Reasonable Doubt: Building the Case for Flexibility, The Catalyst Series on Flexibility In Canadian Law Firms, Catalyst: New York (2005).

Catalyst, Flexible Work Arrangements III: A Ten-Year Retrospective of Part-Time Arrangements for Managers and Professionals: New York (2000).

Catalyst, Women In Law: Making The Case, Catalyst: New York (2001).

Center for Women's Business Research, 2004 *Key Facts About Women-Owned Businesses*, (Pamphlet; 2005 Update *available at* http://www.womensbusinessresearch.org/researchstudies.html).

Chanen, Jill Schachner, *Home Again: More Law Firms Create Alumni Programs to Foster Personal, Business Relationships*, 91 ABA Journal, June 2005.

Chen, Vivia, *Cracks In the Ceiling*, The American Lawyer, June 2003.

Chen, Vivia, *Pride and Prejudice*, The American Lawyer, July 2005.

Chicago Bar Association, CBA Alliance for Women, *Call to Action: Focus On Diversity, available at* http://chicagobar.org/calltoaction/default.htm.

Chiu, Charlotte, *Do Professional Women Have Lower Job Satisfaction Then Professional Men? Lawyers as a Case Study*, 38 Sex Roles: A Journal Of Research 521 (April 1998), *available at* http://www.findarticles.com/cf_0/m2294/mag.jhtml?issue=1.

Choosing Community: Girls Get Together to Be Themselves, Girls Inc. News, *at* http://www.girls-inc.org/ic/page.php?id=2.4.10.

Collins, Jim, Good to Great, HarperCollins Publishers: New York (2001).

Coster, Helen, *The Inflation Temptation*, The American Lawyer, October 2004.

Coulter, Silvia L., The Woman Lawyer's Rainmaking Game: How to Build a Successful Law Practice, Glasser Legalworks: New Jersey (2004).

Cowley, Geoffrey, *Why We Strive For Status*, Newsweek, June 16, 2003.

Crittenden, Ann, The Price of Motherhood: Why the Most Important Job In the World is Still the Least Valued, A Metropolitan/Owl Book, An Imprint of Henry Holt and Company, LLC: New York (2001).

Cruden, John C., *The Case For More Women Leaders In the Profession*, Washington Lawyer, November 2005.

Cuddy, Amy J.C., Fiske, Susan T. & Glick, Peter, *When Professionals Become Mothers, Warmth Doesn't Cut the Ice*, 60 Journal Of Social Issues, 2004.

Cunningham, Keith, *Father Time: Flexible Work Arrangements and the Law Firm's Failure of the Family*, 53 Stanford Law Review, April 2001.

D'Alessandro, David, *The Boys of the Boardroom*, Boston Globe, January 28, 2005.

Darling, Diane, C., The Networking Survival Guide: Get the Success You Want By Tapping Into the People You Know, McGraw Hill: New York (2003).

Davidson, Justin, *The Changing Man*, Newsday, July 1, 2002.

Davis, Jenny B., *Distinction With a Difference*, ABA Journal, April 2003, *available at* http://www.abanet.org/careercounsel/abajournalarchives/distinctionwithadifference.html.

Davolos-Harden, Stephanie; Presser, Judith, & Rosathe, Marta T., *Who Cares?: Building Cross-Sector Partnerships For Family Care,* (presentation summary From Spring 2004 Program), MIT Workplace Center, Mit Sloan School Of Management: Massachusetts, 2005.

Deloitte & Touche, *The Year In Review*, Team Bulletin, May 1994.

Dershowitz, Alan, Letters to a Young Lawyer, Basic Books, A Member of Perseus Books Group: New York (2001).

Dillon, Sam, *Harvard Chief Defends His Talk on Women*, New York Times, January 18, 2005.

Drachman, Virginia G., Sisters In Law: Women Lawyers In Modern American History, Harvard University Press: Massachusetts (1998).

Dreessen, Kathleen, *The Work/Life Challenge: Not Just a Women's Issue*, (Parts 1 & 2), Diversity & the Bar, (Minority Corporate Counsel Association), July/August and September/October 2005.

Drucker, Peter F., The Essential Drucker: The Best of Sixty Years of Peter Drucker's Essential Writings on Management, HarperBusiness, An Imprint of HarperCollins Publishers:New York (2003).

Dugan, Hannah C., *Does Gender Still Matter In the Legal Profession?,* 75

Wisconsin Lawyer, October 2002, *available at* http://www.wisbar.org.

Ehrenreich, Barbara, Nickel & Dimed: On (Not) Getting By in America, A Metropolitan /Owl Book, An Imprint of Henry Holt & Company, LLC: New York (2001).

Eichbaum, June, *Becoming a General Counsel: The New Track To the Top*, Diversity & The Bar®, (Minority Corporate Counsel Association), September/October 2005.

Eliasberg, Kristen, *Tapping On the Glass,* Law Firm Inc., October, 2005.

English, Holly, Gender on Trial: Sexual Stereotypes and Work/Life Balance In the Legal Workplace, ALM Publishing: New York (2003).

Epstein, Cynthia Fuchs, Sauté, Robert, Oglensky, Bonnie & Gever, Martha, *Glass Ceilings and Open Doors: Women's Advancement In the Legal Profession*, A Report to the Committee on Women In the Profession, The Association of the Bar of the City of New York, 64 Fordham Law Review, 1995.

Epstein, Cynthia Fuchs, Seron, Carroll, Oglensky, Bonnie, & Sauté, Robert, The Part-Time Paradox: Time Norms, Professional Life, Family, and Gender, Routledge: New York (1999).

Epstein, Phyllis Horn, Women-at-Law: Lessons Learned Along the Pathways to Success, American Bar Association: Illinois (2004).

Estrich, Susan, Sex & Power, Riverhead Books, The Berkley Publishing

Group, A Division of Penguin Putnam Inc.: New York (2000).

Ferrazzi, Keith & Raz, Tahl, Never Eat Alone and Other Secrets to Success, One Relationship at a Time, A Currency Book, Doubleday, A Division of Random House, Inc.: New York (2005).

Figuratively Speaking, The American Lawyer, July 2005.

First Year Enrollment In ABA Approved Law Schools 1947-2002 (Percentage of Women), American Bar Association, *at* http://www.abanet.org/legaled/statistics/femstats.html (June 20, 2003).

Flahardy, Cathleen, *The Hire Power: Legal Departments Add Lawyers to the Payroll*, Corporate Legal Times, May 2005.

Fleischer, Matt, *Women at Leading Firms Hit Glass Plateau,* New York Law Journal, December 5, 2000.

Fletcher, Joyce K., Disappearing Acts: Gender, Power, and Relational Practice at Work, MIT Press: Massachusetts (1999).

Florida Bar Association, Report and Recommendations of the Florida Bar Special Committee for Gender Equality in the Profession (July 1992) *available at* http://www.flabar.org.

Foster, Elizabeth S., *The Glass Ceiling In the Legal Profession: Why Do Law Firms Still Have So Few Female Partners?*, 42 UCLA Law Review, 1995.

Fox, Eleanor M., *Being a Woman, Being a Lawyer and Being a Human Being*

- Woman and Change, 57 Fordham Law Review, 1989.

Frank, David E., *Networking: Golf's No Longer the Only Game In Town*, Massachusetts Lawyers Weekly, October 3, 2005, *available at* http://www.masslawyersweekly.com/subscriber/archives_FTS.cfm.

Frankel, Alison, *The Case of the Missing Associate*, The American Lawyer, July 2005.

Frankel, Alison, *Veil of Tiers*, The American Lawyer, July 2004.

Frankel, Lois P., Nice Girls Don't Get the Corner Office: 101 Unconscious Mistakes Women Make That Sabotage Their Careers, Warner Business Books, Time Warner Book Group: New York (2004).

Friedman, Stewart D.; Christensen, Perry & Degroot, Jessica, *Work and Life: The End of the Zero-Sum Game*, Harvard Business Review, Reprint No. 98605, November/December 1998.

Frisman, Paul, *Toughest Case May Be Family v. Career*, Connecticut Law Tribune, July 12, 1999.

Fuegen, Kathleen, Biernat, Monica, Haines, Elizabeth & Deaux, Kay, *Mothers and Fathers in the Workplace: How Gender and Parental Status Influence Judgments of Job-Related Competence*, 60 Journal Of Social Issues, 2004.

Futter, Ellen V., *Women Professionals: The Slow Rise to the Top*, 57 Fordham Law Review, 1989.

Gaber, Paula, *"Just Trying to Be Human In This Place": The Legal Education of Twenty Women*, 10 Yale Journal of Law and Feminism, 1998.

Galanter, Marc & Palay, Thomas, Tournament of Lawyers: The Transformation of the Big Law Firm, University of Chicago Press: Illinois and London (1991).

Gallagher, Stephen P., *Family v. Career: More Lawyers Caught In the Middle*, State Bar News, New York State Bar Association, July/August 1999.

Gallina v. Mintz, Levin, Cohn, Ferris, Glovsky & Popeo, P.C., U.S. Ct. App. 4th Cir. No. 03-1883 (February 2, 2005) Unpublished Opinion.

Generation & Gender In the Workplace, An issue brief by Families and Work Institute, American Business Collaboration (October, 2004).

Georgia Association for Women Lawyers, Atlanta Bar Association Women In the Profession Committee, Georgia Commission on Women, It's About Time: Part-Time Policies and Practices In Atlanta Law Firms (2004) *available at* http://www.gawl.org/gawl/docs/Its%20About%20TimeFinal.pdf.

Gilson, Ronald J. & Mnookin, Robert H., *Coming of Age In a Corporate Law Firm: The Economics of Associate Career Patterns,* 41 Stanford Law Review, 1989.

Gladwell, Malcolm, The Tipping Point: How Little Things Can Make a Big Difference, Back Bay Books, Little Brown & Company, Time Warner Book Group: New York (2002).

Glendon, Mary Ann, A Nation Under Lawyers: How the Crisis In the Legal Profession Is Transforming American Society, Farrar, Straus & Giroux: New York (1994).

Glendon, Mary Ann, *Feminism & The Family: An Indissoluble Marriage*, Commonweal, February 14, 1997.

Goodman, Ellen, *Summers' Teachable Moment*, Boston Globe, February 24, 2005.

Gordon, Leslie A., *Women Mean Business: Firms Marketing to Female Clients Offer Book Readings, Spa Retreats*, 91 ABA Journal, August 2005.

Graham, Deborah, Getting Down to Business: Marketing and Women Lawyers, Glasser Legalworks: New Jersey (1996, 1997).

Griffith, Cary, *Creative Billing: Is the Reign of the Almighty Billable Hour Over,* Lawcrossing, *available at* http://www.lawcrossing.com/article/index.php?printerflag=P&id=627.

Groysberg, Boris, Nanda, Ashish & Nohria, Nitin, *The Risky Business of Hiring Stars*, Harvard Business Review, May 2004.

Guinier, Lani, Fine, Michelle & Balin, Jane, Becoming Gentlemen: Women, Law School and Institutional Change, Beacon Press: Massachusetts (2002).

Haapaniemi, Peter, *Key Word: Leadership*, Law Biz, Summer/Fall 2005.

Hales, Dianne, Just Like a Woman: How Gender Science is Redefining What Makes Us Female, Bantam Books, A Division of Random House, Inc.: New York (2000).

Hall, Karen, *Take the Money and Run*, The American Lawyer, October 2000.

Hancock, Amy Sladczyk & Parvin, Cordell, *What Firms Can Do to Help Associates Take Responsibility for Their Careers*, 17 NALP Bulletin, November 2004.

Harrington, Mona, *Is Time-Out for Family Unprofessional?*, Trial, February 1997.

Harrington, Mona, Women Lawyers: Rewriting the Rules, Plume, A Division of the Penguin Group: New York (1995).

Hedaa, Maryann, *Attracting - And Keeping - The Best & Brightest*, Hildebrandt International (Spring 2001) *at* http://www.hildebrandt.com/documents.aspx?doc_id=827.

Heim, Pat, Murphy, Susan A. with Golant, Susan K., In the Company of Women, Tarcher/Putnam, Penguin Group (Usa) Inc.: New York (2003).

Heinz, John P., Hull, Kathleen E. & Harter, Ava A., *Lawyers And Their Discontents: Findings From a Survey of the Chicago Bar*, 74 Indiana Law Journal, 1995.

Hennessey, John, Hockfield, Susan & Tilghman, Shirley, *Women and Science: The Real Issue*, Boston Globe, February 12, 2005.

Henry, Deborah Epstein, *The Case for Flex-Time and Part-Time Lawyering*, 23 Pennslyvania Lawyer, 2001.

Hewlett, Sylvia Ann, *Executive Women and the Myth of Having It All*, Harvard Business Review OnPoint, Product No. 9616, April 2002.

Hewlett, Sylvia Ann & Luce, Carolyn Buck, *Off-Ramps and On-Ramps: Keeping Talented Women On the Road to Success*, Harvard Business Review, March 2005.

Hewlett, Sylvia Ann & West, Cornel, *Not Our Kind of People, 2005*, Boston Sunday Globe, October 30, 2005.

Hochschild, Arlie Russell, The Time Bind: When Work Becomes Home and Home Becomes Work, A Metropolitan/Owl Book, An Imprint of Henry Holt And Company, Inc.: New York (1997).

It's The Manager, Stupid, The Economist, August 8, 1998, Thomson Gale Document No. A21000938.

Jackson, Maggie, *Family-Friendly Europe Offers a Model For Redefining U.S. Workplace Policies*, Boston Sunday Globe, November 21, 2004, *available at* http://bostonworks.boston.com/globe/archives/112104.shtml.

Jackson, Maggie, *Flex Time, Mentoring For Women Help Create a New Business Culture*, Boston Globe, October 24, 2004.

Jackson, Maggie, *Work-Life Issues Can Test Managers*, Boston Sunday Globe, August 28, 2005.

Kanter, Rosabeth Moss, Confidence: How Winning Streaks & Losing Streaks Begin & End, Crown Publishing Group, A Division of Random House: New York (2004).

Kanter, Rosabeth Moss, Men and Women of the Corporation, Basic Books, A Member of the Perseus Books Group: New York (1977) (1993).

Kanter, Rosabeth Moss, *The Rhythm of Change*, Women's Business, April 2001.

Kanter, Rosabeth Moss And Roessner, Jane, *Deloitte & Touche (A): A Hole In the Pipeline,* Harvard University Business School 9-300-012, (May 2, 2003).

Kanter, Rosabeth Moss & Roessner, Jane, *Deloitte & Touche (B): Changing the Workplace,* Harvard University Business School 9-300-013, (May 2, 2003).

Kanter, Rosabeth Moss & Stein, Barry A., A Tale of "O" On Being Different in an Organization, Harper & Row: New York, and Fitzhenry & Whiteside Limited: Toronto (1980).

Kantrowitz, Barbara, *Sex and Science*, Newsweek, January 31, 2005.

Kay, Herma Hill, *Symposium Celebration of the Tenth Anniversary of Justice Ruth Bader Ginsburg's Appointment to the Supreme Court of the United States*, 104 Columbia Law Review, January 2004.

Kaye, Judith S., *A Prologue In the Guise of an Epilogue*, 57 Fordham Law Review, 1989.

Kaye, Judith S., *Women Lawyers In Big Firms: A Study In Progress Toward Gender Equality*, 57 Fordham Law Review, 1988.

Keeva, Steven, *Take Care of Yourself*, 90 ABA Journal, December 2004.

Kelly, Erin & Dobbin, Frank, *Civil Rights Law Work: Sex Discrimination and the Rise of Maternity Leave Policies,* 105 American Journal of Sociology, 1999.

Klingelsmith, M. C., *A Pioneer Woman Lawyer of Pennsylvania*, 9 Women Lawyers' Journal, 1920.

Kolbert, Elizabeth, *The Climate Of Man - III: What Can Be Done?*, The New Yorker, May 9, 2005.

Kolker, Carlyn, *Keeping Score*, The American Lawyer, September 2005.

Kolker, Carlyn, *The Wages of Denial*, The American Lawyer, March 2005.

Kolz, Amy, *Can You Hear Me Now?*, The American Lawyer, October 2005.

Kolz, Amy, *Don't Call Them Slackers*, The American Lawyer, October 2005.

Koppel, Nathan, *Hello, I Must Be Going*, The American Lawyer, March 2005.

Koppel, Nathan, *The High-Priced Spread*, The American Lawyer, July 2005.

Korzec, Rebecca, *Gender Bias: Continuing Challenges and Opportunities*, 29 Litigation, Spring 2003.

Kropf, Marcia Brumit, *Inspiring Girls to Be Strong, Smart, and Bold*, 14 Regional Review Federal Reserve Bank Boston (Q1 2005).

Lambreth, Susan Raridon, Address at the Developing Women Leaders In the Legal Profession Conference, June 10, 2005, Sponsored by the Hildebrandt Institute (http://www.hildebrandt.com/ hdbtinstitute.aspx?wp_id=271).

Lambreth, Susan Raridon & Yanuklis, Amanda J., *Achieving the Benefits of Practice Management*, Hildebrant International, August 30, 2001, *at* http://www.hildebrandt.com/documents.aspx?doc_id=547.

Lambreth, Susan Raridon & Yanuklis, Amanda J., *Practice Groups— Selecting The Most Effective Partners As Leaders,* Hildebrandt International, (as reprinted from New York Law Journal, September 11, 2001, Copyright 2001 NLP IP Co.), *at* http://www.hildebrandt.com/documents.aspx?doc_id=1062.

Landers, Renée M., *A Profession of Students, Practitioners, Professors, and Judges,* Boston Bar Journal, November/December 2003.

Landers, Renée M., Rebitzer, James B. & Lowell J. Taylor, *Rat Race Redux: Adverse Selection In the Determination of Work Hours in Law Firms,* 86 American Economic Review, 1996.

Levty, Ron, *Law of Gravity Pulls Down Brobeck,* San Francisco Business Times, *at* http://www.bizjournals.com/sanfrancisco, May 13, 2002.

Levy, Paul F., *Teamwork on the Field and at Work,* 14 Regional Review: Federal Reserve Bank Boston, (Q1 2005).

Lewis, Diane E., *A Look Back, and Forward,* Boston Sunday Globe, May 30, 1999.

Lewis, Diane E., *Hale & Dorr Hikes Lawyers' Pay,* Boston Globe, February 9, 2000.

Lewis, Diane E., *Happy Right Here,* Boston Sunday Globe, July 17, 2005.

Lewis, Diane E., *High Anxiety Over Attorneys' Soaring Pay,* Boston Globe, February 11, 2000.

Lewis, Diane E., *How to Brag Like a Professional: Consultant Urges Women to Talk Themselves Up the Corporate Ladder,* Boston Sunday Globe, September 5, 2004.

Lewis, Diane E., *Law Firms Up Salary Ante to Fight Associates' Flight to Dot-Coms,* Boston Globe, February 8, 2000.

Lin, Angela, *Sunday Offers a Good Time to Get Work Done,* Boston Sunday Globe, September 12, 2004.

Llewellyn-Williams, Michael for The Committee Of 200, *The C200 Business Leadership Index 2004: Annual Report On Women's Clout In Business,* Northern Trust Corporation: Illinois, 2001-2004.

Longstreth, Andrew, *Partner in Name Only?,* The American Lawyer, March 2005.

Lovell, Sharon E., Kahn, Arnold S., Anton, Jennifer, Davidson, Amanda, Dowling, Elizabeth, Post, Dawn & Mason, Chandra, *Does Gender Affect the Link Between Organizational Citizenship Behavior And Performance Evaluation?,* 41 Sex Roles: A Journal of Research, September 1999, *available at* http://www.findarticles.com/p/articles/mi_m2294/is_1999_sept/ai_58469481.

Lowe, Suzanne C., Marketplace Masters: How Professional Service Firms Compete to Win, Praeger Publishers, An Imprint of Greenwood Publishing Group, Inc.: Connecticut (2004).

Lublin, Joann S., *Women Aspire to Be Chief as Much as Men Do*, Wall Street Journal, June 23, 2004.

MacCrate, Robert, *What Women are Teaching a Male-Dominated Profession*, 57 Fordham Law Review, 1989.

Maister, David H., Managing the Professional Service Firm, The Free Press, A Division of Simon & Schuster, Inc.: New York (1993).

Maister, David H., True Professionalism: The Courage To Care About Your People, Your Clients, and Your Career, The Free Press, A Division of Simon & Schuster, Inc.: New York (1997).

Maister, David H.; Green, Charles H. & Galford, Robert M., The Trusted Advisor, Touchstone: New York (2000).

Marks, Roger, *Has Mentoring Become a Forgotten Ritual?*, Corporate Legal Times, January 2005.

McCollam, Douglas, *The Future of Time*, Litigation (Supplement to the American Lawyer & Corporate Counsel) 2005.

McCracken, Douglas M., *Winning the Talent War for Women: Sometimes it Takes a Revolution*, Harvard Business Review, November/December 2000, Reprint R00611.

McFedries, Paul, *Tipping Point*, Word Spy *at* http://www.wordspy.com/words/tippingpoint.asp.

McGinn, Daniel, *The Guy of the Storm*, Newsweek, January 31, 2005.

McGuire, Elizabeth, *Still Seeking a Perfect Balance*, New York Times, August 11, 1998.

Mckenna, Patrick J. & Maister, David H., F1rst Among Equals, Free Press, Simon & Shuster, Inc.: New York (2002).

Meyerson, Debra, & Fletcher, Joyce K., *A Modest Manifesto for Shattering the Glass Ceiling*, Harvard Business Review, January-February 2000, Reprint R00107.

Minding the Gap, The American Lawyer, May 2004.

Minority Corporate Counsel Association, *The Myth of the Meritocracy: A Report on the Bridges and Barriers to Success In Large Law Firms*, 2003 MCCA Pathways, *available at* http://www.mcca.com/site/data/researchprograms/purplepathways/index.html.

Miller, Leslie Anne, *Special Report on Women and Minorities in the Profession: Women in the Legal Profession: Where Are We Now?*, 25 The Pennsylvania Lawyer, January/February 2003.

Minow, Martha, Making All the Difference: Inclusion, Exclusion, and American Law, Cornell University Press: New York (1990).

Moll, Richard W., The Lure of the Law, Penguin Books: New York (1990).

Morello, Karen Berger, The Invisible Bar: The Woman Lawyer in America 1638 to the Present, Beacon Press: Massachusetts (1988).

Murolo, Priscilla, The Common Ground of Womanhood: Class, Gender, and

Working Girls' Clubs, 1884-1928, University of Illinois Press: Illinois (1997).

Murphy, Evelyn with Graff, E.J., Getting Even: Why Women Don't Get Paid Like Men—and What to Do About It, Touchstone, Simon & Schuster, Inc.: New York (2005).

NALP Foundation for Law Career Research and Education and the American Bar Foundation, After the JD: First Results of a National Study of Legal Careers: NALP Foundation, Kansas and the American Bar Foundation: Illinois (2004).

NALP Foundation for Law Career Research and Education, In Pursuit of Attorney Work-Life Balance: Best Practices In Management, NALP Foundation: Kansas (2005).

NALP Foundation, Keeping the Keepers II: Mobility and Management of Associates, Entry-Level and Lateral Hiring and Attrition 1998-2003, NALP Foundation: Kansas (2003).

NALP Foundation, Presence of Women and Attorneys of Color in Large Law Firms Continues to Rise Slowly but Steadily, NALP Foundation: Kansas: (October 3, 2002), *at* http://www.nalp.org/press/details.php?id=18.

National Association of Minority & Women Owned Law Firms (NAMWOLF) *at* www.namwolf.org.

Nash, Laura & Stevenson, Howard, Just Enough: Tools for Creating Success In Your Work and Life, John Wiley & Sons, Inc.: New Jersey (2004).

Nash, Laura & Stevenson, Howard, *Success That Lasts*, Harvard Business Review, February 2004.

Neil, Martha, *Who Is a Partner?* 91 ABA Journal, June 2005.

Neil, Martha, *Working 9-5, or 10-3, or 1-4?*, 91 ABA Journal, December 2003.

Nelson, Robert L., Partners with Power: The Social Transformation of the Large Law Firm, University of California Press: California (1988).

New York County Lawyer's Association Task Force to Increase Diversity In the Legal Profession, Report of the Task Force to Increase Diversity In the Legal Profession (2002).

New York State Bar Association Committee on Women in Law, Gender Equity in the Legal Profession: A Survey, Observations and Recommendations (2001), *available at* http://www.nysba.org/content/contentgroups/news1/reports3/womeninlawreport-recs.pdf.

New York State Bar Association Committee on Women in the Law, Report and Sample Policy on Alternative Work Arrangements (1995).

Nossel, Suzanne & Westfall, Elizabeth, Presumed Equal: What America's Top Women Lawyers Really Think About Their Firms, Career Press, Inc. New Jersey (1998).

Olson, Scott, *Few Women Scale Managing Partner Peak*, 25 Indianapolis Business Journal, June 28, 2004.

Orchant, Alison G., *The Status of Women In the Legal Profession*, Monster

Legal, *at* http://legal.monster.com/ articles/womenstatus.

Ostrow, Ellen, *Is Thinking "Like A Lawyer" Holding You Back?*, 28 Beyond The Billable Hour? (2005) *at* http:// lawyerslifecoach.com/newsletters/ issue28.html.

Parsa, T.Z., *The Drudge Report,* New York Magazine, June 21, 1999.

Pipher, Mary, Reviving Ophelia: Saving the Selves of Adolescent Girls, Ballantine Books, A Division of Random House, Inc.: New York (1994).

Pratt, Mary K., *Her Place at the Table*, Boston Business Journal, June 11-17, 2004.

Press, Aric, *Adding Value*, The American Lawyer, July 2005.

Press, Aric & Beck, Susan, *Almost a Revolution*, The American Lawyer, May 2004.

Provosty, Shelly Hammond, *Dri Task Force Examines the Status of Women Litigators at Law Firms*, Of Counsel, July 2005.

Qualters, Sheri, *Going Where Business Is: Law Firms Target Women*, Boston Business Journal, July 19-25, 2002.

Qualters, Sheri, *Hurdles on the Partner Track*, Boston Business Journal, April 1, 2005, at http://www.bizjournals.com/boston/stories/2005/04/04/story1.html.

Qualters, Sheri, *Women Lawyers Hone Rainmaking Skills*, Boston Business Journal, August 1, 2005, *available at* http://boston.bizjournals.com/ boston/stories/2005/08/01/ focus3.html.

Quindlen, Anna, Being Perfect, Random House, Inc., New York (2005).

Quindlen, Anna, *Still Needing the F Word*, Newsweek, October 20, 2003.

Quinn, Jane Bryant, *Revisiting the Mommy Track*, Newsweek, July 17, 2000.

Rader, Michael, *Building a Fence Around the Law*, Boston Bar Journal, November/December 2004.

Raggi, Reena, *Prosecutors' Offices: Where Gender is Irrelevant*, 57 Fordham Law Review (1989).

Ranalli, Ralph, *Pleas Of Frustration - Lawyers Questioning, Abandoning Their Profession*, Boston Globe, August 18, 2003.

Reeves, Arin N., *Five Principles for Creating Diversity In Law Firms,* Practical Lawyer, October 2002.

Reichman, Nancy J. & Sterling, Joyce S., Gender Penalties Revisited, University of Denver: Colorado (2004).

Reichman, Nancy J. & Sterling, Joyce S., *Recasting the Brass Ring: Deconstructing and Reconstructing Workplace Opportunities for Women Lawyers*, 29 Capital University Law Review, 2002.

Reigning Women, 32 Massachusetts Lawyers Weekly, February 23, 2004.

Reskin, Paula, *Unconsciousness Raising*, 14 Regional Review, Federal Reserve Bank Boston (Q1 2005).

Rhode, Deborah L., In the Interests of Justice: Reforming the Legal Profession, Oxford University Press, Inc.: New York (2000).

Rhode, Deborah L., The Difference "Difference" Makes: Women and Leadership, Stanford University Press: California (2003).

Ridgeway, Cecilia L. & Correll, Shelley J., *Motherhood as a Status Characteristic*, 60 Journal of Social Issues, 2004.

Rikleen, Lauren Stiller, *Female In-House Counsel Can Wield Economic Power to Level Playing Field in Hiring Outside Lawyers*, New England In-House, February 3, 2004, *available at* http://www.newenglandinhouse.com.

Robertson, Tatsha, *Between Work and Life There's Balance: But Do You Have to Sacrifice Career Goals to Get It?*, Boston Sunday Globe, June 19, 2005.

Rose, Joel A., *Is Your Firm's Culture an Asset or a Liability?*, Of Counsel, April 2005.

Rund, Bryan & Kisliuk, Bill, *D. C. Salary Watch: Hiring Strategies to Match A Hot Market*, Legal Times, February 1, 2001, *available at* http://store.law.com/newswire_results.asp?lqry=salary+watch&x=8&y=8.

Sachdev, Ameet, *Hourly Legal Fees under Attack*, Chicago Tribune, April 18, 2005, *available at* http://pqasb.pqarchiver.com/chicagotribune/advancedsearch.html.

Samborn, Hope Viner, *Higher Hurdles for Women*, 86 ABA Journal, September 2000.

Sandburg, Brenda, *Brobeck Cuts Paralegal Supervisors*, March 15, 2002 *at* http://www.law.com.

Sandburg, Brenda, *The New Math, at* http://www.law.com, April 27, 2004.

Sandman, James J., *The Business Case for Effective Part-Time Programs*, Women Lawyers Journal, Winter 2003.

Sandman, Jim, *What a Difference a Dad Makes*, Remarks at the Working Mother WorkLife Congress, October 1, 2003.

Schwartz, Felice N., *It Costs to Employ Women, But Pays a Talent Dividend*, Los Angeles Times, March 17, 1989.

Segal, Jonathan A., *Mirror-Image Mentoring*, HR Magazine, March 2000.

Share, John, *Big Clients Pressuring Firms on Diversity*, The Business Journal (Minneapolis St. Paul) October 17, 2003, *available at* http://twincities.bizjournals.com/twincities/stories/2003/10/20/story3.html.

Shellenbarger, Sue, *Companies are Finding It Really Pays to Be Nice to Employees*, Wall Street Journal, July 22, 1997.

Shellenbarger, Sue, *Those Lists Ranking Best Place to Work are Rising in Influence*, Wall Street Journal, August 26, 1998.

Smith, Larry, Inside/Outside: How Businesses Buy Legal Services, ALM Publishing/ALM Inc.: New York (2001).

Smith, Larry, *Publicity Equals Communications Equals Case Management*, 24 No. 5 of Counsel, May 2005, *at* http://www.westlaw.com.

Solomon, Charlene Marmer, *Cracks in the Glass Ceiling*, 79 WorkForce, September 2000, available at http://

condor.depaul.edu/~mwilson/extra/discover/glassceil.html.

Stacy, Caren Ulrich, *Incentivizing Partner Participation in Professional Development*, NALP Bulletin, August 2004.

Stewart, James B., The Partners: Inside America's Most Powerful Law Firms, Simon & Schuster: New York (1983).

Story, Louise, *Many Women at Elite Colleges Set Career Path to Motherhood*, New York Times, September 20, 2005, *available at* http://www.nytimes.com/2005/09/20/national/20women.html?3i=5070&en=88d5272285b1.

Sullivan, Marianne, *Women Very Much in Minority among Equity Partners*, Boston Business Journal, July 30, 2004, *available at* http://www.bizjournals.com/boston/stories/2004/08/02/focus2.html.

Summers, Lawrence H., *Remarks at NBER Conference on Diversifying the Science and Engineering Workforce*, Office of the President of Harvard College, http://www.president.harvard.edu/speeches/2005/nber.html, January 14, 2005.

Supreme Court Historical Society, *Sandra Day O'Connor*, March 2, 2000, *available at* http://www.supremecourthistory.org/myweb/justice/o'connor.htm.

Sussman, Fern S., *The Large Law Firm Structure: An Historic Opportunity*, 57 Fordham Law Review, 1989.

Tanenbaum, Leora, Catfight: Rivalries Among Women—From Diets to Dating, From the Boardroom to the Delivery Room, Seven Stories Press, HarperCollins Publishers, Inc.: New York (2002).

Tannen, Deborah, *The Power of Talk: Who Gets Heard and Why*, Harvard Business Review, September/October 1995, Reprint 95510.

Tebo, Graham, *The Debt Conundrum*, 87 ABA Journal, March 2001.

"*The A-List*," The American Lawyer, September 2005.

The Am Law 100, The American Lawyer, July 2005.

The Am Law 200, The American Lawyer, August 2005

The Crucial Next Phase: Facilitating the Success of Women in Private Practice, 2003 Levick Strategic Commission & Northstar Conference.

Travis, Michelle A., *Equality In the Virtual Workplace*, 24 Berkeley Journal of Employment and Labor Law, 2003.

Trunk, Penelope, *A New Generation Puts the Focus On Family*, Boston Globe, April 17, 2005.

Tulgan, Bruce, Managing Generation X: How to Bring Out the Best in Young Talent, W.W. Norton & Company, Inc.: New York (2000).

United States Court of Appeals, First Circuit, Report of the First Circuit Gender, Race and Ethnic Bias Task Forces (1999).

United States Equal Employment Opportunity Commission, Diversity In Law Firms (2003), *at* http://

www.eeoc.gov/stats/reports/diversitylaw/index.html.

United States Equal Employment Opportunity Commission, Press Release, EEOC Charges Sidley & Austin with Age Discrimination (January 13, 2005) at http://www.eeoc.gov/press/1-13-05.html.

WFD Consulting,"When Talented Women Leave Your Company: Is it Push or Pull?" It's About Time, Winter 2004, available at http://www.wfd.com.

Ward, Stephanie Francis, 2,000+ Club Stays Open 24/7, 91 ABA Journal, February 2005.

Ward, Stephanie Francis, Billing Basics: Associates Need to Learn Nuances of Billing Before Starting Big Projects, 90 ABA Journal, October 2004.

Ward, Stephanie Francis, Coming of Age: When It Comes to Mentoring, Younger Is Sometimes Better, 90 ABA Journal, January 2004.

Ward, Stephanie Francis, Part-Time Possibilities, ABA Journal, April 2004.

Washington State Superior Court, Commission on Gender & Justice and The Glass Ceiling Task Force, 2001 Self-Audit for Gender and Racial Equity: A Survey of Washington Law Firms (Final Report administered by the NorthWest Research Group) (2001).

Weisman, Robert, Hear Women Roar as Technology, Business Force, Boston Sunday Globe, November 2, 2003.

Wellington, Sheila, Making the Case: Women In Law, in The Difference

"Difference" Makes: Women and Leadership, Stanford University Press: California (2003).

Wen, Patricia, GenX Dad, Boston Globe Magazine, January 16, 2005.

"What's My Line?" 1950-1967 Version: How the Game Was Played, A Tribute to "What's My Line?" at http://www.geocities.com/televisioncity/4439/wml50.html.

Wilkins, David B., Symposium: Brown At Fifty: From "Separate is Inherently Unequal" to "Diversity is Good For Business": The Rise of Market-Based Diversity Arguments and the Fate of the Black Corporate Bar, 117 Harvard Law Review, March 2004.

Wilkins, David B., Do Clients Have Ethical Obligations to Lawyers? Some Lessons From the Diversity Wars, 11 Georgetown Journal of Legal Ethics, Summer 1998.

Williams, Joan, Unbending Gender: Why Family and Work Conflict and What to Do About It, Oxford University Press, Inc.: New York (2000).

Williams, Joan C., & Calvert, Cynthia Thomas, Balanced Hours: Effective Part-Time Policies for Washington Law Firms, American University Washington College of Law, Project for Attorney Retention, Final, 2nd Ed., (2001).

Williams, Joan C., & Cooper, Holly Cohen, The Public Policy of Motherhood, 60 Journal of Social Issues, 2004.

Wilmsen, Steven, Law and the Disorder It Can Bring to Family Life, Boston Globe, June 24, 1999.

Wilmsen, Steven, *Law Suitless: Change In Clientele Spurs Casual Dress at Legal Firms*, Boston Globe, November 19, 1999.

Wiseman, Rosalind, Queen Bees & Wannabes: Helping Your Daughter Survive Cliques, Gossip, Boyfriends, and Other Realities of Adolescence, Three Rivers Press, Random House, Inc.: New York (2002).

Wolf, Naomi, Misconceptions: Truth, Lies, and the Unexpected on the Journey to Motherhood, First Anchor Books, A Division of Random House: New York (2003).

Women's Bar Association of D.C., Women's Bar Association Foundation of D.C. and American University Washington College of Law, Gender, Work and Family Project Report, *Results of* Lawyers, Work & Family: A Study of Alternative Schedule Programs at Law Firms In the District of Columbia (2000).

Women's Bar Association Of Masssachusetts, A Report of the Employment Issues Committee, More than Part-Time: The Effect of Reduced-Hours Arrangements on the Retention, Recruitment and Success of Women Attorneys In Law Firms (2000).

Women Lawyers of Utah, Report on 20th Anniversary Survey of Utah Women Lawyers, (October 13, 2001).

Yale Law School Career Development Office, *The Truth About the Billable Hour, at* http://www.law.yale.edu/outside/pdf/career_development/cdo-billable_hour.pdf.

Young, Eric, *Silicon Valley Law Giant to Dissolve*, San Francisco Business Times, January 27, 2003.

Yurko, Richard J., *Mentoring: A Guide for Both Sides*, Boston Bar Journal, November/December 2003.

INDEX

ABBOTT, IDA O.
Mentoring, 338-340

ADOLESCENTS
Pipher, Saving the Selves of Adolescent Girls, 216

AGE DISCRIMINATION
Partner retirement, 345

ALUMNI PROGRAMS
Chanen, More Law Firms Create Alumni Programs etc., 193, 199

APPEARANCE
Professional appearance, 379-380

ASSIGNMENT PROCESS
Generally, 43-52
Amorphous nature of process, 46
Assumptions about women's preferences, 46
Career advancement, using assignments as tool of, 46
Client contact, 45-46
Complex matters, selection process, 46-47
Discrimination, unconscious, 47
Disparate results, 48-49
Due diligence vs. negotiations, 47
Equal access to challenging assignments, 306
Gender, impact of, 44, 46
Importance to associates, 44-45
Leadership and oversight, 293
Link to professional growth, 44-45
Managing partner perspective, 244
Non-client billable projects, 189-190
Part-time workers, 144-145, 150
Political skills, men vs. women associates, 45-46
Powerful partners, seeking assignments from, 43 et seq.
Pro bono work, 46

COMPETITION

CONFIDENCE

CONTINGENCY FEES

COSTER, HELEN

COULTER, SILVIA

COUNSEL

CRUDEN, JOHN C.

CUDDY, ET AL.

CULTURE

ENVIRONMENT
Work Environment, this index

EPSTEIN, ET AL.
Glass Ceilings and Open Doors etc., 45-47, 51, 57, 62, 68, 72, 75, 77-78, 82-83, 89-90, 105-106, 109-110, 112-113, 116, 118, 126, 128, 130, 134, 153, 156, 161-165, 169-170, 174, 195, 275, 278, 343-344, 348-349, 379, 381, 384

EPSTEIN, PHYLLIS HORN
Women-at-Law etc., 212, 229

ESTRICH, SUSAN
Sex and Power, 47, 52, 116, 128, 296, 301, 381, 384

EVALUATION PROCESS
Accountability for results, link to, 306
Bottom-up evaluations, 305
Compensation, tie to, 305
Criteria, ambiguous, 159
Feedback, importance of, 161, 305
Gender bias, 157
Gender-neutral process, 304-306
In-group favoritism, 157
Leniency bias, 158
Long-term negative impact of one bad evaluation, 159
Measuring success, 303-307
Organizational citizenship behavior and, 46
Stereotyping, 160, 304
Subjectivity, 161-162

FAMILY OBLIGATIONS
Bailyn et al., Work-Family Policy Network etc., 63, 73, 344, 349, 352, 365
Boynton, Balancing Work & Family, 273, 277
Chanow, Lawyers, Work & Family etc., 273-274, 278, 296, 301
Davolos-Harden et al., Building Cross-Sector Partnerships for Family Care, 351, 365
Flexibility, this index
Gallagher, Family v. Career etc., 289, 300
Generational changes, 272 et seq.
Harrington, Is Time-Out for Family Unprofessional?, 403-404

MERITOCRACY

MEYERSON & FLETCHER

MILLER, LESLIE ANNE

MOLL, RICHARD W.

MORELLO, KAREN BERGER

MOTHERHOOD

MURPHY, EVELYN

MYTHS